STATISTICS
Plain and Simple

THIRD EDITION

Sherri L. Jackson
Jacksonville University

WADSWORTH
CENGAGE Learning·

Australia · Brazil · Japan · Korea · Mexico · Singapore · Spain · United Kingdom · United States

Statistics Plain and Simple, **Third Edition**
Sherri L. Jackson

Publisher: Jon-David Hague

Acquisitions Editor: Tim Matray

Assistant Editor: Jessica Alderman

Editorial Assistant: Nicole Richards

Media Editor: Mary Noel

Brand Manager: Liz Rhoden

Market Development Manager: Chris Sosa

Art and Cover Direction, Production
Management, and Composition:
PreMediaGlobal

Manufacturing Planner: Karen Hunt

Rights Acquisitions Specialist: Roberta Broyer

Cover Image: Zketch/Shutterstock

For product information and technology assistance, contact us at
Cengage Learning Customer & Sales Support, 1-800-354-9706.

For permission to use material from this text or product,
submit all requests online at **www.cengage.com/permissions.**
Further permissions questions can be e-mailed to
permissionrequest@cengage.com.

Library of Congress Control Number: 2012940372

ISBN-13: 978-1-133-31253-6

ISBN-10: 1-133-31253-5

Wadsworth
20 Davis Drive
Belmont, CA 94002-3098
USA

Cengage Learning is a leading provider of customized learning solutions with office locations around the globe, including Singapore, the United Kingdom, Australia, Mexico, Brazil, and Japan. Locate your local office at **www.cengage.com/global.**

Cengage Learning products are represented in Canada by Nelson Education, Ltd.

To learn more about Wadsworth, visit **www.cengage.com/wadsworth**

Purchase any of our products at your local college store or at our preferred online store **www.cengagebrain.com.**

Printed in the United States of America
2 3 4 5 6 7 16 15 14 13

About the Author

Sherri L. Jackson is Professor of Psychology at Jacksonville University, where she has taught since 1988. At JU, she has won Excellence in Teaching, Scholarship, and University Service awards, the university-wide Professor of the Year Award in 2004, the Woman of the Year Award in 2005, and the Institutional Excellence Award in 2007. She received her M.S. and Ph.D. in cognitive/experimental psychology from the University of Florida. Her research interests include human reasoning and the teaching of psychology. She has published numerous articles in both areas. In 1997, she received a research grant from the Office of Teaching Resources in Psychology (APA Division 2) to develop *A Compendium of Introductory Psychology Textbooks 1997–2000*. She is also the author of *Research Methods and Statistics: A Critical Thinking Approach*, 4th ed. (Belmont, CA: Wadsworth, 2012), *Research Methods: A Modular Approach*, 2nd ed. (Belmont, CA: Wadsworth, 2011), and *A Concise Guide to Statistical Analyses Using Excel, SPSS, and the TI-84 Calculator*, (Belmont, CA: Wadsworth, 2013).

Brief Contents

Contents

6 Standard Scores (*z* Scores) 82

CHAPTER THREE SUMMARY AND REVIEW 95

CHAPTER THREE STATISTICAL SOFTWARE RESOURCES 99

CHAPTER 4

Probability and Hypothesis Testing 111

7 Probability 112

8 Hypothesis Testing and Inferential Statistics 125

CHAPTER 5

The *z* and *t* Tests   139

CHAPTER 6

Two-Group *t* Tests   175

CHAPTER 7

Introduction to Analysis of Variance (ANOVA)   215

CHAPTER 8

Repeated Measures and Two-Factor ANOVAs   251

20 Advanced Correlational Techniques: Regression Analysis   331

CHAPTER NINE SUMMARY AND REVIEW   337

CHAPTER NINE STATISTICAL SOFTWARE RESOURCES   341

CHAPTER 10

Nonparametric Procedures   353

21 Chi-Square Tests   355

Preface

Statistics Plain and Simple, 3rd edition, was written to provide students and instructors with a simple, straightforward approach to learning and teaching statistics. The text is designed to be used in a variety of classroom situations—as a statistics text in an undergraduate course, as a supplement to a combined statistics and methodology course, or as a quick review at the graduate level. Most of the statistical concepts typically covered in briefer statistics texts are covered here along with some additional statistical concepts not typically found in such texts (for example, effect size, confidence intervals, repeated measures ANOVAs, and Wilcoxon tests).

One of my goals in writing this text was to be *concise yet comprehensive.* The text is organized into ten chapters, each divided into brief modules. This modular format allows students to digest smaller chunks and teachers to have greater flexibility in reading assignments and the amount of material covered in each class. Most modules are brief, just 6 to15 pages in length. However, despite the brevity of the modules, most statistics covered in the typical undergraduate course are covered here. Moreover, the coverage of each statistical test is divided into four clear subsections. The first describes the statistical test and what it does for a researcher. The second subsection provides the formulas for the test and an example of how to apply the formulas. In the third subsection I demonstrate how to interpret the results from the test and how to report these results in APA publication format. In the final subsection, I discuss the assumptions that underlie the test. Using the same format for the discussion of each test means that students become familiar with what to expect with each new statistical test. Moreover, these subsections also serve to break the material down into chunks that are easier to understand and digest.

In addition, I have made every attempt to use a straightforward, easy-to-understand *writing style.* I present the information in a simple, direct, clear fashion. Because statistics is one of the more difficult courses for many students, I also try to write in an engaging, conversational style, much as if the reader were a student seated in front of me in my classroom. I hope, through this writing style, to help students better understand some of the more troublesome concepts without losing their interest.

Pedagogical Aids

The text uses several pedagogical aids. Each chapter begins with a *chapter outline* followed by *learning objectives* at the beginning of each module. A *running glossary* appears in the margins of each module and is alphabetized at the end of the book. *In Review* summary matrices occur at the end of major subsections in each module, providing a tabular review of the major concepts within that subsection. The summary matrices are immediately followed by *Critical Thinking Checks,* which vary in length and format but typically involve a series of application questions concerning the information in the preceding subsection. The questions are designed to foster analytical and critical thinking skills in students in addition to reviewing the module subsection information. Thus, students can study the *In Review* summary after reading a module subsection and then respond to the *Critical Thinking Check* on that information. At the end of each module, the *Module Exercises* allow students to further review and apply the knowledge gained in the module. At the end of each chapter, a *Chapter Summary and Review* provides a built-in study guide consisting of a chapter summary, Fill-in Self-Test Questions, Multiple-Choice Self-Test Questions, and Self-Test Problems. Answers to the Critical Thinking Checks are provided at the end of each module. Answers to the odd-numbered Module Exercises and all Chapter Summary and Review Exercises are included in Appendix B.

New to This Edition

The major change to the third edition of *Statistics Plain and Simple* is that the Excel, SPSS, and TI-84 material that previously appeared in Appendix C has now been integrated into the book and appears as a Statistical Software Resources section at the end of relevant chapters. In addition the coverage of various procedures in Excel and SPSS has increased. Lastly, two new non-parametric statistics have been added to Module 22—the Kruskal-Wallis test and the Friedman test. The SPSS procedures for each of these is also covered.

Acknowledgments

I must acknowledge several people for their help with this project. I thank my husband, Richard Griggs, for his careful proofreading and insightful comments, and Percy for the encouragement of her ever-wagging tail. In addition, I would like to thank those who reviewed the text in its various stages. The reviewers include Patricia L. Tomich, Kent State University; Christine Ferri, Richard Stockton College of New Jersey; Brendan Morse, Bridgewater State College; and Tina Jameson, Bridgewater State College.

Special thanks to Timothy Matray, Acquiring Sponsoring Editor, for his support and guidance, and Jon-David Hague, Publisher; Nicole Richards,

Editorial Assistant; Janay Pryor, Associate Marketing Program Manager; Talia Wise, Marketing Programs Director; Brenda Carmichael, Art Director; Karen Hunt, Manufacturing Planner; and Roberta Broyer, Rights Acquisition Specialist, all of Wadsworth/Cengage Learning. Finally, thanks to Dewanshu Ranjan and PreMediaGlobal for their production expertise and to Pamela Rockwell for her excellent copyediting skills.

Sherri L. Jackson

Science and Statistics

Learning Objectives
- Explain the goals of science.
- Identify and compare descriptive methods.
- Identify and compare predictive (relational) methods.
- Describe the explanatory method. Your description should include independent variable, dependent variable, control group, and experimental group.
- Explain how we "do" science and how proof and disproof relate to doing science.

You may be wondering why you are enrolled in a statistics class. Most students take statistics because it is a requirement in their major field, and often students do not understand *why* it is a requirement. Scientists and researchers use statistics to describe data and draw inferences. Thus, no matter whether your major is in the behavioral sciences, the natural sciences, or in more applied areas such as business or education, statistics are necessary to your discipline. Why? Statistics are necessary because scientists and researchers collect data and test hypotheses with these data using statistics. A **hypothesis** is a prediction regarding the outcome of a study. This prediction concerns the potential relationship between at least two variables (a **variable** is an event or behavior that has at least two values). Hypotheses are stated in such a way that they are testable. When we test our hypotheses, statistics may lead us to conclude that our hypothesis is or is not supported by our observations.

In science, the goal of testing hypotheses is to arrive at or test a **theory**—an organized system of assumptions and principles that attempts to explain certain phenomena and how they are related. Theories help us to organize and explain the data gathered in research studies. In other words, theories allow us to develop a framework regarding the facts in a certain area. For example, Darwin's theory organizes and explains facts related to evolution. In addition to helping us organize and explain facts, theories also help in producing new knowledge by steering researchers toward specific observations of the world.

hypothesis A prediction regarding the outcome of a study involving the potential relationship between at least two variables.

variable An event or behavior that has at least two values.

theory An organized system of assumptions and principles that attempts to explain certain phenomena and how they are related.

Students are sometimes confused about the differences between a hypothesis and a theory. A *hypothesis* is a prediction regarding the outcome of a single study. Many hypotheses may be tested and several research studies conducted before a comprehensive theory on a topic is put forth. Once a *theory* is developed, it may aid in generating future hypotheses. In other words, researchers may have additional questions regarding the theory that help them to generate new hypotheses to test. If the results from these additional studies further support the theory, we are likely to have greater confidence in the theory. However, every time we test a hypothesis, statistics are necessary.

Goals of Science

Scientific research has three basic goals: (1) to describe, (2) to predict, and (3) to explain. All of these goals lead to a better understanding of behavior and mental processes.

Description   Description begins with careful observation. Behavioral scientists might describe patterns of behavior, thought, or emotions in humans. They might also describe the behavior(s) of other animals. For example, researchers might observe and describe the type of play behavior exhibited by children or the mating behavior of chimpanzees. Description allows us to learn about behavior and when it occurs. Let's say, for example, that you were interested in the channel-surfing behavior of males and females. Careful observation and description would be needed in order to determine whether or not there were any gender differences in channel-surfing. Description allows us to observe that two events are systematically related to one another. Without description as a first step, predictions cannot be made.

description   Carefully observing behavior in order to describe it.

Prediction   Prediction allows us to identify the factors that indicate when an event or events will occur. In other words, knowing the level of one variable allows us to predict the approximate level of the other variable. We know that if one variable is present at a certain level, then there is a greater likelihood that the other variable will be present at a certain level. For example, if we observed that males channel-surf with greater frequency than females, we could then make predictions about how often males and females might change channels when given the chance.

prediction   Identifying the factors that indicate when an event or events will occur.

Explanation   Finally, **explanation** allows us to identify the causes that determine when and why a behavior occurs. In order to explain a behavior, we need to demonstrate that we can manipulate the factors needed to produce or eliminate the behavior. For example, in our channel-surfing example, if gender predicts channel-surfing, what might cause it? It could be genetic or environmental. Maybe males have less tolerance for commercials and thus channel-surf at a greater rate. Maybe females are more interested

explanation   Identifying the causes that determine when and why a behavior occurs.

in the content of commercials and are thus less likely to change channels. Maybe the attention span of females is greater. Maybe something associated with having a Y chromosome increases channel-surfing, or something associated with having two X chromosomes leads to less channel-surfing. Obviously the possible explanations are numerous and varied. As scientists, we test these possibilities to identify the best explanation of why a behavior occurs. When we try to identify the best explanation for a behavior, we must systematically eliminate any alternative explanations. To eliminate alternative explanations, we must impose control over the research situation. We will discuss the concepts of control and alternative explanations shortly.

An Introduction to Research Methods in Science ●●

The goals of science map very closely onto the research methods that scientists use. In other words, there are methods that are descriptive in nature, predictive in nature, and explanatory in nature. I will briefly introduce these methods here.

Descriptive Methods

observational method
Making observations of human or other animal behavior.

Behavioral scientists use three types of descriptive methods. First is the **observational method**—simply making observations of human or other animal behavior. Scientists approach observation in two ways. *Naturalistic observation* involves observing humans or other animals behave in their natural habitat. Observing the mating behavior of chimpanzees in their natural setting would be an example of this approach. *Laboratory observation* involves observing behavior in a more contrived and controlled situation, usually the laboratory. Bringing children to a laboratory playroom to observe play behavior would be an example of this approach. Observation involves description at its most basic level. One advantage of the observational method, as well as other descriptive methods, is the flexibility to change what one is studying. A disadvantage of descriptive methods is that the researcher has little control. As we use more powerful methods, we gain control but lose flexibility.

case study method
An in-depth study of one or more individuals.

A second descriptive method is the **case study method**. A case study is an in-depth study of one or more individuals. Freud used case studies to develop his theory of personality development. Similarly, Jean Piaget used case studies to develop his theory of cognitive development in children. This method is descriptive in nature, as it involves simply describing the individual(s) being studied.

survey method Questioning individuals on a topic or topics and then describing their responses.

The third method that relies on description is the **survey method**—questioning individuals on a topic or topics and describing their responses. Surveys can be administered by mail, over the phone, on the Internet, or as a personal interview. One advantage of the survey method over the other descriptive methods is that it allows researchers to study larger groups of individuals more easily. This method has disadvantages, however. One concern has to do with the wording of questions. Are they easy to understand? Are they written in such a manner that they bias the respondents' answers? Such concerns relate to the validity of the data collected. Another concern relevant to the survey method (and most other research methods) is whether the group of people who participate in the study (the **sample**) is representative of all the people about whom the study is meant to generalize (the **population**). This concern can usually be overcome through random sampling. A *random sample* is achieved when, through random selection, each member of the population is equally likely to be chosen as part of the sample.

sample The group of people who participate in a study.

population All of the people about whom a study is meant to generalize.

Predictive (Relational) Methods

Two methods allow researchers to not only describe behaviors but also predict from one variable to another. The first, the **correlational method,** assesses the degree of relationship between two measured variables. If two variables are correlated with each other, we can predict from one variable to the other with a certain degree of accuracy. For example, height and weight are correlated. The relationship is such that an increase in one variable (height) is generally accompanied by an increase in the other variable (weight). Knowing this, we can predict an individual's approximate weight, with a certain degree of accuracy, given the person's height.

correlational method A method that assesses the degree of relationship between two variables.

One problem with correlational research is that it is often misinterpreted. Frequently, people assume that because two variables are correlated, there must be some sort of causal relationship between the variables. This is not so. *Correlation does not imply causation.* Remember that a correlation simply means that the two variables are related in some way. For example, being a certain height does not cause you to also be a certain weight. It would be nice if it did, because then we would not have to worry about being either under- or overweight. What if I told you that watching violent TV and displaying aggressive behavior were correlated? What could you conclude based on this correlation? Many people might conclude that watching violent TV causes one to act more aggressively. Based on the evidence given (a correlational study), however, we cannot draw this conclusion. All we can conclude is that those who watch more violent television programs also tend to act more aggressively. It is possible that the violent TV causes aggression, but we cannot draw this conclusion based only on correlational data. It is also possible that those who are aggressive by nature are attracted to more violent television programs, or that some other variable is causing both aggressive behavior and violent TV watching. The point is that observing a correlation between two variables simply means that they are related to each other.

The correlation between height and weight, or violent TV and aggressive behavior, is a **positive relationship**: As one variable (height) increases, we observe an increase in the second variable (weight). Some correlations indicate a **negative relationship:** As one variable increases, the other variable systematically decreases. Can you think of an example of a negative

positive relationship A relationship between two variables in which an increase in one variable is accompanied by an increase in the other variable.

negative relationship A relationship between two variables in which an increase in one variable is accompanied by a decrease in the other variable.

relationship between two variables? Consider this: As mountain elevation increases, temperature decreases. Negative correlations also allow us to predict from one variable to another. If I know the mountain elevation, it will help me predict the approximate temperature.

Besides the correlational method, a second method that allows us to describe and predict is the **quasi-experimental method.** Quasi-experimental research allows us to compare naturally occurring groups of individuals. For example, we could examine whether alcohol consumption by students in a fraternity or sorority differs from that of students not in such organizations. You will see in a moment that this method differs from the experimental method, described below, in that the groups studied occur naturally. In other words, we do not assign people to join a Greek organization or not. They have chosen their groups on their own, and we are simply looking for differences (in this case, in the amount of alcohol typically consumed) between these naturally occurring groups. This is often referred to as a *subject* or *participant variable*—a characteristic inherent in the participants that cannot be changed. Because we are using groups that occur naturally, any differences that we find may be due to the variable of being a Greek member or not, or the differences may be due to other factors that we were unable to control in this study. For example, maybe those who like to drink more are also more likely to join a Greek organization. Once again, if we find a difference between these groups in amount of alcohol consumed, we can use this finding to predict what type of student (Greek or non-Greek) is likely to drink more. However, we cannot conclude that belonging to a Greek organization *causes* one to drink more because the participants came to us after choosing to belong to these organizations. In other words, what is missing when we use predictive methods such as the correlational and quasi-experimental methods is control.

When using predictive methods, we do not systematically manipulate the variables of interest; we only measure them. This means that, although we may observe a relationship between variables (such as that described between drinking and Greek membership), we cannot conclude that it is a causal relationship. Why? Because there could be other, *alternative explanations* for this relationship. An **alternative explanation** is the idea that it is possible that some other, uncontrolled, extraneous variable may be responsible for the observed relationship. For example, maybe those who choose to join Greek organizations come from higher-income families and have more money to spend on such things as alcohol. Or maybe those who choose to join Greek organizations are more interested in socialization and drinking alcohol before they even join the organization. Thus, because these methods leave the possibility for alternative explanations, we cannot use them to establish cause-and-effect relationships.

Explanatory Method

When using the experimental method, researchers pay a great deal of attention to eliminating alternative explanations by using the proper controls. Because of this, the **experimental method** allows researchers not only to describe and predict but also to determine whether there is a cause-and-effect

quasi-experimental method Research that compares naturally occurring groups of individuals; the variable of interest cannot be manipulated.

alternative explanation The idea that it is possible that some other, uncontrolled, extraneous variable may be responsible for the observed relationship.

experimental method A research method that allows a researcher to establish a cause-and-effect relationship through manipulation of a variable and control of the situation.

relationship between the variables of interest. In other words, this method enables researchers to know when and why a behavior occurs. Many preconditions must be met in order for a study to be experimental in nature. Here, we will simply consider the basics—the minimum requirements needed for an experiment.

The basic premise of experimentation is that the researcher controls as much as possible in order to determine whether there is a cause-and-effect relationship between the variables being studied. Let's say, for example, that a researcher is interested in whether taking vitamin C supplements leads to fewer colds. The idea behind experimentation is that the researcher manipulates at least one variable (known as the **independent variable**) and measures at least one variable (known as the **dependent variable**). In our study, what should the researcher manipulate? If you identified amount of vitamin C, then you are correct. If amount of vitamin C is the independent variable, then number of colds is the dependent variable. For comparative purposes, the independent variable has to have at least two groups or conditions. We typically refer to these two groups or conditions as the control group and the experimental group. The **control group** is the group that serves as the baseline or "standard" condition. In our vitamin C study, the control group is the group that does not take vitamin C supplements. The **experimental group** is the group that receives the treatment—in this case, those who take vitamin C supplements. Thus, in an experiment, one thing that we control is the level of the independent variable that participants receive.

What else should we control to help eliminate alternative explanations? Well, we need to control the type of participants in each of the treatment conditions. We should begin by drawing a random sample of participants from the population. Once we have our sample of participants, we have to decide who will serve in the control group versus the experimental group. In order to gain as much control as possible, and eliminate as many alternative explanations as possible, we should use **random assignment**—assigning participants to conditions in such a way that every participant has an equal probability of being placed in any condition. How does random assignment help us to gain control and eliminate alternative explanations? By using random assignment we should minimize or eliminate differences between the groups. In other words, we want the two groups of participants to be as alike as possible. The only difference we want between the groups is that of the independent variable we are manipulating—amount of vitamin C. Once participants are assigned to conditions, we keep track of the number of colds they have over a specified time period (the dependent variable).

Let's review some of the controls we have used in the present study. We have controlled who is in the study (we want a sample representative of the population about whom we are trying to generalize), who participates in each group (we should randomly assign participants to the two conditions), and the treatment each group receives as part of the study (some take vitamin C supplements and some do not). Can you identify other variables that we might need to consider controlling in the present study? How about amount of sleep

independent variable
The variable in a study that is manipulated by the researcher.

dependent variable
The variable in a study that is measured by the researcher.

control group   The group of participants that does not receive any level of the independent variable and serves as the baseline in a study.

experimental group
The group of participants that receives some level of the independent variable.

random assignment
Assigning participants to conditions in such a way that every participant has an equal probability of being placed in any condition.

control Manipulating the independent variable in an experiment or any other extraneous variables that could affect the results of a study.

received each day, type of diet, and amount of exercise (all variables that might contribute to general health and well-being)? There are undoubtedly other variables we would need to control if we were to complete this study. The basic idea is that when using the experimental method, we try to **control** as much as possible by manipulating the independent variable and controlling any other extraneous variables that could affect the results of the study. Randomly assigning participants also helps to control for participant differences between the groups. What does all of this control gain us? If, after completing this study with the proper controls, we found that those in the experimental group (those who took vitamin C supplements) did in fact have fewer colds than those in the control group, we would have evidence supporting a cause-and-effect relationship between these variables. In other words, we could conclude that taking vitamin C supplements reduces the frequency of colds.

IN REVIEW

AN INTRODUCTION TO RESEARCH METHODS

Goal Met	Research Methods	Advantages/Disadvantages
Description	Observational method	Descriptive methods allow description of behavior(s)
	Case study method	Descriptive methods do not support reliable predictions
	Survey method	Descriptive methods do not support cause-and-effect explanations
Prediction	Correlational method	Predictive methods allow description of behavior(s)
	Quasi-experimental method	Predictive methods support reliable predictions from one variable to another
		Predictive methods do not support cause-and-effect explanations
Explanation	Experimental method	Allows description of behavior(s)
		Supports reliable predictions from one variable to another
		Supports cause-and-effect explanations

CRITICAL THINKING CHECK 1.1

1. In a recent study, researchers found a negative correlation between income level and incidence of psychological disorders. Jim thinks this means that being poor leads to psychological disorders. Is he correct in his conclusion? Why or why not?
2. In a study designed to assess the effects of exercise on life satisfaction, participants were assigned to groups based on whether they reported exercising or not. All participants then completed a life satisfaction inventory.
   a. What is the independent variable?
   b. What is the dependent variable?
   c. Is the independent variable a participant variable or a true manipulated variable?

3. What type of method would you recommend researchers use to answer the following questions?
   a. What percentage of cars runs red lights?
   b. Do student athletes spend as much time studying as student nonathletes?
   c. Is there a relationship between type of punishment used by parents and aggressiveness in children?
   d. Do athletes who are randomly assigned to a group using imagery techniques perform better than those who are randomly assigned to a group not using such techniques?

Doing Science

Although the experimental method can establish a cause-and-effect relationship, most researchers would not wholeheartedly accept a conclusion from only one study. Why is that? Any one of a number of problems can occur in a study. For example, there may be control problems. Researchers may believe they have controlled for everything but miss something, and the uncontrolled factor may affect the results. In other words, a researcher may believe that the manipulated independent variable caused the results when, in reality, it was something else.

Another reason for caution in interpreting experimental results is that a study may be limited by the technical equipment available at the time. For example, in the early part of the 19th century, many scientists believed that studying the bumps on a person's head allowed them to know something about the internal mind of the individual being studied. This movement, known as phrenology, was popularized through the writings of physician Joseph Gall (1758–1828). At the time that it was popular, phrenology appeared very "scientific" and "technical." With hindsight and with the technological advances that we have today, the idea of phrenology seems laughable to us now.

Finally, we cannot completely rely on the findings of one study because a single study cannot tell us everything about a theory. The idea of science is that it is not static; the theories generated through science change. For example, we often hear about new findings in the medical field, such as "Eggs are so high in cholesterol that you should eat no more than two a week." Then, a couple of years later, we might read "Eggs are not as bad for you as originally thought. New research shows that it is acceptable to eat them every day." You may have heard people confronted with such contradictory findings complain, "Those doctors, they don't know what they're talking about. You can't believe any of them. First they say one thing, and then they say completely the opposite. It's best to just ignore all of them." The point is that when testing a theory scientifically, we may obtain contradictory results. These contradictions may lead to new, very valuable information that subsequently leads to a theoretical change. Theories evolve and change over time based on the consensus of the research. Just because a particular idea or theory is supported by data from one study does not mean that the research on that topic ends and that we just accept the theory as it currently stands and never do any more research on that topic.

Proof and Disproof

When scientists test theories, they do not try to prove them true. Theories can be supported based on the data collected, but obtaining support for something does not mean it is true in all instances. Proof of a theory is logically impossible. As an example, consider the following problem, adapted from Griggs and Cox (1982). This is known as the Drinking Age Problem (the reason for the name will become readily apparent).

> On this task imagine that you are a police officer responsible for making sure the drinking-age rule is being followed. The four cards below represent information about four people sitting at a table. One side of a card indicates what the person is drinking and the other side of the card indicates the person's age. The rule is: "If a person is drinking alcohol, then the person is 21 or over." In order to check that the rule is true or false, which card or cards below would you turn over? Turn over only the card or cards that you need to check to be sure.

Drinking a beer	16 years old	Drinking a coke	22 years old

Does turning over the beer card and finding that the person is 21 years of age or older prove that the rule is always true? No—the fact that one person is following the rule does not mean that it is always true. How, then, do we test a hypothesis? We test a hypothesis by attempting to falsify or disconfirm it. If it cannot be falsified, then we say we have support for it. Which cards would you choose in an attempt to falsify the rule in the drinking age problem? If you identified the beer card as being able to falsify the rule, then you were correct. If we turn over the beer card and find that the individual is under 21 years of age, then the rule is false. Is there another card that could also falsify the rule? Yes, the 16 years of age card can. How? If we turn that card over and find that the individual is drinking alcohol, then the rule is false. These are the only two cards that can potentially falsify the rule. Thus, they are the only two cards that need to be turned over.

ScienceCartoonsPlus.com

Even though disproof or disconfirmation is logically sound in terms of testing hypotheses, falsifying a hypothesis does not always mean that the hypothesis is false. Why? There may be design problems in the study, as described earlier. Thus, even when a theory is falsified, we need to be cautious in our interpretation. We do not want to completely discount a theory based on a single study.

REVIEW OF KEY TERMS

alternative explanation (p. 6)
case study method (p. 4)
control (p. 8)
control group (p. 7)
correlational method (p. 5)
dependent variable (p. 7)
description (p. 3)
experimental group (p. 7)

experimental method (p. 6)
explanation (p. 3)
hypothesis (p. 2)
independent variable (p. 7)
negative relationship (p. 5)
observational method (p. 4)
population (p. 5)
positive relationship (p. 5)

prediction (p. 3)
quasi-experimental method (p. 6)
random assignment (p. 7)
sample (p. 5)
survey method (p. 4)
theory (p. 2)
variable (p. 2)

MODULE EXERCISES

(Answers to odd-numbered questions appear in Appendix B.)

1. After describing your medical symptoms to your doctor, he claims he has a possible "theory" to explain your symptoms. What is wrong with his statement? How might he better state his beliefs?

2. Identify and briefly describe the three goals of science.

3. Identify advantages and disadvantages of naturalistic observation versus laboratory observation.
4. Identify the two predictive (relational) methods and describe each.
5. In a study of the effects of type of study on exam performance, participants are randomly assigned to one of two conditions. In one condition, participants study alone using notes they took during class lectures. In a second condition, participants study in interactive groups with notes from class lectures. The amount of time spent studying is held constant. All students then take the same exam on the material.
   a. What is the independent variable in this study?
   b. What is the dependent variable in this study?
   c. Identify the control and experimental groups in this study.
   d. Is the independent variable manipulated or a participant variable?
6. Researchers interested in the effects of caffeine on anxiety have randomly assigned participants to one of two conditions in a study, the no caffeine condition or the caffeine condition. After drinking two cups of either regular or decaffeinated coffee, participants will take an anxiety inventory.
   a. What is the independent variable in this study?
   b. What is the dependent variable in this study?
   c. Identify the control and experimental groups in this study.
   d. Is the independent variable manipulated or a participant variable?
7. Gerontologists interested in the effects of age on reaction time have two groups of participants take a test in which they must indicate as quickly as possible whether a probe word was a member of a previous set of words. One group of participants is between the age of 25 and 45, whereas the other group of participants is between the age of 55 and 75. The time it takes to make the response is measured.
   a. What is the independent variable in this study?
   b. What is the dependent variable in this study?
   c. Identify the control and experimental groups in this study.
   d. Is the independent variable manipulated or a participant variable?

CRITICAL THINKING CHECK ANSWERS

Critical Thinking Check 1.1

1. Jim is incorrect because he is inferring causation based on correlational evidence. He is assuming that because the two variables are correlated, one must be causing changes in the other. In addition, he is assuming the direction of the inferred causal relationship—that a lower income level causes psychological disorders, not that having a psychological disorder leads to a lower income level. The correlation simply indicates that these two variables are related in an inverse manner. That is, those with psychological disorders also tend to have lower income levels.
2. a. The independent variable is exercise.
   b. The dependent variable is life satisfaction.
   c. The independent variable is a participant variable.
3. a. Naturalistic observation
   b. Quasi-experimental method
   c. Correlational method
   d. Experimental method

WEB RESOURCES

The book-specific website at CengageBrain.com offers students a variety of study tools and useful resources such as glossaries, flashcards, quizzes, and Statistics and Research Methods Workshops.

Variables and Measurement

Learning Objectives
- Explain and give examples of an operational definition.
- Explain the four properties of measurement and how they are related to the four scales of measurement.
- Explain the difference between a discrete variable and a continuous variable.

An important step when designing a study is to define the variables in your study. A second important step is to determine the level of measurement of the dependent variable, which will ultimately help to determine which statistics are appropriate for analyzing the data collected.

Operationally Defining Variables

Some variables are fairly easy to define, manipulate, and measure. For example, if a researcher were studying the effects of exercise on blood pressure, she could manipulate the amount of exercise by varying the length of time that individuals exercised or by varying the intensity of the exercise (as by monitoring target heart rates). She could also measure blood pressure periodically during the course of the study; a machine already exists that will take this measure in a consistent and accurate manner. Does this mean that the measure will always be accurate? No. There is always the possibility for measurement error. In other words, the machine may not be functioning properly, or there may be human error contributing to the measurement error.

Now let's suppose that a researcher wants to study a variable that is not as concrete or easily measured as blood pressure. For example, many people study abstract concepts such as aggression, attraction, depression, hunger, or anxiety. How would we either manipulate or measure any of these variables? My definition of what it means to be hungry may be quite different from yours. If I decided to measure hunger by simply asking participants in an experiment if they were hungry, the measure would not be accurate because each individual may define hunger in a different way. What we need

operational definition
A definition of a variable in terms of the operations (activities) a researcher uses to measure or manipulate it.

is an **operational definition** of hunger—a definition of the variable in terms of the operations (activities) the researcher uses to measure or manipulate it.

As this is a somewhat circular definition, let's reword it in a way that may make more sense. An operational definition specifies the activities of the researcher in measuring and/or manipulating a variable (Kerlinger, 1986). In other words, we might define hunger in terms of specific activities, such as not having eaten for 12 hours. Thus, one operational definition of hunger could be that simple: Hunger occurs when 12 hours have passed with no food intake. Notice how much more concrete this definition is than simply saying hunger is that "gnawing feeling" that you get in your stomach. Specifying hunger in terms of the number of hours without food is an operational definition, whereas defining hunger as that "gnawing feeling" is not an operational definition.

In research, it is necessary to operationally define all variables—those measured (dependent variables) and those manipulated (independent variables). One reason for doing this is to ensure that the variables are measured consistently or manipulated in the same way during the course of the study. Another reason is to help us communicate our ideas to others. For example, what if a researcher said that he measured anxiety in his study? I would need to know how he defined anxiety operationally because it can be defined in many different ways. Thus, it can be measured in many different ways. For example, anxiety could be defined as the number of nervous actions displayed in a 1-hour time period, as a person's score on a GSR (galvanic skin response) machine, as a person's heart rate, or as a person's score on the Taylor Manifest Anxiety Scale. Some measures are better than others—*better* meaning more consistent and valid. Once I understand how a researcher has defined a variable operationally, I can replicate the study if I desire. I can begin to have a better understanding of the study and whether or not it may have problems. I can also better design my study based on how the variables were operationally defined in other research studies.

Properties of Measurement

identity A property of measurement in which objects that are different receive different scores.

magnitude A property of measurement in which the ordering of numbers reflects the ordering of the variable.

equal unit size A property of measurement in which a difference of 1 means the same amount throughout the entire scale.

In addition to operationally defining independent and dependent variables, you must consider the level of measurement of the dependent variable. There are four levels of measurement, each based on the characteristics or properties of the data. These properties include identity, magnitude, equal unit size, and absolute zero. When a measure has the property of **identity,** objects that are different receive different scores. For example, if participants in a study had different political affiliations, they would receive different scores. Measurements have the property of **magnitude** (also called *ordinality*) when the ordering of the numbers reflects the ordering of the variable. In other words, numbers are assigned in order so that some numbers represent more or less of the variable being measured than others.

Measurements have an **equal unit size** when a difference of 1 is the same amount throughout the entire scale. For example, the difference between people who are 64 inches tall and 65 inches tall is the same as the difference between people who are 72 inches tall and 73 inches tall. The difference in each situation (1 inch) is identical. Notice how this differs from the property of magnitude. Were we to simply line up and rank a group of individuals based on their height, the scale would have the properties of identity and magnitude, but not equal unit size. Can you think about why this would be so? We would not actually measure people's height in inches, but simply order them in terms of how tall they appear, from shortest (the person receiving a score of 1) to tallest (the person receiving the highest score). Thus, our scale would not meet the criteria of equal unit size. In other words, the difference in height between the two people receiving scores of 1 and 2 might not be the same as the difference in height between the two people receiving scores of 3 and 4.

Lastly, measures have an **absolute zero** when assigning a score of zero indicates an absence of the variable being measured. For example, time spent studying would have the property of absolute zero because a score of 0 on this measure would mean an individual spent no time studying. However, a score of 0 is not always equal to the property of absolute zero. As an example, think about the Fahrenheit temperature scale. That measurement scale has a score of 0 (the thermometer can read 0 degrees), but does that score indicate an absence of temperature? No, it indicates a very cold temperature. Hence, it does not have the property of absolute zero.

absolute zero A property of measurement in which assigning a score of 0 indicates an absence of the variable being measured.

Scales of Measurement

As noted previously, the level or scale of measurement depends on the properties of the data. There are four scales of measurement (nominal, ordinal, interval, and ratio), and each of these scales has one or more of the properties described in the previous section. We will discuss the scales in order, from the one with the fewest properties to the one with the most properties—that is, from least to most sophisticated. As we will see in later modules, it is important to establish the scale of measurement of your data in order to determine the appropriate statistical test to use when analyzing the data.

Nominal Scale A **nominal scale** is one in which objects or individuals are broken into categories that have no numerical properties. Nominal scales have the characteristic of identity but lack the other properties. Variables measured on a nominal scale are often referred to as *categorical variables* because the measuring scale involves dividing the data into categories. However, the categories carry no numerical weight. Some examples of categorical variables, or data measured on a nominal scale, include ethnicity, gender, and political affiliation.

nominal scale A scale in which objects or individuals are broken into categories that have no numerical properties.

We can assign numerical values to the levels of a nominal variable. For example, for ethnicity, we could label Asian Americans as 1, African Americans as 2, Latin Americans as 3, and so on. However, these scores do not carry any numerical weight; they are simply names for the categories. In other words, the scores are used for identity, but not for magnitude, equal unit size, or absolute value. We cannot order the data and claim that 1s are more than or less than 2s. We cannot analyze these data mathematically. It would not be appropriate, for example, to report that the mean ethnicity was 2.56. We cannot say that there is a true zero where someone would have no ethnicity. We can, however, form frequency distributions based on the data, calculate a mode, and use the chi-square test to analyze data measured on a nominal scale. If you are unfamiliar with these statistical concepts, don't worry. They will be discussed in later modules.

ordinal scale A scale in which objects or individuals are categorized and the categories form a rank order along a continuum.

Ordinal Scale An **ordinal scale** is one in which objects or individuals are categorized and the categories form a rank order along a continuum. Data measured on an ordinal scale have the properties of identity and magnitude but lack equal unit size and absolute zero. Ordinal data are often referred to as *ranked* data because the data are ordered from highest to lowest, or biggest to smallest. For example, reporting how students did on an exam based simply on their rank (highest score, second highest, and so on) would be an ordinal scale. This variable would carry identity and magnitude because each individual receives a rank (a number) that carries identity, and beyond simple identity it conveys information about order or magnitude (how many students performed better or worse in the class). However, the ranking score does not have equal unit size (the difference in performance on the exam between the students ranked 1 and 2 is not necessarily the same as the difference between the students ranked 2 and 3), or an absolute zero. We can calculate a mode or a median based on ordinal data; it is less meaningful to calculate a mean. We can also use nonparametric tests such as the Wilcoxon rank-sum test or a Spearman rank-order correlation coefficient (again, these statistical concepts will be explained in later modules).

interval scale A scale in which the units of measurement (intervals) between the numbers on the scale are all equal in size.

Interval Scale An **interval scale** is one in which the units of measurement (intervals) between the numbers on the scale are all equal in size. When using an interval scale, the properties of identity, magnitude, and equal unit size are met. For example, the Fahrenheit temperature scale is an interval scale of measurement. A given temperature carries identity (days with different temperatures receive different scores on the scale), magnitude (cooler days receive lower scores and hotter days receive higher scores), and equal unit size (the difference between 50 and 51 degrees is the same as that between 90 and 91 degrees.) However, the Fahrenheit scale does not have an absolute zero. Because of this, we are not able to form ratios based on this scale (for example, 100 degrees is not twice as hot as 50 degrees). Because interval data can be added and subtracted, we can calculate the mean, median, or mode for interval data. We can also use *t* tests, ANOVAs, or Pearson product-moment correlation coefficients to analyze interval data (once again, these statistics will be discussed in later modules).

ratio scale A scale in which, in addition to order and equal units of measurement, there is an absolute zero that indicates an absence of the variable being measured.

Ratio Scale A **ratio scale** is one in which, in addition to order and equal units of measurement, there is an absolute zero that indicates an absence of the variable being measured. Ratio data have all four properties of measurement—identity, magnitude, equal unit size, and absolute zero. Examples of ratio scales of measurement include weight, time, and height. Each of these scales has identity (individuals who weigh different amounts would receive different scores), magnitude (those who weigh less receive lower scores than those who weigh more), and equal unit size (1 pound is the same weight anywhere along the scale and for any person using the scale). These scales also have an absolute zero, which means a score of zero reflects an absence of that variable. This also means that ratios can be formed. For example, a weight of 100 pounds is twice as much as a weight of 50 pounds. As with interval data, mathematical computations can be performed on ratio data. This means that the mean, median, and mode can be computed. In addition, as with interval data, t tests, ANOVAs, or the Pearson product-moment correlation can be computed.

Notice that the same statistics are used for both interval and ratio scales. For this reason, many behavioral scientists simply refer to the category as *interval-ratio data* and typically do not distinguish between these two types of data. You should be familiar with the differences between interval and ratio data but aware that the same statistics are used with both types of data.

FEATURES OF SCALES OF MEASUREMENT

IN REVIEW

	Nominal	**Ordinal**	**Interval**	**Ratio**
		SCALE OF MEASUREMENT		
Examples	Ethnicity	Class rank	Temperature	Weight
	Religion	Letter grade	(Fahrenheit and Celsius)	Height
	Sex			Time
			Many psychological tests	
Properties	Identity	Identity	Identity	Identity
		Magnitude	Magnitude	Magnitude
			Equal unit size	Equal unit size
				Absolute zero
Mathematical Operations	None	Rank order	Add	Add
			Subtract	Subtract
			Multiply	Multiply
			Divide	Divide
Typical Statistics Used	Mode	Mode	Mode	Mode
	Chi-square	Median	Median	Median
		Wilcoxon tests	Mean	Mean
			t test	t test
			ANOVA	ANOVA

CRITICAL THINKING CHECK 2.1

1. Provide several operational definitions of *anxiety*. Include nonverbal measures and physiological measures. How would your operational definitions differ from a dictionary definition?
2. Identify the scale of measurement for each of the following:
   a. Phone area code
   b. Grade of egg (large, medium, small)
   c. Amount of time spent studying
   d. Score on the SAT
   e. Class rank
   f. Number on a volleyball jersey
   g. Miles per gallon

Discrete and Continuous Variables

discrete variables
Variables that usually consist of whole-number units or categories and are made up of chunks or units that are detached and distinct from one another.

Another means of classifying variables is in terms of whether they are discrete or continuous in nature. **Discrete variables** usually consist of whole-number units or categories. They are made up of chunks or units that are detached and distinct from one another. A change in value occurs a whole unit at a time, and decimals do not make sense with discrete scales. Most nominal and ordinal data are discrete. For example, gender, political party, and ethnicity are discrete scales. Some interval or ratio data can be discrete. For example, the number of children someone has would be reported as a whole number (discrete data), yet it is also ratio data (you can have a true zero and form ratios).

continuous variables
Variables that usually fall along a continuum and allow for fractional amounts.

Continuous variables usually fall along a continuum and allow for fractional amounts. The term *continuous* means that it "continues" between the whole-number units. Examples of continuous variables are age (22.7 years), height (64.5 inches), and weight (113.25 pounds). Most interval and ratio data are continuous in nature.

REVIEW OF KEY TERMS

absolute zero (p. 15)
continuous variables (p. 18)
discrete variables (p. 18)
equal unit size (p. 14)

identity (p. 14)
interval scale (p. 16)
magnitude (p. 14)
nominal scale (p. 15)

operational definition (p. 14)
ordinal scale (p. 16)
ratio scale (p. 16)

MODULE EXERCISES

(Answers to odd-numbered questions appear in Appendix B.)

1. What does it mean to define variables operationally?
2. Which of the following is the best operational definition of depression?

a. Depression is defined as that low feeling you get sometimes.
b. Depression is defined as what happens when a relationship ends.
c. Depression is defined as your score on a 50-item depression inventory.

d. Depression is defined as the number of boxes of tissues that you cry your way through.
3. Identify and describe the four properties of measurement.
4. Describe the similarities and differences between a nominal scale and an ordinal scale.
5. Describe the similarities and differences between an interval scale and a ratio scale.

6. Identify the type of scale of measurement for each of the following.
   a. Number correct on a 100-point exam
   b. Distance walked (in miles) on a treadmill
   c. Religious affiliation
   d. Placement in a beauty contest
7. Is number of college classes completed a discrete or continuous variable? Explain your answer. Identify the scale of measurement for this variable.

CRITICAL THINKING CHECK ANSWERS

Critical Thinking Check 2.1

1. Some operational definitions are suggested in the text. These definitions are quantifiable and based on measurable events. They are not conceptual, as a dictionary definition would be.

2. nominal
   ordinal
   ratio
   interval
   ordinal
   nominal
   ratio

WEB RESOURCES

The book-specific website at CengageBrain.com offers students a variety of study tools and useful resources such as glossaries, flashcards, quizzes, and Statistics and Research Methods Workshops.

CHAPTER ONE SUMMARY AND REVIEW
Getting Started

CHAPTER SUMMARY

We began the chapter by stressing the importance of statistics to scientists and researchers. The three goals of science (description, prediction, and explanation) were discussed and related to the research methods used by behavioral scientists. Methods that are descriptive in nature include observation, case study, and survey methods. Those that are predictive in nature include correlational and quasi-experimental methods. The experimental method allows for explanation of cause-and-effect relationships. The practicalities of doing research and proof and disproof in science were discussed, including the idea that testing a hypothesis involves attempting to falsify it. Lastly, we discussed defining variables operationally, identifying the scale of measurement for dependent variables, and the difference between discrete and continuous variables.

CHAPTER 1 REVIEW EXERCISES

(Answers to exercises appear in Appendix B.)

Fill-in Self-Test

Answer the following questions. If you have trouble answering any of the questions, restudy the relevant material before going on to the multiple-choice self-test.

1. A _____ is a prediction regarding the outcome of a study that often involves a prediction regarding the relationship between two variables in a study.
2. The three goals of science are _____, _____, and _____.
3. A _____ is an in-depth study of one or more individuals.
4. All of the people about whom a study is meant to generalize make up the _____.
5. The _____ method is a method in which the degree of relationship between at least two variables is assessed.
6. A characteristic inherent in the participants that cannot be changed is known as a _____ variable.
7. The variable in a study that is manipulated is the _____ variable.
8. The _____ group is the group of participants that serves as the baseline in a study.
9. A definition of a variable in terms of the activities a researcher uses to measure or manipulate it is an _____.
10. _____ is a property of measurement in which the ordering of numbers reflects the ordering of the variable.

11. A(n) _____ scale is a scale in which objects or individuals are broken into categories that have no numerical properties.

12. A(n) _____ scale is a scale in which the units of measurement between the numbers on the scale are all equal in size.

Multiple-Choice Self-Test

Select the single best answer for each of the following questions. If you have trouble answering any of the questions, restudy the relevant material.

1. A prediction regarding the outcome of a study is to _____ and an organized system of assumptions and principles that attempts to explain certain phenomena and how they are related is to _____.
   a. theory; hypothesis
   b. hypothesis; theory
   c. independent variable; dependent variable
   d. dependent variable; independent variable

2. Ray was interested in the mating behavior of squirrels, so he went into the field to observe them. Ray is using the _____ method of research.
   a. case study method
   b. laboratory observational
   c. naturalistic observational
   d. correlational

3. Negative correlation is to _____ and positive correlation is to
   _____.
   a. increasing or decreasing together; moving in opposite directions
   b. moving in opposite directions; increasing or decreasing together
   c. independent variable; dependent variable
   d. dependent variable; independent variable

4. Which of the following is a participant (subject) variable?
   a. Amount of time given to study a list of words
   b. Fraternity membership
   c. The number of words in a memory test
   d. All of the above

5. If a researcher assigns subjects to groups based on, for example, their earned GPA, the researcher would be using
   a. a manipulated independent variable.
   b. random assignment.
   c. a participant variable.
   d. a manipulated dependent variable.

6. In an experimental study of the effects of time spent studying on grade, time spent studying would be the
   a. control group.
   b. independent variable.
   c. experimental group.
   d. dependent variable.

7. Baseline is to treatment as _____ is to _____.
   a. independent variable; dependent variable
   b. dependent variable; independent variable
   c. experimental group; control group
   d. control group; experimental group

8. In a study of the effects of alcohol on driving performance, driving performance would be the
   a. control group.
   b. independent variable.
   c. experimental group.
   d. dependent variable.

9. Gender is to the _____ property of measurement and time is to the _____ property of measurement.
   a. magnitude; identity
   b. equal unit size; magnitude
   c. absolute zero; equal unit size
   d. identity; absolute zero

10. Arranging a group of individuals from heaviest to lightest represents the _____ property of measurement.
    a. identity
    b. magnitude
    c. equal unit size
    d. absolute zero

11. Letter grade on a test is to the _____ scale of measurement and height is to the _____ scale of measurement.
    a. ordinal; ratio
    b. ordinal; nominal
    c. nominal; interval
    d. interval; ratio

12. Weight is to the _____ scale of measurement and political affiliation is to the _____ scale of measurement.
    a. ratio; ordinal
    b. ratio; nominal
    c. interval; nominal
    d. ordinal; ratio

13. Measuring in whole units is to _____ and measuring in whole units and/or fractional amounts is to _____.
    a. discrete variable; continuous variable
    b. continuous variable; discrete variable
    c. nominal scale; ordinal scale
    d. Both b and c

CHAPTER 2
Descriptive Statistics I

In this chapter, and the next, we discuss what to do with the observations made when conducting a study—namely, how to describe the data set through the use of descriptive statistics. First, we consider ways of organizing the data. We need to take the large number of observations made during the course of a study and present them in a manner that is easier to read and understand. Then, we discuss some simple descriptive statistics. These statistics allow us to do some "number crunching"—to condense a large number of observations into a summary statistic or set of statistics. The concepts and statistics described in this section can be used to draw conclusions from data. They do not come close to covering all that can be done with data gathered from a study. They do, however, provide a place to start.

Organizing Data

Learning Objectives
- Organize data in a frequency distribution.
- Organize data in a class interval frequency distribution.
- Graph data in a bar graph.
- Graph data in a histogram.
- Graph data in a frequency polygon.

We will discuss two methods of organizing data: frequency distributions and graphs.

Frequency Distributions

To illustrate the processes of organizing and describing data, let's use the data set presented in Table 3.1. These data represent the scores of 30 students on an introductory psychology exam. One reason for organizing data and using statistics is so that meaningful conclusions can be drawn. As you can see from Table 3.1, our list of exam scores is simply that—a list in no particular order. As shown here, the data are not especially meaningful. One of the first steps in organizing these data might be to rearrange them from highest to lowest or lowest to highest.

Once this is accomplished (see Table 3.2), we can try to condense the data into a **frequency distribution**—a table in which all of the scores are listed along with the frequency with which each occurs. We can also show a relative frequency distribution, which indicates the proportion of the total observations included in each score. When the relative frequency distribution is multiplied by 100, it is read as a percentage. A frequency distribution and a relative frequency distribution of our exam data are presented in Table 3.3.

The frequency distribution is a way of presenting data that makes the pattern of the data easier to see. We can make the data set even easier to

frequency distribution
A table in which all of the scores are listed along with the frequency with which each occurs.

TABLE 3.1 Exam scores for 30 students

SCORE	SCORE
56	74
69	70
78	90
80	74
47	59
85	86
82	92
74	60
95	63
65	45
54	94
60	93
87	82
76	77
75	78

TABLE 3.2 Exam scores ordered from lowest to highest

SCORE	SCORE
45	76
47	77
54	78
56	78
59	80
60	82
60	82
63	85
65	86
69	87
70	90
74	92
74	93
74	94
75	95

read (especially desirable with large data sets) if we group the scores and create a **class interval frequency distribution.** We can combine individual scores into categories, or intervals, and list them along with the frequency of scores in each interval. In our exam score example, the scores range from 45 to 95—a 50-point range. A rule of thumb when creating class intervals is to have between 10 and 20 categories (Hinkle, Wiersma, & Jurs, 1988). A quick method of calculating what the width of the interval should be is to subtract the smallest score from the largest score and then divide by the number of intervals you would like (Schweigert, 1994). If we wanted 10 intervals in our example, we would proceed as follows:

class interval frequency distribution A table in which the scores are grouped into intervals and listed along with the frequency of scores in each interval.

$$\frac{95 - 45}{10} = \frac{50}{10} = 5$$

The frequency distribution using the class intervals with a width of 5 is provided in Table 3.4. Notice how much more compact the data appear when presented in a class interval frequency distribution. Although such distributions have the advantage of reducing the number of categories, they have the disadvantage of not providing as much information as a regular frequency distribution. For example, although we can see from the class interval frequency distribution that five people scored between 75 and 79, we do not know their exact scores within the interval.

TABLE 3.3 Frequency and relative frequency distributions of exam data

SCORE	f (FREQUENCY)	rf (RELATIVE FREQUENCY)
45	1	.033
47	1	.033
54	1	.033
56	1	.033
59	1	.033
60	2	.067
63	1	.033
65	1	.033
69	1	.033
70	1	.033
74	3	.100
75	1	.033
76	1	.033
77	1	.033
78	2	.067
80	1	.033
82	2	.067
85	1	.033
86	1	.033
87	1	.033
90	1	.033
92	1	.033
93	1	.033
94	1	.033
95	1	.033
	$N = 30$	1.00

Graphing Data

Frequency distributions can provide valuable information, but sometimes a picture is of greater value. Several types of pictorial representations can be used to represent data. The choice depends on the type of data collected and what the researcher hopes to emphasize or illustrate. The most common graphs used by psychologists are bar graphs, histograms, and frequency polygons (line graphs). Graphs typically have two coordinate axes, the x-axis (the horizontal axis) and the y-axis (the vertical axis). Most commonly, the y-axis is shorter than the x-axis, typically 60% to 75% of the length of the x-axis.

TABLE 3.4 A class interval distribution of exam data

CLASS INTERVAL	f	rf
45–49	2	.067
50–54	1	.033
55–59	2	.067
60–64	3	.100
65–69	2	.067
70–74	4	.133
75–79	5	.167
80–84	3	.100
85–89	3	.100
90–94	4	.133
95–99	1	.033
	$N = 30$	1.00

Bar Graphs and Histograms

Bar graphs and histograms are frequently confused. When the data collected are on a nominal scale, or if the variable is a **qualitative variable** (a categorical variable for which each value represents a discrete category), then a bar graph is most appropriate. A **bar graph** is a graphical representation of a frequency distribution in which vertical bars are centered above each category along the *x*-axis and are separated from each other by a space, indicating that the levels of the variable represent distinct, unrelated categories.

If the variable is a **quantitative variable** (the scores represent a change in quantity), or if the data collected are ordinal, interval, or ratio in scale, then a histogram can be used. A **histogram** is also a graphical representation of a frequency distribution in which vertical bars are centered above scores on the *x*-axis, but in a histogram the bars touch each other to indicate that the scores on the variable represent related, increasing values.

In both a bar graph and a histogram, the height of each bar indicates the frequency for that level of the variable on the *x*-axis. The spaces between the bars on the bar graph indicate not only the qualitative differences among the categories but also that the order of the values of the variable on the *x*-axis is arbitrary. In other words, the categories on the *x*-axis in a bar graph can be placed in any order. The fact that the bars are contiguous in a histogram indicates not only the increasing quantity of the variable but also that the variable has a definite order that cannot be changed.

A bar graph is illustrated in Figure 3.1. For a hypothetical distribution, the frequencies of individuals who affiliate with various political parties are indicated. Notice that the different political parties are listed on the *x*-axis, whereas frequency is recorded on the *y*-axis. Although the political parties are presented in a certain order, this order could be rearranged because the variable is qualitative.

qualitative variable
A categorical variable for which each value represents a discrete category.

bar graph A graphical representation of a frequency distribution in which vertical bars are centered above each category along the x-axis and are separated from each other by a space, indicating that the levels of the variable represent distinct, unrelated categories.

quantitative variable
A variable for which the scores represent a change in quantity.

histogram A graphical representation of a frequency distribution in which vertical bars centered above scores on the x-axis touch each other to indicate that the scores on the variable represent related, increasing values.

FIGURE 3.1
Bar graph
representing
political affiliation
for a distribution
of 30 individuals

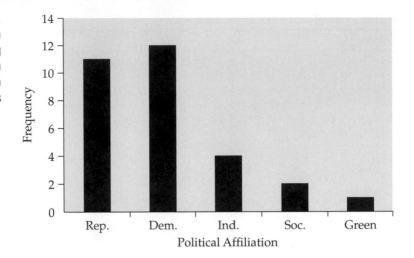

Figure 3.2 illustrates a histogram. In this figure, the frequencies of intelligence test scores from a hypothetical distribution are indicated. A histogram is appropriate because the IQ score variable is quantitative. The variable has a specific order that cannot be rearranged. You can see how to use Excel and SPSS to create both bar graphs and histograms in the Statistical Software Resources section at the end of this chapter. If you are unfamiliar with Excel or SPSS, see Appendix C to get started with these tools.

Frequency Polygons

frequency polygon
A line graph of the frequencies of individual scores.

We can also depict the data in a histogram as a **frequency polygon**—a line graph of the frequencies of individual scores or intervals. Again, scores (or intervals) are shown on the x-axis and frequencies on the y-axis. Once all the frequencies are plotted, the data points are connected. You can see the frequency polygon for the intelligence score data in Figure 3.3.

FIGURE 3.2
Histogram
representing IQ
score data for
30 individuals

FIGURE 3.3
Frequency polygon of IQ score data for 30 individuals

Frequency polygons are appropriate when the variable is quantitative or the data are ordinal, interval, or ratio. In this respect, frequency polygons are similar to histograms. Frequency polygons are especially useful for continuous data (such as age, weight, or time) in which it is theoretically possible for values to fall anywhere along the continuum. For example, an individual can weigh 120.5 pounds or be 35.5 years of age. Histograms are more appropriate when the data are discrete (measured in whole units)—for example, number of college classes taken or number of siblings. You can see how to use Excel and SPSS to create frequency polygons in the Statistical Software Resources section at the end of this chapter. If you are unfamiliar with Excel or SPSS, see Appendix C to get started with these tools.

DATA ORGANIZATION

IN REVIEW

TYPE OF ORGANIZATIONAL TOOL

	Frequency Distribution	Bar Graph	Histogram	Frequency Polygon
Description	A list of all scores occurring in the distribution along with the frequency of each	A pictorial graph with bars representing the frequency of occurrence of items for qualitative variables	A pictorial graph with bars representing the frequency of occurrence of items for quantitative variables	A pictorial line graph representing the frequency of occurrence of items for quantitative variables
Use with	Nominal, ordinal, interval, or ratio data	Nominal data	Typically ordinal, interval, or ratio data—most appropriate for discrete data	Typically ordinal, interval, or ratio data—more appropriate for continuous data

<table>
<tr>
<td>

CRITICAL
THINKING
CHECK
3.1

</td>
<td>

1. What do you think might be the advantage of a graphical representation of data over a frequency distribution?
2. A researcher observes driving behavior on a roadway, noting the gender of the drivers, the type of vehicle driven, and the speed at which they are traveling. The researcher wants to organize the data in graphs but cannot remember when to use bar graphs, histograms, or frequency polygons. Which type of graph should be used to describe each variable?

</td>
</tr>
</table>

REVIEW OF KEY TERMS

bar graph (p. 29)
class interval frequency
    distribution (p. 27)

frequency distribution (p. 26)
frequency polygon (p. 30)
histogram (p. 29)

qualitative variable (p. 29)
quantitative variable (p. 29)

MODULE EXERCISES

(Answers to odd-numbered questions appear in Appendix B.)

Exercises 1–3: The following data represent a distribution of speeds at which individuals were traveling on a highway.

64	64
76	67
65	68
67	70
67	65
80	70
79	72
73	65
65	62
68	64

1. Organize the data into a frequency distribution with frequency (f) and relative frequency (rf) columns.
2. Organize the data into a class interval frequency distribution with 10 intervals and frequency (f) and relative frequency (rf) columns.
3. Which type of figure should be used to represent these data—a bar graph, histogram, or frequency polygon? Why? Draw the appropriate figure for these data.
4. Differentiate a qualitative variable from a quantitative variable.
5. Explain when it would be appropriate to use a bar graph versus a histogram.
6. Explain when it would be appropriate to use a histogram versus a frequency polygon.

CRITICAL THINKING CHECK ANSWERS

Critical Thinking Check 3.1

1. One advantage is that it is easier to "see" the data set in a graphical representation. In other words, with a picture it is easier to determine where the majority of the scores are in the distribution. With a frequency distribution, there is more reading involved before a judgment can be made about the shape of the distribution.

2. Gender and type of vehicle driven are qualitative variables, measured on a nominal scale; thus, a bar graph should be used. The speed at which the drivers are traveling is a quantitative variable, measured on a ratio scale. Either a histogram or a frequency polygon could be used, although a frequency polygon might be better because of the continuous nature of the variable.

WEB RESOURCES

The book-specific website at CengageBrain.com offers students a variety of study tools and useful resources such as glossaries, flashcards, quizzes, and Statistics and Research Methods Workshops.

MODULE 4
Measures of Central Tendency

Learning Objectives
- Differentiate measures of central tendency.
- Know how to calculate the mean, median, and mode.
- Know when it is most appropriate to use each measure of central tendency.

descriptive statistics
Numerical measures that describe a distribution by providing information on the central tendency of the distribution, the width of the distribution, and the shape of the distribution.

measure of central tendency A number intended to characterize an entire distribution.

mean A measure of central tendency; the arithmetic average of a distribution.

Organizing data into tables and graphs can help make a data set more meaningful. These methods, however, do not provide as much information as numerical measures. **Descriptive statistics** are numerical measures that describe a distribution by providing information on the central tendency of the distribution, the width of the distribution, and the distribution's shape. A **measure of central tendency** characterizes an entire set of data in terms of a single representative number. Measures of central tendency measure the "middleness" of a distribution of scores in three ways: the mean, median, and mode.

Mean

The most commonly used measure of central tendency is the **mean**—the arithmetic average of a group of scores. You are probably familiar with this idea. We can calculate the mean for our distribution of exam scores (from the previous module) by adding all of the scores together and dividing by the total number of scores. Mathematically, this would be:

$$\mu = \frac{\sum X}{N}$$

where

μ (pronounced "mu") represents the symbol for the population mean
Σ represents the symbol for "the sum of"
X represents the individual scores, and
N represents the number of scores in the distribution

34

To calculate the mean, then, we sum all of the Xs, or scores, and divide by the total number of scores in the distribution (N). You may have also seen this formula represented as follows:

$$\overline{X} = \frac{\sum X}{N}$$

In this case $\overline{X}$ represents a sample mean.

We can use either formula (they are the same) to calculate the mean for the distribution of exam scores used in Module 3. These scores are presented again in Table 4.1, along with a column showing frequency (f) and another

TABLE 4.1 Frequency distribution of exam scores, including an fX column

X	f	fX
45	1	45
47	1	47
54	1	54
56	1	56
59	1	59
60	2	120
63	1	63
65	1	65
69	1	69
70	1	70
74	3	222
75	1	75
76	1	76
77	1	77
78	2	156
80	1	80
82	2	164
85	1	85
86	1	86
87	1	87
90	1	90
92	1	92
93	1	93
94	1	94
95	1	95
	30	2220 = $\sum X$

column showing the frequency of the score multiplied by the score (f times X). The sum of all the values in the fX column is the sum of all the individual scores (ΣX). Using this sum in the formula for the mean, we have:

$$\mu = \frac{\Sigma X}{N} = \frac{2{,}220}{30} = 74.00$$

You can also calculate the mean using SPSS, Excel, or the Stats function on most calculators. As an example, the procedure for calculating the mean using each of these tools is presented in the Statistical Software Resources section at the end of this chapter. If you are unfamiliar with Excel or SPSS, see Appendix C to get started with these tools. Use of the mean is constrained by the nature of the data. It is appropriate for interval and ratio data, but it is not appropriate for ordinal or nominal data.

Median

Another measure of central tendency, the median, is used in situations in which the mean might not be representative of a distribution. Let's use a different distribution of scores to demonstrate when it might be appropriate to use the median rather than the mean. Imagine that you are considering taking a job with a small computer company. When you interview for the position, the owner of the company informs you that the mean income for employees at the company is approximately $100,000 and that the company has 25 employees. Most people would view this as good news. Having learned in a statistics class that the mean might be influenced by extreme scores, you ask to see the distribution of 25 incomes. The distribution is shown in Table 4.2.

The calculation of the mean for this distribution is:

$$\frac{\Sigma X}{N} = \frac{2{,}498{,}000}{25} = 99{,}920$$

Notice that, as claimed, the mean income of company employees is very close to $100,000. Notice also, however, that the mean in this case is not very representative of central tendency, or "middleness." In this distribution, the mean is thrown off center or inflated by one very extreme score of $1,800,000 (the income of the company's owner, needless to say). This extremely high income pulls the mean toward it and thus increases or inflates the mean. Thus, in distributions with one or a few extreme scores (either high or low), the mean will not be a good indicator of central tendency. In such cases, a better measure of central tendency is the median.

median A measure of central tendency; the middle score in a distribution after the scores have been arranged from highest to lowest or lowest to highest.

The **median** is the middle score in a distribution after the scores have been arranged from highest to lowest or lowest to highest. The distribution of incomes in Table 4.2 is already ordered from lowest to highest. To determine the median, we simply have to find the middle score. In this situation, with 25 scores, that would be the 13th score. You can see that the median of the distribution would be an income of $27,000, which is far more representative of the central tendency for this distribution of incomes.

TABLE 4.2   Yearly salaries for 25 employees

INCOME	FREQUENCY	fX
15,000	1	15,000
20,000	2	40,000
22,000	1	22,000
23,000	2	46,000
25,000	5	125,000
27,000	2	54,000
30,000	3	90,000
32,000	1	32,000
35,000	2	70,000
38,000	1	38,000
39,000	1	39,000
40,000	1	40,000
42,000	1	42,000
45,000	1	45,000
1,800,000	1	1,800,000
	$N = 25$	$\Sigma X = 2{,}498{,}000$

Why is the median not as influenced as the mean by extreme scores? Think about the calculation of each of these measures. When calculating the mean, we must add in the atypical income of $1,800,000, thus distorting the calculation. When determining the median, however, we do not consider the size of the $1,800,000 income; it is only a score at one end of the distribution whose numerical value does not have to be considered in order to locate the middle score in the distribution. The point to remember is that the median is not affected by extreme scores in a distribution because it is only a positional value. The mean is affected because its value is determined by a calculation that has to include the extreme value.

In the income example, the distribution had an odd number of scores ($N = 25$). Thus, the median was an actual score in the distribution (the 13th score). In distributions with an even number of observations, the median is calculated by averaging the two middle scores. In other words, we determine the middle point between the two middle scores. Look back at the distribution of exam scores in Table 4.1. This distribution has 30 scores. The median would be the average of the 15th and 16th scores (the two middle scores). Thus, the median would be 75.5—not an actual score in the distribution, but the middle point nonetheless. Notice that in this distribution, the median (75.5) is very close to the mean (74.00). Why are they so similar? Because this distribution contains no extreme scores, both the mean and the median are representative of the central tendency of the distribution.

Like the mean, the median can be used with ratio and interval data and is inappropriate for use with nominal data, but unlike the mean, the median can be used with most ordinal data.

Mode ●○

mode A measure of central tendency; the score in the distribution that occurs with the greatest frequency.

The third measure of central tendency is the **mode**—the score in a distribution that occurs with the greatest frequency. In the distribution of exam scores, the mode is 74 (similar to the mean and median). In the distribution of incomes, the mode is $25,000 (similar to the median, but not the mean). In some distributions, all scores occur with equal frequency; such a distribution has no mode. In other distributions, several scores occur with equal frequency. Thus, a distribution may have two modes (bimodal), three modes (trimodal), or even more. The mode is the only indicator of central tendency that can be used with nominal data. Although it can also be used with ordinal, interval, or ratio data, the mean and median are more reliable indicators of the central tendency of a distribution, and the mode is seldom used.

IN REVIEW

MEASURES OF CENTRAL TENDENCY			
	TYPE OF CENTRAL TENDENCY MEASURE		
	Mean	**Median**	**Mode**
Definition	The arithmetic average	The middle score in a distribution of scores organized from highest to lowest or lowest to highest	The score occurring with greatest frequency
Use with	Interval and ratio data	Ordinal, interval, and, ratio data	Nominal, ordinal, interval, or ratio data
Caution	Not for use with distributions with a few extreme scores		Not a reliable measure of central tendency

CRITICAL THINKING CHECK 4.1

1. In the example described in Critical Thinking Check 3.1, a researcher collected data on drivers' gender, type of vehicle, and speed of travel. What would be an appropriate measure of central tendency to calculate for each type of data?
2. If one driver was traveling at a rate of 100 mph (25 mph faster than anyone else), which measure of central tendency would you recommend against using?

REVIEW OF KEY TERMS

descriptive statistics (p. 34)   measure of central tendency (p. 34)   mode (p. 38)
mean (p. 34)   median (p. 36)

MODULE EXERCISES

(Answers to odd-numbered questions appear in Appendix B.)

1. The following data represent a distribution of speeds at which individuals were traveling on a highway.

64	73	65
76	65	70
65	68	72
67	64	65
67	67	62
80	68	64
79	70	

Calculate the mean, median, and mode for the speed distribution data set.

2. For the distribution in Exercise 1, which measure of central tendency is most appropriate and why?

Exercises 3–6: Calculate the mean, median, and mode for the following four distributions.

3. 2, 2, 4, 5, 8, 9, 10, 11, 11, 11

4. 1, 2, 3, 4, 4, 5, 5, 5, 6, 6, 8, 9

5. 1, 3, 3, 3, 5, 5, 8, 8, 8, 9, 10, 11

6. 2, 3, 4, 5, 6, 6, 6, 7, 8, 8

7. For the following two distributions, indicate which measure(s) of central tendency would be appropriate for each.

Distribution A: 10, 11, 11, 12, 12, 12, 13, 13, 14

Distribution B: 10, 11, 11, 12, 12, 12, 13, 13, 100

CRITICAL THINKING CHECK ANSWERS

Critical Thinking Check 4.1

1. Because gender and type of vehicle driven are nominal data, the mode can be determined. However, it is inappropriate to use the median or the mean with these data. The speed at which the drivers are traveling is ratio in scale; thus, the mean, median, or mode could be used. The mean and median would be better indicators of central tendency.

2. In this case, the mean should not be used because of the single outlier in the distribution.

WEB RESOURCES

The book-specific website at CengageBrain.com offers students a variety of study tools and useful resources such as glossaries, flashcards, quizzes, and Statistics and Research Methods Workshops.

CHAPTER TWO SUMMARY AND REVIEW
Descriptive Statistics I

CHAPTER SUMMARY

This chapter discussed data organization and descriptive statistics. Several methods of data organization were presented, including how to design a frequency distribution, a bar graph, a histogram, and a frequency polygon. The type of data appropriate for each of these methods was also discussed. One category of descriptive statistics that summarizes a large data set includes measures of central tendency (mean, median, and mode). These statistics provide information about the central tendency, or "middleness," of a distribution of scores. The mean is the arithmetic average; the median is the middle score in a distribution of scores after the scores have been ordered from highest to lowest, or lowest to highest; and the mode is the score that occurs with the greatest frequency.

CHAPTER 2 REVIEW EXERCISES

(Answers to exercises appear in Appendix B.)

Fill-in Self-Test

Answer the following questions. If you have trouble answering any of the questions, restudy the relevant material before going on to the multiple-choice self-test.

1. A _____ is a table in which all of the scores are listed along with the frequency with which each occurs.
2. A categorical variable for which each value represents a discrete category is a _____ variable.
3. A graphical representation of a frequency distribution in which vertical bars centered above scores on the *x*-axis touch each other to indicate that the scores on the variable represent related, increasing values is a _____.
4. Measures of _____ are numbers intended to characterize an entire distribution.
5. The _____ is the middle score in a distribution after the scores have been arranged from highest to lowest or lowest to highest.

Multiple-Choice Self-Test

Select the single best answer for each of the following questions. If you have trouble answering any of the questions, restudy the relevant material.

1. A _____ is graphical representation of a frequency distribution in which vertical bars are centered above each category along the *x*-axis and are separated from

each other by a space indicating that the levels of the variable represent distinct, unrelated categories.
a. histogram
b. frequency polygon
c. bar graph
d. class interval histogram

2. Qualitative variable is to quantitative variable as ____ is to ____.
a. categorical variable; numerical variable
b. numerical variable; categorical variable
c. bar graph; histogram
d. categorical variable and bar graph; numerical variable and histogram

3. Seven Girl Scouts reported the following individual earnings from their sale of cookies: $17, $23, $13, $15, $12, $19, and $13. In this distribution of individual earnings, the mean is ____ the mode and ____ the median.
a. equal to; equal to
b. greater than; equal to
c. equal to; less than
d. greater than; greater than

4. When Dr. Thomas calculated her students' history test scores, she noticed that one student had an extremely high score. Which measure of central tendency should be used in this situation?
a. mean
b. standard deviation
c. median
d. either the mean or the median

5. Imagine that 4,999 people who are penniless live in Medianville. An individual whose net worth is $500,000,000 moves to Medianville. Now the mean net worth in this town is ____ and the median net worth is ____.
a. 0; 0
b. $100,000; 0
c. 0; $100,000
d. $100,000; $100,000

6. Middle score in the distribution is to ____ as score occurring with the greatest frequency is to ____.
a. mean; median
b. median; mode
c. mean; mode
d. mode; median

7. Mean is to ____ as mode is to ____.
a. ordinal, interval, and ratio data only; nominal data only
b. nominal data only; ordinal data only
c. interval and ratio data only; all types of data
d. None of the above

Self-Test Problems

1. For the following distribution, organize the data into a frequency distribution with frequency (f) and relative frequency(rf) columns.
   1, 1, 2, 2, 4, 5, 8, 9, 10, 11, 11, 11

2. Calculate the mean, median, and mode for the distribution in Problem 1.

CHAPTER TWO
Statistical Software Resources

If you need help getting started with Excel or SPSS, please see Appendix C: Getting Started with Excel and SPSS.

 MODULE 3 Organizing Data

Using Excel to Create a Bar Graph

Begin by entering the data from Figure 3.1 in Module 3 into an Excel spreadsheet, as follows. Please note that the column headings of "Affiliation" and "Frequency" are entered into the spreadsheet. Once the data are entered, highlight all of the data including the column headers.

Now select the **Insert** ribbon and then **Column** (please note that there is a **Bar** option for figures but that this produces horizontal bars, whereas the bars in a bar graph should be vertical). Select the top left option from the

Column options (2-D column chart). This should produce the following bar graph:

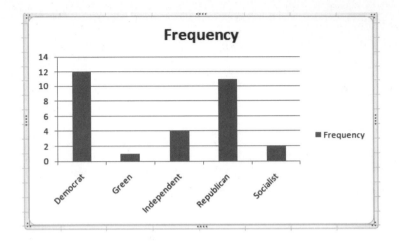

Notice that the different political parties are listed on the *x*-axis, whereas frequency is recorded on the *y*-axis. Excel provides **Chart Tools** so that we can modify the appearance of a graph. For example, if you want the bar graph to conform to APA style, you could use **Chart Tools** to modify the appearance of the chart. To use **Chart Tools**, make sure that you have clicked on the chart in Excel after which the three ribbons under **Chart Tools**, (**Design**, **Layout**, and **Format**) will become accessible. Using these menus, you can change the appearance of the chart to, for example, add **Axis Titles** (under the **Layout** ribbon), remove the horizontal **Gridlines** (under the **Layout** ribbon), or change the color of the bars (Excel uses blue as the default) by using the **Format** ribbon, clicking one of the bars, and selecting **Shape Fill**. After making these modifications, your chart will appear as follows:

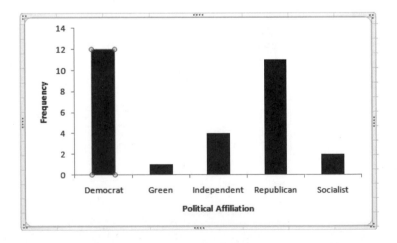

Please also note that although the political parties are presented in a certain order, this order could be rearranged because the variable is qualitative.

Using Excel to Create a Histogram

To illustrate the difference between a bar graph and a histogram, let's use the data from the table below, which lists the frequencies of intelligence test scores from a hypothetical distribution of 30 individuals. A histogram is appropriate for these data because the IQ score variable is quantitative. The variable has a specific order that cannot be rearranged.

IQ Score Data for 30 Individuals

Score	Frequency
83	1
86	1
89	1
92	2
98	3
101	4
107	5
110	3
113	2
116	3
119	2
125	1
131	1
134	1

Begin by entering the data into an Excel spreadsheet, as follows. Please note that the column headings of "Score" and "Frequency" are entered into the spreadsheet. Once the data are entered, highlight only the "Frequency" data as is illustrated in the next screen capture.

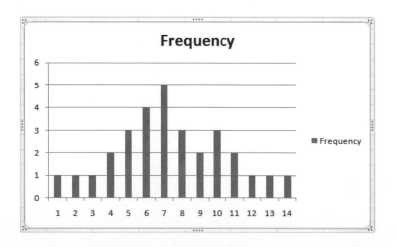

Because Excel does not have a histogram option in which the bars in the graph touch, we'll have to use special formatting to create the histogram. Click on the **Insert** ribbon and then **Column**. Select the option in the top left corner, as we did when creating bar graphs. This should produce the following graph:

We'll begin editing the graph by removing the spaces between the bars. To do so, right-click on any of the bars and select **Format Data Series** to produce the following pop-up window:

Move the **Gap Width** tab to zero as is indicated in the window and then close the window. Your figure should now more closely resemble a histogram. Now you can use the **Chart Tools** to modify your figure so that it more closely resembles what you desire. This should include axis labels on the x- and y-axes and changing the values on the x-axis to reflect the range of intelligence scores that were measured. To accomplish the latter, right-click on a value on the *x*-axis and choose **Select Data…** to produce the following pop-up window:

Click on the Edit window under **Horizontal (Category) Axis Labels**. You'll receive the following pop-up window:

Highlight the IQ scores from the spreadsheet and they will be inserted into the **Axis label range:** box. Then click **OK**. Click **OK** a second time to close the original pop-up window. You can now use the **Chart Tools** to format your histogram so that it more closely resembles a graph appropriate for APA style. This would include adding axis labels to the *x*- and *y*-axes, changing the bars from blue to black, and removing the gridlines from the graph. After making these changes, your figure should look as follows:

Using Excel to Create a Frequency Polygon (Line Graph)

Begin by entering the intelligence test score data from the table presented in the previous example into an Excel spreadsheet, as follows. Then, highlight only the Frequency data as is illustrated in the next screen capture.

	A	B
1	Score	Frequency
2	83	1
3	86	1
4	89	1
5	92	2
6	98	3
7	101	4
8	107	5
9	110	3
10	113	2
11	116	3
12	119	2
13	125	1
14	131	1
15	134	1

Next, click on the **Insert** ribbon and then **Line**. Select the option in the top left corner (the first 2-D line option). This should produce the following graph:

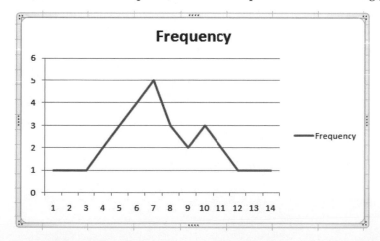

Now, right-click on a value on the *x*-axis and then click **Select Data...** to produce the following pop-up window:

Click on the Edit window under **Horizontal (Category) Axis Labels**. You'll receive the following pop-up window:

Highlight the IQ scores from the spreadsheet and they will be inserted into the **Axis label range:** box. Then click **OK**. Click **OK** a second time to close the original pop-up window. You can now use the **Chart Tools** to format your frequency polygon so that it more closely resembles line graphs appropriate for APA style. This would include adding axis labels to the *x*- and *y*-axes, changing the line from blue to black, and removing the gridlines from the graph. After making these changes, your figure should look as follows:

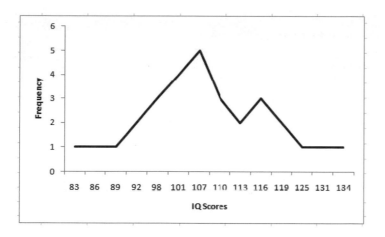

Using SPSS to Create a Bar Graph

We'll use the same data as in the earlier example (Figure 3.1 in Module 3) to illustrate how to use SPSS to create a bar graph. To begin, we enter the data into the SPSS spreadsheet. As with Excel we use two columns, one labeled Affiliation and one labeled Frequency, as can be seen in the following screen capture.

	Affiliation	Frequency	var	var	var	var	var	var
1	Democrat	12.00						
2	Green	1.00						
3	Independ	4.00						
4	Republic	11.00						
5	Socialis	2.00						
6								
7								
8								

File Edit View Data Transform Analyze Direct Marketing Graphs Utilities Add-ons Window Help

Next, we click on the **Graphs** menu and then **Chart Builder**. From the Gallery menu on the bottom of the dialog box select Bar and then double click the first bar graph icon in the top row to produce the following dialog box.

You can see that the two variables are listed in the top left **Variables** box. Drag the Affiliation variable to the *x*-axis box in the figure on the top right, and then drag the Frequency variable to the *y*-axis box in the figure on the top right. The dialog box should now look as follows:

Next, click on the **Element Properties...** box on the right-hand side of the dialog box to receive the following dialog box.

Highlight **Y-Axis 1 (Bar 1)** and change the name of the variable from Mean Frequency to simply Frequency, and then click **Apply** and **OK**. Finally, click **OK** in the original dialog box. SPSS will then produce an output file with the following bar graph.

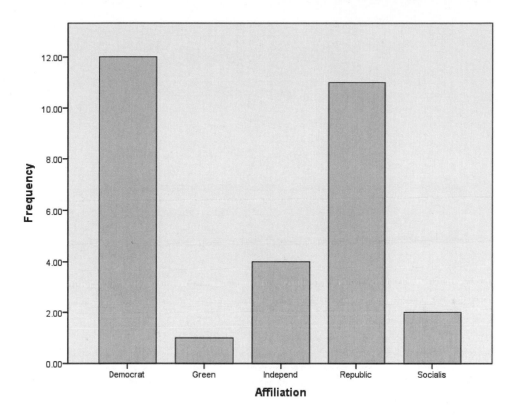

Using SPSS to Create a Histogram

Let's use the same data set as in the Excel histogram example to create a histogram with SPSS. Thus, we'll enter the IQ score data into the SPSS spreadsheet. However, in this case, each individual score is entered. This is illustrated in the screen capture below in which all 30 scores have been entered into SPSS (Please note that due to screen size constraints, the final four scores do not show in the screen capture. Thus, make sure you use the IQ data from the earlier table that we used when creating a histogram using Excel.)

File	Edit	View	Data	Transform	Analyze	Dire

10 :

	IQscore	var	var
4	92.00		
5	92.00		
6	98.00		
7	98.00		
8	98.00		
9	101.00		
10	101.00		
11	101.00		
12	101.00		
13	107.00		
14	107.00		
15	107.00		
16	107.00		
17	107.00		
18	110.00		
19	110.00		
20	110.00		
21	113.00		
22	113.00		
23	116.00		
24	116.00		
25	116.00		
26	119.00		

Data View | Variable View

The variable was named **IQscore** using the **Variable View** screen and it was designated a **Numeric** variable with the **Scale** level of measurement. To name the variable, click on the **Variable View** tab at the bottom of the window and type the name you wish to give the variable in the highlighted **Name** box. The variable name cannot have any spaces in it. Because these data represent intelligence score data, we'll type in **IQscore.** Note also that the **Type** of data is Numeric. Once the variable is named, highlight the **Data View** tab on the bottom left of the screen in order to get back to the data spreadsheet. (See Appendix C: "Getting Started with Excel and SPSS," if you are unfamiliar with naming variables.) From the **Data View** spreadsheet screen, select **Graphs**, and then **Chart Builder...** to receive the following dialog boxes.

Select **Histogram** and then double click on the first example of a histogram. In the dialog box on the top left of the screen, click on **IQscore** and drag it to the *x*-axis box in the histogram on the right. Then, in the **Element Properties** box on the right highlight **Bar1,** as in the screen capture above and then click on **Set Parameters** to receive the following dialog box:

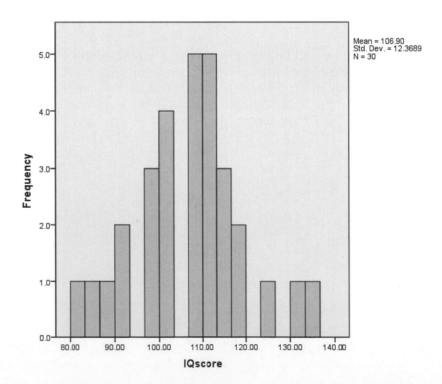

Make sure that **Automatic** is selected as the option in the first box. In the second box, select **Custom** and set the **Number of intervals** at 18 (the number of different IQ scores received by the 30 participants in the study). Then click **Continue** and then **Apply**. Finally, click **OK** in the dialog box on the left and you should receive the histogram in the output file.

Notice that the bars are touching, except for those instances in which there were missing scores.

Using SPSS to Create a Frequency Polygon (Line Graph)

We'll once again use the intelligence test score data to illustrate how to create a frequency polygon using SPSS. Enter the data in the same manner we did when we created a histogram in SPSS. In other words, enter each individual score on a separate line in SPSS so that all 30 scores in the distribution are entered individually as we did earlier in the module when creating the histogram. Once the data are entered, named, and coded as numeric with the scale level of measurement, click on **Graphs** and then **Chart Builder** to receive the following dialog boxes:

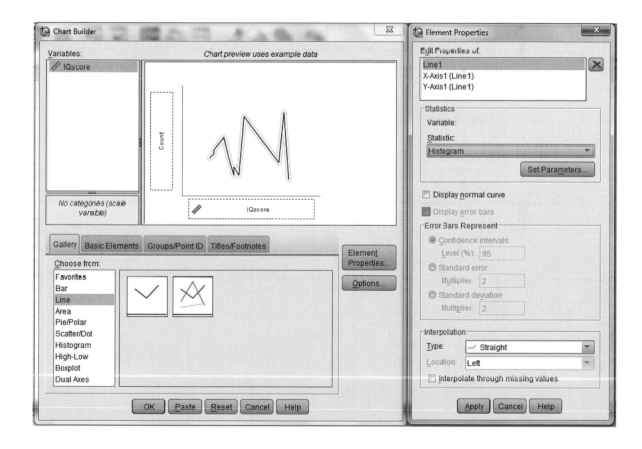

Double click on the **Line** graph option in the lower left of the screen, and then drag the **IQscore** variable from the top left of the screen to *x*-axis box. In the **Element Properties** dialog box on the right of the screen, highlight

Line 1 and then **Histogram** in the **Statistic** box. Click on the **Set Parameters** box to receive the following dialog box:

Select **Automatic** in the first box, and then **Custom** in the second box indicating that the number of intervals should be 52 (the total range of IQ scores for our group of 30 individuals). Click **Continue** and then **Apply**. Finally, click **OK** to execute the procedure. You should receive the following frequency polygon.

MODULE 4 Measures of Central Tendency

Using Excel to Calculate the Mean, Median, and Mode

To begin using Excel to conduct data analyses, the data must be entered into an Excel spreadsheet. This simply involves opening Excel and entering the data into the spreadsheet. You can see in the following spreadsheet that I have entered the exam grade data from Table 4.1 in Module 4 into an Excel spreadsheet.

Once the data have been entered, we use the Data Analysis tool to calculate descriptive statistics. This is accomplished by clicking on the **Data** tab or ribbon and then clicking the **Data Analysis** icon on the top right side of the window. Once the Data Analysis tab is active, a dialog box of options will appear (see next).

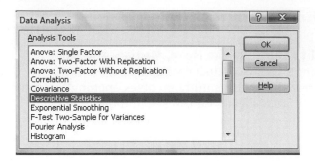

Select **Descriptive Statistics** as is indicated in the preceding box, and then click **OK**. This will lead to the following dialog box:

With the cursor in the **Input Range** box, highlight the data that you want analyzed from column A in the Excel spreadsheet so that they appear in the input range. In addition, check the **Summary statistics** box. Once you have done this, click **OK**. The summary statistics will appear in a new Worksheet, as seen next.

	A	B
1	*Column1*	
2		
3	Mean	74
4	Standard Error	2.532546762
5	Median	75.5
6	Mode	74
7	Standard Deviation	13.8713299
8	Sample Variance	192.4137931
9	Kurtosis	-0.60744581
10	Skewness	-0.391850234
11	Range	50
12	Minimum	45
13	Maximum	95
14	Sum	2220
15	Count	30

As you can see, there are several descriptive statistics reported, including all three measures of central tendency (mean, median, and mode).

Using SPSS to Calculate the Mean

As with the Excel exercise above, we will once again be using the data from Table 4.1 in Module 4 to calculate descriptive statistics. We begin by entering the data from Table 4.1 into an SPSS spreadsheet. This simply involves opening SPSS and entering the data into the spreadsheet. You can see in the following spreadsheet that I have entered the exam grade data from Table 4.1 into an SPSS spreadsheet.

File	Edit	View	Data	Transform	Analyze	Graphs	Utilities	Add-ons	Window	Help

	VAR00001	var	var	var	var	var	var	var	var	var	var
1	45.00										
2	47.00										
3	54.00										
4	56.00										
5	59.00										
6	60.00										
7	60.00										
8	63.00										
9	65.00										
10	69.00										
11	70.00										
12	74.00										
13	74.00										
14	74.00										
15	75.00										
16	76.00										
17	77.00										
18	78.00										
19	78.00										
20	80.00										
21	82.00										
22	82.00										
23	85.00										
24	86.00										
25	87.00										
26	90.00										
27	92.00										
28	93.00										
29	94.00										
30	95.00										
31											

Notice that the variable is simply named VAR00001. To rename the variable to something appropriate for your data set, click on the **Variable View** tab on the bottom left of the screen. You will see the following window:

| File | Edit | View | Data | Transform | Analyze | Graphs | Utilities | Add-ons | Window | Help |

	Name	Type	Width	Decimals	Label	Values	Missing	Columns	Align	Measure	Role
1	VAR00001	Numeric	8	2		None	None	8	Right	Scale	Input
2											
3											
4											
5											
6											
7											
8											
9											
10											
11											
12											
13											
14											
15											
16											
17											
18											
19											
20											
21											
22											
23											
24											
25											
26											
27											
28											
29											
30											
31											
32											
33											
34											
35											
36											

Data View Variable View

Type the name you wish to give the variable in the highlighted **Name** box. The variable name cannot have any spaces in it. Because these data represent exam grade data, we'll type in **Examgrade**. Note also that the **Type** of data is Numeric. Once the variable is named, highlight the **Data View** tab on the bottom left of the screen in order to get back to the data spreadsheet. Once you've navigated back to the data spreadsheet, click on the **Analyze** tab at the top of the screen and a drop-down menu with various statistical analyses will appear. Select **Descriptive Statistics** and then **Descriptive.** The following dialog box will appear:

Examgrade will be highlighted, as above. Click on the arrow in the middle of the window and the Examgrade variable will be moved over to the **Variables** box. Then click on **Options** to receive the following dialog box:

You can see that the Mean, Standard Deviation, Minimum, and Maximum are all checked. However, you could select any of the descriptive statistics you want calculated. After making your selections, click **Continue** and then **OK**. The output will appear on a separate page as an Output file like the one below where you can see the minimum and maximum scores for this distribution along with the mean exam score of 74. Please note that if you had more than one set of data—for example, two classes of exam scores—they could each occupy one column in your SPSS spreadsheet and you could conduct analyses on both variables at the same time. In this situation, separate descriptive statistics would be calculated for each data set.

Descriptives

Descriptive Statistics

	N	Minimum	Maximum	Mean	Std. Deviation
Exam Grade	30	45.00	95.00	74.0000	13.87133
Valid N (listwise)	30				

Using the TI-84 to Calculate the Mean

Follow the steps below to use your TI-84 calculator to calculate the mean for the data set from Table 4.1 in Module 4.

1. With the calculator on, press the STAT key.
2. EDIT will be highlighted. Press the ENTER key.
3. Under L1 enter the data from Table 4.1.
4. Press the STAT key again and highlight CALC.
5. Number 1: 1—VAR STATS will be highlighted. Press ENTER.
6. Press ENTER once again.

The statistics for the single variable on which you entered data will be presented on the calculator screen. The mean is presented on the first line of output as $\overline{X}$.

CHAPTER 3

Descriptive Statistics II

Measures of Variation

Learning Objectives
- Differentiate measures of variation.
- Know how to calculate the range, average deviation, and standard deviation.
- Explain the difference between a normal distribution and a skewed distribution.
- Differentiate the types of kurtosis.
- Explain the difference between a positively skewed distribution and a negatively skewed distribution.

measure of variation
A number that indicates how dispersed scores are around the mean of the distribution.

A measure of central tendency provides information about the "middleness" of a distribution of scores, but not about the width or spread of the distribution. To assess the width of a distribution, we need a measure of variability or dispersion. A **measure of variation** indicates how scores are dispersed around the mean of the distribution. As an illustration, consider the two very small distributions represented in Table 5.1. Each represents a small distribution of exam scores. Notice that the mean for each distribution is the same. If these data represented two very small classes of students, reporting that the two classes had the same mean on the exam might lead one to conclude that they performed essentially the same. Notice, however, how different the distributions are. Providing a measure of variability along with a measure of central tendency would convey the information that even though the distributions have the same mean, the spread of the distributions is very different.

TABLE 5.1 Two distributions of exam scores

CLASS 1	CLASS 2
0	45
50	50
100	55
$\Sigma = 150$	$\Sigma = 150$
$\mu = 50$	$\mu = 50$

We will discuss three measures of variability: the range, the average deviation, and the standard deviation. The range can be used with any type of data. However, the standard deviation and average deviation are appropriate only for interval and ratio data.

Range

range A measure of variation; the difference between the lowest and the highest scores in a distribution.

The simplest measure of variation is the **range**—the difference between the lowest and the highest score in a distribution. To find the range, simply subtract the lowest score from the highest score. In our hypothetical distributions of exam scores, the range for Class 1 is 100 points, whereas the range for Class 2 is 10 points. Thus, the range provides some information concerning the difference in the spread of the distributions. In this simple measure of variation, however, only the highest and lowest scores enter the calculation, and all other scores are ignored. For example, referring back to Module 4 and the distribution of 30 exam scores in Table 4.1, only 2 of the 30 scores would be used in calculating the range ($95 - 45 = 50$). Thus, the range is easily distorted by one unusually high or low score in a distribution.

Average Deviation and Standard Deviation

More sophisticated measures of variation use all of the scores in the distribution in their calculation. The most commonly used measure of variation is the *standard deviation*. Most people have heard this term before and may even have calculated a standard deviation if they have taken a statistics class. However, many people who know how to calculate a standard deviation do not really appreciate the information it provides.

To begin, let's think about what the phrase *standard deviation* means. Other words that might be substituted for the word *standard* include *average*, *normal*, or *usual*. The word *deviation* means to *diverge*, *move away from*, or *digress*. Putting these terms together, we see that the standard deviation means the average movement away from something. But what? It is the average movement away from the center of the distribution—the mean.

The **standard deviation,** then, is the average distance of all of the scores in the distribution from the mean or central point of the distribution—or, as we shall see shortly, the square root of the average squared deviation from the mean. Think about how you would calculate the average distance of all of the scores from the mean of the distribution. First, you would have to determine how far each score is from the mean; this is the deviation, or difference, score. Then, you would have to average these scores. This is the basic idea behind calculating the standard deviation.

The data from Table 4.1 are presented again in Table 5.2. Let's use these data to calculate the average distance from the mean. We will begin with a calculation that is slightly simpler than the standard deviation, known as the **average deviation.** The average deviation is essentially what the name implies—the average distance of all of the scores from the mean of the distribution. Referring to Table 5.2, you can see that we begin by determining how much each score deviates from the mean, or

$$X - \mu$$

where

X = each individual score, and
μ = the population mean

Then we need to sum the deviation scores. Notice, however, that if we were to sum these scores, they would add to zero. Therefore, we first take the absolute value of the deviation scores (the distance from the mean, irrespective of

standard deviation
A measure of variation; the average difference between the scores in the distribution and the mean or central point of the distribution, or more precisely, the square root of the average squared deviation from the mean.

average deviation An alternative measure of variation that also indicates the average difference between the scores in a distribution and the mean of the distribution.

TABLE 5.2 Calculations for the sum of the absolute values of the deviation scores ($\mu = 74$)

X	$X - \mu$	$|X - \mu|$
45	−29.00	29.00
47	−27.00	27.00
54	−20.00	20.00
56	−18.00	18.00
59	−15.00	15.00
60	−14.00	14.00
60	−14.00	14.00
63	−11.00	11.00
65	−9.00	9.00
69	−5.00	5.00
70	−4.00	4.00
74	0.00	0.00
74	0.00	0.00
74	0.00	0.00
75	1.00	1.00
76	2.00	2.00
77	3.00	3.00
78	4.00	4.00
78	4.00	4.00
80	6.00	6.00
82	8.00	8.00
82	8.00	8.00
85	11.00	11.00
86	12.00	12.00
87	13.00	13.00
90	16.00	16.00
92	18.00	18.00
93	19.00	19.00
94	20.00	20.00
95	21.00	21.00
		$332.00 = \Sigma|X - \mu|$

direction), as shown in the third column of Table 5.2. To calculate the average deviation, we sum (Σ) the absolute value of each deviation score:

$$\Sigma |X - \mu|$$

Then we divide by the total number of scores (N) to find the average deviation:

$$AD = \frac{\Sigma |X - \mu|}{N}$$

Using the data from Table 5.2, we would calculate the average deviation as follows:

$$AD = \frac{\Sigma |X - \mu|}{N} = \frac{332}{30} = 11.07$$

Thus, for the exam score distribution, the scores fall an average of 11.07 points from the mean of 74.00.

Although the average deviation is fairly easy to compute, it is not as useful as the standard deviation because, as we will see in later modules, the standard deviation is used in many other statistical procedures.

The standard deviation is very similar to the average deviation. The only difference is that rather than taking the absolute value of the deviation scores, we use another method to "get rid of" the negative deviation scores—we square the deviation scores. This procedure is illustrated in Table 5.3. Notice that this table is very similar to Table 5.2. It includes the distribution of exam scores, the deviation scores, and the squared deviation scores. The formula for the standard deviation is:

$$\sigma = \sqrt{\frac{\Sigma (X - \mu)^2}{N}}$$

where

X = each individual score
μ = the population mean
N = the total number of scores, and
Σ = summation of

This formula represents the standard deviation for a population. The symbol for the population standard deviation is σ (pronounced "sigma"). To derive the standard deviation for a sample, the calculation is the same but the symbols differ. This will be discussed later in the module.

Notice that the formula is similar to that for the average deviation. We determine the deviation scores, square the deviation scores, sum the squared deviation scores, and divide by the number of scores in the distribution. Lastly, we take the square root of that number. Why? Squaring the deviation scores has inflated them. We now need to bring the squared deviation scores back to the same level of measurement as the mean so that the standard deviation is measured on the same scale as the mean.

TABLE 5.3   Calculations for the sum of the squared deviation scores

X	$X - \mu$	$(X - \mu)^2$
45	−29.00	841.00
47	−27.00	729.00
54	−20.00	400.00
56	−18.00	324.00
59	−15.00	225.00
60	−14.00	196.00
60	−14.00	196.00
63	−11.00	121.0
65	−9.00	81.00
69	−5.00	25.00
70	−4.00	16.00
74	0.00	0.00
74	0.00	0.00
74	0.00	0.00
75	1.00	1.00
76	2.00	4.00
77	3.00	9.00
78	4.00	16.00
78	4.00	16.00
80	6.00	36.00
82	8.00	64.00
82	8.00	64.00
85	11.00	121.00
86	12.00	144.00
87	13.00	169.00
90	16.00	256.00
92	18.00	324.00
93	19.00	361.00
94	20.00	400.00
95	21.00	441.00
		$5,580.00 = \Sigma(X - \mu)^2$

Now, using the sum of the squared deviation scores (5,580.00) from Table 5.3, we can calculate the standard deviation:

$$\sigma = \sqrt{\frac{\sum(X - \mu)^2}{N}} = \sqrt{\frac{5,580.00}{30}} = \sqrt{186.00} = 13.64$$

Compare this number to the average deviation calculated on the same data ($AD = 11.07$). The standard deviation tells us that the exam scores fall an average of 13.64 points from the mean of 74.00. The standard deviation is slightly larger than the average deviation of 11.07 and will always be larger whenever both of these measures of variation are calculated on the same distribution of scores. Can you see why? It is because we are squaring the deviation scores and thus giving more weight to those that are farther from the mean of the distribution. The scores that are lowest and highest will have the largest deviation scores; squaring them exaggerates the difference. When all of the squared deviation scores are summed, these large scores will contribute disproportionately to the numerator and, even after dividing by N and taking the square root, will result in a larger number than what we see for the average deviation.

If you have taken another statistics class, you may have used the "raw-score formula" to calculate the standard deviation. The raw-score or computational formula is shown in Table 5.4, where it is used to calculate the standard deviation for the same distribution of exam scores. The numerator represents an algebraic transformation from the original formula that is somewhat shorter to use. Although the raw-score formula is slightly easier to use, it is more difficult to equate this formula with what the standard deviation actually is—a means of determining the average deviation (or distance) from the mean for all of the scores in the distribution.

As mentioned previously, the calculation of the standard deviation for a sample (S) differs from the calculation for the standard deviation for a population (σ) only in the symbols used to represent each term. The formula for a sample is:

$$S = \sqrt{\frac{\sum(X - \overline{X})^2}{N}}$$

where

S = sample standard deviation
X = each individual score
$\overline{X}$ = sample mean
N = number of scores in the distribution
$\sum$ = summation of

TABLE 5.4   Standard deviation raw-score formula

$$\sigma = \sqrt{\frac{\sum X^2 - \frac{(\sum X)^2}{N}}{N}} = \sqrt{\frac{169,860 - \frac{(2,220)^2}{30}}{30}} = \sqrt{\frac{169,860 - \frac{4,928,400}{30}}{30}}$$

$$= \sqrt{\frac{169,860 - 164,280}{30}} = \sqrt{\frac{5,580.00}{30}} = \sqrt{186.00} = 13.64$$

Note that the only difference is in the notation for the mean ($\overline{X}$ rather than μ). This difference simply reflects the scientific notation for the population mean versus the sample mean. However, the calculation is exactly the same as that for σ. Thus, if we were to use the data set from Table 5.3 to calculate S, we would arrive at exactly the same answer as we did for σ, 13.64.

If, however, you are using sample data to estimate the population standard deviation, then the standard deviation formula must be slightly modified. The modification provides what is called an "unbiased estimator" of the population standard deviation based on sample data. The modified formula is:

$$s = \sqrt{\frac{\sum(X - \overline{X})^2}{N - 1}}$$

where

s = unbiased estimator of population standard deviation
X = each individual score
$\overline{X}$ = sample mean
N = number of scores in the distribution
$\sum$ = summation of

Notice that the symbol for the unbiased estimator of the population standard deviation is s (lowercase), whereas the symbol for the sample standard deviation is S. The main difference, however, is in the denominator—dividing by $N - 1$ versus N. The reason is that the standard deviation within a small sample may not be representative of the population; that is, there may not be as much variability in the sample as there actually is in the population. We therefore divide by $N - 1$, because dividing by a smaller number increases the standard deviation and thus provides a better estimate of the population standard deviation.

We can use the formula for s to calculate the standard deviation on the same set of exam score data. Before we even begin the calculation, we know that because we are dividing by a smaller number ($N - 1$), s should be larger than σ and S (which were 13.64 for the same distribution of scores). Normally we would not compute both σ and s on the same distribution of scores because σ is the standard deviation for the population and s is the unbiased estimator of the population standard deviation based on sample data. I am doing so here simply to illustrate the difference in the formulas.

$$s = \sqrt{\frac{\sum(X - \overline{X})^2}{N - 1}} = \sqrt{\frac{5{,}580.00}{30 - 1}} = \sqrt{\frac{5{,}580.00}{29}} = \sqrt{192.41} = 13.87$$

Note that s (13.87) is slightly larger than σ and S (13.64). The procedures for calculating σ, S, and s using Excel, SPSS, and the TI-84 calculator are shown in the Statistical Software Resource Section at the end of this chapter.

One final measure of variability is called the *variance*. The variance is equal to the standard deviation squared. Thus, the variance for a population would be σ^2 and for a sample, S^2. Because variance is not as useful a descriptive statistic as the standard deviation, we will not discuss it here.

We will see, however, that it is used in more advanced statistical procedures presented later in the text.

The formulas for the average deviation, standard deviation, and variance all use the mean. Thus, it is appropriate to use these measures with interval or ratio data, but not with ordinal and nominal data.

IN REVIEW

MEASURES OF VARIATION

TYPE OF VARIATION MEASURE

	Range	Average Deviation	Standard Deviation
Definition	The difference between the lowest and highest scores in the distribution	The average distance of all of the scores from the mean of the distribution	The square root of the average squared deviation from the mean of a distribution
Use with	Primarily interval and ratio data, but can be used with any type of data	Only interval and ratio data	Only interval and ratio data
Caution	A simple measure that does not use all scores in the distribution in its calculation	A more sophisticated measure in which all scores are used, but which may not weight extreme scores adequately	The most sophisticated and most frequently used measure of variation

CRITICAL THINKING CHECK 5.1

1. For a distribution of scores, what information does a measure of variation add that a measure of central tendency does not convey?
2. Today's weather report included information on the normal rainfall for this time of year. The amount of rain that fell today was 1.5 inches above normal. To decide whether this is an abnormally high amount of rain, you need to know that the standard deviation for rainfall is .75 inches. What would you conclude about how normal the amount of rainfall was today? Would your conclusion be different if the standard deviation were 2 inches rather than .75 inches?
3. Draw two distributions with the same mean but different standard deviations in one graph. Draw a second set of distributions on another graph with different means but the same standard deviation.

Types of Distributions

In addition to knowing the central tendency and width or spread of a distribution, it is also important to know about the shape of the distribution.

Normal Distributions

When a distribution of scores is very large, it tends to approximate a pattern called a normal distribution. When plotted as a frequency polygon, a normal distribution forms a symmetrical, bell-shaped pattern often called a **normal curve** (see Figure 5.1). We say that the pattern approximates a normal distribution because a true normal distribution is a theoretical construct not actually observed in the real world.

The **normal distribution** is a theoretical frequency distribution that has certain special characteristics. First, it is bell-shaped and symmetrical—the right half is a mirror image of the left half. Second, the mean, median, and mode are equal and are located at the center of the distribution. Third, the normal distribution is *unimodal*—it has only one mode. Fourth, most of the observations are clustered around the center of the distribution, with far fewer observations at the ends, or "tails," of the distribution. Lastly, when standard deviations are used on the *x*-axis, the percentage of scores falling between the mean and any point on the *x*-axis is the same for all normal curves. This important property of the normal distribution will be discussed more fully in Module 6.

normal curve A symmetrical, bell-shaped frequency polygon representing a normal distribution.

normal distribution A theoretical frequency distribution having certain special characteristics.

Kurtosis

Although we typically think of the normal distribution as being similar to the curve depicted in Figure 5.1, there are variations in the shape of normal distributions. **Kurtosis** refers to how flat or peaked a normal distribution is. In other words, kurtosis refers to the degree of dispersion among the scores, or whether the distribution is tall and skinny or short and fat. The normal distribution depicted in Figure 5.1 is called mesokurtic—*meso* means "middle." **Mesokurtic** curves have peaks of medium height and the distributions are moderate in breadth. Now look at the two distributions depicted in Figure 5.2.

The normal distribution on the left is leptokurtic—*lepto* means "thin." **Leptokurtic** curves are tall and thin, with only a few scores in the middle of the distribution having a high frequency. Last, see the curve on the right side of Figure 5.2. This is a platykurtic curve—*platy* means "broad" or "flat." **Platykurtic** curves are short and more dispersed (broader). In a platykurtic curve, there are many scores around the middle score that all have a similar frequency.

kurtosis How flat or peaked a normal distribution is.

mesokurtic Normal curves that have peaks of medium height and distributions that are moderate in breadth.

leptokurtic Normal curves that are tall and thin, with only a few scores in the middle of the distribution having a high frequency.

platykurtic Normal curves that are short and more dispersed (broader).

**FIGURE 5.1
A normal
distribution**

*mean
median
mode*

Leptokurtic   Platykurtic

FIGURE 5.2
Types of distributions: Leptokurtic and platykurtic

Positively Skewed Distributions

Most distributions do not approximate a normal or bell-shaped curve. Instead, they are skewed, or lopsided. In a skewed distribution, scores tend to cluster at one end or the other of the *x*-axis, with the tail of the distribution extending in the opposite direction. In a **positively skewed distribution,** the peak is to the left of the center point and the tail extends toward the right, or in the positive direction. (See Figure 5.3.)

Notice that what is skewing the distribution, or throwing it off center, are the scores toward the right or positive direction. A few individuals have extremely high scores that pull the distribution in that direction. Notice also what this does to the mean, median, and mode. These three measures do not have the same value, nor are they all located at the center of the distribution as they are in a normal distribution. The mode—the score with the highest frequency—is the high point on the distribution. The median divides the distribution in half. The mean is pulled in the direction of the tail of the distribution; that is, the few extreme scores pull the mean toward them and inflate it.

positively skewed distribution A distribution in which the peak is to the left of the center point and the tail extends toward the right or in the positive direction.

Negatively Skewed Distributions

The opposite of a positively skewed distribution is a **negatively skewed distribution**—a distribution in which the peak is to the right of the center point and the tail extends toward the left, or in the negative direction. The term *negative* refers to the direction of the skew. As can be seen in Figure 5.3, in a negatively skewed distribution, the mean is pulled toward the left by the few extremely low scores in the distribution. As in all distributions, the

negatively skewed distribution A distribution in which the peak is to the right of the center point and the tail extends toward the left or in the negative direction.

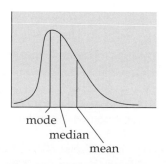

mode
median
mean

positively skewed distribution

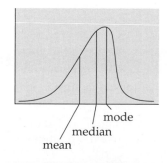

mode
median
mean

negatively skewed distribution

FIGURE 5.3
Positively and negatively skewed distributions

median divides the distribution in half, and the mode is the most frequently occurring score in the distribution.

Knowing the shape of a distribution provides valuable information concerning the distribution. For example, would a class of students prefer to have a negatively or positively skewed distribution of exam scores for an exam they have taken? Students will frequently answer that they would prefer a positively skewed distribution, because they think the term *positive* means good. Keep in mind that positive and negative describe the skew of the distribution, not whether the distribution is "good" or "bad." Assuming that the exam scores span the entire possible range (say from 0 to 100), you should prefer a negatively skewed distribution—meaning that most people have high scores and only a few people have low scores.

Another example of the value of knowing the shape of a distribution is provided by Harvard paleontologist Stephen Jay Gould (1985). Gould was diagnosed in 1982 with a rare form of cancer. He immediately began researching the disease and learned that it was incurable and had a median mortality rate of only 8 months after discovery. Rather than immediately assuming that he would be dead in 8 months, Gould realized this meant that half of the patients lived longer than 8 months. As he was diagnosed with the disease in its early stages and was receiving high-quality medical treatment, he reasoned that he could expect to be in the half of the distribution that lived beyond 8 months. The other piece of information that Gould found encouraging was the shape of the distribution. Look again at the two distributions in Figure 5.3, and decide which you would prefer in this situation. With a positively skewed distribution, the cases to the right of the median could stretch out for years; this is not true for a negatively skewed distribution. The distribution of life expectancy for Gould's disease was positively skewed, and Gould was obviously in the far right-hand tail of the distribution because he lived and remained professionally active for another 20 years.

REVIEW OF KEY TERMS

average deviation (p. 71)
kurtosis (p. 78)
leptokurtic (p. 78)
measure of variation (p. 70)
mesokurtic (p. 78)

negatively skewed
    distribution (p. 79)
normal curve (p. 78)
normal distribution (p. 78)
platykurtic (p. 78)

positively skewed
    distribution (p. 79)
range (p.70)
standard deviation (p. 71)

MODULE EXERCISES

(Answers to odd-numbered questions appear in Appendix B.)

Calculate the range, average deviation, and standard deviation for the following five distributions (Exercises 1–5).

1. 1, 2, 3, 4, 5, 6, 7, 8, 9
2. −4, −3, −2, −1, 0, 1, 2, 3, 4
3. 10, 20, 30, 40, 50, 60, 70, 80, 90
4. .1, .2, .3, .4, .5, .6, .7, .8, .9
5. 100, 200, 300, 400, 500, 600, 700, 800, 900

6. What is the difference in calculation and use of σ, S, and s?
7. Using the data from question 1 in Module 4, determine whether the data represent a normal or skewed distribution. If skewed, what type of skew do the data represent?
8. Describe the difference between mesokurtic, leptokurtic, and platykurtic curves.

CRITICAL THINKING CHECK ANSWERS

Critical Thinking Check 5.1

1. A measure of variation tells us about the spread of the distribution. In other words, are the scores clustered closely about the mean, or are they spread over a wide range?
2. The amount of rainfall for the indicated day is 2 standard deviations above the average. I would therefore conclude that the amount of rainfall was well above average. If the standard deviation were 2 rather than .75, then the amount of rainfall for the indicated day would be less than 1 standard deviation above average—above average, but not greatly above average.

3.

Same Mean, Different Standard Deviations

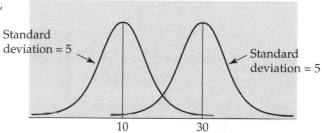

Same Standard Deviation, Different Means

WEB RESOURCES

The book-specific website at CengageBrain.com offers students a variety of study tools and useful resources such as glossaries, flashcards, quizzes, and Statistics and Research Methods Workshops.

Standard Scores (*z* Scores)

Learning Objectives
- Describe what a *z* score is.
- Know how to calculate a *z* score.
- Describe what a percentile rank is.
- Know how to calculate a percentile rank.

Introduction to Standard Scores (*z* Scores)

The descriptive statistics and types of distributions discussed so far are valuable for describing a sample or group of scores. Sometimes, however, we want information about a single score. For example, in our exam score distribution, we may want to know how one person's exam score compares with those of others in the class. Or we may want to know how an individual's exam score in one class, say psychology, compares with the same person's exam score in another class, say English. Because the two distributions of exam scores are different (different means and standard deviations), simply comparing the raw scores on the two exams will not provide this information.

Let's say an individual who was in the psychology exam distribution used as an example in Module 3 (Table 3.1) scored 86 on the exam. Remember, from Modules 4 and 5 that the exam had a mean of 74.00 with a standard deviation (*S*) of 13.64. Assume that the same person took an English exam and got a score of 91 and that the English exam had a mean of 85 with a standard deviation of 9.58. On which exam did the student do better? Most people would immediately say the English exam because the score on this exam was higher. However, we are interested in how well this student did in comparison to everyone else who took the exams. In other words, did the individual do better on the psychology exam in comparison to those taking that exam than on the English exam in comparison to those taking the English exam?

Calculation of *z* scores

To answer this question, we need to convert the exam scores into a form we can use to make comparisons. A **standard score,** or **z score,** is a measure of how many standard deviation units an individual raw score falls from the mean of the distribution. We can convert each exam score to a *z* score and then compare the *z* scores because they will be in the same unit of measurement. We can think of *z* scores as a translation of raw scores into scores of the same language for comparative purposes. The formulas for *z* score transformations are:

$$z = \frac{X - \overline{X}}{S}$$

and

$$z = \frac{X - \mu}{\sigma}$$

where *z* is the symbol for the standard score. The difference between the two formulas is simply that the first is used when calculating a *z* score for an individual in comparison to a sample (thus, the use of the sample mean and sample standard deviation in the formula), and the second when calculating a *z* score for an individual in comparison to a population (thus, the use of the population mean and population standard deviation in the formula). Notice that they do exactly the same thing—indicate the number of standard deviations an individual score is from the mean of the distribution.

Conversion to a *z* score is a statistical technique that is appropriate for use with data measured on a ratio or interval scale of measurement (scales for which means are calculated). Let's use the formula to calculate the *z* scores for the previously mentioned student's psychology and English exam scores. The necessary information is summarized in Table 6.1.

To calculate the *z* score for the English test, we first calculate the difference between the score and the mean and then divide by the standard deviation. We use the same process to calculate the *z* score for the psychology exam. These calculations are as follows:

$$z_{\text{English}} = \frac{X - \overline{X}}{S} = \frac{91 - 85}{9.58} = \frac{6}{9.58} = +0.626$$

$$z_{\text{Psychology}} = \frac{X - \overline{X}}{S} = \frac{86 - 74}{13.64} = \frac{12}{13.64} = +0.880$$

TABLE 6.1   Raw score (*X*), sample mean (*X̄*), and standard deviation (*S*) for English and psychology exams

	X	(*X̄*)	*S*
English	91	85	9.58
Psychology	86	74	13.64

The individual's z score for the English test is 0.626 standard deviations above the mean, and the z score for the psychology test is 0.880 standard deviations above the mean. Thus, even though the student answered more questions correctly on the English exam (had a higher raw score) than on the psychology exam, the student performed better on the psychology exam relative to other students in the psychology class than on the English exam in comparison to other students in the English class.

The z scores calculated in the previous example were both positive, indicating that the individual's scores were above the mean in both distributions. When a score is below the mean, the z score is negative, indicating that the individual's score is lower than the mean of the distribution. Let's go over another example so that you can practice calculating both positive and negative z scores.

Suppose you administered a test to a large sample of people and computed the mean and standard deviation of the raw scores, with the following results:

$$\overline{X} = 45$$
$$S = 4$$

Suppose also that four of the individuals who took the test had the following scores:

Person	Score (X)
Rich	49
Debbie	45
Pam	41
Henry	39

Let's calculate the z score equivalents for the raw scores of these individuals, beginning with Rich.

$$z_{Rich} = \frac{X_{Rich} - \overline{X}}{S} = \frac{49 - 45}{4} = \frac{4}{4} = +1$$

Notice that we substitute Rich's score (X_{Rich}) and then use the group mean ($\overline{X}$) and the group standard deviation (S). The positive sign (+) indicates that the z score is positive, or above the mean. We find that Rich's score of 49 is 1 standard deviation above the group mean of 45.

Now let's calculate Debbie's z score.

$$z_{Debbie} = \frac{X_{Debbie} - \overline{X}}{S} = \frac{45 - 45}{4} = \frac{0}{4} = 0$$

Debbie's score is the same as the mean of the distribution. Therefore, her z score is 0, indicating that she scored neither above nor below the mean. Keep in mind that a z score of 0 does not indicate a low score; it indicates a score right at the mean or average. See if you can calculate the z scores for Pam and Henry on your own. Did you get $z_{Pam} = -1$ and $z_{Henry} = -1.5$? Good work!

In summary, the z score tells you if an individual raw score is above the mean (a positive z score) or below the mean (a negative z score), and it tells you how many standard deviations the raw score is above or below the mean. Thus, z scores are a means of transforming raw scores to standard scores for purposes of comparison in both normal and skewed distributions. The procedure for calculating z scores using Excel is shown in the Statistical Software Resource section at the end of this chapter.

z Scores and the Standard Normal Distribution ●●

If the distribution of scores for which you are calculating transformations (z scores) is normal (symmetrical and unimodal), then it is referred to as the **standard normal distribution**—a normal distribution with a mean of 0 and a standard deviation of 1. The standard normal distribution is actually a theoretical distribution defined by a specific mathematical formula. All other normal curves approximate the standard normal curve to a greater or lesser extent. The value of the standard normal curve is that it can provide information about the proportion of scores that are higher or lower than any other score in the distribution. A researcher can also determine the probability of occurrence of a score that is higher or lower than any other score in the distribution. The proportions under the standard normal curve hold only for normal distributions—not for skewed distributions. Even though z scores can be calculated on skewed distributions, the proportions under the standard normal curve do not hold for skewed distributions.

Take a look at Figure 6.1, which represents the area under the standard normal curve in terms of standard deviations. Based on this figure, we see that approximately 68% of the observations in the distribution fall between −1.0 and +1.0 standard deviations from the mean. This approximate percentage holds for all data that are normally distributed. Notice also that approximately 13.5% of the observations fall between −1.0 and −2.0 and another 13.5% between +1.0 and +2.0, and that approximately 2% of the

standard normal distribution A normal distribution with a mean of 0 and a standard deviation of 1.

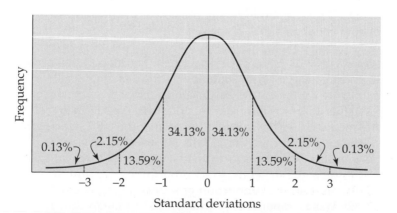

FIGURE 6.1
Area under the standard normal curve

observations fall between −2.0 and −3.0 and another 2% between +2.0 and +3.0. Only .13% of the scores are beyond a z score of either ±3.0. If you sum the percentages in Figure 6.1, you will have 100%—all of the area under the curve, representing everybody in the distribution. If you sum half of the curve, you will have 50%—half of the distribution.

With a curve that is normal or symmetrical, the mean, median, and mode are all at the center point; thus, 50% of the scores are above this number and 50% are below this number. This property helps us determine probabilities. For example, what is the probability of randomly choosing a score that falls above the mean? The probability is equal to the proportion of scores in that area, or .50. Figure 6.1 gives us a rough estimate of the proportions under the normal curve. Luckily for us, statisticians have determined the exact proportion of scores that will fall between any two z scores—for example, between z scores of +1.30 and +1.39. This information is provided in Table A.1 in Appendix A at the back of the text. A small portion of this table is shown in Table 6.2.

The columns along the top of the table are labeled z, Area Between Mean and z, and Area Beyond z. The column heads also include pictorial representations. The z columns refer to the z score with which you are working. The Area Between Mean and z represents the area under the curve between the mean of the distribution (where $z = 0$) and the z score with which you are working—that is, the proportion of scores between the mean and the z score in column 1. The Area Beyond z is the area under the curve from the z score out to the tail end of the distribution. Notice that the entire table only goes as far as a z score of 4.00, because it is very unusual for a normally distributed population of scores to include scores larger than this. Notice also that the table provides information only about positive z scores, even though the distribution of scores actually ranges from approximately −4.00 to +4.00. Because the distribution is symmetric, the areas between the mean and z and beyond the z scores are the same whether the z score is positive or negative.

Let's use some of the examples from earlier in the module to illustrate how to use these proportions under the normal curve. Assume that the test data described earlier (with $\overline{X} = 45$ and $S = 4$) are normally distributed, so that the proportions under the normal curve apply. We calculated z scores for four individuals who took the test—Rich, Debbie, Pam, and Henry. Let's use Rich's z score to illustrate the use of the normal curve table. Rich had a z score equal to +1.00—1 standard deviation above the mean. I like to begin by drawing a picture representing the normal curve, and sketching in the z score with which I am working. Thus, Figure 6.2 shows a representation of the normal curve, with a line drawn at a z score of +1.00.

Before we look at the proportions under the normal curve, we can begin to gather information from this picture. We see that Rich's score is above the mean. Using the information from Figure 6.1, we see that roughly 34% of the area under the curve falls between his z score and the mean of the distribution, whereas approximately 16% of the area falls beyond his z score. Using Table A.1 to get the exact proportions, we find (from the Area Beyond z column) that the proportion of scores falling above the z score of +1.0 is .1587. This number can be interpreted to mean that 15.87% of the scores

TABLE 6.2   A portion of the standard normal curve table

	AREAS UNDER THE STANDARD NORMAL CURVE FOR VALUES OF Z				
Z	AREA BETWEEN MEAN AND Z	AREA BEYOND Z	Z	AREA BETWEEN MEAN AND Z	AREA BEYOND Z
0.00	.0000	.5000	0.32	.1255	.3745
0.01	.0040	.4960	0.33	.1293	.3707
0.02	.0080	.4920	0.34	.1331	.3669
0.03	.0120	.4880	0.35	.1368	.3632
0.04	.0160	.4840	0.36	.1406	.3594
0.05	.0199	.4801	0.37	.1443	.3557
0.06	.0239	.4761	0.38	.1480	.3520
0.07	.0279	.4721	0.39	.1517	.3483
0.08	.0319	.4681	0.40	.1554	.3446
0.09	.0359	.4641	0.41	.1591	.3409
0.10	.0398	.4602	0.42	.1628	.3372
0.11	.0438	.4562	0.43	.1664	.3336
0.12	.0478	.4522	0.44	.1770	.3300
0.13	.0517	.4483	0.45	.1736	.3264
0.14	.0557	.4443	0.46	.1772	.3228
0.15	.0596	.4404	0.47	.1808	.3192
0.16	.0636	.4364	0.48	.1844	.3156
0.17	.0675	.4325	0.49	.1879	.3121
0.18	.0714	.4286	0.50	.1915	.3085
0.19	.0753	.4247	0.51	.1950	.3050
0.20	.0793	.4207	0.52	.1985	.3015
0.21	.0832	.4268	0.53	.2019	.2981
0.22	.0871	.4129	0.54	.2054	.2946
0.23	.0910	.4090	0.55	.2088	.2912
0.24	.0948	.4052	0.56	.2123	.2877
0.25	.0987	.4013	0.57	.2157	.2843
0.26	.1026	.3974	0.58	.2190	.2810
0.27	.1064	.3936	0.59	.2224	.2776
0.28	.1103	.3897	0.60	.2257	.2743
0.29	.1141	.3859	0.61	.2291	.2709
0.30	.1179	.3821	0.62	.2324	.2676
0.31	.1217	.3783	0.63	.2357	.2643

(continued)

TABLE 6.2   A portion of the standard normal curve table (*continued*)

AREAS UNDER THE STANDARD NORMAL CURVE FOR VALUES OF Z					
z	AREA BETWEEN MEAN AND Z	AREA BEYOND Z	z	AREA BETWEEN MEAN AND Z	AREA BEYOND Z
0.64	.2389	.2611	0.74	.2704	.2296
0.65	.2422	.2578	0.75	.2734	.2266
0.66	.2454	.2546	0.76	.2764	.2236
0.67	.2486	.2514	0.77	.2794	.2206
0.68	.2517	.2483	0.78	.2823	.2177
0.69	.2549	.2451	0.79	.2852	.2148
0.70	.2580	.2420	0.80	.2881	.2119
0.71	.2611	.2389	0.81	.2910	.2090
0.72	.2642	.2358	0.82	.2939	.2061
0.73	.2673	.2327	0.83	.2967	.2033

Source: Lehman, R. S. (1995). *Statistics in the Behavioral Sciences: A Conceptual Introduction*. Pacific Grove, CA: Brooks/Cole Publishing.

FIGURE 6.2
Standard normal curve with z score of +1.00 indicated

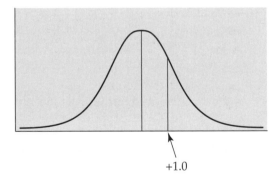

+1.0

were higher than Rich's score, or that the probability of randomly choosing a score with a z score greater than +1.00 is .1587. To determine the proportion of scores falling below Rich's z score, we need to use the Area Between Mean and z column and add .50 to this proportion. According to the table, the area between the mean and the z score is .3413. Why must we add .50 to this number? The table provides information about only one side of the standard normal distribution. We must add in the proportion of scores represented by the other half of the distribution, which is always .50. Look back at Figure 6.2. Rich's score is +1.00 above the mean, which means that he did better than those between the mean and his z score (.3413) and also better than everybody below the mean (.50). Hence, the proportion of scores below Rich's score is .8413.

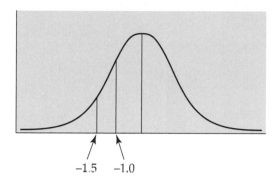

FIGURE 6.3
**Standard normal
curve with *z* scores
of −1.0 and −1.5
indicated**

Let's use Debbie's *z* score to further illustrate the use of the table. Debbie's *z* score was 0.00—right at the mean. We know that if she is at the mean (*z* = 0), then half of the distribution is below her score and half is above her score. Does this match what Table A.1 tells us? According to the table, .5000 (50%) of scores are beyond this *z* score, so the information in the table does agree with our reasoning.

Using the table with Pam and Henry's *z* scores will be slightly more difficult, because both Pam and Henry had negative *z* scores. Remember, Pam had a *z* score of –1.00, and Henry had a *z* score of –1.50. Let's begin by drawing a normal distribution and then marking where both Pam and Henry fall on that distribution. This information is represented in Figure 6.3.

Before even looking at the *z* table, let's think about what we know from Figure 6.3. We know that both Pam and Henry scored below the mean, that they are in the lower 50% of the class, that the proportion of people scoring higher than them is greater than .50, and that the proportion of people scoring lower than them is less than .50. Keep this overview in mind as we use Table A.1. Using Pam's *z* score of –1.0, see if you can determine the proportion of scores lying above and below her score. If you determined that the proportion of scores above hers was .8413 and that the proportion below was .1587, then you were correct!

Why is the proportion above her score .8413? We begin by looking in the table at a *z* score of 1.0 (remember, there are no negatives in the table). The Area Between Mean and *z* is .3413, and then we need to add the proportion of .50 in the top half of the curve. Adding these two proportions, we get .8413. The proportion below her score is represented by the area in the tail, or the Area Beyond *z* of .1587. Now see if you can compute the proportions above and below Henry's *z* score of –1.5. Did you get .9332 above his score and .0668 below his score? Good work!

Now, let's try something slightly more difficult by determining the proportion of scores that fall between Henry's *z* score of –1.5 and Pam's *z* score of –1.0. Referring back to Figure 6.3, you can see that we are targeting the area between the two *z* scores represented on the curve. Again, we use Table A.1 to provide the proportions. The area between the mean and Henry's *z* score of –1.5 is .4332, whereas the area between the mean and Pam's *z* score of –1.0 is .3413. To determine the proportion of scores that fall between the two, we subtract .3413 from .4332, obtaining a difference of .0919. This result is illustrated in Figure 6.4.

FIGURE 6.4
Proportion of scores
between z scores of
−1.0 and −1.5

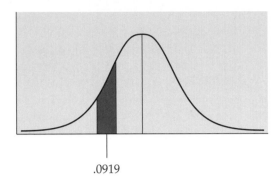

.0919

Percentile Ranks

percentile rank A score that indicates the percentage of people who scored at or below a given raw score.

The standard normal curve can also be used to determine an individual's **percentile rank**—the percentage of scores equal to or below the given raw score, or the percentage of scores the individual's score is higher than. To determine a percentile rank, we must first know the individual's z score. Let's say we wanted to calculate an individual's percentile rank based on this person's score on an intelligence test. The scores on the intelligence test are normally distributed, with $\mu = 100$ and $\sigma = 15$. Let's suppose the individual scored 119. Using the z score formula, we have:

$$z = \frac{X - \mu}{\sigma} = \frac{119 - 100}{15} = \frac{19}{15} = 1.27$$

Looking at the Area Between Mean and z column in Table A.1 in Appendix A for a score of +1.27, we find the proportion .3980. To determine all of the area below the score, we must add .50 to .3980; the entire area below a z score of +1.27, then, is .8980. If we multiply this proportion by 100, we can describe the intelligence test score of 119 as being in the 89.80th percentile.

To practice calculating percentile ranks, see if you can calculate the percentile ranks for Rich, Debbie, Pam, and Henry from our previous example. You should arrive at the following percentile ranks.

Person	Score (X)	z Score	Percentile Rank
Rich	49	+1.0	84.13th
Debbie	45	0.0	50.00th
Pam	41	−1.0	15.87th
Henry	39	−1.5	6.68th

Students most often have trouble determining percentile ranks from negative z scores. Always draw a figure representing the normal curve with the z scores indicated; this will help you determine which column to use from the z table. When the z score is negative, the proportion of the curve representing those who scored lower than the individual is found in the Area Beyond z. We then multiply this proportion by 100 to determine the percentile rank. When the z score is positive, the proportion of the curve representing those who scored lower than the individual is found by using the Area Between Mean and z, adding .50 (the bottom half of the distribution) to this proportion, and then multiplying by 100 to determine the percentile rank.

What if we know an individual's percentile rank and want to determine this person's raw score? Let's say we know that an individual scored at the 75th percentile on the intelligence test described previously. We want to know what score has 75% of the scores below it. We begin by using Table A.1 to determine the z score for this percentile rank. If the individual is at the 75th percentile, we know the Area Between Mean and z is .25. How do we know this? The person scored higher than the 50% of people in the bottom half of the curve, and .75 − .50 = .25. Therefore, we look in the column labeled Area Between Mean and z and find the proportion that is closest to .25. The closest we come to .25 is .2486, which corresponds to a z score of 0.67.

Remember the z score formula is:

$$z = \frac{X - \mu}{\sigma}$$

We know that $\mu = 100$ and $\sigma = 15$, and now we know that $z = 0.67$. What we want to find is the person's raw score, X. So, let's solve the equation for X.

$$z = \frac{X - \mu}{\sigma}$$

$$z\sigma = X - \mu$$

$$z\sigma + \mu = X$$

Substituting the values we have for μ, σ, and z,

$$X = z\sigma + \mu$$

$$X = 0.67(15) + 100$$

$$= 10.05 + 100$$

$$= 110.05$$

As you can see, the standard normal distribution is useful for determining how a single score compares with a population or sample of scores and also for determining probabilities and percentile ranks. Knowing how to use the proportions under the standard normal curve increases the information we can derive from a single score.

Z SCORES AND PERCENTILE RANKS			
	TYPE OF DISTRIBUTION		
	Normal	**Positively Skewed**	**Negatively Skewed**
z score transformations applicable?	Yes	Yes	Yes
Percentile ranks and proportions under standard normal curve applicable?	Yes	No	No

IN REVIEW

CRITICAL
THINKING
CHECK
6.1

1. Why is it not possible to use the proportions under the standard normal curve with skewed distributions?
2. Students in the Psychology Department at General State University have an average SAT score of 1025 with a standard deviation of 175. The distribution is normal.
   a. What proportion of students scored equal to or greater than 1,000?
   b. What proportion of students scored equal to or greater than 1,150?
   c. What proportion of students scored between 1,000 and 1,150?
   d. What is the percentile rank for an individual who scored 950?
   e. What score would an individual at the 75th percentile have?
3. Based on what you have learned about z scores, percentile ranks, and the use of the area under the standard normal curve, fill in the missing information in the following table representing performance on an exam that is normally distributed with $\overline{X} = 55$ and $S = 6$.

	X	z Score	Percentile Rank
John	63		
Ray		−1.66	
Betty			72

REVIEW OF KEY TERMS

percentile rank (p. 90)   standard normal distribution (p. 85)   z score (standard score) (p. 83)

MODULE EXERCISES

(Answers to odd-numbered questions appear in Appendix B.)

Exercises 1–6 are based on the following data: The results of a recent survey indicate that the average new car costs $23,000 with a standard deviation of $3,500. The price of cars is normally distributed.

1. If someone bought a car for $32,000, what proportion of cars cost an equal amount or more than this?
2. If someone bought a car for $16,000, what proportion of cars cost an equal amount or more than this?
3. At what percentile rank is a car that sold for $30,000?

4. At what percentile rank is a car that sold for $12,000?
5. What proportion of cars were sold for an amount between $12,000 and $30,000?
6. For what price would a car at the 16th percentile have sold?

Exercises 7–12 are based on the following data: A survey of college students was conducted during final exam week to assess the number of hours spent studying each day. The mean number of hours was 5 with a standard deviation of 1.5 hours. The distribution was normal.

7. What proportion of students studied 7 or more hours per day?

8. What proportion of students studied 2 or more hours per day?
9. What proportion of individuals studied between 2 and 7 hours per day?
10. How many hours would an individual at the 60th percentile rank study?
11. What is the percentile rank for an individual who studied 4 hours per day?
12. What is the percentile rank for an individual who studied 7.5 hours per day?

13. Fill in the missing information in the following table representing performance on an exam that is normally distributed with $\overline{X} = 75$ and $S = 9$.

	X	z Score	Percentile Rank
Ken	73	—	—
Drew	—	1.55	—
Cecil	—	—	82

CRITICAL THINKING CHECK ANSWERS

Critical Thinking Check 6.1

1. The proportions hold only for normal (symmetrical) distributions in which one half of the distribution is equal to the other. If the distribution were skewed, this condition would be violated.
2. a. .5557
   b. .2388
   c. 3169
   d. 33.36
   e. 1,142

3.

	X	z Score	Percentile Rank
John	63	+1.33	90.82
Ray	45.05	−1.66	4.85
Betty	58.48	+0.58	72

WEB RESOURCES

The book-specific website at CengageBrain.com offers students a variety of study tools and useful resources such as glossaries, flashcards, quizzes, and Statistics and Research Methods Workshops.

CHAPTER THREE SUMMARY AND REVIEW
Descriptive Statistics II

CHAPTER SUMMARY

In this chapter, we have discussed some additional descriptive statistics. Descriptive statistics that tell us about the spread or dispersion of the distribution are known as measures of variation (range, average deviation, and standard deviation). A distribution may be normal, positively skewed, or negatively skewed. The shape of the distribution affects the relationship among the mean, median, and mode. Finally, we discussed the calculation of z score transformations as a means of standardizing raw scores for comparative purposes. Although z scores can be used with either normal or skewed distributions, the proportions under the standard normal curve can be applied only to data that approximate a normal distribution.

Based on our discussion of these descriptive methods, you can begin to organize and summarize a large data set and also compare the scores of individuals to the entire sample or population.

CHAPTER 3 REVIEW EXERCISES

(Answers to exercises appear in Appendix B.)

Fill-in Self-Test

Answer the following questions. If you have trouble answering any of the questions, restudy the relevant material before going on to the multiple-choice self-test.

1. Measures of _____ are numbers that indicate how dispersed scores are around the mean of the distribution.
2. An alternative measure of variation that indicates the average difference between the scores in a distribution and the mean of the distribution is the _____.
3. When we divide the squared deviation scores by $N - 1$ rather than by N, we are using the _____ of the population standard deviation.
4. σ represents the _____ standard deviation and S represents the _____ standard deviation.
5. A distribution in which the peak is to the left of the center point and the tail extends toward the right is a _____ skewed distribution.
6. A number that indicates how many standard deviation units a raw score is from the mean of a distribution is a _____.
7. The normal distribution with a mean of 0 and a standard deviation of 1 is the _____.

Multiple-Choice Self-Test

Select the single best answer for each of the following questions. If you have trouble answering any of the questions, restudy the relevant material.

1. The calculation of the standard deviation differs from the calculation of the average deviation in that the deviation scores are
   a. squared.
   b. converted to absolute values.
   c. squared and converted to absolute values.
   d. It does not differ.

2. Imagine that distribution A contains the following scores: 11, 13, 15, 18, 20. Imagine that distribution B contains the following scores: 13, 14, 15, 16, 17. Distribution A has a _____ standard deviation and a _____ average deviation in comparison to distribution B.
   a. larger; larger
   b. smaller; smaller
   c. larger; smaller
   d. smaller; larger

3. Which of the following is not true?
   a. All scores in the distribution are used in the calculation of the range.
   b. The average deviation is a more sophisticated measure of variation than the range; however, it may not weight extreme scores adequately.
   c. The standard deviation is the most sophisticated measure of variation because all scores in the distribution are used and because it weights extreme scores adequately.
   d. None of the other alternatives is false.

4. If the shape of a frequency distribution is lopsided, with a long tail projecting longer to the left than to the right, how would the distribution be skewed?
   a. Normally
   b. Negatively
   c. Positively
   d. Average

5. If Jack scored 15 on a test with a mean of 20 and a standard deviation of 5 what is his z score?
   a. 1.5
   b. −1.0
   c. 0.0
   d. Cannot be determined.

6. Faculty in the Physical Education department at State University consume an average of 2,000 calories per day with a standard deviation of 250 calories. The distribution is normal. What proportion of faculty consumes an amount between 1,600 and 2,400 calories?
   a. .4452
   b. .8904
   c. .50
   d. None of the above.

7. If the average weight for women is normally distributed with a mean of 135 pounds and a standard deviation of 15 pounds, then approximately 68% of all women should weigh between _____ and _____ pounds.
   a. 120; 150
   b. 120; 135
   c. 105; 165
   d. Cannot say from the information given.
8. Sue's first philosophy exam score is −1 standard deviation from the mean in a normal distribution. The test has a mean of 82 and a standard deviation of 4. Sue's percentile rank would be approximately
   a. 78%.
   b. 84%.
   c. 16%.
   d. Cannot say from the information given.

Self-Test Problems

1. Calculate the range, average deviation, and standard deviation for the following distribution:
   2, 2, 3, 4, 5, 6, 7, 8, 8.
2. The results of a recent survey indicate that the average new home costs $100,000 with a standard deviation of $15,000. The price of homes is normally distributed.
   a. If someone bought a home for $75,000, what proportion of homes cost an equal amount or more than this?
   b. At what percentile rank is a home that sold for $112,000?
   c. For what price would a home at the 20th percentile have sold?

CHAPTER THREE
Statistical Software Resources

If you need help getting started with Excel or SPSS, please see Appendix C: Getting Started with Excel and SPSS.

MODULE 5 Measures of Variation

The data we'll be using to illustrate how to calculate measures of variation are exam score data for a class of 30 students and are presented in the Table 5.1 in Module 5.

Using Excel

To begin using Excel to conduct this analysis, the data must be entered into an Excel spreadsheet. This simply involves opening Excel and entering the data into the spreadsheet.

You can see in the following image that I have entered the exam grade data from Table 5.1 into an Excel spreadsheet.

Once the data have been entered, we use the Data Analysis tool to calculate descriptive statistics. This is accomplished by clicking on the **Data** tab or ribbon and then clicking the **Data Analysis** icon on the far top right side of the window. Once the Data Analysis tab is active, a dialog box of options will appear (see next).

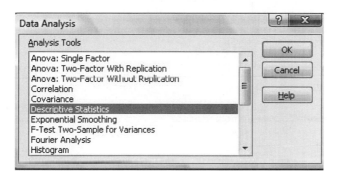

Select **Descriptive Statistics** as is indicated in the preceding box, and then click **OK**. This will lead to the following dialog box:

With the cursor in the **Input Range** box, highlight the data that you want analyzed from column A in the Excel spreadsheet so that they appear in the input range. In addition, check the **Summary statistics** box. Once you have done this, click **OK**. The summary statistics will appear in a new Worksheet, as seen next.

	A	B
1	Column1	
2		
3	Mean	74
4	Standard Error	2.532546762
5	Median	75.5
6	Mode	74
7	Standard Deviation	13.8713299
8	Sample Variance	192.4137931
9	Kurtosis	-0.60744581
10	Skewness	-0.391850234
11	Range	50
12	Minimum	45
13	Maximum	95
14	Sum	2220
15	Count	30

As you can see, there are several descriptive statistics reported, including measures of variation (range, standard deviation, and variance).

Using SPSS

As with the Excel exercise above, we will once again be using the data from Table 5.1 to calculate measures of variation. We begin by entering the data from Table 5.1 into an SPSS spreadsheet. This simply involves opening SPSS and entering the data into the spreadsheet. You can see in the following image that I have entered the exam grade data from Table 5.1 into an SPSS spreadsheet:

| File | Edit | View | Data | Transform | Analyze | Graphs | Utilities | Add-ons | Window | Help |

	VAR00001	var	var	var	var	var	var	var	var	var	var
1	45.00										
2	47.00										
3	54.00										
4	56.00										
5	59.00										
6	60.00										
7	60.00										
8	63.00										
9	65.00										
10	69.00										
11	70.00										
12	74.00										
13	74.00										
14	74.00										
15	75.00										
16	76.00										
17	77.00										
18	78.00										
19	78.00										
20	80.00										
21	82.00										
22	82.00										
23	85.00										
24	86.00										
25	87.00										
26	90.00										
27	92.00										
28	93.00										
29	94.00										
30	95.00										
31											

Notice that the variable is simply named VAR00001. To rename the variable to something appropriate for your data set, click on the **Variable View** tab on the bottom left of the screen. You will see the following window:

File	Edit	View	Data	Transform	Analyze	Graphs	Utilities	Add-ons	Window	Help

	Name	Type	Width	Decimals	Label	Values	Missing	Columns	Align	Measure	Role
1	VAR00001	Numeric	8	2		None	None	8	Right	Scale	Input
2											
3											
4											
5											
6											
7											
8											
9											
10											
11											
12											
13											
14											
15											
16											
17											
18											
19											
20											
21											
22											
23											
24											
25											
26											
27											
28											
29											
30											
31											
32											
33											
34											
35											
36											

Data View   Variable View

Type the name you wish to give the variable in the highlighted **Name** box. The variable name cannot have any spaces in it. Because these data represent exam grade data, we'll type in **Examgrade**. Note also that the **Type** of data is Numeric. Once the variable is named, highlight the **Data View** tab on the bottom left of the screen in order to get back to the data spreadsheet.

Once you've navigated back to the data spreadsheet, click on the **Analyze** tab at the top of the screen and a drop-down menu with various statistical analyses will appear. Select **Descriptive Statistics** and then **Descriptives....** The following dialog box will appear:

Examgrade will be highlighted, as above. Click on the arrow in the middle of the window and the Examgrade variable will be moved over to the **Variables** box. Then click on **Options** to receive the following dialog box:

You can see that the Mean, Standard Deviation, Minimum, and Maximum are all checked. However, you could select any of the descriptive statistics you want calculated. After making your selections, click **Continue** and then **OK**. The output will appear on a separate page as an Output file like the one below where you can see the minimum and maximum scores for this distribution along with the mean exam score of 74 and the standard deviation of 13.87. Please note that if you had more than one set of data, for example, two classes of exam scores, they could each occupy one column in your SPSS spreadsheet and you could conduct analyses on both variables at the same time. In this situation, separate descriptive statistics would be calculated for each data set.

Descriptives

Descriptive Statistics

	N	Minimum	Maximum	Mean	Std. Deviation
Exam Grade	30	45.00	95.00	74.0000	13.87133
Valid N (listwise)	30				

Using the TI-84

Follow the steps below to use your TI-84 calculator to calculate the standard deviation for the data set from Table 5.1.

TI-84 Exercise: Calculation of σ (standard deviation for population) and s (estimated population standard deviation).

1. With the calculator on, press the STAT key.
2. EDIT will be highlighted. Press the ENTER key.
3. Under L1 enter the data from Table 5.1.
4. Press the STAT key once again and highlight CALC.
5. Number 1: 1—VAR STATS will be highlighted. Press ENTER.
6. Press ENTER once again.

Descriptive statistics for the single variable on which you entered data will be shown. The population standard deviation (σ) is indicated by the symbol σ_X. The unbiased estimator of the population standard deviation (s) is indicated by the symbol S_X.

MODULE 6 Standard Scores or z Scores

Using Excel to Determine z Scores

To illustrate how to calculate z scores, we'll use the example in Module 6, also presented in the following table. We can see in the table the mean and standard deviation for two groups of students—one group who took an English exam and a second group who took a psychology exam.

Mean and standard deviation for English and psychology exams for two classes.

	Mean	Standard Deviation
English	85	9.58
Psychology	74	13.64

The scores for two of the students who took each of these exams follow:

Person	English Exam	Psychology Exam
Rich	91	88
Debbie	82	80

We'll use Excel to calculate the z scores for each of these individuals on the two exams. To calculate z scores using Excel, we use a function other than the Data Analysis ToolPak. Open Excel and click on the **Formulas** tab. You can see in the following Excel worksheet that this tab is highlighted:

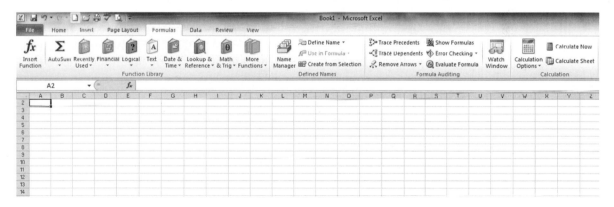

We'll start with the English exam data from the preceding table to calculate Rich's z score. You can see from that table that the English exam had a mean of 85 and a standard deviation of 9.58. To calculate the first z score, click on the *fX* button on the far left side of the formulas ribbon. You should receive the following dialog box:

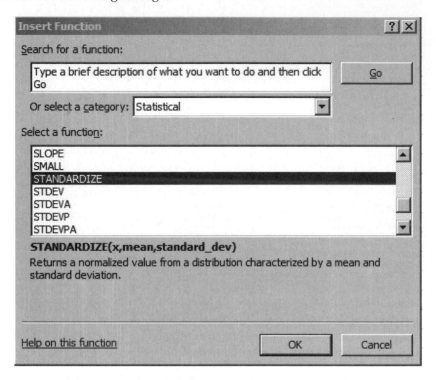

Make sure that **Statistical** is selected in the "Or select a category" field and then scroll down and select **STANDARDIZE** as in the preceding window. Finally select **OK** to receive the following dialog box. Enter Rich's English exam score into the *X* box and the mean and standard deviation where indicated. Then click **OK**.

Excel will give you the preceding output, where you can see the z score of +0.6263 in the A2 cell. This z score indicates that Rich scored 0.63 standard deviations above the mean on the English exam. If we want to compare this score to his performance on the psychology exam, or to Debbie's performance on the English exam, we must calculate these z scores also. Thus, to calculate Rich's z score on the psychology exam we use the same procedure as above. Use this procedure to calculate Rich's z score on the psychology exam and Debbie's z scores for both the English and psychology exams. You should receive the following results:

Rich's psychology exam z score = +1.03
Debbie's English exam z score = −.31
Debbie's psychology exam z score = +.44

Thus, we can see that although Rich's English exam score was higher than his psychology exam score (91 vs. 88), his z score on the psychology exam was larger than his z score on the English exam, indicating that he was 1.03 standard deviations above the mean on the psychology exam, but only .63 standard deviation above the mean on the English exam. Debbie, on the other hand, had a negative z score on the English exam, indicating that she scored −.31 standard deviation below the class mean. However, her psychology z score was +.44 standard deviation above the mean of the class, even though her raw score on the psychology exam was lower than her raw score on the English exam (80 vs. 82).

CHAPTER 4
Probability and Hypothesis Testing

In this chapter you will be introduced to the concepts of probability and hypothesis testing. **Probability** is the study of likelihood and uncertainty. Most decisions that we make are probabilistic in nature. Thus, probability plays a critical role in most professions and in our everyday decisions. We will discuss basic probability concepts along with how to compute probabilities and the use of the standard normal curve in making probabilistic decisions.

Hypothesis testing is the process of determining whether a hypothesis is supported by the results of a research project. Our introduction to hypothesis testing will include a discussion of the null and alternative hypotheses, Type I and Type II errors, and one- and two-tailed tests of hypotheses as well as an introduction to statistical significance and probability as they relate to inferential statistics.

probability The study of likelihood and uncertainty; the number of ways a particular outcome can occur, divided by the total number of outcomes.

hypothesis testing The process of determining whether a hypothesis is supported by the results of a research study.

MODULE 7
Probability

Learning Objectives

- Understand how probability is used in everyday life.
- Know how to compute a probability.
- Understand and be able to apply the multiplication rule.
- Understand and be able to apply the addition rule.
- Understand the relationship between the standard normal curve and probability.

In order to better understand the nature of probabilistic decisions, consider the following court case of *The People v. Collins*, 1968. In this case, the robbery victim was unable to identify his assailant. All that the victim could recall was that the assailant was female with a blonde pony tail. In addition, he remembered that she fled the scene in a yellow convertible that was driven by an African American male who had a full beard. The suspect in the case fit the description given by the victim, so the question was "Could the jury be sure, beyond a reasonable doubt, that the woman on trial was the robber?" The evidence against her was as follows: She was blonde and often wore her hair in a pony tail; her codefendant friend was an African American male with a moustache, beard, and a yellow convertible. The attorney for the defense stressed the fact that the victim could not identify *this* woman as the woman who robbed him, and that therefore there should be reasonable doubt on the part of the jury.

The prosecutor, on the other hand, called an expert in probability theory who testified to the following: The probability of all of the above conditions (being blonde *and* often having a pony tail *and* having an African American male friend *and* his having a full beard, *and* his owning a yellow convertible) co-occurring when these characteristics are independent was 1 in 12 million. The expert further testified that the combination of characteristics was so unusual that the jury could in fact be certain "beyond a reasonable doubt" that the woman was the robber. The jury returned a verdict of "guilty" (Arkes & Hammond, 1986; Halpern, 1996).

As can be seen in the previous example, the legal system operates on probability and recognizes that we can never be absolutely certain when deciding whether an individual is guilty. Thus, the standard of "beyond a reasonable doubt" was established and jurors base their decisions on probability, whether they realize it or not. Most decisions that we make on a daily basis are, in fact, based on probabilities. Diagnoses made by doctors, verdicts produced by juries, decisions made by business executives regarding expansion and what products to carry, decisions regarding whether individuals are admitted to colleges, and most everyday decisions all involve using probability. In addition, all games of chance (for example, cards, horse racing, the stock market) involve probability.

If you think about it, there is very little in life that is certain. Therefore, most of our decisions are probabilistic and having a better understanding of probability will help you with those decisions. In addition, because probability also plays an important role in science, that is another important reason for us to have an understanding of it. As we will see in later modules, the laws of probability are critical in the interpretation of research findings.

Basic Probability Concepts ● ●

Probability refers to the number of ways a particular outcome (event) can occur divided by the total number of outcomes (events). (Please note that the words *outcome* and *event* will be used interchangeably in this module.) Probabilities are often presented or expressed as proportions. Proportions vary between 0.0 and 1.0, where a probability of 0.0 means the event certainly will not occur and a probability of 1.0 means that the event is certain to occur. Thus, any probability between 0.0 and 1.0 represents an event with some degree of uncertainty to it. How much uncertainty depends on the exact probability with which we are dealing. For example, a probability close to 0.0 represents an event that is almost certain not to occur, and a probability close to 1.0 represents an event that is almost certain to occur. On the other hand, a probability of .50 represents maximum uncertainty. In addition, keep in mind that probabilities tell us about the likelihood of events in the long run, not the short run.

Let's start with a simplistic example of probability. What is the probability of getting a "head" when tossing a coin? In this example, we have to consider how many ways there are to get a "head" on a coin toss (there is only one way, the coin lands heads up) and how many possible outcomes there are (there are two possible outcomes, either a "head" or a "tail"). So, the probability of a "head" in a coin toss is:

$$p(\text{head}) = \frac{\text{Number of ways to get a head}}{\text{Number of possible outcomes}} = \frac{1}{2} = .50$$

This means that in the long run, we can expect a coin to land heads up 50% of the time.

Let's consider some other examples. How likely would it be for an individual to roll a 2 in one roll of a die? Once again, let's put this into basic probability terms. There is only one way to roll a 2, the die lands with the 2 side up. How many possible outcomes are there in a single roll of a die? There are six possible outcomes (any number between 1 and 6 could appear on the die). Hence, the probability of rolling a 2 on a single roll of a die would be 1/6, or about .17. Representing this in a formula as we did for the previous example:

$$p(2) = \frac{\text{Number of ways to get a 2}}{\text{Number of possible outcomes}} = \frac{1}{6} = .17$$

Let's make it a little more difficult. What is the probability of rolling an odd number in a single roll of a die? Well, there are three odd numbers on any single die (1, 3, and 5). Thus, there are three ways that an odd number can occur. Once again, how many possible outcomes are there in a single roll of a die? Six (any number between 1 and 6). Therefore, the probability of rolling an odd number on a single roll is 3/6, or .50. Represented as a formula this would be:

$$p(\text{odd number}) = \frac{\text{Number of ways to get an odd number}}{\text{Number of possible outcomes}} = \frac{3}{6} = .50$$

What if I asked you what the probability of rolling a single-digit number is in a single roll of a die? A die has six numbers on it, and each is a single-digit number. Thus, there are six ways to get a single-digit number. How many possible outcomes are there in a single roll of a die? Once again, six. Hence, the probability of rolling a single-digit number is 6/6, or 1.0. If someone asked you to place a bet on this occurring, you could not lose on this bet! Once again, as a formula this would be:

$$p(\text{single-digit number}) = \frac{\text{Number of ways to get a single-digit number}}{\text{Number of possible outcomes}}$$

$$= \frac{6}{6} = 1.0$$

Now that you have a basic idea of where probabilities come from, let's talk a little bit more about how we use probabilities. Keep in mind that probabilities tell us something about what will happen in the long run. Therefore, when we think about using some of the probabilities that we just calculated, we have to think about using them in the long run. For example, we determined that the probability of rolling a 2 on a single roll of a die was .17. This means that over many rolls of the die, it will land with the 2 side up about 17% of the time. We cannot predict what will happen on any single roll of the die, but over many rolls of the die, we will roll a 2 with a probability of .17. This means that with a very large number of trials, we can predict with great accuracy what proportion of the rolls will end up as 2s. However, we cannot predict which particular rolls will yield a 2. So when we think about using probabilities, we need to think about using them for predictions in the long run, not the short run.

CRITICAL THINKING CHECK 7.1

1. What is the probability of pulling a king from a standard (52-card) deck of playing cards?
2. What is the probability of pulling a spade from a standard deck of playing cards?
3. What is the probability of rolling an even number on a single roll of a die?
4. Imagine that you have a bag that contains 4 black poker chips and 7 red poker chips. What is the probability of pulling a black poker chip from the bag?

The Rules of Probability ●●

Often we are concerned with the probability of two or more events occurring and not just the probability of a single event occurring. For example, what is the probability of rolling at least one 4 in two rolls of a die, or what is the probability of getting two tails in two flips of a coin?

FIGURE 7.1
Tree diagram of
possible coin toss
outcomes

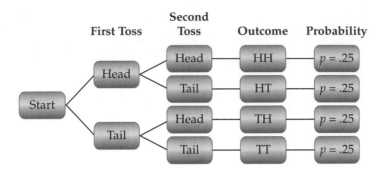

FIGURE 7.1
Tree diagram of
possible coin toss
outcomes

Let's use the coin-toss example to determine the probability of two tails occurring in two flips of a coin. Based on what we discussed in the previous section, we know that the probability of a tail on one flip of a coin is 1/2, or .50. The same is true for the second toss, the probability of a tail is 1/2, or .50. However, let's think about the possible outcomes for two tosses of a coin. One outcome is a head on the first toss and a head on the second toss (HH). The other outcomes would be a head followed by a tail (HT), a tail followed by a head (TH), and a tail followed by a tail (TT). These four possible outcomes are illustrated in the tree diagram in Figure 7.1.

Notice that the probability of two tails or any one of the other three possible outcomes is 1/4, or .25. But how are these probabilities calculated? The general rule that we apply here is known as the multiplication rule, or the *and* rule. When the events are independent and we want to know the probability of one event "and" another event, we use this rule.

multiplication rule
A probability rule stating that the probability of a series of outcomes occurring on successive trials is the product of their individual probabilities, when the sequence of outcomes is independent.

The **multiplication rule** says that the probability of a series of outcomes occurring on successive trials is the product of their individual probabilities, when the events are independent (do not impact one another). Thus, when using the multiplication rule, we *multiply* the probability of the first event by the probability of the second event. Therefore, for the present problem, the probability of a tail in the first toss is 1/2, or .50, *and* the probability of a tail in the second toss is 1/2, or .50. When we multiply these two probabilities, we have .50 × .50 = .25. This should make some sense to you because the probability of both events occurring should be less than that of either event alone. We can represent the problem as follows:

$$p(\text{tail on first toss and tail on second toss}) = p(\text{tail on first toss})$$
$$\times p(\text{tail on second toss})$$

Let's try another example. Assuming that the probabilities of having a girl and having a boy are both .50 for single-child births, what is the probability that a couple planning a family of three children would have the children in the following order: girl, girl, boy?

You can see in the tree diagram in Figure 7.2 that the probability of girl, girl, boy is .125. Let's use the *and* rule to double-check this probability. The

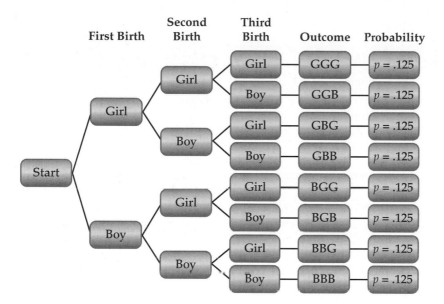

FIGURE 7.2
Tree diagram of
possible birth orders

probability of a girl as the first child is 1/2, or .50. The same is true for the probability of a girl as the second child (.50) and the probability of a boy as the third child (.50). In order to determine the probability of this sequence of births, we multiply: $.50 \times .50 \times .50 = .125$.

In addition to being able to calculate probabilities based on a series of independent events (as in the preceding examples), we can also calculate the probability of one event or another event occurring on a single trial when the events are mutually exclusive. Mutually exclusive means that only one of the events can occur on a single trial. For example, a coin toss can either be heads or tails on a given trial, but not both. When dealing with mutually exclusive events, we apply what is known as the **addition rule,** which states that the probability of one outcome *or* the other outcome occurring on a particular trial is the sum of their individual probabilities. In other words, we are *adding* the two probabilities together. Thus, the probability of having either a girl or a boy when giving birth would be:

addition rule A probability rule stating that the probability of one outcome or another outcome occurring on a particular trial is the sum of their individual probabilities, when the outcomes are mutually exclusive.

$$p(\text{girl } or \text{ boy}) = p(\text{girl}) + p(\text{boy}) = .50 + .50 = 1.00$$

This is sometimes referred to as the *or* rule because we are determining the probability of one event *or* the other event.

Let's try another problem using the *or* rule. What is the probability of drawing either a club or a heart when drawing one card from a deck of cards? The probability of drawing a club is 13/52, or .25. The same holds for drawing a heart (13/52 = .25). Thus, the probability of drawing either a club or a heart card on a single draw would be .25 + .25 = .50.

$$p(\text{club or heart}) = p(\text{club}) + p(\text{heart}) = .25 + .25 = .50$$

IN REVIEW

THE RULES OF PROBABILITY		
Rule	**Explanation**	**Example**
The Multiplication Rule	The probability of a series of independent outcomes occurring on successive trials is the product of their individual probabilities. This is also known as the *and* rule because we want to know the probability of one event *and* another event.	In order to determine the probability of one coin toss of a head followed by (*and*) another coin toss of a head, we multiply the probability of each individual event: .50 × .50 = .25
The Addition Rule	The probability of one outcome or another outcome occurring on a particular trial is the sum of their individual probabilities when the two outcomes are mutually exclusive. This is also known as the *or* rule because we want to know the probability of one event *or* another event.	In order to determine the probability of tossing a head *or* a tail on a single coin toss, we sum the probability of each individual event: .50 + .50 = 1.0

CRITICAL THINKING CHECK 7.2

1. Which rule, the multiplication rule or the addition rule, would be applied in each of the following situations?
   a. What is the probability of a couple having a girl as their first child followed by a boy as their second child?
   b. What is the probability of pulling a spade or a diamond from a standard deck of cards on a single trial?
   c. What is the probability of pulling a spade (and then putting it back in the deck) followed by pulling a diamond from a standard deck of cards?
   d. What is the probability of pulling a jack or a queen from a standard deck of cards on a single trial?
2. Determine the probability for each of the examples in exercise 1.

Probability and the Standard Normal Distribution

As you might remember from Chapter 3, z scores can be used to determine proportions under the standard normal curve. In that chapter, we used z scores and the area under the standard normal curve to determine percentile ranks. We will now use z scores and the area under the standard normal curve (Table A.1) to determine probabilities. As you might remember, the standard normal curve has a mean of 0 and a standard deviation of 1.

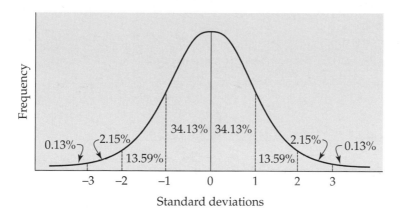

FIGURE 7.3
Area under the
standard normal
curve

In addition, as discussed in Chapter 3, the standard normal curve is symmetrical and bell shaped and the mean, median, and mode are all the same. Take a look at Figure 7.3, which represents the area under the standard normal curve in terms of standard deviations. We looked at this figure in the previous module (Figure 6.1), and based on this figure, we see that approximately 68% of the observations in the distribution fall between −1.0 and +1.0 standard deviations from the mean. This approximate percentage holds for all data that are normally distributed. Notice also that approximately 13.5% of the observations fall between −1.0 and −2.0 and another 13.5% between +1.0 and +2.0, and that approximately 2% of the observations fall between −2.0 and −3.0 and another 2% between +2.0 and +3.0. Only .13% of the scores are beyond a z score of either ±3.0. If you sum the percentages in Figure 7.3, you will have 100%—all of the area under the curve, representing everybody in the distribution. If you sum half of the curve, you will have 50%—half of the distribution.

We can use the areas under the standard normal curve to determine the probability that an observation falls within a certain area under the curve. Let's use a distribution that is normal to illustrate what we mean. Intelligence test scores are normally distributed with a mean of 100 and a standard deviation of 15. We could use the standard normal curve to determine the probability of randomly selecting someone from the population who had an intelligence score as high or higher than a certain amount. For example, if a school psychologist wanted to know the probability of selecting a student from the general population who had an intelligence test score of 119 or higher, we could use the area under the standard normal curve to determine this. First we have to convert the intelligence test score to a z score. As you might remember, the formula for a z score is:

$$z = \frac{X - \mu}{\sigma}$$

where X represents the individual's score on the intelligence test, μ represents the population mean, and σ represents the population standard

FIGURE 7.4
Standard normal
curve with $z = +1.27$
indicated

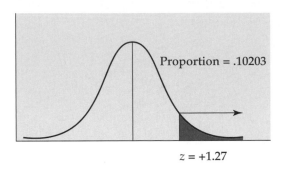

$z = +1.27$

deviation. Using this formula, we can calculate the individual's z score as follows:

$$z = \frac{X - \mu}{\sigma} = \frac{119 - 100}{15} = \frac{19}{15} = +1.27$$

Thus, we know that this individual's z score falls +1.27 standard deviations above the mean. As in Chapter 3, it is helpful to represent this on a figure where the z score of +1.27 is indicated. This is illustrated in Figure 7.4.

Now, in order to determine the probability of selecting a student with an intelligence test score of 119 or higher, we need to turn to Table A.1 in Appendix A. We begin by looking up a z score of 1.27 and find that for this score, a proportion of .39797 of the scores fall between the score and the mean of the distribution and a proportion of .10203 of the scores fall beyond the score. Referring to Figure 7.4, we see that the proportion of the curve in which we are interested is the area beyond the score, or .10203. This means that the probability of randomly selecting a student with an intelligence test score of 119 or higher is .10203, or just slightly higher than 10%. We can represent this problem in standard probability format as follows:

$$p(X \geq 119) = .10203$$

Let's try a couple more probability problems using the intelligence test score distribution. First, what is the probability of the school psychologist randomly selecting a student with an intelligence test score of 85 or higher? Secondly, what is the probability of the school psychologist selecting a student with an intelligence test score of 70 or lower?

Let's begin with the first problem. We need to convert the intelligence test score to a z score and then consult Table A.1.

$$z = \frac{X - \mu}{\sigma} = \frac{85 - 100}{15} = \frac{-15}{15} = -1.0$$

When we consult Table A.1, we find that for a z score of –1.0, .15866 of the scores fall below this score and .34134 of the scores fall between this score and the mean of the distribution. This z score is illustrated in Figure 7.5 along with the area in which we are interested—the probability of a student with an intelligence test score of 85 or higher being selected.

Proportion = .34134 + .50 = .84134

$z = -1.0$

FIGURE 7.5
Standard normal
curve with $z = -1.0$
indicated

In order to determine the *probability* of selecting a student with an intelligence test score this high or higher, we take the area between the mean and the z score (.34134) and add the .50 from the other half of the distribution to it. Hence, the probability of selecting a student with an intelligence test score of 85 or higher is .84134, or approximately 84%. You should see that the probability of this happening is fairly high because when we look at Figure 7.5 we are talking about a large proportion of people who fit this description. This can be represented as follows:

$p(X \geq 85) = .84134$

Let's work the second problem, the probability of selecting a student with an intelligence test score of 70 or lower. Once again we begin by converting this score into a z score.

$$z = \frac{X - \mu}{\sigma} = \frac{70 - 100}{15} = \frac{-30}{15} = -2.0$$

Next, we represent this on a figure with the z score indicated along with the area in which we are interested (anyone with this score or a lower score). This is illustrated in Figure 7.6.

Consulting Table A.1, we find that for a z score of –2.0, .02275 of the scores are below the score (beyond it) and .47725 of the scores are between the score and the mean of the distribution. We are interested in the probability

Proportion = .02275

$z = -2.0$

FIGURE 7.6
Standard normal
curve with $z = -2.0$
indicated

of selecting a student with an intelligence test score of 70 or lower. Can you figure out what that would be? If you answered .02275, you are correct. Therefore, there is slightly more than a 2% chance of selecting a student with an intelligence test score this low or lower—a fairly low probability event. This can be represented as follows:

$$p(X \leq 70) = .02275$$

Let's apply what we have learned about using the standard normal curve to calculate probabilities together with the addition rule from earlier in the module to determine the probability of selecting a child whose intelligence test score is 70 or lower or 119 or higher. We have already determined the z scores for each of these intelligence test scores in our previous problems. The intelligence test score of 70 converts to a z score of -2.0 and the intelligence test score of 119 converts to a z score of $+1.27$. Moreover, we have already determined that the probability of selecting a student with a score of 70 or lower is .02275 and that the probability of selecting a student with an intelligence test score of 119 or higher is .10203. Thus, applying the addition rule, the probability of selecting a student with a score that is 70 or lower *or* 119 or higher would be the sum of these two probabilities, or .02275 + .10203. These two probabilities sum to .12478, or just about 12.5%. This can be represented as follows:

$$= p(X \leq 70 \text{ or } X \geq 119) = p(X \leq 70) + p(X \geq 119)$$
$$= p(X \leq 70 \text{ or } X \geq 119) = (.02275) + (.10203)$$
$$= p(X \leq 70 \text{ or } X \geq 119) = .12478$$

Now let's turn to using the multiplication rule, discussed earlier in the module, with the area under the standard normal curve (Table A.1). In this case, we want to determine the probability of selecting two students who fit different descriptions. For example, what is the probability of selecting one student with an intelligence test score equal to or below 80, followed by another student with an intelligence test score equal to or above 125? Once again, we begin by converting the scores to z scores.

$$z = \frac{X - \mu}{\sigma} = \frac{80 - 100}{15} = \frac{-20}{15} = -1.33$$

$$z = \frac{X - \mu}{\sigma} = \frac{125 - 100}{15} = \frac{25}{15} = +1.67$$

Consequently, the intelligence test scores convert to z scores of -1.33 and $+1.67$, respectively. Next we use Table A.1 to determine the probability of each of these events. Consulting Table A.1, we find that the probability of selecting a student with a score of 80 or lower is .09175 and the probability of selecting a student with a score of 125 or higher is .04745. These z scores and proportions are represented in Figure 7.7.

We now apply the multiplication rule to determine the probability of selecting the first person followed by the second person. Thus, we multiply

FIGURE 7.7
Standard normal
curve with $z = -1.33$
and $z = +1.67$
indicated

the first probability by the second probability, or $.09175 \times .04745 = .00435$. This can be represented as follows:

$$p(X \leq 80 \text{ and } X \geq 125) = p(X \leq 80) + p(X \geq 125)$$
$$p(X \leq 80 \text{ and } X \geq 125) = (.09175) + (.04745)$$
$$p(X \leq 80 \text{ and } X \geq 125) = .00435$$

Thus, the probability of the first event followed by the second event has a very low probability of less than 1%.

---

1. If SAT scores are normally distributed with a mean of 1,000 and a standard deviation of 200, what is the probability of a student scoring 1,100 or higher on the SAT?
2. For this hypothetical SAT distribution, what is the probability of a student scoring 910 or lower on the SAT?
3. For this hypothetical SAT distribution, what is the probability of a student scoring 910 or lower or 1,100 or higher?
4. For this hypothetical SAT distribution, what is the probability of selecting a student who scored 910 or lower followed by a student who scored 1,100 or higher on the SAT?

CRITICAL THINKING CHECK 7.3

REVIEW OF KEY TERMS

addition rule (p. 117)
hypothesis testing (p. 111)

multiplication rule (p. 116)
probability (p. 111)

MODULE EXERCISES

(Answers to odd-numbered questions appear in Appendix B.)

1. Imagine that I have a jar that contains 50 blue marbles and 20 red marbles.

a. What is the probability of selecting a red marble from the jar?
b. What is the probability of selecting a blue marble from the jar?

c. What is the probability of selecting either a red or a blue marble from the jar?

d. What is the probability of selecting a red marble (with replacement) followed by a blue marble?

2. What is the probability of a couple having children in the following birth order: boy, boy, boy, boy?

3. What is the probability of selecting either a 2 or a 4 (of any suit) from a standard deck of cards?

4. If height is normally distributed with a mean of 68 inches and a standard deviation of 5 inches,

what is the probability of selecting someone who is 70 inches or taller?

5. For the distribution described in exercise 4, what is the probability of selecting someone who is 64 inches or shorter?

6. For the distribution described in exercise 4, what is the probability of selecting someone who is 70 inches or taller or 64 inches or shorter?

7. For the distribution described in exercise 4, what is the probability of selecting someone who is 70 inches or taller followed by someone who is 64 inches or shorter?

CRITICAL THINKING CHECK ANSWERS

Critical Thinking Check 7.1

1. $\dfrac{4}{52} = .077$

2. $\dfrac{13}{52} = .25$

3. $\dfrac{3}{6} = .50$

4. $\dfrac{4}{11} = .36$

Critical Thinking Check 7.2

1. (a) Multiplication rule
   (b) Addition rule
   (c) Multiplication rule
   (d) Addition rule

2. (a) $.50 \times .50 = .25$

   (b) $\left(\dfrac{13}{52}\right) + \left(\dfrac{13}{52}\right) = .25 + .25 = .50$

   (c) $\left(\dfrac{13}{52}\right) \times \left(\dfrac{13}{52}\right) = .25 \times .25 = .0625$

   (d) $\left(\dfrac{4}{52}\right) + \left(\dfrac{4}{52}\right) = .077 + .077 = .154$

Critical Thinking Check 7.3

1. $z = +.50, p = .30854$
2. $z = -.45, p = .32634$
3. $.32634 + .30854 = .63488$
4. $.32634 \times .30854 = .101$

WEB RESOURCES

The book-specific website at CengageBrain.com offers students a variety of study tools and useful resources such as glossaries, flashcards, quizzes, and Statistics and Research Methods Workshops.

Hypothesis Testing and Inferential Statistics

Learning Objectives

- Differentiate null and alternative hypotheses.
- Differentiate one- and two-tailed hypothesis tests.
- Explain how Type I and Type II errors are related to hypothesis testing.
- Explain what statistical significance means.
- Explain the difference between a parametric test and a nonparametric test.

Research is usually designed to answer a specific question, for example, "Do science majors score higher on tests of intelligence than students in the general population?" The process of determining whether this statement is supported by the results of the research project is referred to as hypothesis testing.

Suppose a researcher wants to examine the relationship between type of after-school program attended by a child and intelligence level. The researcher is interested in whether students who attend an after-school program that is academically oriented (math, writing, computer use) score higher on an intelligence test than students who do not attend such programs. The researcher will form a hypothesis. The hypothesis might be that children in academic after-school programs will have higher IQ scores than children in the general population. Because most intelligence tests are standardized with a mean score (μ) of 100 and a standard deviation (σ) of 15, the students in the academic after-school program would have to score higher than 100 for the hypothesis to be supported.

Null and Alternative Hypotheses

Most of the time, researchers are interested in demonstrating the truth of some statement. In other words, they are interested in supporting their hypothesis. It is impossible statistically, however, to demonstrate that something is true. In fact, statistical techniques are much better at demonstrating that something is not true. This presents a dilemma for researchers. They want to support their hypotheses, but the techniques available to them are better for showing that something is false. What are they to do? The logical route is to propose exactly the opposite of what they want to demonstrate to be true, then disprove or falsify that hypothesis. What is left (the initial hypothesis) must then be true (Kranzler, 2007).

Let's use our sample hypothesis to demonstrate what we mean. We want to show that children who attend academic after-school programs have different (higher) IQ scores from those who do not. We understand that statistics cannot demonstrate the truth of this statement. We therefore construct what is known as a **null hypothesis** (symbol H_0). Whatever the research topic, the null hypothesis always predicts that there is no difference between the groups being compared. This is typically what the researcher does not expect to find. Think about the meaning of null—nothing or zero. The null hypothesis means you have found nothing—no difference between the groups.

For the sample study, the null hypothesis would be that children who attend academic after-school programs are of the same intelligence level as other children. Remember, we said that statistics allow us to disprove or falsify a hypothesis. Therefore, if the null hypothesis is not supported, our original hypothesis—that children who attend academic after-school programs have different IQs from other children—is all that is left. In statistical notation, the null hypothesis for this study would be:

$$H_0: \mu_0 = \mu_1, \text{ or } \mu_{\text{academic program}} = \mu_{\text{general population}}$$

The purpose of the study, then, is to decide whether H_0 is probably true or probably false.

The hypothesis that the researcher wants to support is known as the **alternative hypothesis** (H_a), or the **research hypothesis** (H_1). The statistical notation for H_a is:

$$H_a: \mu_0 > \mu_1, \text{ or } \mu_{\text{academic program}} > \mu_{\text{general population}}$$

When we use inferential statistics, we are trying to reject H_0, which means that H_a is supported.

One- and Two-Tailed Hypothesis Tests   ●●

The manner in which the previous research hypothesis (H_a) was stated reflects what is known statistically as a **one-tailed hypothesis**, or a **directional hypothesis.** In this case, the researcher predicted the direction of the difference, namely, that those in the academic after-school programs would do better than those in the general population. When we use a directional alternative hypothesis, the null hypothesis is also, in some sense, directional. If the alternative hypothesis is that children in academic after-school programs will have higher intelligence test scores, then the null hypothesis is that being in academic after-school programs either will have no effect on intelligence test scores or will decrease intelligence test scores. Thus, the null

null hypothesis The hypothesis predicting that no difference exists between the groups being compared.

alternative hypothesis (research hypothesis) The hypothesis that the researcher wants to support, predicting that a significant difference exists between the groups being compared.

one-tailed hypothesis (directional hypothesis) An alternative hypothesis in which the researcher predicts the direction of the expected difference between the groups.

hypothesis for the one-tailed directional test might more appropriately be written as:

$H_0: \mu_0 \leq \mu_1$, or $\mu_{\text{academic program}} \leq \mu_{\text{general population}}$

The alternative to a one-tailed or directional test is a **two-tailed hypothesis,** or a **nondirectional hypothesis**—an alternative hypothesis in which the researcher expects to find differences between the groups but is unsure what the differences will be. In our example, the researcher would predict a difference in IQ scores between children in the academic after-school program and those in the general population, but the direction of the difference would not be predicted. Those in the academic program would be expected to be either higher or lower on IQ, but not the same as the general population of children. The statistical notation for a two-tailed test is as follows:

$H_0: \mu_0 = \mu_1$, or $\mu_{\text{academic program}} = \mu_{\text{general population}}$

$H_a: \mu_0 \neq \mu_1$, or $\mu_{\text{academic program}} \neq \mu_{\text{general population}}$

In our example, a two-tailed hypothesis does not really make sense.

Assume that the researcher has selected a random sample of children from the academic after-school program in order to compare their intelligence level to that of the general population of children (as noted above, we know that the mean IQ for the population is 100). If we were to collect data and find that the mean intelligence level of the children in the academic after-school program is "significantly" (a term that will be discussed shortly) higher than the mean intelligence level for the population, we could reject the null hypothesis. Remember that the null hypothesis states that there is no difference between the sample and the population. Thus, the researcher concludes that the null hypothesis—that there is no difference—is not supported. When the null hypothesis is rejected, the alternative hypothesis— that those in the academic programs have a higher IQ score than those in the population—is supported. We can say that the evidence suggests that the sample of children in the academic after-school programs represents a specific population that scores higher on the IQ test than the general population.

If, on the other hand, the mean IQ score of the children in the academic after-school program is not significantly different from the population mean, then the researcher has failed to reject the null hypothesis and, by default, has failed to support the alternative hypothesis. In this case, the alternative hypothesis that the children in the academic programs will have a higher IQ than the general population would not be supported.

two-tailed hypothesis (nondirectional hypothesis) An alternative hypothesis in which the researcher predicts that the groups being compared differ but does not predict the direction of the difference.

Type I and Type II Errors in Hypothesis Testing ●●

Any time we make a decision using statistics, there are four possible outcomes (see Table 8.1). Two of the outcomes represent correct decisions, whereas two represent errors. Let's use our example to illustrate these possibilities.

TABLE 8.1 The four possible outcomes in statistical decision making

THE RESEARCHER'S DECISION	THE TRUTH (UNKNOWN TO THE RESEARCHER)	
	H_0 is true	H_0 is false
Reject H_0 (say it is false)	Type I error	Correct decision
Fail to reject H_0 (say it is true)	Correct decision	Type II error

Type I error An error in hypothesis testing in which the null hypothesis is rejected when it is true.

If we reject the null hypothesis (the hypothesis stating that there is no IQ difference between groups), we may be correct in our decision, or we may be incorrect. If our decision to reject H_0 is correct, that means there truly is a difference in IQ between children in academic after-school programs and the general population of children. However, our decision could be incorrect. The result may have been due to chance. Even though we observed a significant difference in IQ between the children in our study and the general population, the result might have been a fluke—maybe the children in our sample just happened to guess correctly on a lot of the questions. In this case, we have made what is known as a **Type I error**—we rejected H_0 when in reality we should have failed to reject it (it is true that there really is no IQ difference between the sample and population). Type I errors can be thought of as false alarms—we said there was a difference, but in reality there is no difference.

What if our decision is to not reject H_0, meaning we conclude that there is no difference in IQ between the children in the academic after-school program and children in the general population? This decision could be correct, meaning that in reality there is no IQ difference between the sample and the population. However, it could also be incorrect. In this case, we would be making a **Type II error**—saying there is no difference between groups when in reality there is a difference. Somehow we have missed the difference that really exists and have failed to reject the null hypothesis when it is false. All of these possibilities are summarized in Table 8.1.

Type II error An error in hypothesis testing in which there is a failure to reject the null hypothesis when it is false.

Probability, Statistical Significance, and Errors ●●

Suppose we actually did the study on IQ level and academic after-school programs. In addition, suppose we found that there was a difference between the IQ levels of children in academic after-school programs and children in the general population (those in the academic programs scored higher). Lastly, suppose that this difference is statistically significant at the .05 (or the 5%) level (also known as the .05 alpha level). To say that a result has **statistical significance** at the .05 level means that a difference as big as or bigger than what we observed between the sample and the population could have occurred by chance only 5 times or fewer out of 100. In other

statistical significance An observed difference between two descriptive statistics (such as means) that is unlikely to have occurred by chance.

words, the likelihood that this result is due to chance is small. If the result is not due to chance, then it is most likely due to a true or real difference between the groups. If our result were statistically significant, we would reject the null hypothesis and conclude that we have observed a significant difference in IQ scores between the sample and the population.

Remember, however, that when we reject the null hypothesis, we could be correct in our decision, or we could be making a Type I error. Maybe the null hypothesis is true, and this is one of those 5 or fewer times out of 100 when the observed differences between the sample and the population did occur by chance. This means that when we adopt the .05 level of significance (the .05 alpha level), as often as 5 times out of 100 we could make a Type I error. The .05 level, then, is the probability of making a Type I error (for this reason, it is also referred to as a *p value*, which means *probability value*—the probability of a Type I error). In the social and behavioral sciences, alpha is typically set at .05 (as opposed to .01 or .08 or anything else). This means that researchers in these areas are willing to accept up to a 5% risk of making a Type I error.

What if you want to reduce your risk of making a Type I error and decide to use the .01 alpha level, reducing the risk of a Type I error to 1 out of 100 times? This seems simple enough: Simply reduce alpha to .01, and you have reduced your chance of making a Type I error. By doing this, however, you have now increased your chance of making a Type II error. Do you see why? If I reduce my risk of making a false alarm—saying a difference is there when it really is not—I increase my risk of missing a difference that really is there. When we reduce the alpha level, we have insisted on more stringent conditions for accepting our research hypothesis, making it more likely that we could miss a significant difference when it is present. We will return to Type I and Type II errors in the next module when we cover statistical power and discuss alternative ways of addressing this problem.

Which type of error, Type I or Type II, do you think is considered more serious by researchers? Most researchers consider a Type I error more serious. They would rather miss a result (Type II error) than conclude that there is a meaningful difference when there really is not (Type I error). What about in other arenas—for example, in the courtroom? A jury could make a correct decision in a case (find guilty when truly guilty, or find innocent when truly innocent). They could also make either a Type I error (say guilty when innocent) or Type II error (say innocent when guilty). Which is more serious here? Most people believe that a Type I error is worse in this situation also. How about in the medical profession? Imagine a doctor attempting to determine whether or not a patient has cancer. Here again, the doctor could make one of the two correct decisions or could make one of the two types of errors. What would the Type I error be? This would be saying that cancer is present when in fact it is not. What about the Type II error? This would be saying that there is no cancer when in fact there is. In this situation, most people would consider a Type II error to be more serious.

IN REVIEW

	HYPOTHESIS TESTING	
Concept	**Description**	**Example**
Null Hypothesis	The hypothesis stating that the independent variable has no effect and that there will be no difference between the two groups	H_0: $\mu_0 = \mu_1$ (two-tailed) H_0: $\mu_0 \leq \mu_1$ (one-tailed) H_0: $\mu_0 \geq \mu_1$ (one-tailed)
Alternative Hypothesis or Research Hypothesis	The hypothesis stating that the independent variable has an effect and that there will be a difference between the two groups	H_a: $\mu_0 \neq \mu_1$ (two-tailed) H_a: $\mu_0 > \mu_1$ (one-tailed) H_a: $\mu_0 < \mu_1$ (one-tailed)
Two-Tailed or Nondirectional Test	An alternative hypothesis stating that a difference is expected between the groups, but there is no prediction as to which group will perform better or worse	The mean of the sample will be different from or unequal to the mean of the general population
One-Tailed or Directional Test	An alternative hypothesis stating that a difference is expected between the groups, and it is expected to occur in a specific direction	The mean of the sample will be greater than the mean of the population, or the mean of the sample will be less than the mean of the population
Type I Error	The error of rejecting H_0 when we should have failed to reject it	This error in hypothesis testing is equivalent to a "false alarm," saying that there is a difference when in reality there is no difference between the groups
Type II Error	The error of failing to reject H_0 when we should have rejected it	This error in hypothesis testing is equivalent to a "miss," saying that there is not a difference between the groups when in reality there is difference between the groups
Statistical Significance	When the probability of a Type I error is low (.05 or less)	The difference between the groups is so large that we conclude it is due to something other than chance

CRITICAL THINKING CHECK 8.1

1. A researcher hypothesizes that children from the South weigh less (because they spend more time outside) than the national average. Identify H_0 and H_a. Is this a one- or two-tailed test?
2. A researcher collects data on children's weights from a random sample of children in the South and concludes that children from the South weigh less than the national average. The researcher, however, did not realize that the sample included many children who were small for their age and that in reality there is no difference

in weight between children in the South and the national average. What type of error was made?

3. If a researcher decides to use the .10 level rather than using the conventional .05 level of significance, what type of error is more likely to be made? Why? If the .01 level is used, what type of error is more likely? Why?

Using Inferential Statistics

Now that we have an understanding of the concept of hypothesis testing, we can begin to discuss how hypothesis testing is used. The simplest type of study involves only one group and is known as a **single-group design.** The single-group design lacks a comparison group—there is not a control group of any sort. We can, however, compare the performance of the group (the sample) to the performance of the population (assuming that population data are available).

single-group design
A research study in which there is only one group of participants.

Earlier in the module, we illustrated hypothesis testing using a single-group design—comparing the IQ scores of children in academic after-school programs (the sample) to the IQ scores of children in the general population. The null and alternative hypotheses for this study were:

$H_0: \mu_0 \leq \mu_1$, or $\mu_{\text{academic program}} \leq \mu_{\text{general population}}$

$H_a: \mu_0 > \mu_1$, or $\mu_{\text{academic program}} > \mu_{\text{general population}}$

To compare the performance of the sample to that of the population, we need to know the population mean (μ) and the population standard deviation (σ). We know that for IQ tests, $\mu = 100$ and $\sigma = 15$. We also need to decide who will be in the sample. Random selection will increase our chances of getting a representative sample of children enrolled in academic after-school programs. How many children do we need in the sample? We will see in later modules that the larger the sample, the greater the power of the study. We will also see that one of the assumptions of the statistical procedure we will be using to test our hypothesis is a sample size of 30 or more.

Once we have chosen our sample, we need to collect the data. To collect IQ score data, we could either administer an intelligence test to the children or look at their academic files to see whether they had already taken such a test.

Once the data are collected, we can begin to analyze them using **inferential statistics**—procedures for drawing conclusions about a population based on data collected from a sample. Inferential statistics involve the use of procedures for drawing conclusions based on the scores collected in a research study and going beyond them to make inferences about a population. In the following chapter (Chapter 5) we will describe two inferential statistical tests—the z test and t test. Both of these are **parametric tests**—tests that require us to make certain assumptions about estimates

inferential statistics
Procedures for drawing conclusions about a population based on data collected from a sample.

parametric test A statistical test that involves making assumptions about estimates of population characteristics, or parameters.

of population characteristics, or parameters. These assumptions typically involve knowing the mean (μ) and standard deviation (σ) of the population and that the population distribution is normal. Parametric tests are generally used with interval or ratio data. The alternative to a parametric test is a **nonparametric test**; that is, it does not involve the use of any population parameters. In other words, μ and σ are not needed, and the underlying distribution does not have to be normal. Nonparametric tests are most often used with ordinal or nominal data and will be discussed more fully in Chapter 10.

nonparametric test
A statistical test that does not involve the use of any population parameters— μ and σ are not needed, and the underlying distribution does not have to be normal.

IN REVIEW

SINGLE-SAMPLE RESEARCH AND INFERENTIAL STATISTICS		
Concept	**Description**	**Examples**
Parametric Inferential Statistics	Inferential statistical procedures that require certain assumptions about the parameters of the population represented by the sample data, such as knowing μ and σ and that the distribution is normal Most often used with interval or ratio data	z test t test (discussed in Chapter 5)
Nonparametric Inferential Statistics	Inferential procedures that do not require assumptions about the parameters of the population represented by the sample data; μ and σ are not needed, and the underlying distribution does not have to be normal Most often used with ordinal or nominal data	Chi-square tests Wilcoxon tests (discussed in Chapter 10)

CRITICAL THINKING CHECK 8.2

1. How do inferential statistics differ from descriptive statistics?
2. How does single-sample research involve the use of hypothesis testing? In other words, in a single-group design, what hypothesis is tested?

REVIEW OF KEY TERMS

alternative hypothesis (research hypothesis) (p. 126)
inferential statistics (p. 131)
nonparametric test (p. 132)
null hypothesis (p. 126)

one-tailed hypothesis (directional hypothesis) (p. 126)
parametric test (p. 131)
single-group design (p. 131)
statistical significance (p. 128)

two-tailed hypothesis (nondirectional hypothesis) (p. 127)
Type I error (p. 128)
Type II error (p. 128)

MODULE EXERCISES

(Answers to odd-numbered questions appear in Appendix B.)

1. The admissions counselors at Brainy University believe that the freshman class they have just recruited is the brightest yet. If they wanted to test this belief (that the freshmen are brighter than the other classes), what would the null and alternative hypotheses be? Is this a one- or two-tailed hypothesis test?

2. To test the hypothesis in exercise 1, the admissions counselors select a random sample of freshmen and compare their scores on the SAT to those of the population of upper-classmen. They find that the freshmen do in fact have a higher mean SAT score. However, what they are unaware of is that the sample of freshmen was not representative of all freshmen at Brainy University. In fact, the sample over-represented those with high scores and under-represented those with low scores. What type of error (Type I or Type II) did the counselors make?

3. A researcher believes that family size has increased in the last decade in comparison to the previous decade—that is, people are now having more children than they were before. What would the null and alternative hypotheses be in a study designed to assess this? Is this a one- or two-tailed hypothesis test?

4. What are the appropriate H_0 and H_a for each of the following research studies? In addition, note whether the hypothesis test is one- or two-tailed.
   a. A study in which researchers want to test whether there is a difference in spatial ability between left- and right-handed people
   b. A study in which researchers want to test whether nurses who work 8-hour shifts deliver higher-quality work than those who work 12-hour shifts
   c. A study in which researchers want to determine whether crate-training puppies is superior to training without a crate

5. Assume that each of the following conclusions represents an error in hypothesis testing. Indicate whether each of the statements is a Type I or II error.
   a. Based on the data, the null hypothesis was rejected.
   b. There was no significant difference in quality of work between nurses who work 8- and 12-hour shifts.
   c. There was a significant difference between right- and left-handers in their ability to perform a spatial task.
   d. The researcher failed to reject the null hypothesis based on these data.

6. Explain the difference between parametric and nonparametric statistics.

CRITICAL THINKING CHECK ANSWERS

Critical Thinking Check 8.1

1. $H_0: \mu_{\text{Southern children}} = \mu_{\text{children in general}}$, or
   $H_0: \mu_{\text{Southern children}} \geq \mu_{\text{children in general}}$
   $H_a: \mu_{\text{Southern children}} < \mu_{\text{children in general}}$
   This is a one-tailed test.

2. The researcher concluded that there was a difference when in reality there was no difference between the sample and the population. This is a Type I error.

3. With the .10 level of significance, the researcher is willing to accept a higher probability that the result may be due to chance. Therefore, a Type I error is more likely to be made than if the researcher used the more traditional .05 level of significance. With a .01 level of significance, the researcher is willing to accept only a .01 probability that the result may be due to chance. In this case, a true result is more likely to be missed, meaning that a Type II error is more likely.

Critical Thinking Check 8.2

1. Inferential statistics allow researchers to make inferences about a population based on sample data. Descriptive statistics simply describe a data set.

2. Single-sample research allows researchers to compare sample data to population data. The hypothesis tested is whether the sample performs similarly to the population or whether the sample differs significantly from the population and, thus, represents a different population.

WEB RESOURCES

The book-specific website at CengageBrain.com offers students a variety of study tools and useful resources such as glossaries, flashcards, quizzes, and Statistics and Research Methods Workshops.

CHAPTER FOUR SUMMARY AND REVIEW
Probability and Hypothesis Testing

CHAPTER SUMMARY

This chapter consisted of an introduction to probability and hypothesis testing. There was a discussion of how to calculate basic probabilities, how to use the multiplication and addition rules, and lastly how to use the area under the normal curve to calculate probabilities. With respect to hypothesis testing, there was a discussion of the null and alternative hypotheses, one- and two-tailed hypothesis tests, and Type I and Type II errors in hypothesis testing. In addition, the concept of statistical significance was defined. The most simplistic use of hypothesis testing—a single-group design—in which the performance of a sample is compared to the general population was presented to illustrate the use of inferential statistics in hypothesis testing.

CHAPTER 4 REVIEW EXERCISES

(Answers to exercises appear in Appendix B.)

Fill-in Self-Test

Answer the following questions. If you have trouble answering any of the questions, restudy the relevant material before going on to the multiple-choice self test.

1. _____ is the study of likelihood and uncertainty.
2. The rule that says that the probability of a series of outcomes occurring on successive trials is the product of their individual probabilities is the _____ rule.
3. The rule that says that the probability of one outcome or the other outcome occurring on a particular trial is the sum of their individual probabilities is the _____ rule.
4. The hypothesis predicting that no difference exists between the groups being compared is the _____.
5. An alternative hypothesis in which the researcher predicts the direction of the expected difference between the groups is a _____.
6. An error in hypothesis testing in which the null hypothesis is rejected when it is true is a _____.
7. When an observed difference, say between two means, is unlikely to have occurred by chance, we say that the result has _____.
8. _____ tests are statistical tests that do not involve the use of any population parameters.

Multiple-Choice Self-Test

Select the single best answer for each of the following questions. If you have trouble answering any of the questions, restudy the relevant material.

1. The study of likelihood and uncertainty is to _____ and the process of determining whether a hypothesis is supported by the results of a research project is to _____.
   a. hypothesis testing; probability
   b. hypothesis testing; inferential statistics
   c. probability; hypothesis testing
   d. inferential statistics; probability

2. The *and* rule is to _____ and the *or* rule is to _____.
   a. multiplication rule; addition rule
   b. addition rule; multiplication rule
   c. multiplication rule; multiplication rule
   d. addition rule; addition rule

3. The probability of rolling a 5 on one roll of a standard die is
   a. .25
   b. .50
   c. .20
   d. .17

4. The probability of rolling either a 2 or a 5 on one roll of a standard die is
   a. .34
   b. .25
   c. .50
   d. .03

5. The probability of rolling a 2 followed by a 6 on a standard die is:
   a. .34
   b. .25
   c. .50
   d. .03

6. If a psychology exam is normally distributed with a mean of 75 and a standard deviation of 5, what is the probability of someone scoring 80 or higher on the exam?
   a. .15866
   b. .34134
   c. .84134
   d. .30598

7. If a psychology exam is normally distributed with a mean of 75 and a standard deviation of 5, what is the probability of someone scoring 65 or higher on the exam?
   a. .02275
   b. .47725
   c. .52275
   d. .97725

8. Inferential statistics allow us to infer something about the _____ based on the _____.
   a. sample; population
   b. population; sample
   c. sample; sample
   d. population; population

9. The hypothesis predicting that differences exist between the groups being compared is the _____ hypothesis.
   a. null
   b. alternative
   c. one-tailed
   d. two-tailed

10. Null hypothesis is to alternative hypothesis as _____ is to _____.
    a. effect; no effect
    b. Type I error; Type II error
    c. no effect; effect
    d. None of the alternatives is correct.

11. One-tailed hypothesis is to directional hypothesis as _____ hypothesis is to _____ hypothesis.
    a. null; alternative
    b. alternative; null
    c. two-tailed; nondirectional
    d. two-tailed; one-tailed

12. When using a one-tailed hypothesis, the researcher predicts
    a. the direction of the expected difference between the groups.
    b. that the groups being compared will differ in some way.
    c. nothing.
    d. only one thing.

13. In a study of the effects of caffeine on driving performance, researchers predict that those in the group that is given more caffeine will exhibit worse driving performance. The researchers are using a _____ hypothesis.
    a. two-tailed
    b. directional
    c. one-tailed
    d. both directional and one-tailed

14. In a recent study, researchers concluded that caffeine significantly increased anxiety levels. What the researchers were unaware of, however, was that several of the participants in the no-caffeine group were also taking antianxiety medications. The researchers' conclusion is a(n) _____ error.
    a. Type II
    b. Type I
    c. null hypothesis
    d. alternative hypothesis

15. When alpha is .05, this means that
    a. the probability of a Type II error is .95.
    b. the probability of a Type II error is .05.
    c. the probability of a Type I error is .95.
    d. the probability of a Type I error is .05.

CHAPTER 5
The *z* and *t* Tests

In this chapter, we continue our discussion of inferential statistics—procedures for drawing conclusions about a population based on data collected from a sample. We will address two different statistical tests: the z test and *t* test. After reading this chapter, engaging in the Critical Thinking checks, and working through the problems at the end of each module and at the end of the chapter, you should understand the differences between the two tests covered in this chapter, when to use each test, how to use each to test a hypothesis, and the assumptions of each test.

MODULE 9
The Single-Sample z Test

Learning Objectives
- Explain what a z test is and what it does.
- Calculate a z test.
- Explain what statistical power is and how to make statistical tests more powerful.
- List the assumptions of the z test.
- Calculate confidence intervals using the z distribution.

The *z* Test: What It Is and What It Does

z test A parametric inferential statistical test of the null hypothesis for a single sample where the population variance is known.

The **z test** is a parametric statistical test that allows you to test the null hypothesis for a single sample when the population variance is known. This procedure allows us to compare a sample to a population in order to assess whether the sample differs significantly from the population. If the sample was drawn randomly from a certain population (children in academic after-school programs) and we observe a difference between the sample and a broader population (all children), we can then conclude that the population represented by the sample differs significantly from the comparison population.

Let's return to our example from the previous module and assume that we have actually collected IQ scores from 75 students enrolled in academic after-school programs. We want to determine whether the sample of children in academic after-school programs represents a population with a mean IQ greater than the mean IQ of the general population of children. As stated previously, we already know μ (100) and σ (15) for the general population of children. The null and alternative hypotheses for a one-tailed test are:

$H_0: \mu_0 \leq \mu_1$, or $\mu_{\text{academic program}} \leq \mu_{\text{general population}}$

$H_a: \mu_0 > \mu_1$, or $\mu_{\text{academic program}} > \mu_{\text{general population}}$

In Module 6 we learned how to calculate a *z* score for a single data point (or a single individual's score). To review, the formula for a *z* score is:

$$z = \frac{X - \mu}{\sigma}$$

where

X = each individual score
μ = the population mean
σ = the population standard deviation

Remember that a *z* score tells us how many standard deviations above or below the mean of the distribution an individual score falls. When using the *z* test, however, we are not comparing an individual score to the population mean. Instead, we are comparing a sample mean to the population mean. We therefore cannot compare the sample mean to a population distribution of individual scores. We must compare it instead to a distribution of sample means, known as the sampling distribution.

The Sampling Distribution

If you are becoming confused, think about it this way. A **sampling distribution** is a distribution of sample means based on random samples of a fixed size from a population. Imagine that we have drawn many different samples of some size (say 75) from the population (children whose IQ can be measured). For each sample that we draw, we calculate the mean; then we plot the means of all the samples. What do you think the distribution will look like? Well, most of the sample means will probably be similar to the population mean of 100. Some of the sample means will be slightly lower than 100; some will be slightly higher than 100; and others will be right at 100. A few of the sample means, however, will not be similar to the population mean. Why? Based on chance, some samples will contain some of the rare individuals with either very high IQ scores or very low IQ scores. Thus, the means for those samples will be much lower than 100 or much higher than 100. Such samples, however, will be few in number. Hence, the sampling distribution (the distribution of sample means) will be normal (bell-shaped), with most of the sample means clustered around 100 and a few sample means in the tails or the extremes. Therefore, the mean for the sampling distribution will be the same as the mean for the distribution of individual scores (100).

sampling distribution A distribution of sample means based on random samples of a fixed size from a population.

The Standard Error of the Mean

Here is a more difficult question: Would the standard deviation of the sampling distribution, known as the **standard error of the mean,** be the same as that for a distribution of individual scores? We know that $\sigma = 15$ for the distribution of individual IQ test scores. Would the variability in the sampling distribution be as great as it is in a distribution of individual scores? Let's think about it. The sampling distribution is a distribution of sample means.

standard error of the mean The standard deviation of the sampling distribution.

In our example, each sample has 75 people in it. Now, the mean for a sample of 75 people could never be as low or as high as the lowest or highest individual score. Why? Most people have IQ scores around 100. This means that in each of the samples, most people will have scores around 100. A few people will have very low scores, and when they are included in the sample, they will pull the mean for that sample down. A few others will have very high scores, and these scores will raise the mean for the sample in which they are included. A few people in a sample of 75, however, can never pull the mean for the sample as low as a single individual's score might be or as high as a single individual's score might be. For this reason, the standard error of the mean (the standard deviation for the sampling distribution) can never be as large as σ (the standard deviation for the distribution of individual scores).

How does this relate to the z test? A z test uses the mean and standard deviation for the sampling distribution to determine whether the sample mean is significantly different from the population mean. Thus, we need to know the mean (μ) and the standard error of the mean ($\sigma_{\overline{X}}$) for the sampling distribution. We have already said that μ for the sampling distribution is the same as μ for the distribution of individual scores—100. How will we determine what $\sigma_{\overline{X}}$ is?

To find the standard error of the mean, we would need to draw a number of samples from the population, determine the mean for each sample, and then calculate the standard deviation for this distribution of sample means. This is hardly feasible. Luckily for us, there is a method of finding the standard error of the mean without doing all of this. This is based on the central limit theorem. The central limit theorem is a precise description of the distribution that would be obtained if you selected every possible sample, calculated every sample mean, and constructed the distribution of sample means. The **central limit theorem** states that for any population with mean μ and standard deviation σ, the distribution of sample means for sample size N will have a mean of μ and a standard deviation of $\sigma/\sqrt{N}$ and will approach a normal distribution as N approaches infinity. Thus, according to the central limit theorem, in order to determine the standard error of the mean (the standard deviation for the sampling distribution) we take the standard deviation for the population (σ) and divide by the square root of the sample size ($\sqrt{N}$):

central limit theorem
A theorem which states that for any population with mean μ and standard deviation σ, the distribution of sample means for sample size N will have a mean of μ and a standard deviation of $\sigma/\sqrt{N}$ and will approach a normal distribution as N approaches infinity.

$$\sigma_{\overline{X}} = \frac{\sigma}{\sqrt{N}}$$

We can now use this information to calculate the z test. The formula for the z test is

$$z = \frac{\overline{X} - \mu}{\sigma_{\overline{X}}}$$

where

$\overline{X}$ = sample mean
μ = mean of the sampling distribution
$\sigma_{\overline{X}}$ = standard deviation of the sampling distribution, or standard error of the mean

	THE *z* TEST (PART I)		IN REVIEW

Concept	Description	Use
Sampling Distribution	A distribution of sample means where each sample is the same size (*N*)	Used for comparative purposes for *z* tests—a sample mean is compared with the sampling distribution to assess the likelihood that the sample is part of the sampling distribution
Standard Error of the Mean ($\sigma_{\bar{X}}$)	The standard deviation of a sampling distribution, determined by dividing σ by $\sqrt{N}$	Used in the calculation of *z*
z Test	Indication of the number of standard deviation units the sample mean is from the mean of the sampling distribution	An inferential test that compares a sample mean with the sampling distribution in order to determine the likelihood that the sample is part of the sampling distribution

1. Explain how a sampling distribution differs from a distribution of individual scores.
2. Explain the difference between $\sigma_{\bar{X}}$ and σ.
3. How is a *z* test different from a *z* score?

CRITICAL THINKING CHECK 9.1

Calculations for the One-Tailed *z* Test

You can see that the formula for a *z* test represents finding the difference between the sample mean ($\overline{X}$) and the population mean (μ) and then dividing by the standard error of the mean ($\sigma_{\bar{X}}$). This will tell us how many standard deviation units a sample mean is from the population mean, or the likelihood that the sample is from that population. We already know μ and σ, so all we need is to find the mean for the sample ($\overline{X}$) and to calculate $\sigma_{\bar{X}}$ based on a sample size of 75.

Suppose we find that the mean IQ score for the sample of 75 children enrolled in academic after-school programs is 103.5. We can calculate $\sigma_{\bar{X}}$ based on knowing the sample size and σ.

$$\sigma_{\bar{X}} = \frac{\sigma}{\sqrt{N}} = \frac{15}{\sqrt{75}} = \frac{15}{8.66} = 1.73$$

We now use $\sigma_{\overline{X}}$ (1.73) in the z test formula.

$$z = \frac{\overline{X} - \mu}{\sigma_{\overline{X}}} = \frac{103.5 - 100}{1.73} = \frac{3.5}{1.73} = +2.02$$

Instructions on using the TI-84 calculator to conduct this one-tailed z test appear in the Statistical Software Resources section at the end of this chapter.

Interpreting the One-Tailed z Test

Figure 9.1 represents where the sample mean of 103.5 lies with respect to the population mean of 100. The z test score of 2.02 can be used to test our hypothesis that the sample of children in the academic after-school program represents a population with a mean IQ greater than the mean IQ for the general population. To do this, we need to determine whether the probability is high or low that a sample mean as large as 103.5 would be chosen from this sampling distribution. In other words, is a sample mean IQ score of 103.5 far enough away from, or different enough from, the population mean of 100 for us to say that it represents a significant difference with an alpha level of .05 or less?

How do we determine whether a z score of 2.02 is statistically significant? Because the sampling distribution is normally distributed, we can use the area under the normal curve (Table A.1 in Appendix A). When we discussed z scores in Module 6, we saw that Table A.1 provides information on the proportion of scores falling between μ and the z score and the proportion of scores beyond the z score. To determine whether a z test is significant, we can use the area under the curve to determine whether the chance of a given score's occurring is 5% or less. In other words, is the score far enough away from (above or below) the mean that only 5% or less of the scores are as far or farther away?

Using Table A.1, we find that the z score that marks off the top 5% of the distribution is 1.645. This is referred to as the z **critical value,** or z_{cv}. For us to conclude that the sample mean is significantly different from the population mean, then, the sample mean must be at least ± 1.645 standard deviations (z units) from the mean. The critical value of 1.645 is illustrated in Figure 9.2. The z we obtained for our sample mean (z_{obt}) is 2.02, and this value falls

critical value The value of a test statistic that marks the edge of the region of rejection in a sampling distribution, where values equal to it or beyond it fall in the region of rejection.

FIGURE 9.1
The obtained mean in relation to the population mean

100   103.5
 μ $\overline{X}$

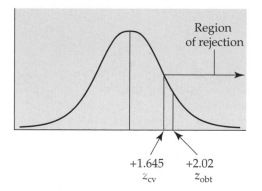

within the region of rejection for the null hypothesis. We therefore reject H_0 which states that the sample mean represents the general population mean and support our alternative hypothesis that the sample mean represents a population of children in academic after-school programs whose mean IQ is greater than 100. We make this decision because the z test score for the sample is larger than (further out in the tail than) the critical value of ±1.645. In APA style, it would be reported as follows: z ($N = 75$) = 2.02, $p < .05$ (one-tailed).

Keep in mind that when a result is significant, the p value (the α level, or probability of a Type I error) is reported as less than (<) .05 (or some smaller probability) not greater than (>)—an error commonly made by students. Remember the p value, or alpha level, indicates the probability of a Type I error. We want this probability to be small, meaning we are confident that there is only a small probability that our results were due to chance. This means it is highly probable that the observed difference between the sample mean and the population mean is truly a meaningful difference.

The test just conducted was a one-tailed test, because we predicted that the sample would score higher than the population. What if this were reversed? For example, imagine I am conducting a study to see whether children in athletic after-school programs weigh less than children in the general population. Can you determine what H_0 and H_a are for this example?

H_0: $\mu_0 \geq \mu_1$, or $\mu_{\text{weight of children in athletic programs}} \geq \mu_{\text{weight of children in general population}}$

H_a: $\mu_0 < \mu_1$, or $\mu_{\text{weight of children in athletic programs}} < \mu_{\text{weight of children in general population}}$

Assume that the mean weight of children in the general population (μ) is 90 pounds, with a standard deviation (σ) of 17 pounds. You take a random sample ($N = 50$) of children in athletic after-school programs and find a mean weight ($\overline{X}$) of 86 pounds. Given this information, you can now test the hypothesis that the sample of children in the athletic after-school program represents a population with a mean weight that is less than the mean weight for the general population of children.

First, we calculate the standard error of the mean ($\sigma_{\overline{X}}$).

$$\sigma_{\overline{X}} = \frac{\sigma}{\sqrt{N}} = \frac{17}{\sqrt{50}} = \frac{17}{7.07} = 2.40$$

Now, we enter $\sigma_{\overline{X}}$ into the z test formula.

$$z = \frac{\overline{X} - \mu}{\sigma_{\overline{X}}} = \frac{86 - 90}{2.40} = \frac{-4}{2.40} = -1.67$$

The z score for this sample mean is -1.67, meaning that it falls 1.67 standard deviations below the mean. The critical value for a one-tailed test was 1.645 standard deviations. This means the z score has to be at least 1.645 standard deviations away from (above *or* below) the mean in order to fall in the region of rejection. In other words, the critical value for a one-tailed z test is ± 1.645.

Is our z score at least that far away from the mean? It is, but just barely. Therefore, we reject H_0 and support H_a—that children in the athletic after-school programs weigh significantly less than children in the general population and hence represent a population of children who weigh less. In APA style, this would be written as $z\,(N = 50) = -1.67, p < .05$ (one-tailed). Instructions on using the TI-84 calculator to conduct this one-tailed z test appear in the Statistical Software Resources section at the end of this chapter.

Calculations for the Two-Tailed z Test

So far, we have completed two z tests, both one-tailed. Let's turn now to a two-tailed z test. Remember that a two-tailed test is also known as a nondirectional test—a test in which the prediction is simply that the sample will perform differently from the population, with no prediction as to whether the sample mean will be lower or higher than the population mean.

Suppose that in the previous example we used a two-tailed rather than a one-tailed test. We expect the weight of the children in the athletic after-school program to differ from that of children in the general population, but we are not sure whether they will weigh less (because of the activity) or more (because of greater muscle mass). H_0 and H_a for this two-tailed test appear next. See if you can determine what they would be before you continue reading.

H_0: $\mu_0 = \mu_1$, or $\mu_{\text{athletic programs}} = \mu_{\text{general population}}$

H_a: $\mu_0 \neq \mu_1$, or $\mu_{\text{athletic programs}} \neq \mu_{\text{general population}}$

Let's use the same data as before: The mean weight of children in the general population (μ) is 90 pounds, with a standard deviation (σ) of 17 pounds; for children in the sample ($N = 50$), the mean weight ($\overline{X}$) is 86 pounds. Using this information, you can now test the hypothesis that children in athletic after-school programs differ in weight from those in the general population. Notice that the calculations will be exactly the same for this z test. That is, $\sigma_{\overline{X}}$ and the z score will be exactly the same as before. Why? All of the measurements are exactly the same. To review:

$$\sigma_{\overline{X}} = \frac{\sigma}{\sqrt{N}} = \frac{17}{\sqrt{50}} = \frac{17}{7.07} = 2.40$$

$$z = \frac{\overline{X} - \mu}{\sigma_{\overline{X}}} = \frac{86 - 90}{2.40} = \frac{-4}{2.40} = -1.67$$

Interpreting the Two-Tailed *z* Test

If we end up with the same *z* score, how does a two-tailed test differ from a one-tailed test? The difference is in the *z* critical value (z_{cv}). In a two-tailed test, both halves of the normal distribution have to be taken into account. Remember that with a one-tailed test, the z_{cv} was ±1.645; this *z* score was so far away from the mean (*either* above *or* below) that only 5% of the scores were beyond it. How will the z_{cv} for a two-tailed test differ?

With a two-tailed test, the z_{cv} has to be so far away from the mean that a *total* of only 5% of the scores are beyond it (*both* above *and* below the mean). A z_{cv} of ±1.645 leaves 5% of the scores above the positive z_{cv} and 5% below the negative z_{cv}. If we take both sides of the normal distribution into account (which we do with a two-tailed test because we do not predict whether the sample mean will be above or below the population mean), then 10% of the distribution will fall beyond the two critical values. Thus, ±1.645 cannot be the critical value for a two-tailed test because this leaves too much chance (10%) operating.

To determine the z_{cv} for a two-tailed test, then, we need to find the *z* score that is far enough away from the population mean that only 5% of the distribution— taking into account both halves of the distribution—is beyond the score. Because Table A.1 represents only half of the distribution, we need to look for the *z* score that leaves only 2.5% of the distribution beyond it. Then, when we take into account both halves of the distribution, 5% of the distribution will be accounted for (2.5% + 2.5% = 5%). Can you determine what *z* score this would be, using Table A.1?

If you concluded that it would be ±1.96, then you are correct. This is the *z* score that is far enough away from the population mean (using both halves of the distribution) that only 5% of the distribution is beyond it. The critical values for both one- and two-tailed tests are illustrated in Figure 9.3.

$z_{critical} = -1.645$ μ_{null}

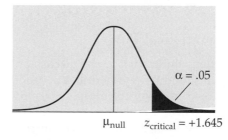

μ_{null} $z_{critical} = +1.645$

FIGURE 9.3
Regions of rejection and critical values for one-tailed versus two-tailed tests

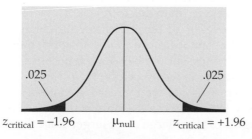

$z_{critical} = -1.96$ μ_{null} $z_{critical} = +1.96$

FIGURE 9.4
The *z* critical value
and the *z* obtained
for the two-tailed
z test example

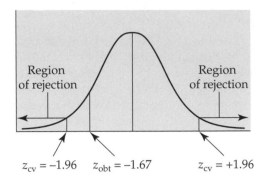

FIGURE 9.4
The *z* critical value
and the *z* obtained
for the two-tailed
z test example

Okay, what do we do with this critical value? We use it exactly the same way as we did the z_{cv} for a one-tailed test. In other words, the z_{obt} has to be as large as or larger than the z_{cv} in order for us to reject H_0. Is our z_{obt} as large as or larger than ±1.96? No (this is illustrated in Figure 9.4). Our z_{obt} was −1.67 and not in the region of rejection. We therefore fail to reject H_0 and conclude that the weight of children in the athletic after-school program does not differ significantly from the weight of children in the general population. Instructions on using the TI-84 calculator to conduct this two-tailed *z* test appear in the Statistical Software Resources section at the end of this chapter.

With exactly the same data (sample size, μ, σ, $\overline{X}$, and $\sigma_{\overline{X}}$), we rejected H_0 using a one-tailed test and failed to reject H_0 with a two-tailed test. How can this be? The answer is that a one-tailed test is statistically a more powerful test than a two-tailed test. **Statistical power** refers to the probability of correctly rejecting a false H_0. With a one-tailed test, you are more likely to reject H_0 because the z_{obt} does not have to be as large (as far away from the population mean) to be considered significantly different from the population mean. (Remember, the z_{cv} for a one-tailed test is ±1.645, but for a two-tailed test, it is ±1.96.)

statistical power
The probability of correctly rejecting a false H_0.

Statistical Power

Let's think back to the discussion of Type I and Type II errors in the previous module. We said that in order to reduce your risk of a Type I error, you need to lower the alpha level—for example, from .05 to .01. We also noted, however, that lowering the alpha level increases the risk of a Type II error. How, then, can we reduce our risk of a Type I error but not increase our risk of a Type II error? As we just noted, a one-tailed test is more powerful—you do not need as large a z_{cv} in order to reject H_0. Here, then, is one way to maintain an alpha level of .05 but increase your chances of rejecting H_0. Of course, ethically you cannot simply choose to adopt a one-tailed test for this reason. The one-tailed test should be adopted because you truly believe that the sample will perform above (*or* below) the mean.

By what other means can we increase statistical power? Look back at the *z* test formula. We know that the larger the z_{obt}, the greater the chance that it will be significant (as large as or larger than the z_{cv}) and that we can therefore reject H_0. What could we change in our study that might increase the size of the z_{obt}? Well, if the denominator in the *z* formula were a smaller number, then the z_{obt} would be larger and more likely to fall in the region of rejection. How can we make the denominator smaller? The denominator is $\sigma_{\overline{X}}$. Do you remember the formula for $\sigma_{\overline{X}}$?

$$\sigma_{\overline{X}} = \frac{\sigma}{\sqrt{N}}$$

It is very unlikely that we can change or influence the standard deviation for the population (σ). What part of the $\sigma_{\overline{X}}$ formula can we influence? The sample size (N).

If we increase sample size, what will happen to $\sigma_{\overline{X}}$? Let's see. We'll use the same example as before, a two-tailed test with all of the same measurements. The only difference will be in sample size. Thus, the null and alternative hypotheses will be

$H_0: \mu_0 = \mu_1$, or

$\mu_{\text{weight of children in athletic after-school programs}} = \mu_{\text{weight of children in general population}}$

$H_a: \mu \neq \mu_1$, or

$\mu_{\text{weight of children in athletic after-school programs}} \neq \mu_{\text{weight of children in general population}}$

The mean weight of children in the general population (μ) is once again 90 pounds, with a standard deviation (σ) of 17 pounds, and the sample of children in the after-school program again has a mean ($\overline{X}$) weight of 86 pounds. The only difference will be in sample size. In this case, our sample has 100 children in it. Let's test the hypothesis (conduct the *z* test) for these data.

$$\sigma_{\overline{X}} = \frac{17}{\sqrt{100}} = \frac{17}{10} = 1.70$$

$$z - \frac{86 - 90}{1.70} = \frac{-4}{1.70} = -2.35$$

Do you see what happened when we increased sample size? The standard error of the mean ($\sigma_{\overline{X}}$) decreased (we will discuss why in a minute), and the z_{obt} increased—in fact, it increased to the extent that we can now reject H_0 with this two-tailed test because our z_{obt} of -2.35 is further away from the mean than the z_{cv} of -1.96. Therefore, another way to increase statistical power is to increase sample size.

Why does increasing sample size decrease ($\sigma_{\overline{X}}$)? Well, you can see why based on the formula, but let's think back to our earlier discussion about $\sigma_{\overline{X}}$. We said that it was the standard deviation for a sampling distribution—a distribution of sample means of a set size. If you recall the IQ example we used in our discussion of $\sigma_{\overline{X}}$ and the sampling distribution, we said that $\mu = 100$ and $\sigma = 15$. We discussed what $\sigma_{\overline{X}}$ would be for a sampling distribution in which each sample mean was based on a sample size of 75. We further noted that $\sigma_{\overline{X}}$ would always be smaller (have less variability) than

σ because it represents the standard deviation of a distribution of sample means, not a distribution of individual scores. What, then, will increasing sample size do to $\sigma_{\bar{X}}$? If each sample in the sampling distribution had 100 people in it rather than 75, what do you think this would do to the distribution of sample means?

As we noted earlier, most people in a sample will be close to the mean (100), with only a few people in each sample representing the tails of the distribution. If we increase sample size to 100, we will have 25 more people in each sample. Most of them will probably be close to the population mean of 100; therefore, each sample mean will probably be closer to the population mean of 100. Thus, a sampling distribution based on samples of $N = 100$ rather than $N = 75$ will have less variability, which means that $\sigma_{\bar{X}}$ will be smaller.

Assumptions and Appropriate Use of the z Test

As noted earlier in the module, the z test is a parametric inferential statistical test for hypothesis testing. Parametric tests involve the use of parameters or population characteristics. With a z test, the parameters, such as μ and σ, are known. If they are not known, the z test is not appropriate. Because the z test involves the calculation and use of a sample mean, it is appropriate for use with interval or ratio data. In addition, because we use the area under the normal curve (Table A.1), we are assuming that the distribution of random samples is normal. Small samples often fail to form a normal distribution. Therefore, if the sample size is small ($N < 30$), the z test may not be appropriate. In cases where the sample size is small, or where σ is not known, the appropriate test would be the t test, discussed in the next module.

IN REVIEW

THE z TEST (PART II)		
Concept	**Description**	**Examples**
One-Tailed z Test	A directional inferential test in which a prediction is made that the population represented by the sample will be either above or below the general population	$H_a: \mu_0 < \mu_1$ or $H_a: \mu_0 > \mu_1$
Two-Tailed z Test	A nondirectional inferential test in which the prediction is made that the population represented by the sample will differ from the general population, but the direction of the difference is not predicted	$H_a: \mu_0 \neq \mu_1$
Statistical Power	The probability of correctly rejecting a false H_0	One-tailed tests are more powerful; increasing sample size increases power

CRITICAL
THINKING
CHECK
9.2

1. Imagine that I want to compare the intelligence level of psychology majors to the intelligence level of the general population of college students. I predict that psychology majors will have higher IQ scores. Is this a one- or two-tailed test? Identify H_0 and H_a.
2. Conduct the z test for the previous example. Assume that $\mu = 100$, $\sigma = 15$, $\overline{X} = 102.75$, and $N = 60$. Should we reject H_0 or fail to reject H_0?

Confidence Intervals Based on the *z* Distribution

In this text, hypothesis tests such as the previously described z test are the main focus. However, sometimes social and behavioral scientists use estimation of population means based on confidence intervals rather than statistical hypothesis tests. For example, imagine that you want to estimate a population mean based on sample data (a sample mean). This differs from the previously described z test in that we are not determining whether the sample mean differs significantly from the population mean; rather, we are estimating the population mean based on knowing the sample mean. We can still use the area under the normal curve to accomplish this—we simply use it in a slightly different way.

Let's use the previous example in which we know the sample mean weight of children enrolled in athletic after-school programs ($\overline{X} = 86$), σ (17), and the sample size ($N = 100$). However, imagine that we do not know the population mean (μ). In this case, we can calculate a confidence interval based on knowing the sample mean and σ. A **confidence interval** is an interval of a certain width, which we feel "confident" will contain μ. We want a confidence interval wide enough that we feel fairly certain it contains the population mean. For example, if we want to be 95% confident, we want a 95% confidence interval.

How can we use the area under the standard normal curve to determine a confidence interval of 95%? We use the area under the normal curve to determine the z scores that mark off the area representing 95% of the scores under the curve. If you consult Table A.1, you will find that 95% of the scores will fall between ±1.96 standard deviations above and below the mean. Thus, we could determine which scores represent ±1.96 standard deviations from the mean of 86. This seems fairly simple, but we must remember that we are dealing with a distribution of sample means (the sampling distribution) and not with a distribution of individual scores. Thus, we must convert the standard deviation (σ) to the standard error of the mean ($\sigma_{\overline{X}}$, the standard deviation for a sampling distribution) and use the standard error

confidence interval
An interval of a certain width that we feel confident will contain μ.

of the mean in the calculation of a confidence interval. Remember we calculate $\sigma_{\overline{X}}$ by dividing σ by the square root of N.

$$\sigma_{\overline{X}} = \frac{17}{\sqrt{100}} = \frac{17}{10} = 1.70$$

We can now calculate the 95% confidence interval using the following formula:

$$CI = \overline{X} \pm z(\sigma_{\overline{X}})$$

where

$\overline{X}$ = the sample mean
$\sigma_{\overline{X}}$ = the standard error of the mean, and
z = the z score representing the desired confidence interval

Thus:

$$CI = 86 \pm 1.96(1.70)$$
$$= 86 \pm 3.332$$
$$= 82.668\text{--}89.332$$

Thus, the 95% confidence interval ranges from 82.67 to 89.33. We would conclude, based on this calculation, that we are 95% confident that the population mean lies within this interval.

What if we wanted to have greater confidence that our population mean is contained in the confidence interval? In other words, what if we want to be 99% confident? We would have to construct a 99% confidence interval. How would we go about doing this?

We would do exactly what we did for the 95% confidence interval. First, we would consult Table A.1 to determine what z scores mark off 99% of the area under the normal curve. We find that z scores of ± 2.58 mark off 99% of the area under the curve. We then apply the same formula for a confidence interval used previously.

$$CI = \overline{X} \pm z(\sigma_{\overline{X}})$$
$$CI = 86 \pm 2.58(1.70)$$
$$= 86 \pm 4.386$$
$$= 81.614\text{--}90.386$$

Thus, the 99% confidence interval ranges from 81.61 to 90.39. We would conclude, based on this calculation, that we are 99% confident that the population mean lies within this interval.

Typically, statisticians recommend using a 95% or a 99% confidence interval. However, using Table A.1 (the area under the normal curve), you could construct a confidence interval of 55%, 70%, or any percentage you desire.

It is also possible to do hypothesis testing with confidence intervals. For example, if you construct a 95% confidence interval based on knowing a sample mean and then determine that the population mean is not in the confidence interval, the result is significant. For example, the 95% confidence interval we constructed earlier of 82.67–89.33 did not include the actual population mean reported earlier in the module ($\mu = 90$). Thus, there is less than a 5% chance that this sample mean could have come from this population—the same conclusion we reached when using the *z* test earlier in the module.

REVIEW OF KEY TERMS

central limit theorem (p. 142)
confidence interval (p. 151)
critical value (p. 144)

sampling distribution (p. 141)
standard error of the
    mean (p. 141)

statistical power (p. 148)
z test (p. 140)

MODULE EXERCISES

(Answers to odd-numbered questions appear in Appendix B.)

1. What is a sampling distribution?
2. Explain why the mean of a sampling distribution is the same as the mean for a distribution of individual scores but the standard deviation for a sampling distribution differs from the standard deviation of a distribution of individual scores.
3. Explain why the z_{cv} for a one-tailed test differs from that for a two-tailed test.
4. Explain what statistical power is and how we can increase power.
5. A researcher is interested in whether students who attend private high schools have higher average SAT scores than students in the general population of high school students. A random sample of 90 students at a private high school is tested and has a mean SAT score of 1,050. The average for public high school students is 1,000 ($\sigma = 200$).
   a. Is this a one- or two-tailed test?
   b. What are H_0 and H_a for this study?
   c. Compute z_{obt}.
   d. What is z_{cv}?

   e. Should H_0 be rejected? What should the researcher conclude?
   f. Determine the 95% confidence interval for the population mean, based on the sample mean.
6. The producers of a new toothpaste claim that it prevents more cavities than other brands of toothpaste. In other words, those who use the new toothpaste should have fewer cavities than those who use other brands. A random sample of 60 people uses the new toothpaste for six months. The mean number of cavities at their next checkup is 1.5. In the general population, the mean number of cavities at a six-month checkup is 1.73 ($\sigma = 1.12$).
   a. Is this a one- or two-tailed test?
   b. What are H_0 and H_a for this study?
   c. Compute z_{obt}.
   d. What is z_{cv}?
   e. Should H_0 be rejected? What should the researcher conclude?
   f. Determine the 95% confidence interval for the population mean, based on the sample mean.

CRITICAL THINKING CHECK ANSWERS

Critical Thinking Check 9.1

1. A sampling distribution is a distribution of sample means. Thus, rather than representing scores for individuals, the sampling distribution plots the means of samples of a set size.

2. $\sigma_{\overline{X}}$ is the standard deviation for a sampling distribution. It therefore represents the standard deviation for a distribution of sample means. σ is the standard deviation for a population of individual scores rather than sample means.

3. A z test compares the performance of a sample to the performance of the population by indicating the number of standard deviation units the sample mean is from the mean of the sampling distribution. A z score indicates how many standard deviation units an individual score is from the population mean.

Critical Thinking Check 9.2

1. Predicting that psychology majors will have higher IQ scores makes this a one-tailed test.

H_0: $\mu_{\text{psychology majors}} \leq \mu_{\text{general population}}$
H_a: $\mu_{\text{psychology majors}} > \mu_{\text{general population}}$

2. $\sigma_{\overline{X}} = \dfrac{15}{\sqrt{60}} = \dfrac{15}{7.75} = 1.94$

$z = \dfrac{102.75 - 100}{1.94} = \dfrac{2.75}{1.94} = +1.42$

Because this is a one-tailed test, $z_{cv} = \pm 1.645$. The $z_{obt} = +1.42$. We therefore fail to reject H_0; psychology majors do not differ significantly on IQ scores in comparison to the general population of college students.

WEB RESOURCES

The book-specific website at CengageBrain.com offers students a variety of study tools and useful resources such as glossaries, flashcards, quizzes, and Statistics and Research Methods Workshops.

The Single-Sample *t* Test

Learning Objectives

- Explain what a *t* test is and what it does.
- Calculate a *t* test
- List the assumptions of the *t* test.
- Calculate confidence intervals using the *t* distribution.

The *t* Test: What It Is and What It Does

The **t test** for a single sample is similar to the *z* test in that it is also a parametric statistical test of the null hypothesis for a single sample. As such, it is a means of determining the number of standard deviation units a score is from the mean (μ) of a distribution. With a *t* test, however, the population variance is not known. Another difference is that *t* distributions, although symmetrical and bell-shaped, are *not* normally distributed. This means that the areas under the normal curve that apply for the *z* test do not apply for the *t* test.

t test A parametric inferential statistical test of the null hypothesis for a single sample where the population variance is not known.

Student's *t* Distribution

The *t* distribution, known as **Student's *t* distribution,** was developed by William Sealey Gosset, a chemist, who worked for the Guinness Brewing Company of Dublin, Ireland, at the beginning of the 20th century. Gosset noticed that when working with small samples of beer ($N < 30$) chosen for quality-control testing, the sampling distribution of the means was symmetrical and bell-shaped, but *not* normal. Therefore, the proportions under the standard normal curve did not apply. In other words, with small sample sizes, the curve was symmetrical, but it was not the standard normal curve. As the size of the samples in the sampling distribution increased, the sampling distribution approached the normal distribution and the

Student's *t* distribution
A set of distributions that, although symmetrical and bell-shaped, are not normally distributed.

proportions under the curve became more similar to those under the standard normal curve. He eventually published his findings under the pseudonym "Student"; and with the help of Karl Pearson, a mathematician, he developed a general formula for the t distributions (Peters, 1987; Stigler, 1986; Tankard, 1984).

We refer to t distributions in the plural because unlike the z distribution, of which there is only one, the t distributions are a family of symmetric distributions that differ for each sample size. As a result, the critical value indicating the region of rejection changes for samples of different sizes. As the size of the samples increases, the t distribution approaches the z or normal distribution. Table A.2 in Appendix A at the back of your book provides the t critical values (t_{cv}) for both one- and two-tailed tests for various sample sizes and alpha levels. Notice, however, that although we have said that the critical value depends on sample size, there is no column in the table labeled N for sample size. Instead, there is a column labeled **df**, which stands for **degrees of freedom.** The degrees of freedom are related to sample size. For example, assume that you are given six numbers, 2, 5, 6, 9, 11, and 15. The mean of these numbers is 8. If you are told that you can change the numbers as you like, but that the mean of the distribution must remain at 8, how many numbers can you change arbitrarily? You can change five of the six numbers arbitrarily. Once you have changed five of the numbers arbitrarily, the sixth number is determined by the qualification that the mean of the distribution must equal 8. Therefore, in this distribution of six numbers, five are free to vary. Thus, there are five degrees of freedom. For any single distribution, then, $df = N - 1$.

degrees of freedom (df)
The number of scores in a sample that are free to vary.

Look again at Table A.2, and notice what happens to the critical values as the degrees of freedom increase. Look at the column for a one-tailed test with alpha equal to .05 and degrees of freedom equal to 10. The critical value is ±1.812. This is larger than the critical value for a one-tailed z test, which was ±1.645. Because we are dealing with smaller, nonnormal distributions when using the t test, the t score must be farther away from the mean in order for us to conclude that it is significantly different from the mean. What happens as the degrees of freedom increase? Look in the same column— one-tailed test, alpha = .05—for 20 degrees of freedom. The critical value is ±1.725, smaller than the critical value for 10 degrees of freedom. Continue to scan down the same column, one-tailed test and alpha=.05, until you reach the bottom, where $df = \infty$. Notice that the critical value is ±1.645, the same as it is for a one-tailed z test. Thus, when the sample size is large, the t distribution is the same as the z distribution.

Calculations for the One-Tailed t Test

Let's illustrate the use of the single-sample t test to test a hypothesis. Assume the mean SAT score of students admitted to General University is 1,090. Thus, the university mean of 1,090 is the population mean (μ). The population standard deviation is unknown. The members of the Biology Department believe that students who decide to major in biology have higher

TABLE 10.1   SAT scores for a sample of 10 biology majors

X
1,010
1,200
1,310
1,075
1,149
1,078
1,129
1,069
1,350
1,390
$\Sigma X = 11,760$

$$\bar{X} = \frac{\Sigma X}{N} = \frac{11,760}{10} = 1,176$$

SAT scores than the general population of students at the university. The null and alternative hypotheses are thus

H_0: $\mu_0 \leq \mu_1$, or $\mu_{\text{biology students}} \leq \mu_{\text{general population}}$

H_a: $\mu_0 > \mu_1$, or $\mu_{\text{biology students}} > \mu_{\text{general population}}$

Notice that this is a one-tailed test because the researchers predict that the biology students will perform higher than the general population of students at the university. The researchers now need to obtain the SAT scores for a sample of biology majors. This information is provided in Table 10.1, which shows that the mean SAT score for the sample is 1,176. This sample mean represents our estimate of the population mean SAT score for biology majors.

The Estimated Standard Error of the Mean

The *t* test will tell us whether this mean differs significantly from the university mean of 1,090. Because we have a small sample ($N = 10$) and because we do not know σ, we must conduct a *t* test rather than a *z* test. The formula for the *t* test is

$$t = \frac{\bar{X} - \mu}{s_{\bar{X}}}$$

This looks very similar to the formula for the *z* test that we used in Module 9. The only difference is in the denominator, where $s_{\bar{X}}$ (the **estimated standard error of the mean** of the sampling distribution) has been

estimated standard error of the mean   An estimate of the standard deviation of the sampling distribution.

substituted for $\sigma_{\overline{X}}$. We use $s_{\overline{X}}$ rather than $\sigma_{\overline{X}}$ because we do not know σ (the standard deviation for the population) and thus cannot calculate $\sigma_{\overline{X}}$. We can, however, determine s (the unbiased estimator of the population standard deviation) and, based on this, we can determine $s_{\overline{X}}$. The formula for $s_{\overline{X}}$ is

$$s_{\overline{X}} = \frac{s}{\sqrt{N}}$$

We must first calculate s (the estimated standard deviation for a population, based on sample data) and then use this to calculate the estimated standard error of the mean ($s_{\overline{X}}$). The formula for s, which we learned in Module 3, is

$$s = \sqrt{\frac{\Sigma(X - \overline{X})^2}{N - 1}}$$

Using the information in Table 10.1, we can use this formula to calculate s.

$$s = \sqrt{\frac{156,352}{9}} = \sqrt{17,372.44} = 131.80$$

Thus, the unbiased estimator of the standard deviation (s) is 131.80. We can now use this value to calculate $s_{\overline{X}}$, the estimated standard error of the sampling distribution.

$$s_{\overline{X}} = \frac{s}{\sqrt{N}} = \frac{131.80}{\sqrt{10}} = \frac{131.80}{3.16} = 41.71$$

Finally, we can use this value for $s_{\overline{X}}$ to calculate t.

$$t = \frac{\overline{X} - \mu}{s_{\overline{X}}} = \frac{1,176 - 1,090}{41.71} = \frac{86}{41.71} = +2.06$$

Interpreting the One-Tailed t Test

Our sample mean falls 2.06 standard deviations above the population mean of 1,090. We must now determine whether this is far enough away from the population mean to be considered significantly different. In other words, is our sample mean far enough away from the population mean that it lies in the region of rejection? Because this is a one-tailed alternative hypothesis, the region of rejection is in one tail of the sampling distribution. Consulting Table A.2 for a one-tailed test with alpha $=.05$ and $df = N - 1 = 9$, we see that $t_{cv} = \pm 1.833$. The t_{obt} of 2.06 is therefore within the region of rejection. We reject H_0 and support H_a. In other words, we have sufficient evidence to allow us to conclude that biology majors have significantly higher SAT scores than the rest of the students at General University. In APA style, this would be reported as $t(9) = 2.06, p < .05$ (one-tailed). Figure 10.1 illustrates the obtained t with respect to the region of rejection. Instructions on using Excel, SPSS, or the TI-84 calculator to conduct this one-tailed single sample t test appear in the Statistical Software Resources section at the end of this chapter.

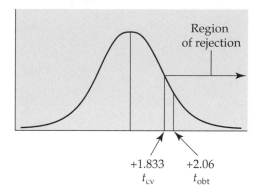

FIGURE 10.1
The *t* critical value and the *t* obtained for the single-sample one-tailed *t* test example

Calculations for the Two-Tailed *t* Test

What if the Biology Department had made no directional prediction concerning the SAT scores of its students? In other words, suppose the members of the department were unsure whether their students' scores would be higher or lower than those of the general population of students and were simply interested in whether biology students differed from the population. In this case, the test of the alternative hypothesis would be two-tailed, and the null and alternative hypotheses would be

H_0: $\mu_0 = \mu_1$, or $\mu_{\text{biology students}} = \mu_{\text{general population}}$

H_a: $\mu_0 \neq \mu_1$, or $\mu_{\text{biology students}} \neq \mu_{\text{general population}}$

Assuming that the sample of biology students is the same, $\overline{X}$, s, and $s_{\overline{X}}$ would all be the same. The population at General University is also the same, so μ would still be 1,090. Using all of this information to conduct the t test, we end up with exactly the same t test score of +2.06. What, then, is the difference for the two-tailed t test? It is the same as the difference between the one- and two-tailed z test—the critical values differ.

Interpreting the Two-Tailed *t* Test

Remember that with a two-tailed alternative hypothesis, the region of rejection is divided evenly between the two tails (the positive and negative ends) of the sampling distribution. Consulting Table A.2 for a two-tailed test with alpha = .05 and $df = N - 1 = 9$, we see that $t_{\text{cv}} = \pm 2.262$. The t_{obt} of 2.06 is therefore not within the region of rejection. We do not reject H_0 and thus cannot support H_a. In other words, we do not have sufficient evidence to allow us to conclude that the population of biology majors differs significantly on SAT scores from the rest of the students at General University. Thus, with exactly the same data, we rejected H_0 with a one-tailed test, but failed to reject H_0 with a two-tailed test, illustrating once again that one-tailed tests are more powerful than two-tailed tests. Figure 10.2 illustrates the obtained t for the two-tailed test in relation to the regions of rejection. Instructions on using Excel, SPSS, or the TI-84 calculator to conduct this two-tailed single-sample t test appear in the Statistical Software Resources section at the end of this chapter.

FIGURE 10.2
The *t* critical value and the *t* obtained for the single-sample two-tailed test example

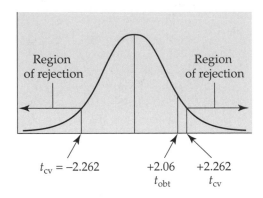

Region
of rejection

Region
of rejection

$t_{cv} = -2.262$ +2.06   +2.262
t_{obt} t_{cv}

Assumptions and Appropriate Use of the Single-Sample *t* Test

The *t* test is a parametric test, as is the *z* test. As a parametric test, the *t* test must meet certain assumptions. These assumptions include that the data are interval or ratio and that the population distribution of scores is symmetrical. The *t* test is used in situations that meet these assumptions and in which the population mean is known but the population standard deviation (σ) is not known. In cases where these criteria are not met, a nonparametric test is more appropriate. Nonparametric tests are covered in Chapter 10.

IN REVIEW

THE *t* TEST		
Concept	**Description**	**Use/Examples**
Estimated standard error of the mean ($s_{\bar{X}}$)	The estimated standard deviation of a sampling distribution, calculated by dividing *s* by $\sqrt{N}$	Used in the calculation of a *t* test
t test	Indicator of the number of standard deviation units the sample mean is from the mean of the sampling distribution	An inferential statistical test that differs from the *z* test in that the sample size is small (usually <30) and σ is not known
One-tailed *t* test	A directional inferential test in which a prediction is made that the population represented by the sample will be either above or below the general population	$H_a: \mu_0 < \mu_1$ or $H_a: \mu_0 > \mu_1$
Two-tailed *t* test	A nondirectional inferential test in which the prediction is made that the population represented by the sample will differ from the general population, but the direction of the difference is not predicted	$H_a: \mu_0 \neq \mu_1$

1. Explain the difference in use and computation between the *z* test and the *t* test.
2. Test the following hypothesis using the *t* test: Researchers are interested in whether the pulse of long-distance runners differs from that of other athletes. They suspect that the runners' pulses will be lower. They obtain a random sample ($N = 8$) of long-distance runners, measure their resting pulse, and obtain the following data: 45, 42, 64, 54, 58, 49, 47, 55. The average resting pulse of athletes in the general population is 60 beats per minute.

CRITICAL THINKING CHECK 10.1

Confidence Intervals Based on the *t* Distribution ●●

You might remember from our discussion of confidence intervals in Module 9 that they allow us to estimate population means based on sample data (a sample mean). Thus, when using confidence intervals, rather than determining whether the sample mean differs significantly fom the population mean, we are estimating the population mean based on knowing the sample mean. We can use confidence intervals with the *t* distribution just as we did with the *z* distribution (the area under the normal curve).

Let's use the previous example in which we know the sample mean SAT score for the biology students ($\overline{X} = 1,176$), the estimated standard error of the mean ($s_{\overline{X}} = 41.71$), and the sample size ($N = 10$). We can calculate a confidence interval based on knowing the sample mean and $s_{\overline{X}}$. Remember that a confidence interval is an interval of a certain width, which we feel "confident" will contain μ. We are going to calculate a 95% confidence interval—in other words, an interval that we feel 95% confident contains the population mean. In order to calculate a 95% confidence interval using the *t* distribution, we use Table A.2 (Critical Values for the Student's *t* Distribution) to determine the critical value of *t* at the .05 level. We use the .05 level because 1 minus alpha tells us how confident we are, and in this case 1 − alpha is 1 − .05 = 95%.

For a one-sample *t* test, the confidence interval is determined with the following formula:

$$\overline{X} \pm t_{cv}(s_{\overline{X}})$$

We already know $\overline{X}$ (1,176) and $s_{\overline{X}}$ (41.71), so all we have left to determine is t_{cv}. We use Table A.2 to determine the t_{cv} for the .05 level and a two-tailed test. We always use the t_{cv} for a two-tailed test because we are describing values both above and below the mean of the distribution. Using Table A.2, we find that the t_{cv} for 9 degrees of freedom (remember $df = N - 1$) is 2.262. We now have all of the values we need to determine the confidence interval.

Let's begin by calculating the lower limit of the confidence interval:

$$1{,}176 - 2.262(41.71) = 1{,}176 - 94.35 = 1{,}081.65$$

The upper limit of the confidence interval is

$$1{,}176 + 2.262(41.71) = 1176 + 94.35 = 1{,}270.35$$

Thus, we can conclude that we are 95% confident that the interval of SAT scores from 1,081.65 to 1,270.35 contains the population mean (μ).

As with the z distribution, we can calculate confidence intervals for the t distribution that give us greater or less confidence (for example a 99% confidence interval or a 90% confidence interval). Typically, statisticians recommend using either the 95% or 99% confidence interval (the intervals corresponding to the .05 and .01 alpha levels in hypothesis testing). You have likely encountered such intervals in real life. They are usually phrased in terms of "plus or minus" some amount, called the *margin of error*. For example, when a newspaper reports that a sample survey showed that 53% of the viewers support a particular candidate, the margin of error is typically also reported—for example, "with a ±3% margin of error." This means that the researchers who conducted the survey created a confidence interval around the 53% and that if they actually surveyed the entire population, μ would be within ±3% of the 53%. In other words, they believe that between 50% and 56% of the viewers support this particular candidate.

REVIEW OF KEY TERMS

degrees of freedom (df)
(p. 156)

estimated standard error
of the mean (p. 157)

Student's t distribution (p. 155)
t test (p. 155)

MODULE EXERCISES

(Answers to odd-numbered questions appear in Appendix B.)

1. Explain how a t test differs from a z test.
2. Explain how $s_{\bar{X}}$ differs from $\sigma_{\bar{X}}$.
3. Why does t_{cv} change when sample size changes? What must be computed in order to determine t_{cv}?
4. Henry performed a two-tailed test for an experiment in which $N = 24$. He could not find his t table, but he remembered the t_{cv} at $df = 13$. He decided to compare his t_{obt} to this t_{cv}. Is he more likely to make a Type I or a Type II error in this situation?
5. A researcher hypothesizes that people who listen to music via headphones have greater hearing loss and will thus score lower on a hearing test than those in the general population. On a standard hearing test, $\mu = 22.5$. The researcher gives this same test to a random sample of 12 individuals who regularly use headphones. Their scores on the test are 16, 14, 20, 12, 25, 22, 23, 19, 17, 17, 21, 20.
   a. Is this a one- or two-tailed test?
   b. What are H_0 and H_a for this study?
   c. Compute t_{obt}.
   d. What is t_{cv}?
   e. Should H_0 be rejected? What should the researcher conclude?
   f. Determine the 95% confidence interval for the population mean, based on the sample mean.
6. A researcher hypothesizes that individuals who listen to classical music will score differently from the general population on a test of spatial ability. On a standardized test of spatial ability, $\mu = 58$. A random sample of 14 individuals who listen to

classical music is given the same test. Their scores on the test are 52, 59, 63, 65, 58, 55, 62, 63, 53, 59, 57, 61, 60, 59.

a. Is this a one- or two-tailed test?

b. What are H_0 and H_a for this study?

c. Compute t_{obt}.

d. What is t_{cv}?

e. Should H_0 be rejected? What should the researcher conclude?

f. Determine the 95% confidence interval for the population mean, based on the sample mean.

CRITICAL THINKING CHECK ANSWERS

Critical Thinking Check 10.1

1. The z test is used when the sample size is greater than 30 and thus normally distributed, and σ is known. The *t* test, on the other hand, is used when the sample is smaller than 30 and bell-shaped but not normal, and σ is not known.

2. For this sample,

$H_0: \mu_{runners} = \mu_{other\ athletes}$, or

$H_0: \mu_{runners} \geq \mu_{other\ athletes}$

$H_a: \mu_{runners} < \mu_{other\ athletes}$

$\overline{X} = 51.75$

$s = 7.32$

$\mu = 60$

$s_{\overline{X}} = \dfrac{7.32}{\sqrt{8}} = \dfrac{7.32}{2.83} = 2.59$

$t = \dfrac{51.75 - 60}{2.59} = \dfrac{-8.25}{2.59} = -3.19$

$df = 8 - 1 = 7$

$t_{cv} = \pm 1.895$

$t_{obt} = -3.19$

Reject H_0. The runners' pulses are significantly lower than the pulses of athletes in general.

WEB RESOURCES

The book-specific website at CengageBrain.com offers students a variety of study tools and useful resources such as glossaries, flashcards, quizzes, and Statistics and Research Methods Workshops.

CHAPTER FIVE SUMMARY AND REVIEW
The z and t Tests

CHAPTER SUMMARY

Two parametric statistical tests were described in this chapter—the z test and the t test. Each compares a sample mean to the general population. Because both are parametric tests, the distributions should be bell-shaped and certain parameters should be known (in the case of the z test, μ and σ must be known; for the t test, only μ is needed). In addition, because they are parametric tests, the data should be interval or ratio in scale. These tests use the sampling distribution (the distribution of sample means). They also use the standard error of the mean (or estimated standard error of the mean for the t test), which is the standard deviation of the sampling distribution. Both z and t tests can test one- or two-tailed alternative hypotheses, but one-tailed tests are more powerful statistically.

CHAPTER 5 REVIEW EXERCISES

(Answers to exercises appear in Appendix B.)

Fill-in Self-Test

Answer the following questions. If you have trouble answering any of the questions, restudy the relevant material before going on to the multiple-choice self-test.

1. A _____ is a distribution of sample means based on random samples of a fixed size from a population.
2. The _____ is the standard deviation of the sampling distribution.
3. A _____ test is used when σ and μ are known and the sample is 30 or larger.
4. The set of distributions that, although symmetrical and bell-shaped, are not normally distributed is called the _____.
5. The _____ is a parametric statistical test of the null hypothesis for a single sample where the population variance is not known.
6. A _____ test is used when μ is known but not σ and the sample is 30 or less.

Multiple-Choice Self-Test

Select the single best answer for each of the following questions. If you have trouble answering any of the questions, restudy the relevant material.

1. The sampling distribution is a distribution of
   a. sample means.
   b. population means.
   c. sample standard deviations.
   d. population standard deviations.

2. A one-tailed z test, $p = .05$, is to _____ and a two-tailed z test, $p = .05$, is to _____.
   a. ± 1.645; ± 1.96
   b. ± 1.96; ± 1.645
   c. Type I error; Type II error
   d. Type II error; Type I error
3. Which of the following is an assumption of the z test?
   a. The data should be ordinal or nominal.
   b. The population distribution of scores should be normal.
   c. The population mean (μ) is known, but not the standard deviation (σ).
   d. The sample size is typically less than 30.
4. Which type of test is more powerful?
   a. A directional test
   b. A nondirectional test
   c. A two-tailed test
   d. All of the alternatives are equally powerful.
5. For a one-tailed test with $df = 11$, what is t_{cv}?
   a. 1.796
   b. 2.201
   c. 1.363
   d. 1.895
6. Which of the following is an assumption of the t test?
   a. The data should be ordinal or nominal.
   b. The population distribution of scores should be normal.
   c. The population mean (μ) and standard deviation (σ) are known.
   d. The sample size is typically less than 30.

Self-Test Problems

1. A researcher is interested in whether students who play chess have higher average SAT scores than students in the general population. A random sample of 75 students who play chess is tested and has a mean SAT score of 1,070. The population average is 1,000 ($\sigma = 200$).
   a. Is this a one- or two-tailed test?
   b. What are H_0 and H_a for this study?
   c. Compute z_{obt}.
   d. What is z_{cv}?
   e. Should H_0 be rejected? What should the researcher conclude?
   f. Determine the 95% confidence interval for the population mean, based on the sample mean.
2. A researcher hypothesizes that people who listen to classical music have higher concentration skills than those in the general population. On a standard concentration test, the overall mean is 15.5. The researcher gave this same test to a random sample of 12 individuals who regularly listen to classical music. Their scores on the test were as follows:
   $$16, 14, 20, 12, 25, 22, 23, 19, 17, 17, 21, 20$$
   a. Is this a one- or two-tailed test?
   b. What are H_0 and H_a for this study?
   c. Compute t_{obt}.
   d. What is t_{cv}?
   e. Should H_0 be rejected? What should the researcher conclude?
   f. Determine the 95% confidence interval for the population mean, based on the sample mean.

CHAPTER FIVE
Statistical Software Resources

If you need help getting started with Excel or SPSS, please see Appendix C: Getting Started with Excel and SPSS.

MODULE 9 Single-Sample z Test

The problems we'll be using to illustrate how to calculate the single-sample z test appear in Module 9.

Using the TI-84 for the One-tailed z Test from Module 9

The z test will be used to test the hypothesis that the sample of children in the academic after-school programs represents a population with a mean IQ greater than the mean IQ for the general population. To do this, we need to determine whether the probability is high or low that a sample mean as large as 103.5 would be chosen from this sampling distribution. In other words, is a sample mean IQ score of 103.5 far enough away from, or different enough from, the population mean of 100 for us to say that it represents a significant difference with an alpha level of .05 or less?

1. With the calculator on, press the STAT key.
2. Highlight TESTS.
3. 1: Z-Test will be highlighted. Press ENTER.
4. Highlight STATS. Press ENTER.
5. Scroll down to μ_0: and enter the mean for the population (100).
6. Scroll down to σ: and enter the standard deviation for the population (15).
7. Scroll down to $\overline{X}$: and enter the mean for the sample (103.5).
8. Scroll down to n: and enter the sample size (75).
9. Lastly, scroll down to μ: and select the type of test (one-tailed), indicating that we expect the sample mean to be greater than the population mean (select $> \mu_0$). Press ENTER.
10. Highlight CALCULATE and press ENTER.

The z score of 2.02 should be displayed followed by the significance level of .02. If you would like to see where the z score falls on the normal distribution, repeat Steps 1–9, then highlight DRAW, and press ENTER.

The z test score is 2.02, and the alpha level or significance level is $p = .02$. Thus, the alpha level is less than .05, and the mean IQ score of children in the sample differs significantly from that of children in the general population. In other words, children in academic after-school programs score significantly higher on IQ tests than children in the general population.

In APA style, it would be reported as follows: $z(N = 75) = 2.02, p < .05$ (one-tailed).

Using the TI-84 for the Two-Tailed z Test from Module 9

The previous example illustrated a one-tailed z test; however, some hypotheses are two-tailed and thus the z test would also be two-tailed. As an example, refer back to the study from Module 9 in which the researcher examined whether children in athletic after-school programs weighed a different amount than children in the general population. In other words, the researcher expected the weight of the children in the athletic after-school programs to differ from that of children in the general population, but he was not sure whether they would weigh less (because of the activity) or more (because of greater muscle mass). Let's use the following data from Module 9: The mean weight of children in the general population (μ) is 90 pounds, with a standard deviation (σ) of 17 pounds; for children in the sample ($N = 50$), the mean weight ($\overline{X}$) is 86 pounds. Using this information, we can now test the hypothesis that children in athletic after-school programs differ in weight from those in the general population using the TI-84 calculator.

1. With the calculator on, press the STAT key.
2. Highlight TESTS.
3. 1: Z-Test will be highlighted. Press ENTER.
4. Highlight STATS. Press ENTER.
5. Scroll down to μ_0: and enter the mean for the population (90).
6. Scroll down to σ: and enter the standard deviation for the population (17).
7. Scroll down to $\overline{X}$: and enter the mean for the sample (86).
8. Scroll down to n: and enter the sample size (50).
9. Lastly, scroll down to μ: and select the type of test (two-tailed), indicating that we expect the sample mean to differ from the population mean (select $\neq \mu_{0)}$. Press ENTER.
10. Highlight CALCULATE and press ENTER.

The z score of -1.66 should be displayed followed by the alpha level of .096, indicating that this test was not significant. We can therefore conclude that the weight of children in the athletic after-school programs did not differ significantly from the weight of children in the general population.

If you would like to see where the z score falls on the normal distribution, repeat Steps 1–9, then highlight DRAW, and press ENTER.

MODULE 10 The Single-Sample *t* Test

Let's illustrate the use of the single-sample t test to test a hypothesis using the example from Module 10. Assume the mean SAT score of students admitted to General University is 1090. Thus, the university mean of 1090 is the population mean (μ). The population standard deviation is unknown.

The members of the Biology Department believe that students who decide to major in biology have higher SAT scores than the general population of students at the university.

Notice that this is a one-tailed test because the researchers predict that the biology students will perform higher than the general population of students at the university. The researchers now need to obtain the SAT scores for a sample of biology majors. This information is provided in Table 10.1 in Module 10, which shows that the mean SAT score for a sample of 10 biology majors is 1176.

Using Excel

To demonstrate how to use Excel to calculate a single-sample t test, we'll use the data from Table 10.1, which represent SAT scores for 10 biology majors at General University. We are testing whether biology majors have higher average SAT scores than the population of students at General University. We begin by entering the data into Excel. We enter the sample data into the A column and the population mean of 1090 into the D column. We enter the population mean next to the score for each individual in the sample. Thus, you can see that I've entered 1090 in Column B ten times, one time for each individual in our sample of 10 biology majors.

Next highlight the **Data** ribbon, and then click on **Data Analysis** in the top right-hand corner. You should now have the following pop-up window:

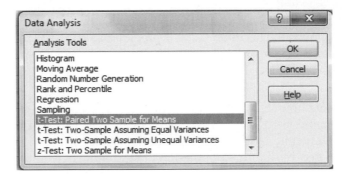

Scroll down to **t-Test: Paired Two Sample for Means,** which is the procedure we'll be using to determine the single-sample *t* test. Then click **OK.** You'll be presented with the following dialog box:

With the cursor in the **Variable 1 Range:** box, highlight the data from column A in the Excel spreadsheet so that they appear in the input range box. Move the cursor to the **Variable 2 Range:** box and enter the data from column B in the spreadsheet into this box by highlighting the data. The dialog box should now appear as follows:

Click **OK** to execute the problem. You will be presented with the following output:

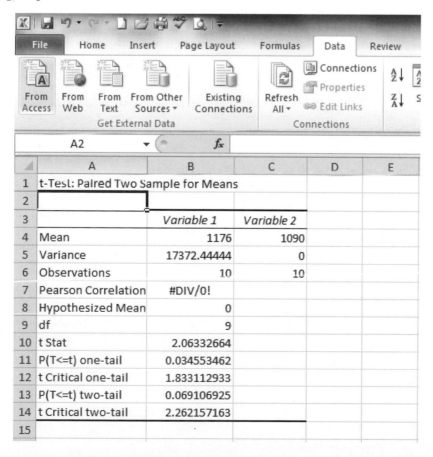

	A	B	C	D	E
1	t-Test: Paired Two Sample for Means				
2					
3		Variable 1	Variable 2		
4	Mean	1176	1090		
5	Variance	17372.44444	0		
6	Observations	10	10		
7	Pearson Correlation	#DIV/0!			
8	Hypothesized Mean	0			
9	df	9			
10	t Stat	2.06332664			
11	P(T<=t) one-tail	0.034553462			
12	t Critical one-tail	1.833112933			
13	P(T<=t) two-tail	0.069106925			
14	t Critical two-tail	2.262157163			
15					

We can see the *t* test score of 2.063 and the one-tailed significance level of $p = .035$. Thus, our sample mean falls 2.06 standard deviations above the population mean of 1090. We must now determine whether this is far enough away from the population mean to be considered significantly different. Because our obtained alpha level (significance level) is .035 and is less than .05, the result is significant. We reject H_0 and support H_a. In other words, we have sufficient evidence to allow us to conclude that biology majors have significantly higher SAT scores than the rest of the students at General University. In APA style, this would be reported as $t(9) = 2.06$, $p = .035$ (one-tailed).

Using SPSS

To demonstrate how to use SPSS to calculate a single-sample *t* test, we'll use the data from Table 10.1 in Module 10, which represent SAT scores for 10 biology majors at General University. We are testing whether biology majors have higher average SAT scores than the population of students at General University. We begin by entering the data into SPSS and naming the variable (if you've forgotten how to name a variable, please refer back to Appendix C).

File	Edit	View	Data	Transform	Analyze	Graphs	Utilities	Add-ons	Window	Help

11 : SATscore

	SATscore	var	var	var	var	var
1	1010.00					
2	1200.00					
3	1310.00					
4	1075.00					
5	1149.00					
6	1078.00					
7	1129.00					
8	1069.00					
9	1350.00					
10	1390.00					

Once the data are entered and the variable named, select the **Analyze** tab and, from the drop-down menu, **Compare Means** followed by **One-Sample T Test.** The following dialog box will appear:

Place the SATscore variable into the **Test Variable** box by utilizing the arrow in the middle of the window. Then let SPSS know what the population mean SAT score is (1090). We enter this population mean in the **Test Value** box as in the following window.

Then click **OK**, and the output for the single-sample *t* test will be produced in an output window as follows:

T-Test

One-Sample Statistics

	N	Mean	Std. Deviation	Std. Error Mean
SATscore	10	1176.0000	131.80457	41.68026

One-Sample Test

	Test Value = 1090					
					95% Confidence Interval of the Difference	
	t	df	Sig. (2-tailed)	Mean Difference	Lower	Upper
SATscore	2.063	9	.069	86.00000	-8.2873	180.2873

We can see the t test score of 2.063 and the two-tailed significance level. Thus, our sample mean falls 2.06 standard deviations above the population mean of 1090. We must now determine whether this is far enough away from the population mean to be considered significantly different. This was a one-tailed test; thus when using SPSS you will need to divide the significance level in half to obtain a one-tailed significance level because SPSS reports only two-tailed significance levels. Our alpha level (significance level) is .035 and is less than .05, meaning the result is significant. We reject H_0 and support H_a. In other words, we have sufficient evidence to allow us to conclude that biology majors have significantly higher SAT scores than the rest of the students at General University. In APA style, this would be reported as $t(9) = 2.06, p = .035$ (one-tailed).

Using the TI-84

Let's use the data from Table 10.1 to conduct the test using the TI-84 calculator.

1. With the calculator on, press the STAT key.
2. EDIT will be highlighted. Press the ENTER key.
3. Under L1 enter the SAT data from Table 10.1.
4. Press the STAT key once again and highlight TESTS.
5. Scroll down to T-Test. Press the ENTER key.
6. Highlight DATA and press ENTER. Enter 1090 (the mean for the population) next to μ_0:. Enter L1 next to List (to do this press the 2nd key followed by the 1 key).
7. Scroll down to μ: and select $>\mu_0$ (for a one-tailed test in which we predict that the sample mean will be greater than the population mean). Press ENTER.
8. Scroll down to and highlight CALCULATE. Press ENTER.

The t score of 2.06 should be displayed, followed by the significance level of .035. In addition, descriptive statistics will be shown. If you would like to see where the t score falls on the distribution, repeat Steps 1–7, then highlight DRAW, and press ENTER.

CHAPTER 6

Two-Group *t* Tests

In this chapter, we discuss the common types of statistical analyses used with simple two-group designs. The inferential statistics discussed in this chapter differ from those presented in Chapter 5 in that in Chapter 5, single samples were being compared to populations (*z* test and *t* test). In this section, the statistics are designed to test differences between two equivalent groups of participants.

Several factors influence which statistic should be used to analyze the data collected. For example, the type of data collected and the number of groups being compared must be considered. Moreover, the statistic used to analyze the data will vary depending on whether the study involves a *between-subjects design*, in which different subjects are used in each of the groups, or a *correlated-groups design,* in which the subjects in the experimental and control groups are related in some way. (Correlated-groups designs are of two types: *within-subjects designs,* in which the same subjects are used repeatedly in each group, and *matched-subjects designs,* in which different subjects are matched between conditions on variables that the researcher believes are relevant to the study.) We will look at the typical inferential statistics used to analyze interval-ratio data for two-group between-subjects designs and correlated-groups designs.

MODULE 11
The *t* Test for Independent Groups (Samples)

Learning Objectives
- Explain when the *t* test for independent groups should be used
- Calculate an independent-groups *t* test.
- Interpret an independent-groups *t* test.
- Calculate and interpret Cohen's *d* and r^2.
- Explain the assumptions of the independent-groups *t* test.
- Calculate confidence intervals.

In the two-group design, two samples (representing two populations) are compared by having one group receive nothing (the control group) and the second group receive some level of the manipulated variable (the experimental group). It is also possible to have two experimental groups and no control group. In this case, members of each group receive a different level of the manipulated variable. The null hypothesis tested in a two-group design is that the populations represented by the two groups do not differ:

$$H_0: \mu_1 = \mu_2$$

The alternative hypothesis may be that we expect differences in performance between the two populations but are unsure which group will perform better or worse (a two-tailed test):

$$H_a: \mu_1 \neq \mu_2$$

or, as discussed in Chapter 5, for a one-tailed test, the null hypothesis is either

$$H_0: \mu_1 \leq \mu_2 \quad \text{or} \quad H_0: \mu_1 \geq \mu_2$$

depending on which alternative hypothesis is being tested:

$$H_a: \mu_1 > \mu_2 \quad \text{or} \quad H_a: \mu_1 < \mu_2, \text{ respectively.}$$

A significant difference between the two groups (samples representing populations) depends on the critical value for the statistical test being conducted. As with the statistical tests described in Chapter 5, alpha is typically set at .05 ($\alpha = .05$).

Remember from Chapter 5 that parametric tests, such as the t test, are inferential statistical tests designed for sets of data that meet certain requirements. The most basic requirement is that the data fit a bell-shaped distribution. In addition, parametric tests involve data for which certain parameters are known, such as the mean (μ) and the standard deviation (σ). Finally, parametric tests use interval-ratio data.

t Test for Independent Groups (Samples): What It Is and What It Does ●●

independent-groups t test
A parametric inferential test for comparing sample means of two independent groups of scores.

The **independent-groups t test** is a parametric statistical test that compares the performance of two different samples of participants. It indicates whether the two samples perform so similarly that we conclude that they are likely from the same population, or whether they perform so differently that we conclude that they represent two different populations. Imagine, for example, that a researcher wants to study the effects on exam performance of massed versus spaced study. All subjects in the experiment study the same material for the same amount of time. The difference between the groups is that one group studies for 6 hours all at once (massed study), whereas the other group studies for 6 hours broken into three 2-hour blocks (spaced study). Because the researcher believes that the spaced-study method will lead to better performance, the null and alternative hypotheses are

H_0: Spaced study $\leq$ Massed study, or $\mu_1 \leq \mu_2$
H_a: Spaced study $>$ Massed study, or $\mu_1 > \mu_2$

The 20 subjects are chosen by random sampling and assigned to the groups randomly. Because of the random assignment of subjects, we are confident that there are no major differences between the groups prior to the study. The dependent variable is the subjects' scores on a 30-item test of the material; these scores are listed in Table 11.1.

Notice that the mean performance of the spaced-study group ($\overline{X}_1 = 22$) is better than that of the massed-study group ($\overline{X}_2 = 16.9$). However, we want to be able to say more than this. In other words, we need to statistically analyze the data to determine whether the observed difference is statistically significant. As you may recall from Chapter 5, statistical significance indicates that an observed difference between two descriptive statistics (such as means) is unlikely to have occurred by chance. For this analysis, we will use an independent-groups t test.

Calculations for the Independent-Groups t Test

The formula for an independent-groups t test is

$$t_{obt} = \frac{\overline{X}_1 - \overline{X}_2}{s_{\overline{X}_1 - \overline{X}_2}}$$

TABLE 11.1 Number of items answered correctly by each subject under spaced-versus massed-study conditions using a between-subjects design ($N = 20$)

SPACED STUDY	MASSED STUDY
23	17
18	18
23	21
22	15
20	15
24	16
21	17
24	19
21	14
24	17
$\overline{X}_1 = 22$	$\overline{X}_2 - 16.9$

This formula resembles that for the single-sample *t* test discussed in Chapter 5. However, rather than comparing a single sample mean to a population mean, we are comparing two sample means. The denominator in the equation represents the **standard error of the difference between means**—the estimated standard deviation of the sampling distribution of differences between the means of independent samples in a two-sample experiment. When conducting an independent-groups *t* test, we are determining how far from the difference between the population means the difference between the sample means falls. If the difference between the sample means is large, it will fall in one of the tails of the distribution (far from the difference between the population means). Remember, our null hypothesis says that the difference between the population means is zero.

To determine how far the difference between sample means is from the difference between the population means, we need to convert our mean differences to standard errors. The formula for this conversion is similar to the formula for the standard error of the mean, introduced in Chapter 5:

$$s_{\overline{X}_1 - \overline{X}_2} = \sqrt{\frac{s_1^2}{n_1} + \frac{s_2^2}{n_2}}$$

The standard error of the difference between the means does have a logical meaning. If you took thousands of pairs of samples from these two populations, and found $\overline{X}_1 - \overline{X}_2$ for each pair, those differences between means would not all be the same. They would form a distribution. The mean

standard error of the difference between means The standard deviation of the sampling distribution of differences between the means of independent samples in a two-sample experiment.

of that distribution would be the difference between the means of the populations ($\mu_1 - \mu_2$), and its standard deviation would be $s_{\overline{X}_1 - \overline{X}_2}$.

Putting all of this together, we see that the formula for determining t is

$$t_{\text{obt}} = \frac{\overline{X}_1 - \overline{X}_2}{\sqrt{\dfrac{s_1^2}{n_1} + \dfrac{s_2^2}{n_2}}}$$

where

$$t_{\text{obt}} = \text{the value of } t \text{ obtained}$$

$\overline{X}_1$ and $\overline{X}_2$ = the means for the two groups

s_1^2 and s_2^2 = the variances of the two groups (the standard deviation squared)

n_1 and n_2 = the number of subjects in each of the two groups (we use n to refer to the subgroups and N to refer to the total number of people in the study)

Let's use this formula to determine whether there are any significant differences between our spaced and massed study groups.

$$\overline{X}_1 = \frac{\sum X_1}{n_1} = \frac{220}{10} = 22 \qquad \overline{X}_2 = \frac{\sum X_2 n_2}{10} = \frac{169}{10} = 16.9$$

$$s_1^2 = \frac{\sum (X_1 - \overline{X}_1)^2}{n_1 - 1} = \frac{36}{9} = 4.00 \qquad s_2^2 = \frac{\sum (X_2 - \overline{X}_2)^2}{n_2 - 1} = \frac{38.9}{9} = 4.32$$

$$t = \frac{\overline{X}_1 - \overline{X}_2}{\sqrt{\dfrac{s_1^2}{n_1} + \dfrac{s_2^2}{n_2}}} = \frac{22 - 16.9}{\sqrt{\dfrac{4.00}{10} + \dfrac{4.32}{10}}} = \frac{5.1}{\sqrt{.832}} = \frac{5.1}{.912} = 5.59$$

"THIS IS THE PART I ALWAYS HATE."

Interpreting the Independent-Groups *t* Test

The $t_{obt} = 5.59$. We must now consult Table A.2 in Appendix A to determine the critical value for t (t_{cv}). First we need to determine the degrees of freedom, which for an independent-groups *t* test are $(n_1 - 1) + (n_2 - 1)$, or $n_1 + n_2 - 2$. In the present study, with 10 subjects in each group, there are 18 degrees of freedom ($10 + 10 - 2 = 18$). The alternative hypothesis was one-tailed, and $\alpha = .05$.

Consulting Table A.2, we find that for a one-tailed test with 18 degrees of freedom, the critical value of *t* at the .05 level is 1.734. Our t_{obt} falls beyond the critical value (is larger than the critical value). Thus, the null hypothesis is rejected, and the alternative hypothesis that subjects in the spaced-study condition performed better on a test of the material than did subjects in the massed-study condition is supported. Because the *t* score was significant at the .05 level, we should check for significance at the .025, .01, .005, and .0005 levels provided in Table A.2. Our t_{obt} of 5.59 is larger than the critical values at all of the levels of significance provided in Table A.2. This result is pictured in Figure 11.1. In APA style, it would be reported as follows: $t(18) = 5.59$, $p < .0005$ (one-tailed). This conveys in a concise manner the *t* score and the degrees of freedom and that the result was significant at the .0005 level. Keep in mind that when a result is significant, the *p* value is reported as less than (<) .05 (or some smaller probability), not greater than (>)—an error commonly made by students. Remember the *p* value, or alpha level, indicates the probability of a Type I error. We want this probability to be small, meaning we are confident that there is only a small probability that our results were due to chance. This means it is highly probable that the observed difference between the groups is truly a meaningful difference—that it is actually due to the independent variable. Instructions on using Excel, SPSS, or the TI-84 calculator to conduct this independent-groups *t* test appear in the Statistical Software Resources section at the end of this chapter.

Look back at the formula for *t*, and think about what will affect the size of the *t* score. We would like the *t* score to be large in order to increase the

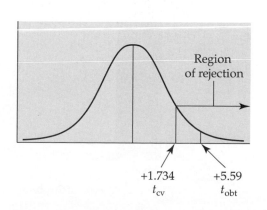

FIGURE 11.1
The obtained *t* score in relation to the *t* critical value

chance that it will be significant. What will increase the size of the t score? Anything that increases the numerator or decreases the denominator in the equation will increase the t score. What will increase the numerator? A larger difference between the means for the two groups (a greater difference produced by the independent variable) will increase the numerator. This difference is somewhat difficult to influence. However, if we minimize chance in our study and the independent variable truly does have an effect, then the means should be different. What will decrease the size of the denominator? Because the denominator is the standard error of the difference between the means $(s_{\overline{X}_1-\overline{X}_2})$ and is derived by using s (the unbiased estimator of the population standard deviation), we can decrease $s_{\overline{X}_1-\overline{X}_2}$ by decreasing the variability within each condition or group or by increasing sample size. Look at the formula and think about why this would be so. In summary, then, three aspects of a study can increase power:

- Greater differences produced by the independent variable
- Smaller variability of raw scores in each condition
- Increased sample size

Graphing the Means

Typically, when a significant difference is found between two means, the means are graphed to provide a pictorial representation of the difference. In creating a graph, we place the independent variable on the x-axis and the dependent variable on the y-axis. As noted in Module 3, the y-axis should be 60% to 75% of the length of the x-axis. For a line graph, we plot each mean and connect them with a line. For a bar graph, we draw separate bars whose heights represent the means. Figure 11.2 shows a bar graph representing the data from the spaced- versus massed-study experiment. Recall that the mean number of items answered correctly by those in the spaced-study condition was 22, compared with a mean of 16.9 for those in the massed-study condition.

FIGURE 11.2
Mean number of items answered correctly under spaced- and massed-study conditions

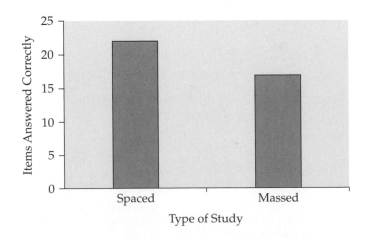

Effect Size: Cohen's *d* and r^2

In addition to the reported statistic, alpha level, and graph, the American Psychological Association (2001a) recommends that we also look at **effect size**—the proportion of variance in the dependent variable that is accounted for by the manipulation of the independent variable. Effect size indicates how big a role the conditions of the independent variable play in determining scores on the dependent variable. Thus, it is an estimate of the effect of the independent variable, regardless of sample size. The larger the effect size, the more consistent is the influence of the independent variable. In other words, the greater the effect size, the more knowing the conditions of the independent variable improves our accuracy in predicting subjects' scores on the dependent variable. For the *t* test, one formula for effect size, known as **Cohen's *d*,** is

effect size The proportion of variance in the dependent variable that is accounted for by the manipulation of the independent variable.

$$d = \frac{\overline{X}_1 - \overline{X}_2}{\sqrt{\dfrac{s_1^2}{2} + \dfrac{s_2^2}{2}}}$$

Cohen's *d* An inferential statistic for measuring effect size when using a *t* test.

Let's begin by working on the denominator, using the data from the spaced-versus massed-study experiment:

$$\sqrt{\frac{s_1^2}{2} + \frac{s_2^2}{2}} = \sqrt{\frac{4.00}{2} + \frac{4.32}{2}} = \sqrt{2.00 + 2.16} = \sqrt{4.16} = 2.04$$

We can now put this denominator into the formula for Cohen's *d*:

$$d = \frac{22 - 16.9}{2.04} = \frac{5.1}{2.04} = 2.50$$

According to Cohen (1988, 1992), a small effect size is one of at least 0.20, a medium effect size is at least 0.50, and a large effect size is at least 0.80. Obviously, our effect size of 2.50 is far greater than 0.80, indicating a very large effect size (most likely a result of using fabricated data). Using APA style, we report that the effect size estimated with Cohen's *d* is 2.50, or you can report Cohen's *d* with the *t* score in the following manner:

$$t(18) = 5.59, p < .0005 \text{ (one-tailed)}, d = 2.50$$

In addition to Cohen's *d*, we can also measure effect size for the independent-groups *t* test using r^2, also known as the coefficient of determination. The **coefficient of determination** (r^2) tells us how much of the variance in one variable can be determined from its relationship with the other variable. When we use it with the *t* test (based on experimental designs with one dependent and one independent variable), we are measuring the proportion of variance accounted for in the dependent variable based on knowing which treatment group the subjects were assigned to for the independent variable. To calculate r^2, use the following formula:

r^2 **(coefficient of determination)** A measure of the proportion of the variance in one variable that is accounted for by another variable.

$$r^2 = \frac{t^2}{t^2 + df}$$

Thus, in our example this would be

$$r^2 = \frac{5.59^2}{5.59^2 + 18} = \frac{31.25}{31.25 + 18} = \frac{31.25}{49.25} = .63$$

According to Cohen (1988), if r^2 is at least .01, the effect size is small; if it is at least .09, it is medium; and if it is at least .25, it is large. Thus, our effect size based on r^2 is large—just as it was when we used Cohen's d.

The preceding example illustrates a t test for independent groups with equal n values (sample sizes). In situations where the n values are unequal, a modified version of the previous formula is used. If you need this formula, you can find it in Appendix D.

Assumptions of the Independent-Groups t Test

The assumptions of the independent-groups t test are similar to those of the single-sample t test. They are as follows:

- The data are interval-ratio scale.
- The underlying distributions are bell-shaped.
- The observations are independent.
- Homogeneity of variance: If we could compute the true variance of the population represented by each sample, the variance in each population would be the same.

If any of these assumptions were violated, it would be appropriate to use another statistic. For example, if the scale of measurement is not interval-ratio or if the underlying distribution is not bell-shaped, it may be more appropriate to use a nonparametric statistic (described in Chapter 10). If the observations are not independent, then it is appropriate to use a statistic for a correlated-groups design (described in the next module).

Confidence Intervals

As with the single-sample z and t tests discussed in Chapter 5, we can also compute confidence intervals for the independent-groups t test. We use the same basic formula we did for computing confidence intervals for the single-sample t test in Chapter 5, except that rather than using the sample mean and the standard error of the mean, we use the difference between the means and the standard error of the difference between means. The formula for the 95% confidence interval would be

$$CI_{95} = \overline{X}_1 - \overline{X}_2 \pm t_{cv}(s_{\overline{X}_1-\overline{X}_2})$$

We have already calculated the means for the two study conditions ($\overline{X}_1$ and $\overline{X}_2$) and the standard error of the difference between means ($s_{\overline{X}_1-\overline{X}_2}$) as part of the previous t test problem. Thus, we simply need to determine t_{cv} to compute the confidence interval, which should contain the difference between the means for the two conditions. Because we are determining a 95% confidence interval, we use t_{cv} at the .05 level, and just as in Chapter 5, we always use the t_{cv} for a two-tailed test because we are determining a confidence interval that contains values both above and below the difference between the means. Consulting Table A.2 in Appendix A for the t_{cv} for 18 degrees of freedom and a two-tailed test, we find that it is 2.101. We can now determine the 95% confidence interval for this problem.

$$CI_{95} = 22 - 16.9 \pm 2.101(.912)$$
$$= 5.1 \pm 1.92$$
$$= 3.18\text{--}7.02$$

Thus, the 95% confidence interval that should contain the difference in mean test scores between the spaced and the massed groups is 3.18–7.02. This means that if someone asked us how big a difference study type makes on test performance, we could answer that we are 95% confident that the difference in performance on the 30-item test between the spaced-versus massed-study groups would be between 3.18 and 7.02 correct answers.

INDEPENDENT-GROUPS *t* TEST   IN REVIEW

What It Is	A parametric test for a two-group between-subjects design
What It Does	Compares performance of the two groups to determine whether they represent the same population or different populations
Assumptions	Interval-ratio data
	Bell-shaped distribution
	Independent observations
	Homogeneity of variance

CRITICAL THINKING CHECK 11.1

1. How is effect size different from significance level? In other words, how is it possible to have a significant result, yet a small effect size?
2. How does increasing sample size affect a *t* test? Why does it affect it in this manner?
3. How does decreasing variability affect a *t* test? Why does it affect it in this manner?

REVIEW OF KEY TERMS

Cohen's *d* (p. 183)
effect size (p. 183)
independent-groups *t* test (p. 178)

r^2 (coefficient of determination) (p. 183)

standard error of the difference between means (p. 179)

MODULE EXERCISES

(Answers to odd-numbered questions appear in Appendix B.)

1. Explain when it would be appropriate to use the independent-groups t test.
2. What is the standard error of the difference between means?
3. Why does APA recommend that we calculate a measure of effect size in addition to calculating the test statistic?
4. A college student is interested in whether there is a difference between male and female students in the amount of time spent studying each week. The student gathers information from a random sample of male and female students on campus. Amount of time spent studying is normally distributed. The data follow:

Males	Females
27	25
25	29
19	18
10	23
16	20
22	15
14	19

   a. What statistical test should be used to analyze these data?
   b. Identify H_0 and H_a for this study.
   c. Conduct the appropriate analysis.
   d. Should H_0 be rejected? What should the researcher conclude?
   e. If significant, compute the effect size and interpret this.
   f. If significant, draw a graph representing the data.
   g. Determine the 95% confidence interval.

5. A student is interested in whether students who study with music playing devote as much attention to their studies as do students who study under quiet conditions. He believes students who study with music do not devote as much attention to their studies as do students who study under quiet conditions. He randomly assigns the 18 subjects to either music or no music conditions and has them read and study the same passage of information for the same amount of time. Participants are then all given the same 10-item test on the material. Their scores appear next. Scores on the test represent interval-ratio data and are normally distributed.

Music	No Music
6	10
5	9
6	7
5	7
6	6
6	6
7	8
8	6
5	9

   a. What statistical test should be used to analyze these data?
   b. Identify H_0 and H_a for this study.
   c. Conduct the appropriate analysis.
   d. Should H_0 be rejected? What should the researcher conclude?
   e. If significant, compute the effect size and interpret this.
   f. If significant, draw a graph representing the data.
   g. Determine the 95% confidence interval.

6. What is a confidence interval?

CRITICAL THINKING CHECK ANSWERS

Critical Thinking Check 11.1

1. The effect size indicates the magnitude of the experimental treatment regardless of sample size. A result can be statistically significant because sample size was very large, but the effect of the independent variable was not so large. Effect size would indicate whether this was the case, because in this type of situation the effect size should be small.

2. In the long run it means that the obtained t is more likely to be significant. This is so because in terms of the formula used to calculate t, increasing sample size will decrease the standard error of the difference between means ($s_{\overline{X}_1 - \overline{X}_2}$). This in turn will increase the size of the obtained t, which means that it is more likely to exceed the critical value and be significant.

3. Decreasing variability also makes a *t* test more powerful (likely to be significant). It does so because decreasing variability also means that $s_{\overline{X}_1 - \overline{X}_2}$ (the standard error of the difference between means) will be smaller. This in turn will increase the size of the obtained *t*, which means that it is more likely to exceed the critical value and be significant.

WEB RESOURCES

The book-specific website at CengageBrain.com offers students a variety of study tools and useful resources such as glossaries, flashcards, quizzes, and Statistics and Research Methods Workshops.

t Test for Correlated Groups (Samples)

Learning Objectives
- Explain when the *t* test for correlated groups should be used.
- Calculate a correlated-groups *t* test.
- Interpret a correlated-groups *t* test.
- Calculate and interpret Cohen's *d* and r^2.
- Explain the assumptions of the correlated-groups *t* test.
- Calculate confidence intervals.

t Test for Correlated Groups: What It Is and What It Does

correlated-groups *t* test
A parametric inferential test used to compare the means of two related (within- or matched-subjects) samples.

The **correlated-groups *t* test,** like the previously discussed *t* test, compares the performance of subjects in two groups. In this case, however, the same people are used in each group (a within-subjects design), or different participants are matched between groups (a matched-subjects design). The test indicates whether there is a difference in sample means and whether this difference is greater than would be expected based on chance. In a correlated-groups design, the sample includes two scores for each person (or matched pair in a matched-subjects design), instead of just one. To conduct the *t* test for correlated groups (also called the *t* test for dependent groups or samples), we must convert the two scores for each person into one score. That is, we compute a difference score for each person by subtracting one score from the other for that person (or for the two individuals in a matched pair). Although this may sound confusing, the dependent-groups *t* test is actually easier to compute than the independent-groups *t* test that we learned about in the previous module. Because the two samples are related, the analysis becomes easier because we work with pairs of scores. The null hypothesis is that there is no difference between the two scores; that is, a person's score in one condition is the same as that (or a matched) person's score in the second condition. The alternative hypothesis is that there is a difference between the paired scores—that the individuals (or matched pairs) performed differently in each condition.

To illustrate the use of the correlated-groups *t* test, imagine that we conduct a study in which participants are asked to learn two lists of words. One list is composed of 20 concrete words (for example, *desk, lamp, bus*); the other is composed of 20 abstract words (for example, *love, hate, deity*). Each participant is tested twice, once in each condition.

Because each participant provides one pair of scores, a correlated-groups *t* test is the appropriate way to compare the means of the two conditions. We expect to find that recall performance is better for the concrete words. Thus, the null hypothesis is

$$H_0: \mu_1 - \mu_2 = 0$$

and the alternative hypothesis is

$$H_a: \mu_1 - \mu_2 > 0$$

representing a one-tailed test of the null hypothesis.

To better understand the correlated-groups *t* test, consider the sampling distribution for the test. This is a sampling distribution of the differences between pairs of sample means. In other words, imagine the population of people who must recall abstract words versus the population of people who must recall concrete words. Further, imagine that samples of 8 participants are chosen (the 8 subjects in each individual sample come from one population), and each sample's mean score in the abstract condition is subtracted from the mean score in the concrete condition. We do this repeatedly until the entire population has been sampled. If the null hypothesis is true, the differences between the sample means should be zero, or very close to zero. If, as the researcher suspects, subjects remember more concrete words than abstract words, the difference between the sample means should be significantly larger than zero.

The data representing each participant's performance are presented in Table 12.1.

TABLE 12.1   Number of abstract and concrete words recalled by each participant using a correlated-groups (within-subjects) design

PARTICIPANT	CONCRETE	ABSTRACT
1	13	10
2	11	9
3	19	13
4	13	12
5	15	11
6	10	8
7	12	10
8	13	13

TABLE 12.2 Number of concrete and abstract words recalled by each participant with difference scores provided

PARTICIPANT	CONCRETE	ABSTRACT	D (DIFFERENCE SCORE)
1	13	10	3
2	11	9	2
3	19	13	6
4	13	12	1
5	15	11	4
6	10	8	2
7	12	10	2
8	13	13	0
			$\Sigma = 20$

Notice that we have two sets of scores, one for the concrete word list and one for the abstract list. Our calculations for the correlated-groups *t* test involve transforming the two sets of scores into one set by determining difference scores. **Difference scores** represent the difference between subjects' performance in one condition and their performance in the other condition. The difference scores for our study are shown in Table 12.2.

difference scores
Scores representing the difference between subjects' performance in one condition and their performance in a second condition.

Calculations for the Correlated-Groups *t* Test

After calculating the difference scores, we have one set of scores representing the performance of participants in both conditions. We can now compare the mean of the difference scores with zero (based on the null hypothesis stated previously). The computations from this point on for the correlated-groups *t* test are similar to those for the single-sample *t* test in Module 10.

$$t = \frac{\overline{D} - 0}{s_{\overline{D}}}$$

where

$\overline{D}$ = the mean of the difference scores
$s_{\overline{D}}$ = the standard error of the difference scores

standard error of the difference scores
The standard deviation of the sampling distribution of mean differences between dependent samples in a two-group experiment.

The **standard error of the difference scores** ($s_{\overline{D}}$) represents the standard deviation of the sampling distribution of mean differences between dependent samples in a two-group experiment. It is calculated in a manner similar to the estimated standard error of the mean ($s_{\overline{X}}$) that we learned how to calculate in Module 10:

$$s_{\overline{D}} = \frac{s_D}{\sqrt{N}}$$

where s_D = the estimated standard deviation of the difference scores. The standard deviation of the difference scores is calculated in the same manner as the standard deviation for any set of scores:

$$s_D = \sqrt{\frac{\Sigma(D - \overline{D})^2}{N - 1}}$$

where

D = each difference score,
$\overline{D}$ = the mean of the difference scores, and
N = the total number of difference scores.

Let's use these formulas to determine s_D, $s_{\overline{D}}$, and the final *t* score.

We begin by determining the mean of the difference scores ($\overline{D}$), which is 20/8 = 2.5, and then use this to determine the difference scores, the squared difference scores, and the sum of the squared difference scores, all needed to calculate the standard deviation (s_D). These are shown in Table 12.3. We then use this sum (24) to determine s_D.

$$s_D = \sqrt{\frac{24}{7}} = \sqrt{3.429} = 1.85$$

Next, we use the standard deviation (s_D = 1.85) to calculate the standard error of the difference scores ($s_{\overline{D}}$):

$$s_{\overline{D}} = \frac{s_D}{\sqrt{N}} = \frac{1.85}{\sqrt{8}} = \frac{1.85}{2.83} = 0.65$$

Finally, we use the standard error of the difference scores ($s_{\overline{D}}$ = .65) and the mean of the difference scores (2.5) in the *t* test formula:

$$t = \frac{\overline{D} - 0}{s_{\overline{D}}} = \frac{2.5 - 0}{0.65} = \frac{2.5}{0.65} = 3.85$$

TABLE 12.3   Difference scores and squared difference scores for concrete and abstract words

D (DIFFERENCE SCORE)	$D - \overline{D}$	$(D - \overline{D})^2$
3	0.5	0.25
2	−0.5	0.25
6	3.5	12.25
1	−1.5	2.25
4	1.5	2.25
2	−0.5	0.25
2	−0.5	0.25
0	−2.5	6.25
		$\Sigma = 24$

Interpreting the Correlated-Groups *t* Test and Graphing the Means

The degrees of freedom for a correlated-groups *t* test are equal to $N - 1$—in this case, $8 - 1 = 7$. We can use Table A.2 in Appendix A to determine t_{cv} for a one-tailed test with $\alpha = .05$ and $df = 7$. Consulting this table, we find that $t_{cv} = 1.895$. Our $t_{obt} = 3.85$ and therefore falls in the region of rejection. Because the *t* score was significant at the .05 level, we should check for significance at the .025, .01, .005, and .0005 levels provided in Table A.2. Our t_{obt} of 3.85 is larger than the critical values of the .025, .01, and .005 levels. Figure 12.1 shows this t_{obt} in relation to the t_{cv}. In APA style, this would be reported as $t(7) = 3.85$, $p < .005$, (one-tailed), indicating that there is a significant difference in the number of words recalled in the two conditions. Instructions on using Excel, SPSS, or the TI-84 calculator to conduct this correlated-groups *t* test appear in the Statistical Software Resources section at the end of this chapter.

This difference in recall performance is illustrated in Figure 12.2, in which the mean number of concrete and abstract words recalled by the participants has been graphed. Thus, we can conclude that subjects performed significantly better in the concrete word condition, supporting the alternative (research) hypothesis.

FIGURE 12.1
The obtained *t* score in relation to the *t* critical value

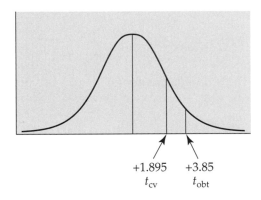

$+1.895$ $+3.85$
t_{cv} t_{obt}

FIGURE 12.2
Mean number of items answered correctly under concrete and abstract study conditions

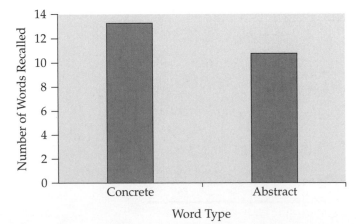

Effect Size: Cohen's *d* and r^2

As with the independent-groups *t* test, we should also compute Cohen's *d* (the proportion of variance in the dependent variable that is accounted for by the manipulation of the independent variable) for the correlated-groups *t* test. Remember, effect size indicates how big a role the conditions of the independent variable play in determining scores on the dependent variable. For the correlated-groups *t* test, the formula for Cohen's *d* is

$$d = \frac{\overline{D}}{s_D}$$

where $\overline{D}$ is the mean of the difference scores and s_D is the standard deviation of the difference scores. We have already calculated each of these as part of the *t* test. Thus,

$$d = \frac{2.5}{1.85} = 1.35$$

Cohen's *d* for a correlated-groups design is interpreted in the same manner as *d* for an independent-groups design. That is, a small effect size is one of at least 0.20, a medium effect size is at least 0.50, and a large effect size is at least 0.80. Obviously, our effect size of 1.35 is far greater than 0.80, indicating a very large effect size.

We can also compute r^2 for the correlated-groups *t* test just as we did for the independent-groups *t* test using the same formula we did in Module 11:

$$r^2 = \frac{t^2}{t^2 + df} = \frac{3.85^2}{3.85^2 + 7} = \frac{14.82}{21.82} = .68$$

Using the guidelines established by Cohen (1988) and noted earlier in the chapter, this is a large effect size.

Assumptions of the Correlated-Groups *t* Test

The assumptions for the correlated-groups *t* test are the same as those for the independent-groups *t* test, except for the assumption that the observations are independent. In this case, the observations are not independent—they are correlated (dependent).

Confidence Intervals

Just as with the independent-groups *t* test, we can calculate confidence intervals based on a correlated-groups *t* test. In this case, we use a formula very similar to that used for the single-sample *t* test from Module 10:

$$CI_{.95} = \overline{D} \pm t_{cv}(s_{\overline{D}})$$

We have already calculated $\overline{D}$ and $s_{\overline{D}}$ as part of the previous *t* test problem. Thus, we only need to determine t_{cv} in order to calculate the 95% confidence interval. Once again, we consult Table A.2 in Appendix A for a two-tailed test (remember we are determining values both above and below the mean, so we use the t_{cv} for a two-tailed test) with 7 degrees of freedom. We find that the t_{cv} is 2.365. Using this, we calculate the confidence interval as follows:

$$CI_{.95} = 2.5 \pm 2.365(0.65)$$
$$= 2.5 \pm 1.54$$
$$= 0.96\text{–}4.04$$

Thus, the 95% confidence interval that should contain the difference in mean test scores between the concrete and the abstract words is 0.96–4.04. This means that if someone asked us how big a difference word type makes on memory performance, we could answer that we are 95% confident that the difference in performance on the 20-item memory test between the two word-type conditions would be between 0.96 and 4.04 words recalled correctly.

IN REVIEW

CORRELATED-GROUPS t TESTS

What It Is	A parametric test for a two-group within-subjects or matched-subjects design
What It Does	Analyzes whether each individual performed in a similar or different manner across conditions
Assumptions	Interval-ratio data
	Bell-shaped distribution
	Correlated (dependent) observations
	Homogeneity of variance

CRITICAL THINKING CHECK 12.1

1. Explain what difference scores are and how they are calculated for a correlated-groups t test.
2. Why is H_0 for a correlated-groups t test H_0: $\mu_1 - \mu_2 = 0$? In other words, why should the difference scores be equal to 0 if H_0 is true?

REVIEW OF KEY TERMS

correlated-groups
  t test (p. 188)

difference scores (p. 190)

standard error of the
  difference scores (p. 190)

MODULE EXERCISES

(Answers to odd-numbered questions appear in Appendix B.)

1. What is the difference between an independent-groups t test and a correlated-groups t test in terms of when each should be used?

2. What are the assumptions of a correlated-groups t test?

3. When using a correlated-groups t test, how do we take the two scores recorded for each participant and "turn them into" one score for each participant?

4. What measures of effect size are used for a correlated-groups *t* test?

5. A researcher is interested in whether participating in sports positively influences self-esteem in young girls. She identifies a group of girls who have not played sports before, but are now planning to begin participating in organized sports. She gives them a 50-item self-esteem inventory before they begin playing sports and administers it again after six months of playing sports. The self-esteem inventory is measured on an interval scale, with higher numbers indicating higher self-esteem. In addition, scores on the inventory are normally distributed. The scores are:

Before	After
44	46
40	41
39	41
46	47
42	43
43	45

a. What statistical test should be used to analyze these data?
b. Identify H_0 and H_a for this study.
c. Conduct the appropriate analysis.
d. Should H_0 be rejected? What should the researcher conclude?
e. If significant, compute the effect size and interpret this.
f. If significant, draw a graph representing the data.
g. Determine the 95% confidence interval.

6. The researcher in exercise number 5 from Module 11 decides to conduct the same study using a within-subjects design in order to control for differences in cognitive ability. He selects a random sample of participants and has them study different material of equal difficulty in both the music and no music conditions. The data appear next. As before, they are measured on an interval-ratio scale and are normally distributed.

Music	No Music
6	10
7	7
6	8
5	7
6	7
8	9
8	8

a. What statistical test should be used to analyze these data?
b. Identify H_0 and H_a for this study.
c. Conduct the appropriate analysis.
d. Should H_0 be rejected? What should the researcher conclude?
e. If significant, compute the effect size and interpret this.
f. If significant, draw a graph representing the data.
g. Determine the 95% confidence interval.

CRITICAL THINKING CHECK ANSWERS

Critical Thinking Check 12.1

1. Difference scores represent the difference in performance for each participant between the score in one condition versus the other condition in the experiment. Thus, we simply take the score from one condition and subtract it from the score in the other condition—always subtracting in the same order (for example, condition one from condition two, or vice versa).

2. If H_0 is true, then the independent variable in the study should not have had any effect. If this is the case, then the difference score for each participant should be zero because the performance in each condition should be the same.

WEB RESOURCES

The book-specific website at CengageBrain.com offers students a variety of study tools and useful resources such as glossaries, flashcards, quizzes, and Statistics and Research Methods Workshops.

CHAPTER SIX SUMMARY AND REVIEW
Two-Group *t* Tests

CHAPTER SUMMARY

Two inferential statistics were presented in this chapter. All statistics discussed in this chapter are parametric and for use with interval-ratio data. The statistics varied based on whether the design was between-subjects or correlated-groups. It is imperative that the appropriate statistic be used to analyze the data collected in an experiment. The first point to consider when determining which statistic to use is whether it should be a parametric or nonparametric statistic. This decision is based on the type of data collected, the type of distribution to which the data conform, and whether any parameters of the distribution are known. Second, we need to know whether the design is between-subjects or correlated-groups when selecting a statistic. Lastly, we need to determine how many groups we are comparing. For designs in which interval-ratio data were collected on two groups, we use a *t* test—independent-groups for between-subjects designs and correlated-groups for within-subjects designs.

CHAPTER 6 REVIEW EXERCISES

(Answers to exercises appear in Appendix B.)

Fill-in Self-Test

Answer the following questions. If you have trouble answering any of the questions, restudy the relevant material before going on to the multiple-choice self-test.

1. A(n) _____ is a parametric inferential test for comparing sample means of two independent groups of scores.
2. _____ is an inferential statistic for measuring effect size with *t* tests.
3. A(n) _____ is a parametric inferential test used to compare the means of two related samples.
4. When using a correlated-groups *t* test, we calculate _____, scores representing the difference between subjects' performance in one condition and their performance in a second condition.
5. The standard deviation of the sampling distribution of mean differences between dependent samples in a two-group experiment is the _____.

Multiple-Choice Self-Test

Select the single best answer for each of the following questions. If you have trouble answering any of the questions, restudy the relevant material.

1. When comparing the sample means for two unrelated groups, we use the
   a. correlated-groups t test.
   b. independent-groups t test.
   c. z test.
   d. single-sample t test.
2. The value of the t test will _____ as sample variance decreases.
   a. increase
   b. decrease
   c. stay the same
   d. not be affected
3. Which of the following t test results has the greatest chance of statistical significance?
   a. $t(28) = 3.12$
   b. $t(14) = 3.12$
   c. $t(18) = 3.12$
   d. $t(10) = 3.12$
4. If the null hypothesis is false, then the t test should be
   a. equal to 0.00.
   b. greater than 1.
   c. greater than .05.
   d. greater than .95.
5. Imagine that you conducted an independent-groups t test with 10 participants in each group. For a one-tailed test, the t_{cv} at $\alpha = .05$ would be
   a. ± 1.729.
   b. ± 2.101.
   c. ± 1.734.
   d. ± 2.093.
6. If a researcher reported for an independent-groups t test that $t(26) = 2.90$, $p < .005$, how many participants were there in the study?
   a. 13
   b. 26
   c. 27
   d. 28
7. $H_a: \mu_1 \neq \mu_2$ is the _____ hypothesis for a _____-tailed test.
   a. null; two
   b. alternative; two
   c. null; one
   d. alternative; one
8. Cohen's d is a measure of _____ for a(n) _____.
   a. significance; t test
   b. significance; ANOVA
   c. effect size; t test
   d. effect size; ANOVA

9. $t_{cv} = \pm 2.15$ and $t_{obt} = -2.20$. Based on these results we _____.
   a. reject H_0
   b. fail to reject H_0
   c. accept H_0
   d. reject H_a

10. If a correlated-groups t test and an independent-groups t test both have $df = 10$, which experiment used fewer participants?
    a. They both used the same number of participants ($n = 10$).
    b. They both used the same number of participants ($n = 11$).
    c. The correlated-groups t test
    d. The independent-groups t test

11. If researchers reported that, for a correlated-groups design, $t(15) = 2.57, p < .05$, you can conclude that
    a. a total of 16 people participated in the study.
    b. a total of 17 people participated in the study.
    c. a total of 30 people participated in the study.
    d. there is no way to determine how many people participated in the study.

Self-Test Problems

1. A college student is interested in whether there is a difference between male and female students in the amount of time spent doing volunteer work each week. The student gathers information from a random sample of male and female students on her campus. Amount of time volunteering (in minutes) is normally distributed. The data appear next. They are measured on an interval-ratio scale and are normally distributed.

Males	Females
20	35
25	39
35	38
40	43
36	50
24	49

   a. What statistical test should be used to analyze these data?
   b. Identify H_0 and H_a for this study.
   c. Conduct the appropriate analysis.
   d. Should H_0 be rejected? What should the researcher conclude?
   e. If significant, compute the effect size and interpret this.
   f. If significant, draw a graph representing the data.
   g. Determine the 95% confidence interval.

2. A researcher is interested in whether studying with music helps or hinders the learner. In order to control for differences in cognitive ability, the researcher decides to use a within-subjects design. He selects a random sample of subjects and has them study different material of equal difficulty in both the music and no music conditions. Subjects then take a 20-item quiz on the material. The study is completely counterbalanced to control for order effects. The data appear next. They are measured on an interval-ratio scale and are normally distributed.

Music	No Music
17	17
16	18
15	17
16	17
18	19
18	18

a. What statistical test should be used to analyze these data?
b. Identify H_0 and H_a for this study.
c. Conduct the appropriate analysis.
d. Should H_0 be rejected? What should the researcher conclude?
e. If significant, draw a graph representing the data.
g. Determine the 95% confidence interval.

CHAPTER SIX
Statistical Software Resources

If you need help getting started with Excel or SPSS, please see Appendix C: Getting Started with Excel and SPSS.

MODULE 11 Independent-Groups *t* Test

The problem we'll be using to illustrate how to calculate the independent-groups *t* test appears in Module 11.

Let's use the example from Module 11 in which a researcher wants to study the effects on exam performance of massed versus spaced study. All participants in the experiment study the same material for the same amount of time. The difference between the groups is that one group studies for 6 hours all at once (massed study), whereas the other group studies for 6 hours broken into three 2-hour blocks (spaced study). The dependent variable is the subjects' scores on a 30-item test of the material; these scores are listed in Table 11.1 in Module 11.

Using Excel

We'll use the data from Table 11.1 to illustrate how to use Excel to calculate an independent-groups *t* test. The data represent number of items answered correctly for two groups of subjects when one group used a spaced-study technique and the other used a massed-study technique. The researcher predicted that those in the spaced-study condition would perform better. The data from Table 11.1 have been entered into the following Excel worksheet, with the data from the spaced condition in column A and the data from the massed condition in column B.

▲	A	B	C
1	Spaced Study	Massed Study	
2	23	17	
3	18	18	
4	23	21	
5	22	15	
6	20	15	
7	24	16	
8	21	17	
9	24	19	
10	21	14	
11	24	14	
12			
13			

Next, with the **Data** ribbon active, we click on **Data Analysis** in the top right corner of the screen and the following dialog box appears:

Data Analysis

Analysis Tools

F-Test Two-Sample for Variances
Fourier Analysis
Histogram
Moving Average
Random Number Generation
Rank and Percentile
Regression
Sampling
t-Test: Paired Two Sample for Means
t-Test: Two-Sample Assuming Equal Variances

OK
Cancel
Help

You can see that I have selected **t-test: Two-Sample Assuming Equal Variances.** After you have done the same, click **OK** and you will then see the following dialog box:

With the cursor in the **Variable 1 Range** box, highlight the data in the A column in the Excel spreadsheet so that they are entered into the **Variable 1 Range** box (do not highlight the column heading of **Spaced Study**). Do the same for column B and enter these data into the **Variable 2 Range** box. Then click **OK.** You will see the following output:

	A	B	C	D
1	t-Test: Two-Sample Assuming Equal Variances			
2				
3		Variable 1	Variable 2	
4	Mean	22	16.9	
5	Variance	4	4.322222222	
6	Observations	10	10	
7	Pooled Variance	4.161111		
8	Hypothesized Mean	0		
9	df	18		
10	t Stat	5.590498		
11	P(T<=t) one-tail	1.32E-05		
12	t Critical one-tail	1.734064		
13	P(T<=t) two-tail	2.63E-05		
14	t Critical two-tail	2.100922		
15				
16				
17				

We are provided with the t test statistic of 5.59 along with the probability and critical values for both one- and two-tailed tests. We can see based on the one-tailed critical value of t that the test is significant at $p = .0000132$. This would be reported in APA style as $t(18) = 5.59, p = .000$ (one-tailed).

Using SPSS

We'll use the same problem to illustrate the use of SPSS for an independent-groups t test. In this study, researchers have subjects use one of two types of study, spaced or massed, and then measure exam performance. The data from Table 11.1 are entered into SPSS as in the following window:

File	Edit	View	Data	Transform	Analyze	Graphs	Utilities	Add-ons	Window	Help

1 . Typeofstudy		1.0					
	Typeofstudy	Examscore	var	var	var	var
1	1.00	23.00				
2	1.00	18.00				
3	1.00	23.00				
4	1.00	22.00				
5	1.00	20.00				
6	1.00	24.00				
7	1.00	21.00				
8	1.00	24.00				
9	1.00	21.00				
10	1.00	24.00				
11	2.00	17.00				
12	2.00	18.00				
13	2.00	21.00				
14	2.00	15.00				
15	2.00	15.00				
16	2.00	16.00				
17	2.00	17.00				
18	2.00	19.00				
19	2.00	14.00				
20	2.00	17.00				
21						

Notice that the independent variable of Type of Study has been converted to a numeric variable where the number 1 represents the spaced-study condition and the number 2 represents the massed-study condition. Thus, the data in rows 1–10 represent spaced-study data, and the data in rows 11–20 represent the massed-study data. Click on the **Analyze** tab and then **Compare Means** followed by **Independent-Samples T Test** as is illustrated next.

The following dialog box will appear:

We'll place the Examscore data into the **Test Variable** (dependent variable) box and the Typeofstudy data into the **Grouping Variable** (independent variable) box by highlighting each variable and using the arrow keys in the middle of the dialog box to move the variables The dialog box should appear as follows once you've completed this task:

Once you have done this, click on the **Grouping Variable** box and the **Define Groups** box below it, which will become active, and you will receive a dialog box as follows:

We have to let SPSS know what values we used to designate the spaced-versus the massed-study groups. Thus, enter a 1 into the **Group 1** box and a 2 into the **Group 2** box and click **Continue**. Then click **OK** in the Independent-Samples T Test dialog box. You should receive output similar to the following:

T-Test

Group Statistics

	Typeofstudy	N	Mean	Std. Deviation	Std. Error Mean
Examscore	1.00	10	22.0000	2.00000	.63246
	2.00	10	16.9000	2.07900	.65744

Independent Samples Test

		Levene's Test for Equality of Variances		t-test for Equality of Means					95% Confidence Interval of the Difference	
		F	Sig.	t	df	Sig. (2-tailed)	Mean Difference	Std. Error Difference	Lower	Upper
Examscore	Equal variances assumed	.022	.884	5.590	18	.000	5.10000	.91226	3.18341	7.01659
	Equal variances not assumed			5.590	17.973	.000	5.10000	.91226	3.18320	7.01680

Descriptive statistics for the two conditions are reported in the first table followed by the t test score of 5.590. Because we are assuming equal variances, we use the df, t score, and other data from that row in the table. Moreover, the two-tailed significance level is provided, but because this was a one-tailed test, you should divide the p-value in half, or consult a critical values table for t in a statistics text. We are also provided with the 95% confidence interval for the t test.

Using the TI-84

Let's use the data from Table 11.1 to conduct the test using the TI-84 calculator.

1. With the calculator on, press the STAT key.
2. EDIT will be highlighted. Press the ENTER key.
3. Under L1 enter the data from Table 11.1 for the spaced-study group.
4. Under L2 enter the data from Table 11.1 for the massed-study group.
5. Press the STAT key once again and highlight TESTS.
6. Scroll down to 2-SampTTest. Press the ENTER key.
7. Highlight DATA. Enter L1 next to List1 (by pressing the 2nd key followed by the 1 key). Enter L2 next to List2 (by pressing the 2nd key followed by the 2 key).
8. Scroll down to μ_1: and select $>\mu_2$ (for a one-tailed test in which we predict that the spaced-study group will do better than the massed-study group). Press ENTER.
9. Scroll down to Pooled: and highlight YES. Press ENTER.
10. Scroll down to and highlight CALCULATE. Press ENTER.

The t score of 5.59 should be displayed followed by the significance level of .000013 and the df of 18. In addition, descriptive statistics for both variables on which you entered data will be shown.

MODULE 12 Correlated-Groups t Test

To illustrate the use of the correlated-groups t test, let's use the example from Module 12 in which subjects are asked to learn two lists of words. One list is composed of 20 concrete words (for example, *desk, lamp, bus*); the other is composed of 20 abstract words (for example, *love, hate, deity*). Each subject is tested twice, once in each condition. Because each subject provides one pair of scores, a correlated-groups t test is the appropriate way to compare the means of the two conditions.

Using Excel

Using Excel to calculate a correlated-groups t test is very similar to using it to calculate an independent-groups t test. We'll use the data from Table 12.1 in Module 12 to illustrate its use. For this t test we are comparing memory for concrete versus abstract words for a group of 8 participants. Each participant served in both conditions. First enter the data from Table 12.1 into an Excel spreadsheet (as seen next). The data for the concrete-word condition are entered into column A and the data for the abstract-word condition into column B.

	A	B	C	D
1	Concrete Words	Abstract Words		
2	13	10		
3	11	9		
4	19	13		
5	13	12		
6	15	11		
7	10	8		
8	12	10		
9	13	13		
10				
11				

Then, with the **Data** ribbon active, click on **Data Analysis** and select **t-test: Paired Two Sample for Means** as indicated in the following dialog box. Click **OK** after doing this.

You will then get the following dialog box into which you will enter the data from column A into the **Variable 1 Range** box by clicking in the **Variable 1 Range** box and then highlighting the data in column A and then doing the same with the data in column B and the **Variable 2 Range** box. After doing this, the dialog box should appear as follows:

Click **OK** and you will receive the output as it appears next.

We can see that $t(7) = 3.82, p = .0033$ (one-tailed).

Using SPSS

To illustrate the correlated-groups t test, we'll use the same problem described above in which a researcher has a group of participants study a list of 20 concrete words and 20 abstract words and then measures recall for the words within each condition. The researcher predicts that the subjects will have better recall for the concrete words. The data from Table 12.1 (in Module 12) are entered into SPSS as follows. We have 8 participants and each serves in both conditions. Thus the scores for each subject in both conditions appear in a single row.

	File	Edit	View	Data	Transform	Analyze	Graphs	Utilities	Add-ons	Window	Help		

1 : Participant	1.0					
	Participant	Concretewords	Abstractwords	var	var	var
1	1.00	13.00	10.00			
2	2.00	11.00	9.00			
3	3.00	19.00	13.00			
4	4.00	13.00	12.00			
5	5.00	15.00	11.00			
6	6.00	10.00	8.00			
7	7.00	12.00	10.00			
8	8.00	13.00	13.00			
9						
10						

Next we click on the **Analyze** tab followed by the **Compare Means** tab and then **Paired-Samples T Test,** as illustrated next.

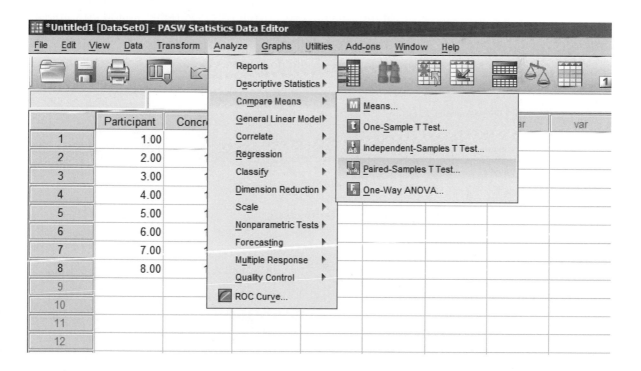

These actions will produce the following dialog box:

Highlight the **Concretewords** variable and then click the arrow button in the middle of the screen. The Concretewords variable should now appear under **Variable1** in the box on the right of the window. Do the same for the **Abstractwords** variable and it should appear under **Variable2** in the box on the right. The dialog box should now appear as follows:

Click **OK** and the output will appear in an output window as below:

T-Test

Paired Samples Statistics

		Mean	N	Std. Deviation	Std. Error Mean
Pair 1	Ccncretewords	13.2500	8	2.76457	.97742
	Abstractwords	10.7500	8	1.83225	.64780

Paired Samples Correlations

		N	Correlation	Sig.
Pair 1	Ccncretewords & Abstractwords	8	.747	.033

Paired Samples Test

		Paired Differences							
					95% Confidence Interval of the Difference				
		Mean	Std. Deviation	Std. Error Mean	Lower	Upper	t	df	Sig. (2-tailed)
Pair 1	Ccncretewords - Abstractwords	2.50000	1.85164	.65465	.95199	4.04801	3.819	7	.007

As in the independent-samples t test in the previous example, descriptive statistics appear in the first table, followed by the correlation between the variables. Lastly, the correlated-groups t test results appear in the third table with the t score of 3.819, 7 degrees of freedom, and the two-tailed significance level. Because this was a one-tailed test, we can find the significance level for this one-tailed t test by dividing the two-tailed significance level in half. Thus, for this problem $t(7) = 3.82, p = .0035$ (one-tailed). As in the previous t test in Module 7, the 95% confidence interval is also reported.

Using the TI-84

Let's use the data from Table 12.1 to conduct the test using the TI-84 calculator.

1. With the calculator on, press the STAT key.
2. EDIT will be highlighted. Press the ENTER key.
3. Under L1 enter the data for Concrete Words.
4. Under L2 enter the data for Abstract Words.
5. Move the cursor so that L3 is highlighted and then enter the following formula: L1 – L2 and press ENTER (to enter L1, press the 2nd key followed by the 1 key; to produce L2, press the 2nd key followed by the 2 key). This will produce a list of difference scores (the Concrete Word scores minus the Abstract Word scores) for each subject.

6. Press the STAT key once again and highlight TESTS.
7. Scroll down to T-Test. Press the ENTER key.
8. Highlight DATA. Enter 0 next to μ_0:. Enter L3 next to List (by pressing the 2nd key followed by the 3 key).
9. Scroll down to μ: and select $> \mu_0$ (for a one-tailed test in which we predict that the difference between the scores for each condition will be greater than 0). Press ENTER.
10. Scroll down to and highlight CALCULATE. Press ENTER.

The t score of 3.82 should be displayed followed by the significance level of .0033. In addition, descriptive statistics will be shown.

In this chapter, we discuss the common types of statistical analyses used with designs involving more than two groups. The inferential statistics discussed in this chapter differ from those presented in the previous two chapters. In Chapter 5, single samples were being compared to populations (z test and t test), and in Chapter 6, two independent or correlated samples were being compared. In this chapter, the statistics are designed to test differences between more than two equivalent groups of subjects.

Several factors influence which statistic should be used to analyze the data collected. For example, the type of data collected and the number of groups being compared must be considered. Moreover, the statistic used to analyze the data will vary depending on whether the study involves a between-subjects design (designs in which different subjects are used in each group) or a correlated-groups design (Remember, correlated-groups designs are of two types: within-subjects designs, in which the same subjects are used repeatedly in each group, and matched-subjects designs, in which different subjects are matched between conditions on variables that the researcher believes are relevant to the study.)

We will look at the typical inferential statistics used to analyze interval-ratio data for between-subjects designs. In Module 13 we discuss the advantages and rationale for studying more than two groups; in Module 14 we discuss the statistics appropriate for use with between-subjects designs involving more than two groups.

MODULE 13
Comparing More than Two Groups

Learning Objectives
- Explain what additional information can be gained by using designs with more than two levels of an independent variable.
- Explain and be able to use the Bonferroni adjustment.
- Identify what a one-way randomized ANOVA is and what it does.
- Describe what between-groups variance is.
- Describe what within-groups variance is.
- Understand conceptually how an F-ratio is derived.

The experiments described so far have involved manipulating one independent variable with only two levels—either a control group and an experimental group or two experimental groups. In this module, we discuss experimental designs involving one independent variable with more than two levels. Examining more levels of an independent variable allows us to address more complicated and interesting questions. Often, experiments begin as two-group designs and then develop into more complex designs as the questions asked become more elaborate and sophisticated.

Using Designs with Three or More Levels of an Independent Variable

Researchers may decide to use a design with more than two levels of an independent variable for several reasons. First, it allows them to compare multiple treatments. Second, it allows them to compare multiple treatments to no treatment (the control group). Third, more complex designs allow researchers to compare a placebo group to control and experimental groups (Mitchell & Jolley, 2001).

Comparing More than Two Kinds of Treatment in One Study

To illustrate this advantage of more complex experimental designs, imagine that we want to compare the effects of various types of rehearsal on memory. We have participants study a list of 10 words using either rote rehearsal (repetition) or some form of elaborative rehearsal. In addition, we specify the type of elaborative rehearsal to be used in the different experimental groups. Group 1 (the control group) uses rote rehearsal, Group 2 uses an imagery mnemonic technique, and Group 3 uses a story mnemonic device. You may be wondering why we do not simply conduct three studies or comparisons. Why don't we compare Group 1 to Group 2, Group 2 to Group 3, and Group 1 to Group 3 in three different experiments? There are several reasons why this is not recommended.

You may remember from Module 11 that a *t* test is used to compare performance between two groups. If we do three experiments, we need to use three *t* tests to determine any differences. The problem is that using multiple tests inflates the Type I error rate. Remember, a Type I error means that we reject the null hypothesis when we should have failed to reject it; that is, we claim that the independent variable has an effect when it does not. For most statistical tests, we use the .05 alpha level, meaning that we are willing to accept a 5% risk of making a Type I error. Although the chance of making a Type I error on one *t* test is .05, the overall chance of making a Type I error increases as more tests are conducted.

Imagine that we conducted three *t* tests or comparisons among the three groups in the memory experiment. The probability of a Type I error on any single comparison is .05. The probability of a Type I error on at least one of the three tests, however, is considerably greater. To determine the chance of a Type I error when making multiple comparisons, we use the formula $1 - (1 - \alpha)^c$, where *c* equals the number of comparisons performed. Using this formula for the present example, we get

$$1 - (1 - .05)^3 = 1 - (.95)^3 = 1 - .86 = .14$$

Thus, the probability of a Type I error on at least one of the three tests is .14, or 14%.

One way of counteracting the increased chance of a Type I error is to use a more stringent alpha level. The **Bonferroni adjustment,** in which the desired alpha level is divided by the number of tests or comparisons, is typically used to accomplish this. For example, if we were using the *t* test to make the three comparisons just described, we would divide .05 by 3 and get .017. By not accepting the result as significant unless the alpha level is .017 or less, we minimize the chance of a Type I error when making multiple comparisons. We know from discussions in previous modules, however, that although using a more stringent alpha level decreases the chance of a Type I error, it increases the chance of a Type II error (failing to reject the null hypothesis when it should have been rejected—missing an effect of an independent variable). Thus, the Bonferroni adjustment is not the best method

Bonferroni adjustment
A means of setting a more stringent alpha level in order to minimize Type I errors.

of handling the problem. A better method is to use a single statistical test that compares all groups rather than using multiple comparisons and statistical tests. Luckily for us, there is a statistical technique that will do this—the analysis of variance (ANOVA), which will be discussed shortly.

Another advantage of comparing more than two kinds of treatment in one experiment is that it reduces both the number of experiments conducted and the number of subjects needed. Once again, refer back to the three-group memory experiment. If we do one comparison with three groups, we can conduct only one experiment, and we need subjects for only three groups. If, however, we conduct three comparisons, each with two groups, we need to perform three experiments, and we need participants for six groups or conditions.

Comparing Two or More Kinds of Treatment with a Control Group

Using more than two groups in an experiment also allows researchers to determine whether each treatment is more or less effective than no treatment (the control group). To illustrate this, imagine that we are interested in the effects of aerobic exercise on anxiety. We hypothesize that the more aerobic activity engaged in, the more anxiety will be reduced. We use a control group that does not engage in any aerobic activity and a high aerobic activity group that engages in 50 minutes per day of aerobic activity—a simple two-group design. Assume, however, that when using this design, we find that both those in the control group and those in the experimental group have high levels of anxiety at the end of the study—not what we expected to find. How could a design with more than two groups provide more information? Suppose we add another group to this study—a moderate aerobic activity group (25 minutes per day)—and get the following results:

Control Group	High Anxiety
Moderate Aerobic Activity	Low Anxiety
High Aerobic Activity	High Anxiety

Based on these data, we have a V-shaped function. Up to a certain point, aerobic activity reduces anxiety. However, when the aerobic activity exceeds a certain level, anxiety increases again. If we had conducted only the original study with two groups, we would have missed this relationship and erroneously concluded that there was no relationship between aerobic activity and anxiety. Using a design with multiple groups allows us to see more of the relationship between the variables.

Figure 13.1 illustrates the difference between the results obtained with the three-group versus the two-group design in this hypothetical study. It also shows the other two-group comparisons—control compared to moderate aerobic activity, and moderate aerobic activity compared to high aerobic activity. This set of graphs allows you to see how two-group designs limit our ability to see the full relationship between variables.

FIGURE 13.1
Determining
relationships with
three-group versus
two-group designs:
(a) three-group
design; (b) two-
group comparison of
control to high
aerobic activity;
(c) two-group
comparison of
control to moderate
aerobic activity;
(d) two-group
comparison of
moderate aerobic
activity to high
aerobic activity

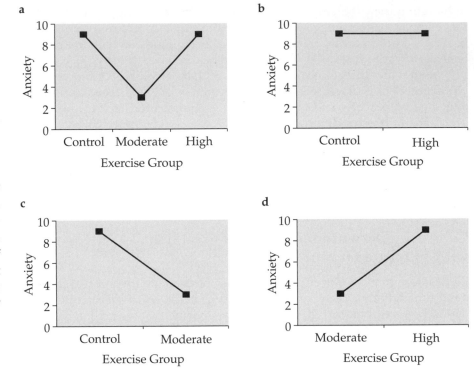

Figure 13.1a shows clearly how the three-group design allows us to assess more fully the relationship between the variables. If we had only conducted a two-group study, such as those illustrated in Figure 13.1b, c, or d, we would have drawn a much different conclusion from that drawn from the three-group design. Comparing only the control to the high aerobic activity group (Figure 13.1b) would have led us to conclude that aerobic activity does not affect anxiety. Comparing only the control to the moderate aerobic activity group (Figure 13.1c) would have led to the conclusion that increasing aerobic activity reduces anxiety. Comparing only the moderate aerobic activity group to the high aerobic activity group (Figure 13.1d) would have led to the conclusion that increasing aerobic activity increases anxiety.

Being able to assess the relationship between the variables means that we can determine the type of relationship that exists. In the previous example, the variables produced a V-shaped function. Other variables may be related in a straight linear manner or in an alternative curvilinear manner (for example, a J-shaped or S-shaped function). In summary, adding levels to the independent variable allows us to determine more accurately the type of relationship that exists between the variables.

Comparing a Placebo Group to the Control and Experimental Groups

A final advantage of designs with more than two groups is that they allow for the use of a *placebo group*—a group of subjects who believe they are receiving treatment but in reality are not. A *placebo* is an inert substance that participants believe is a treatment. How can adding a placebo group improve an experiment? Consider an often-cited study by Paul (1966, 1967) involving children who suffered from maladaptive anxiety in public-speaking situations. Paul used a control group, which received no treatment; a placebo group, which received a placebo that they were told was a potent tranquilizer; and an experimental group, which received desensitization therapy. Of the participants in the experimental group, 85% showed improvement, compared with only 22% in the control condition. If the placebo group had not been included, the difference between the therapy and control groups (85% − 22% = 63%) would overestimate the effectiveness of the desensitization program. The placebo group showed 50% improvement, meaning that the therapy's true effectiveness is much less (85% − 50% = 35%). Thus, a placebo group allows for a more accurate assessment of a therapy's effectiveness because, in addition to spontaneous remission, it controls for participant expectation effects.

DESIGNS WITH MORE THAN TWO LEVELS OF AN INDEPENDENT VARIABLE		**IN REVIEW**

Advantages	Considerations
Allows comparisons of more than two types of treatment	Type of statistical analysis (e.g., multiple *t* tests or ANOVA)
Fewer subjects are needed	Multiple *t* tests increase chance of Type I error; Bonferroni adjustment increases chance of Type II error
Allows comparisons of all treatments to control condition	
Allows for use of a placebo group with control and experimental groups	

Imagine that a researcher wants to compare four different types of treatment. The researcher decides to conduct six individual studies to make these comparisons. What is the probability of a Type I error, with $\alpha = .05$, across these six comparisons? Use the Bonferroni adjustment to determine the suggested alpha level for these six tests.

CRITICAL THINKING CHECK 13.1

Analyzing the Multiple-Group Design

ANOVA (analysis of variance) An inferential parametric statistical test for comparing the means of three or more groups.

As noted previously, *t* tests are not recommended for comparing performance across groups in a multiple-group design because of the increased probability of a Type I error. For multiple-group designs in which interval-ratio data are collected, the recommended parametric statistical analysis is the **ANOVA (analysis of variance).** As its name indicates, this procedure allows us to analyze the variance in a study. You should be familiar with variance from Chapter 3 on descriptive statistics. Nonparametric analyses are also available for designs in which ordinal data are collected (the Kruskal-Wallis analysis of variance) and for designs in which nominal data are collected (chi-square test). We will discuss some of these tests in later modules.

We will begin our coverage of statistics appropriate for multiple-group designs by discussing those used with data collected from a between-subjects design. Recall that a between-subjects design is one in which different participants serve in each condition. Imagine that we conducted the study mentioned at the beginning of the module in which subjects are asked to study a list of 10 words using rote rehearsal or one of two forms of elaborative rehearsal. A total of 24 participants are randomly assigned, 8 to each condition. Table 13.1 lists the number of words correctly recalled by each participant.

one-way randomized ANOVA An inferential statistical test for comparing the means of three or more groups using a between-subjects design.

Because these data represent an interval-ratio scale of measurement and because there are more than two groups, an ANOVA is the appropriate statistical test to analyze the data. In addition, because this is a between-subjects design, we use a **one-way randomized ANOVA.** The term *randomized* indicates that participants have been randomly assigned to conditions in a between-subjects design. The term *one-way* indicates that the design uses only one independent variable—in this case, type of rehearsal. We will discuss statistical tests appropriate for

TABLE 13.1 Number of words recalled correctly in rote, imagery, and story conditions

ROTE REHEARSAL	IMAGERY	STORY	
2	4	6	
4	5	5	
3	7	9	
5	6	10	
2	5	8	
7	4	7	
6	8	10	
3	5	9	
$\bar{X} = 4$	$\bar{X} = 5.5$	$\bar{X} = 8$	Grand Mean = 5.833

correlated-groups designs and tests appropriate for designs with more than one independent variable in Chapter 8. Please note that although the study used to illustrate the ANOVA procedure in this section has an equal number of subjects in each condition, this is not necessary to the procedure.

One-Way Randomized ANOVA: What It Is and What It Does ●●

The analysis of variance (ANOVA) is an inferential statistical test for comparing the means of three or more groups. In addition to helping maintain an acceptable Type I error rate, the ANOVA has the added advantage over using multiple t tests of being more powerful and thus less susceptible to a Type II error. In this section, we will discuss the simplest use of ANOVA—a design with one independent variable with three levels.

Let's continue to use the experiment and data presented in Table 13.1. Remember that we are interested in the effects of rehearsal type on memory. The null hypothesis (H_0) for an ANOVA is that the sample means represent the same population (H_0: $\mu_1 = \mu_2 = \mu_3$). The alternative hypothesis (H_a) is that they represent different populations (H_a: at least one $\mu \neq$ another μ). When a researcher rejects H_0 using an ANOVA, it means that the independent variable affected the dependent variable to the extent that at least one group mean differs from the others by more than would be expected based on chance. Failing to reject H_0 indicates that the means do not differ from each other more than would be expected based on chance. In other words, there is not enough evidence to suggest that the sample means represent at least two different populations.

In our example, the mean number of words recalled in the rote rehearsal condition is 4, for the imagery condition it is 5.5, and in the story condition it is 8. If you look at the data from each condition, you will notice that most subjects in each condition did not score exactly at the mean for that condition. In other words, there is variability within each condition. The overall mean, or **grand mean,** across all participants in all conditions is 5.83. Because none of the participants in any condition recalled exactly 5.83 words, there is also variability between conditions. What we are interested in is whether this variability is due primarily to the independent variable (differences in rehearsal type) or to **error variance**—the amount of variability among the scores caused by chance or uncontrolled variables (such as individual differences between subjects).

The amount of error variance can be estimated by looking at the amount of variability *within* each condition. How will this give us an estimate of error variance? Each subject in each condition was treated similarly—they were each instructed to rehearse the words in the same manner. Because the subjects in each condition were treated in the same manner, any differences observed in the number of words recalled are attributable only to error variance. In other words, some participants may have been more motivated,

grand mean   The mean performance across all participants in a study.

error variance   The amount of variability among the scores caused by chance or uncontrolled variables.

within-groups variance
The variance within each condition; an estimate of the population error variance.

or more distracted, or better at memory tasks—all factors that would contribute to error variance in this case. Therefore, the **within-groups variance** (the variance within each condition or group) is an estimate of the population error variance.

Now compare the means between the groups. If the independent variable (rehearsal type) had an effect, we would expect some of the group means to differ from the grand mean. If the independent variable had no effect on number of words recalled, we would still expect the group means to vary from the grand mean, but only slightly, as a result of error variance attributable to individual differences. In other words, all subjects in a study will not score exactly the same. Therefore, even when the independent variable has no effect, we do not expect that the group means will exactly equal the grand mean, but they should be close to the grand mean. If there were no effect of the independent variable, then the variance between groups would be due to error.

between-groups variance
An estimate of the effect of the independent variable and error variance.

Between-groups variance may be attributed to several sources. There could be systematic differences between the groups, referred to as *systematic variance*. The systematic variance between the groups could be due to the effects of the independent variable (variance due to the experimental manipulation). However, it could also be due to the influence of uncontrolled confounding variables (variance due to extraneous variables). In addition, there will always be some error variance included in any between-groups variance estimate. In sum, between-groups variance is an estimate of systematic variance (the effect of the independent variable *and* any confounds) and error variance.

F-ratio The ratio of between-groups variance to within-groups variance.

By looking at the ratio of between-groups variance to within-groups variance, known as an **F-ratio,** we can determine whether most of the variability is attributable to systematic variance (due, we hope, to the independent variable and not to confounds) or to chance and random factors (error variance):

$$F = \frac{\text{Between-groups variance}}{\text{Within-groups variance}} = \frac{\text{Systematic variance} + \text{error variance}}{\text{Error variance}}$$

Looking at the *F*-ratio, we can see that if the systematic variance (which we assume is due to the effect of the independent variable) is substantially greater than the error variance, the ratio will be substantially greater than 1. If there is no systematic variance, then the ratio will be approximately 1.00 (error variance over error variance). There are two points to remember regarding *F*-ratios. First, in order for an *F*-ratio to be significant (show a statistically meaningful effect of an independent variable), it must be substantially greater than 1 (we will discuss exactly how much larger than 1 in the next module). Second, if an *F*-ratio is approximately 1, then the between-groups variance equals the within-groups variance and there is no effect of the independent variable.

Refer back to Table 13.1, and think about the within-groups versus between-groups variance in this study. Notice that the amount of variance within the groups is small—the scores within each group vary from each individual group mean, but not by very much. The between-groups variance, on the other hand, is large—two of the means across the three conditions vary from the grand mean to a greater extent. With these data, then, it appears that we have a relatively large between-groups variance and a smaller within-groups variance. Our F-ratio will therefore be larger than 1.00. To assess how large it is, we will need to conduct the appropriate calculations (described in the next module). At this point, however, you should have a general understanding of how an ANOVA analyzes variance to determine if there is an effect of the independent variable.

RANDOMIZED ONE-WAY ANOVA

IN REVIEW

Concept	Description
Null hypothesis (H_0)	The independent variable had no effect—the samples all represent the same population
Alternative hypothesis (H_a)	The independent variable had an effect—at least one of the samples represents a different population than the others
F-ratio	The ratio formed when the between-groups variance is divided by the within-groups variance
Between-groups variance	An estimate of the variance of the group means about the grand mean; includes both systematic variance and error variance
Within-groups variance	An estimate of the variance within each condition in the experiment; also known as error variance, or variance due to chance factors

Imagine that the following table represents data from the study just described (the effects of type of rehearsal on number of words recalled from the 10 words given). Do you think that the between-groups and within-groups variances are large, moderate, or small? Would the corresponding F-ratio be greater than, equal to, or less than 1.00?

CRITICAL THINKING CHECK 13.2

Rote Rehearsal	Imagery	Story
2	4	5
4	2	2
3	5	4
5	3	2
2	2	3
7	7	6
6	6	3
3	2	7
$\overline{X} = 4$	$\overline{X} = 3.88$	$\overline{X} = 4$

Grand Mean = 3.96

REVIEW OF KEY TERMS

ANOVA (analysis of variance)
(p. 222)
between-groups variance
(p. 224)

Bonferroni adjustment (p. 218)
error variance (p. 223)
F-ratio (p. 224)
grand mean (p. 223)

one-way randomized
ANOVA (p. 222)
within-groups variance
(p. 224)

MODULE EXERCISES

(Answers to odd-numbered questions appear in Appendix B.)

1. What is/are the advantage(s) of conducting a study with three or more levels of the independent variable?
2. What does the term *one-way* mean with respect to an ANOVA?
3. Explain between-groups variance and within-groups variance.

4. If a researcher decides to use multiple comparisons in a study with three conditions, what is the probability of a Type I error across these comparisons? Use the Bonferroni adjustment to determine the suggested alpha level.
5. If H_0 is true, what should the F-ratio equal or be close to?
6. If H_a is supported, should the F-ratio be greater than, less than, or equal to 1?

CRITICAL THINKING CHECK ANSWERS

Critical Thinking Check 13.1

The probability of a Type I error would be 26.5% $[1 - (1 - .05)^6] = [1 - (.95)^6] = [1 - .735] = 26.5\%$. Using the Bonferroni adjustment, the alpha level would be .008 for each comparison.

Critical Thinking Check 13.2

Both the within-groups and between-groups variances are moderate. This should lead to an F-ratio of approximately 1.

WEB RESOURCES

The book-specific website at CengageBrain.com offers students a variety of study tools and useful resources

such as glossaries, flashcards, quizzes, and Statistics and Research Methods Workshops.

MODULE 14
One-Way Randomized Analysis of Variance (ANOVA)

Learning Objectives
- Identify what a one-way randomized ANOVA is and what it does.
- Use the formulas provided to calculate a one-way randomized ANOVA.
- Interpret the results from a one-way randomized ANOVA.
- Calculate η^2 for a one-way randomized ANOVA.
- Calculate Tukey's post hoc test for a one-way randomized ANOVA.

Calculations for the One-Way Randomized ANOVA

To see exactly how ANOVA works, we begin by calculating the sums of squares (*SS*). This should sound somewhat familiar to you because we calculated sums of squares as part of the calculation for standard deviation in Module 5. The sums of squares in that formula represented the sum of the squared deviation of each score from the overall mean. Determining the sums of squares is the first step in calculating the various types or sources of variance in an ANOVA.

Several types of sums of squares are used in the calculation of an ANOVA. In describing them in this module, I provide *definitional formulas* for each. The definitional formula follows the definition for each sum of squares and should give you the basic idea of how each *SS* is calculated. When dealing with very large data sets, however, the definitional formulas can become somewhat cumbersome. Thus, statisticians have transformed the definitional formulas into *computational formulas.* A computational formula is easier to use in terms of the number of steps required. However, computational formulas do not follow the definition of the *SS* and thus do not necessarily make sense in terms of the definition for each *SS*. If your instructor would prefer that you use the computational formulas, they are provided in Appendix D.

TABLE 14.1   Calculation of SS_{Total} using the definitional formula

ROTE REHEARSAL		IMAGERY		STORY	
X	$(X - \bar{X}_G)^2$	X	$(X - \bar{X}_G)^2$	X	$(X - \bar{X}_G)^2$
2	14.69	4	3.36	6	.03
4	3.36	5	.69	5	.69
3	8.03	7	1.36	9	10.03
5	.69	6	.03	10	17.36
2	14.69	5	.69	8	4.70
7	1.36	4	3.36	7	1.36
6	.03	8	4.70	10	17.36
3	8.03	5	.69	9	10.03
	$\Sigma = 50.88$		$\Sigma = 14.88$		$\Sigma = 61.56$

$SS_{Total} = 50.88 + 14.88 + 61.56 = 127.32$

NOTE: All numbers have been rounded to two decimal places.

total sum of squares   The sum of the squared deviations of each score from the grand mean.

within-groups sum of squares   The sum of the squared deviations of each score from its group mean.

The first sum of squares that we need to describe is the **total sum of squares** (SS_{Total})—the sum of the squared deviations of each score from the grand mean. In a definitional formula, this would be represented as $\Sigma(X - \bar{X}_G)^2$, where X represents each individual score and $\bar{X}_G$ represents the grand mean. In other words, we determine how much each individual subject varies from the grand mean, square that deviation score, and sum all of the squared deviation scores. Using the study from the previous module on the effects of rehearsal type on memory (see Table 13.1), the total sum of squares $(SS_{Total}) = 127.32$. To see where this number comes from, refer to Table 14.1. (For the computational formula, see Appendix D.) Once we have calculated the sum of squares within and between groups (see below), they should equal the total sum of squares when added together. In this way, we can check our calculations for accuracy. If the sum of squares within and between do not equal the sum of squares total, then you know there is an error in at least one of the calculations.

Because an ANOVA analyzes the variance between groups and within groups, we need to use different formulas to determine the amount of variance attributable to these two factors. The **within-groups sum of squares** is the sum of the squared deviations of each score from its group or condition mean and is a reflection of the amount of error variance. In the definitional formula, it would be $\Sigma(X - \bar{X}_g)^2$, where X refers to each individual score and $\bar{X}_g$ refers to the mean for each group or condition. In order to determine this, we find the difference between each score and its group mean, square these deviation scores, and then sum all of the squared deviation scores. The use of this definitional formula to calculate SS_{Within} is illustrated in Table 14.2. The computational formula appears in Appendix D. Thus, rather than comparing every score in the entire study to the grand mean

TABLE 14.2 Calculation of SS_{Within} using the definitional formula

ROTE REHEARSAL		IMAGERY		STORY	
X	$(X - \bar{X}_g)^2$	X	$(X - \bar{X}_g)^2$	X	$(X - \bar{X}_g)^2$
2	4	4	2.25	6	4
4	0	5	.25	5	9
3	1	7	2.25	9	1
5	1	6	.25	10	4
2	4	5	.25	8	0
7	9	4	2.25	7	1
6	4	8	6.25	10	4
3	1	5	.25	9	1
Σ = 24		Σ = 14		Σ = 24	

$SS_{Within} = 24 + 14 + 24 = 62$

NOTE: All numbers have been rounded to two decimal places.

of the study (as is done for SS_{Total}), we compare each score in each condition to the mean of that condition. Thus, SS_{Within} is a reflection of the amount of variability within each condition. Because the subjects in each condition were treated in a similar manner, we would expect little variation among the scores within each group. This means that the within-groups sum of squares (SS_{Within}) should be small, indicating a small amount of error variance in the study. For our memory study, the within-groups sum of squares (SS_{Within}) = 62.

The **between-groups sum of squares** is the sum of the squared deviations of each group's mean from the grand mean, multiplied by the number of subjects in each group. In the definitional formula, this would be $\Sigma[(\bar{X}_g - \bar{X}_G)^2 n]$, where $\bar{X}_g$ refers to the mean for each group, $\bar{X}_G$ refers to the grand mean, and n refers to the number of subjects in each group. The use of the definitional formula to calculate $SS_{Between}$ is illustrated in Table 14.3. The computational formula appears in Appendix D. The between-groups variance is an indication of the systematic variance across the groups (the variance due to the independent variable and any confounds) and error. The basic idea behind the between-groups sum of squares is that if the independent variable had no effect (if there were no differences between the groups), then we would expect all the group means to be about the same. If all the group means were similar, they would also be approximately equal to the grand mean and there would be little variance across conditions. If, however, the independent variable caused changes in the means of some conditions (caused them to be larger or smaller than other conditions), then the condition means not only will differ from each other but will also differ from the grand mean, indicating variance across conditions. In our memory study, $SS_{Between}$ = 65.33.

between-groups sum of squares The sum of the squared deviations of each group's mean from the grand mean, multiplied by the number of subjects in each group.

TABLE 14.3   Calculation of $SS_{Between}$ using the definitional formula

Rote Rehearsal
$(\bar{X}_g - \bar{X}_G)^2 n = (4 - 5.833)^2 8 = (-1.833)^2 8 = (3.36)8 = 26.88$

Imagery
$(\bar{X}_g - \bar{X}_G)^2 n = (5.5 - 5.833)^2 8 = (-.333)^2 8 = (.11)8 = .88$

Story
$(\bar{X}_g - \bar{X}_G)^2 n = (8 - 5.833)^2 8 = (2.167)^2 8 = (4.696)8 = 37.57$

$SS_{Between} = 26.88 + .88 + 37.57 = 65.33$

We can check the accuracy of our calculations by adding the SS_{Within} to the $SS_{Between}$. When added, these numbers should equal SS_{Total}. Thus, SS_{Within} (62) + $SS_{Between}$ (65.33) = 127.33. The SS_{Total} that we calculated earlier was 127.32 and is essentially equal to SS_{Within} + $SS_{Between}$, taking into account rounding errors.

Calculating the sums of squares is an important step in the ANOVA. It is not, however, the end. Now that we have determined SS_{Total}, SS_{Within}, and $SS_{Between}$, we must transform these scores into the mean squares. The term **mean square** (*MS*) is an abbreviation of *mean squared deviation scores*. The *MS* scores are estimates of variance between and within the groups. In order to calculate the *MS* for each group (MS_{Within} and $MS_{Between}$), we divide each *SS* by the appropriate *df* (degrees of freedom). The reason for this is that the *MS* scores are our variance estimates. You may remember from Module 5 that when calculating standard deviation and variance, we divide the sum of squares by *N* (or $N - 1$ for the unbiased estimator) in order to get the average deviation from the mean. In the same manner, we must divide the *SS* scores by their degrees of freedom (the number of scores that contributed to each *SS* minus 1).

mean square An estimate of either variance between groups or variance within groups.

To do this for the present example, we first need to determine the degrees of freedom for each type of variance. Let's begin with the df_{Total}, which we will use to check our accuracy when calculating df_{Within} and $df_{Between}$. In other words, df_{Within} and $df_{Between}$ should sum to the df_{Total}. We determined SS_{Total} by calculating the deviations around the grand mean. We therefore had one restriction on our data—the grand mean. This leaves us with $N - 1$ total degrees of freedom (the total number of participants in the study minus the one restriction). For our study on the effects of rehearsal type on memory,

$$df_{Total} = 24 - 1 = 23$$

Using a similar logic, the degrees of freedom within each group would then be $n - 1$ (the number of subjects in each condition minus 1). However, we have more than one group; we have *k* groups, where *k* refers to the number of groups or conditions in the study. The degrees of freedom within groups is therefore $k(n - 1)$, or $N - k$. For our example,

$$df_{\text{Within}} = 24 - 3 = 21$$

Lastly, the degrees of freedom between groups is the variability of k means around the grand mean. Therefore, df_{Between} equals the number of groups (k) minus 1, or $k - 1$. For our study, this would be

$$df_{\text{Between}} = 3 - 1 = 2$$

Notice that the sum of the df_{Within} and df_{Between} equals df_{Total}: $21 + 2 = 23$. This allows you to check your calculations for accuracy. If the degrees of freedom between and within do not sum to the degrees of freedom total, you know there is a mistake somewhere.

Now that we have calculated the sums of squares and their degrees of freedom, we can use these numbers to calculate our estimates of the variance between and within groups. As stated previously, the variance estimates are called mean squares and are determined by dividing each SS by its corresponding df. In our example,

$$MS_{\text{Between}} = \frac{SS_{\text{Between}}}{df_{\text{Between}}} = \frac{65.33}{2} = 32.67$$

$$MS_{\text{Within}} = \frac{SS_{\text{Within}}}{df_{\text{Within}}} = \frac{62}{21} = 2.95$$

We can now use the estimates of between-groups and within-groups variance to determine the F-ratio:

$$F = \frac{MS_{\text{Between}}}{MS_{\text{Within}}} = \frac{32.67}{2.95} = 11.07$$

The definitional formulas for the sums of squares, along with the formulas for the degrees of freedom, mean squares, and the final F-ratio, are summarized in Table 14.4. The ANOVA summary table for the F-ratio just calculated is presented in Table 14.5. This is a common way of summarizing ANOVA findings. You will sometimes see ANOVA summary tables presented in journal articles because they provide a concise way of presenting the data from an analysis of variance.

TABLE 14.4   ANOVA summary table: definitional formulas

SOURCE	df	SS	MS	F
Between-groups	$k - 1$	$\Sigma[(\bar{X}_g - \bar{X}_G)^2 n]$	$\dfrac{SS_B}{df_B}$	$\dfrac{MS_B}{MS_W}$
Within-groups	$N - k$	$\Sigma(X - \bar{X}_g)^2$	$\dfrac{SS_W}{df_W}$	
Total	$N - 1$	$\Sigma(X - \bar{X}_G)^2$		

TABLE 14.5   ANOVA summary table for the memory study

SOURCE	df	SS	MS	F
Between-groups	2	65.33	32.67	11.07
Within-groups	21	62	2.95	
Total	23	127.33		

Interpreting the One-Way Randomized ANOVA ●●

Our obtained F-ratio of 11.07 is obviously greater than 1.00. However, we do not know whether it is large enough to let us reject the null hypothesis. To make this decision, we need to compare the obtained F (F_{obt}) of 11.07 with an F_{cv}—the critical value that determines the cutoff for statistical significance. The underlying F distribution is actually a family of distributions, each based on the degrees of freedom between and within each group. Remember that the alternative hypothesis is that the population means represented by the sample means are not from the same population. Table A.3 in Appendix A provides the critical values for the family of F distributions when $\alpha = .05$ and when $\alpha = .01$.

To use the table, look at the df_{Within} running down the left side of the table and the $df_{Between}$ running across the top of the table. F_{cv} is found where the row and column of these two numbers intersect. For our example, $df_{Within} = 21$ and $df_{Between} = 2$. Because there is no 21 in the df_{Within} column, we use the next lower number, 20. According to Table A.3, the F_{cv} for the .05 level is 3.49. Because our F_{obt} exceeds this, it is statistically significant at the .05 level. Let's check the .01 level also. The critical value for the .01 level is 5.85. Our F_{obt} is larger than this critical value also. We can therefore conclude that the F_{obt} is significant at the .01 level. In APA publication format, this would be written as $F(2, 21) = 11.07, p < .01$. This means that we reject H_0 and support H_a. In other words, at least one group mean differs significantly from the others. The calculation of this ANOVA using Excel, SPSS, and the TI-84 calculator is presented in the Statistical Software Resources section at the end of this chapter.

Let's consider what factors might affect the size of the final F_{obt}. Because the F_{obt} is derived using the between-groups variance as the numerator and the within-groups variance as the denominator, anything that increases the numerator or decreases the denominator will increase the F_{obt}.

What might increase the numerator? Using stronger controls in the experiment could have this effect because it would make any differences between the groups more noticeable or larger. This means that the $MS_{Between}$ (the numerator in the F-ratio) would be larger and therefore lead to a larger final F-ratio.

What would decrease the denominator? Once again, using better control to reduce overall error variance would have this effect; so would increasing the sample size, which increases df_{Within} and ultimately decreases MS_{Within}. Why would each of these affect the F-ratio in this manner? Each would decrease the size of the MS_{Within}, which is the denominator in the F-ratio. Dividing by a smaller number would lead to a larger final F-ratio and, therefore, a greater chance that it would be significant.

Graphing the Means and Effect Size

As noted in Module 11, we usually graph the means when a significant difference is found between them. As in our previous graphs, the independent variable is placed on the x-axis and the dependent variable on the y-axis. A graph representing the mean performance of each group is shown in Figure 14.1. In this experiment, those in the Rote condition remembered an average of 4 words, those in the Imagery condition remembered an average of 5.5 words, and those in the Story condition remembered an average of 8 words.

In addition to graphing the data, we should also assess the effect size. Based on the F_{obt}, we know that there was more variability between groups than within groups. In other words, the between-groups variance (the numerator in the F-ratio) was larger than the within-groups variance (the denominator in the F-ratio). However, it would be useful to know how much of the variability in the dependent variable can be attributed to the independent variable. In other words, it would be useful to have a measure of effect size. For an ANOVA, effect size can be estimated using **eta-squared** (η^2), which is calculated as follows:

eta-squared An inferential statistic for measuring effect size with an ANOVA.

$$\eta^2 = \frac{SS_{Between}}{SS_{Total}}$$

Because $SS_{Between}$ reflects the differences between the means from the various levels of an independent variable and SS_{Total} reflects the total differences between all scores in the experiment, η^2 reflects the proportion of the total

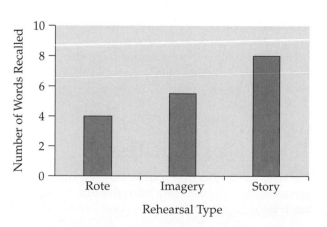

FIGURE 14.1
Number of words recalled as a function of rehearsal type

differences in the scores that is associated with differences between sample means, or how much of the variability in the dependent variable (memory) is attributable to the manipulation of the independent variable (rehearsal type). In other words, η^2 indicates how accurately the differences in scores can be predicted using the levels (conditions) of the independent variable. Referring to the summary table for our example in Table 14.5, η^2 would be calculated as follows:

$$\eta^2 = \frac{65.33}{127.33} = .51$$

In other words, approximately 51% of the variance among the scores can be attributed to the rehearsal condition to which the participant was assigned. In this example, the independent variable of rehearsal type is fairly important in determining the number of words recalled by subjects because the η^2 of 51% represents a considerable effect. There are no specific guidelines delineating what constitutes a meaningful η^2, and whether the amount of variability accounted for is considered meaningful or not depends on the area of research. However, η^2 is useful in determining whether or not a result of statistical significance is also of practical significance. In other words, although researchers might find that an F-ratio is statistically significant, if the corresponding η^2 is negligible, then the result is of little practical significance (Huck & Cormier, 1996).

Assumptions of the One-Way Randomized ANOVA

As with most statistical tests, certain assumptions must be met to ensure that the statistic is being used properly. The assumptions for the randomized one-way ANOVA are similar to those for the t test for independent groups:

- The data are on an interval-ratio scale.
- The underlying distribution is normally distributed.
- The variances among the populations being compared are homogeneous.

Because ANOVA is a robust statistical test, violations of some of these assumptions do not necessarily affect the results. Specifically, if the distributions are slightly skewed rather than normally distributed, it does not affect the results of the ANOVA. In addition, if the sample sizes are equal, the assumption of homogeneity of variances can be violated. However, it is not acceptable to violate the assumption of interval-ratio data. If the data collected in a study are ordinal or nominal in scale, other statistical procedures must be used. These procedures are discussed in a later module.

Tukey's Post Hoc Test

Because the results from our ANOVA indicate that at least one of the sample means differs significantly from the others (represents a different population from the others), we must now compute a post hoc test (a test conducted after the fact—in this case, after the ANOVA). A **post hoc test** involves comparing each of the groups in the study to each of the other groups to determine which ones differ significantly from each other. This may sound familiar to you. In fact, you may be thinking, isn't that what a *t* test does? In a sense, you are correct. However, remember that a series of multiple *t* tests inflates the probability of a Type I error. A post hoc test is designed to permit multiple comparisons and still maintain alpha (the probability of a Type I error) at .05.

The post hoc test presented here is **Tukey's honestly significant difference (HSD).** This test allows a researcher to make all pairwise comparisons among the sample means in a study while maintaining an acceptable alpha (usually .05, but possibly .01) when the conditions have equal *n*. If there is not an equal number of subjects in each condition, then another post hoc test, such as Fisher's protected *t* test, would be appropriate. If you need to use Fisher's protected *t* test, the formula is provided in the Computational Supplement in Appendix D.

Tukey's test identifies the smallest difference between any two means that is significant with $\alpha = .05$ or $\alpha = .01$. The formula for Tukey's HSD is

$$HSD_{.05} = Q(k, df_{Within})\sqrt{\frac{MS_{Within}}{n}}$$

Using this formula, we can determine the HSD for the .05 alpha level. This involves using Table A.4 in Appendix A to look up the value for Q. To look up Q, we need *k* (the number of means being compared—in our study on memory, this is 3) and df_{Within} (found in the ANOVA summary table, Table 14.5). Referring to Table A.4 for $k = 3$ and $df_{Within} = 21$ (because there is no 20 in Table A.4, we use 20 here as we did with Table A.3), we find that at the .05 level, $Q = 3.58$. In addition, we need MS_{Within} from Table 14.5 and *n* (the number of participants in each group). Using these numbers, we calculate the HSD as follows:

$$HSD_{.05} = (3.58)\sqrt{\frac{2.95}{8}} = (3.58)\sqrt{.369} = (3.58)(.607) = 2.17$$

This tells us that a difference of 2.17 or more for any pair of means is significant at the .05 level. In other words, the difference between the means is large enough that it is greater than what would be expected based on chance. Table 14.6 summarizes the differences between the means for each pairwise comparison. Can you identify which comparisons are significant using Tukey's HSD?

post hoc test When used with an ANOVA, a means of comparing all possible pairs of groups to determine which ones differ significantly from each other.

Tukey's honestly significant difference (HSD) A post hoc test used with ANOVAs for making all pairwise comparisons when conditions have equal *n*.

TABLE 14.6 Differences between each pair of means in the memory study

	ROTE REHEARSAL	IMAGERY	STORY
Rote Rehearsal	—	1.5	4.0
Imagery		—	2.5
Story			—

If you identified the differences between the Story condition and the Rote Rehearsal condition and between the Story condition and the Imagery condition as the two honestly significant differences, you were correct. Because the F-ratio was significant at $\alpha = .01$, we should also check the $HSD_{.01}$. To do this, we use the same formula, but we use Q for the .01 alpha level (from Table A.4). The calculations are as follows:

$$HSD_{.01} = (4.64)\sqrt{\frac{2.95}{8}} = (4.64)(.607) = 2.82$$

The only difference significant at this level is between the Rote Rehearsal condition and the Story condition. Thus, based on these data, those in the Story condition recalled significantly more words than those in the Imagery condition ($p < .05$) and those in the Rote Rehearsal condition ($p < .01$).

IN REVIEW

RANDOMIZED ONE-WAY ANOVA	
Concept	Description
F-ratio	The ratio formed when the between-groups variance is divided by the within-groups variance
Between-groups variance	An estimate of the variance of the group means about the grand mean; includes both systematic variance and error variance
Within-groups variance	An estimate of the variance within each condition in the experiment; also known as error variance, or variance due to chance factors
Eta-squared	A measure of effect size—the variability in the dependent variable attributable to the independent variable
Tukey's post hoc test	A test conducted to determine which conditions in a study with more than two groups differ significantly from each other

CRITICAL THINKING CHECK 14.1

1. Of the following four F-ratios, which appears to indicate that the independent variable had an effect on the dependent variable?
   a. 1.25/1.11
   b. 0.91/1.25
   c. 1.95/0.26
   d. 0.52/1.01
2. The following ANOVA summary table represents the results from a study on the effects of exercise on stress. There were three conditions in the study: a control group, a moderate exercise group, and a high exercise group. Each group had 10 subjects and the mean stress levels for each group were Control = 75.0, Moderate Exercise = 44.7, and High Exercise = 63.7. Stress was measured

using a 100-item stress scale, with 100 representing the highest level of stress. Complete the ANOVA summary table, and determine whether the F-ratio is significant. In addition, calculate eta-squared and Tukey's HSD if necessary.

ANOVA Summary Table

Source	df	SS	MS	F
Between		4,689.27		
Within		82,604.20		
Total				

REVIEW OF KEY TERMS

between-groups sum
   of squares (p. 229)
eta-squared (p. 233)
mean square (p. 230)

post hoc test (p. 235)
total sum of squares (p. 228)
Tukey's honestly significant
   difference (HSD) (p. 235)

within-groups sum
   of squares (p. 228)

MODULE EXERCISES

(Answers to odd-numbered questions appear in Appendix B.)

1. A researcher conducts a study on the effects of amount of sleep on creativity. The creativity scores for four levels of sleep (2 hours, 4 hours, 6 hours, and 8 hours) for $n = 5$ subjects (in each group) are presented next.

Amount of Sleep (in hours)

2	4	6	8
3	4	10	10
5	7	11	13
6	8	13	10
4	3	9	9
2	2	10	10

Source	df	SS	MS	F
Between-groups		187.75		
Within-groups		55.20		
Total		242.95		

a. Complete the ANOVA summary table. (If your instructor wants you to calculate the sums of squares, use the preceding data to do so.)
b. Is F_{obt} significant at $\alpha = .05$? at $\alpha = .01$?
c. Perform post hoc comparisons if necessary.

d. What conclusions can be drawn from the F-ratio and the post hoc comparisons?
e. What is the effect size, and what does this mean?
f. Graph the means.

2. In a study on the effects of stress on illness, a researcher tallied the number of colds people contracted during a 6-month period as a function of the amount of stress they reported during the same time period. There were three stress levels: minimal, moderate, and high stress. The sums of squares appear in the following ANOVA summary table. The mean for each condition and the number of participants per condition are also noted.

Source	df	SS	MS	F
Between-groups		22.167		
Within-groups		14.750		
Total		36.917		

Stress Level	Mean	n
Minimal	3	4
Moderate	4	4
High	6	4

a. Complete the ANOVA summary table.
b. Is F_{obt} significant at $\alpha = .05$? at $\alpha = .01$?

c. Perform post hoc comparisons if necessary.
d. What conclusions can be drawn from the F-ratio and the post hoc comparisons?
e. What is the effect size, and what does this mean?
f. Graph the means.

3. A researcher interested in the effects of exercise on stress had subjects exercise for 30, 60, or 90 minutes per day. The mean stress level on a 100-point stress scale (with 100 indicating high stress) for each condition appears next, along with the ANOVA summary table with the sums of squares indicated.

Source	df	SS	MS	F
Between-groups		4,689.27		
Within-groups		82,604.20		
Total		87,293.47		

Exercise Level	Mean	n
30 Minutes	75.0	10
60 Minutes	44.7	10
90 Minutes	63.7	10

a. Complete the ANOVA summary table.
b. Is F_{obt} significant at $\alpha = .05$? at $\alpha = .01$?
c. Perform post hoc comparisons if necessary.
d. What conclusions can be drawn from the F-ratio and the post hoc comparisons?
e. What is the effect size, and what does this mean?
f. Graph the means.

4. A researcher conducted an experiment on the effects of a new "drug" on depression. The control group, a placebo group, received nothing. An experimental group received the "drug." A depression inventory that provided a measure of depression on a 50-point scale was used (50 indicates that an individual is very high on the depression variable). The ANOVA summary table appears next, along with the mean depression score for each condition.

Source	df	SS	MS	F
Between-groups		1,202.313		
Within-groups		2,118.00		
Total		3,320.313		

"Drug" Condition	Mean	n
Control	36.26	15
Placebo	33.33	15
"Drug"	24.13	15

a. Complete the ANOVA summary table.
b. Is F_{obt} significant at $\alpha = .05$? at $\alpha = .01$?
c. Perform post hoc comparisons if necessary.
d. What conclusions can be drawn from the F-ratio and the post hoc comparisons?
e. What is the effect size, and what does this mean?
f. Graph the means.

5. When should post hoc tests be performed?
6. What information does eta-squared (η^2) provide?

CRITICAL THINKING CHECK ANSWERS

Critical Thinking Check 14.1

1. The F-ratio $1.95/0.26 = 7.5$ suggests that the independent variable had an effect on the dependent variable.

2. ANOVA Summary Table

Source	df	SS	MS	F
Between	2	4,689.27	2,344.64	.766
Within	27	82,604.20	3,059.41	
Total	29	87,293.47		

The resulting F-ratio is less than 1 and thus not significant. Although stress levels differed across some of the groups, the difference was not large enough to be significant.

WEB RESOURCES

The book-specific website at CengageBrain.com offers students a variety of study tools and useful resources such as glossaries, flashcards, quizzes, and Statistics and Research Methods Workshops.

CHAPTER SEVEN SUMMARY AND REVIEW
Introduction to Analysis of Variance (ANOVA)

CHAPTER SUMMARY

In this chapter we discussed designs using more than two levels of an independent variable. Advantages to such designs include being able to compare more than two kinds of treatment, using fewer subjects, comparing all treatments to a control group, and using placebo groups. When interval-ratio data are collected using such a design, the parametric statistical analysis most appropriate for use is the ANOVA (analysis of variance). A randomized one-way ANOVA would be used for between-subjects designs. Appropriate post hoc tests (Tukey's HSD) and measures of effect size (eta-squared) were also discussed.

CHAPTER 7 REVIEW EXERCISES

(Answers to exercises appear in Appendix B.)

Fill-in Self-Test

Answer the following questions. If you have trouble answering any of the questions, restudy the relevant material before going on to the multiple-choice self-test.

1. The _____ provides a means of setting a more stringent alpha level for multiple tests in order to minimize Type I errors.
2. A(n) _____ is an inferential statistical test for comparing the means of three or more groups.
3. The mean performance across all subjects is represented by the _____.
4. The _____ variance is an estimate of the effect of the independent variable, confounds, and error variance.
5. The sum of squared deviations of each score from the grand mean is the _____.
6. When we divide an *SS* score by its degrees of freedom, we have calculated a _____.
7. _____ is an inferential statistic for measuring effect size with an ANOVA.
8. For an ANOVA, we use _____ to compare all possible pairs of groups to determine which ones differ significantly from each other.

Multiple-Choice Self-Test

Select the single best answer for each of the following questions. If you have trouble answering any of the questions, restudy the relevant material.

1. The *F*-ratio is determined by dividing _____ by _____.
   a. error variance; systematic variance

    b. between-groups variance; within-groups variance

    c. within-groups variance; between-groups variance

    d. systematic variance; error variance

2. If between-groups variance is large, then we have observed

    a. experimenter effects.

    b. large systematic variance.

    c. large differences due to confounds.

    d. possibly both large systematic variance and large differences due to confounds.

3. The larger the F-ratio, the greater the chance that

    a. a mistake has been made in the computation.

    b. there are large systematic effects present.

    c. the experimental manipulation probably did not have the predicted effects.

    d. the between-groups variation is no larger than would be expected by chance and no larger than the within-groups variance.

4. One reason to use an ANOVA over a t test is to reduce the risk of

    a. a Type II error.

    b. a Type I error.

    c. confounds.

    d. error variance.

5. If the null hypothesis for an ANOVA is false, then the F-ratio should be

    a. greater than 1.00.

    b. a negative number.

    c. 0.00.

    d. 1.00.

6. If in a randomized ANOVA, there are four groups with 15 participants in each group, then the df for the F-ratio is equal to

    a. 60.

    b. 59.

    c. 3, 56.

    d. 3, 57.

7. For an F-ratio with $df = (3, 20)$, the F_{cv} for $\alpha = .05$ would be

    a. 3.10.

    b. 4.94.

    c. 8.66.

    d. 5.53.

8. If a researcher reported an F-ratio with $df = (2, 21)$ for a randomized one-way ANOVA, then there were _____ conditions in the experiment and _____ total subjects.

    a. 2; 21

    b. 3; 23

    c. 2; 24

    d. 3; 24

9. Systematic variance and error variance comprise the _____ variance.

    a. within-groups

    b. total

    c. between-groups

    d. subject

10. If a randomized one-way ANOVA produced $MS_{Between} = 25$ and $MS_{Within} = 5$, then the F-ratio would be
    a. $25/5 = 5$.
    b. $5/25 = .20$.
    c. $25/30 = .83$.
    d. $30/5 = 6$.

Self-Test Problems

Calculate Tukey's HSD and eta-squared for the following ANOVA.

Anova Summary Table

Source	df	SS	MS	F
Between	2	150		
Error	18	100		
Total	20			

CHAPTER SEVEN
Statistical Software Resources

If you need help getting started with Excel or SPSS, please see Appendix C: Getting Started with Excel and SPSS.

MODULES 13 AND 14 One-way Randomized ANOVA

The problem we'll be using to illustrate how to calculate the one-way randomized ANOVA appears in Modules 13 and 14.

Let's use the example from Modules 13 and 14 in which a researcher wants to study the effects on memory performance of rehearsal type. Three types of rehearsal are used (Rote, Imagery, and Story) by three different groups of subjects. The dependent variable is the subjects' scores on a 10-item test of the material. These scores are listed in Table 13.1 in Module 13.

Using Excel

We'll use the data from Table 13.1 (in Module 13) to illustrate the use of Excel to compute a one-way randomized ANOVA. In this study, we had participants use one of three different types of rehearsal (rote, imagery, or story) and then had them perform a recall task. Thus we manipulated rehearsal and measured memory for the 10 words subjects studied. Because there were different participants in each condition, we use a randomized ANOVA. We begin by entering the data into Excel, with the data from each condition appearing in a different column. This can be seen next.

Next, with the **Data** ribbon highlighted, click on the **Data Analysis** tab in the top right corner. You should receive the following dialog box:

Select **Anova: Single Factor,** as in the preceding box, and click **OK.** The following dialog box will appear:

With the cursor in **the Input Range** box, highlight the three columns of data so that they are entered into the Input Range box as they are in the preceding box (highlight only the data, not the column headings). Then click **OK**. The output from the ANOVA will appear on a new Worksheet, as seen next.

	A	B	C	D	E	F	G	H
1	Anova: Single Factor							
2								
3	SUMMARY							
4	*Groups*	*Count*	*Sum*	*Average*	*Variance*			
5	Column 1	8	32	4	3.428571			
6	Column 2	8	44	5.5	2			
7	Column 3	8	64	8	3.428571			
8								
9								
10	ANOVA							
11	*Source of Variation*	*SS*	*df*	*MS*	*F*	*P-value*	*F crit*	
12	Between Groups	65.33333	2	32.66667	11.06452	0.000523	3.4668	
13	Within Groups	62	21	2.952381				
14								
15	Total	127.3333	23					
16								
17								

You can see from the ANOVA Summary Table provided by Excel that $F(2, 21) = 11.06$, $p = .000523$. In addition to the full ANOVA Summary Table, Excel also provides the mean and variance for each condition.

Using SPSS

We'll again use the data from Table 13.1 (in Module 13) to illustrate the use of SPSS to compute a one-way randomized ANOVA. In this study, we had subjects use one of three different types of rehearsal (rote, imagery, or story) and then had them perform a recall task. Thus we manipulated rehearsal and measured memory for the 10 words subjects studied. Because there were different participants in each condition, we use a randomized ANOVA. We begin by entering the data into SPSS. The first column is labeled Rehearsaltype and indicates which type of rehearsal the subjects used (1 for rote, 2 for imagery, and 3 for story). The recall data for each of the three conditions appear in the second column, labeled Recall.

File Edit View Data Transform Analyze Graphs			
27 : Rehearsaltype			
	Rehearsaltype	Recall	var
1	1.00	2.00	
2	1.00	4.00	
3	1.00	3.00	
4	1.00	5.00	
5	1.00	2.00	
6	1.00	7.00	
7	1.00	6.00	
8	1.00	3.00	
9	2.00	4.00	
10	2.00	5.00	
11	2.00	7.00	
12	2.00	6.00	
13	2.00	5.00	
14	2.00	4.00	
15	2.00	8.00	
16	2.00	5.00	
17	3.00	6.00	
18	3.00	5.00	
19	3.00	9.00	
20	3.00	10.00	
21	3.00	8.00	
22	3.00	7.00	
23	3.00	10.00	
24	3.00	9.00	
25			

Next, click on **Analyze,** followed by **Compare Means,** and then **One-Way ANOVA,** as illustrated next.

You should receive the following dialog box:

Enter Rehearsaltype into the **Factor** box by highlighting it and using the appropriate arrow. Do the same for Recall by entering it into the **Dependent List** box. After doing this, the dialog box should appear as follows:

Next click on the **Options** button and select **Descriptive** and **Continue.** Then click on the **Post Hoc** button and select **Tukey** and then **Continue.** Then click on **OK.** The output from the ANOVA will appear in a new Output window as seen next.

Oneway

Descriptives

Recall

	N	Mean	Std. Deviation	Std. Error	95% Confidence Interval for Mean		Minimum	Maximum
					Lower Bound	Upper Bound		
1	8	4.0000	1.85164	.65465	2.4520	5.5480	2.00	7.00
2	8	5.5000	1.41421	.50000	4.3177	6.6823	4.00	8.00
3	8	8.0000	1.85164	.65465	6.4520	9.5480	5.00	10.00
Total	24	5.8333	2.35292	.48029	4.8398	6.8269	2.00	10.00

ANOVA

Recall

	Sum of Squares	df	Mean Square	F	Sig.
Between Groups	65.333	2	32.667	11.065	.001
Within Groups	62.000	21	2.952		
Total	127.333	23			

Post Hoc Tests

Multiple Comparisons

Recall
Tukey HSD

(I) Rehearsaltype	(J) Rehearsaltype	Mean Difference (I-J)	Std. Error	Sig.	95% Confidence Interval	
					Lower Bound	Upper Bound
1.00	2.00	-1.50000	.85912	.212	-3.6655	.6655
	3.00	-4.00000*	.85912	.000	-6.1655	-1.8345
2.00	1.00	1.50000	.85912	.212	-.6655	3.6655
	3.00	-2.50000*	.85912	.022	-4.6655	-.3345
3.00	1.00	4.00000*	.85912	.000	1.8345	6.1655
	2.00	2.50000*	.85912	.022	.3345	4.6655

*. The mean difference is significant at the 0.05 level.

You can see that the descriptive statistics for each condition are provided, followed by the ANOVA Summary Table in which $F(2, 21) = 11.065$, $p = .001$. In addition to the full ANOVA Summary Table, SPSS also calculated Tukey's HSD and provides all pairwise comparisons between the three conditions along with whether or not the comparison was significant.

Using the TI-84
Let's use the data from Table 13.1 (in Module 13) to conduct the analysis.

1. With the calculator on, press the STAT key.
2. EDIT will be highlighted. Press the ENTER key.
3. Under L1 enter the data from Table 13.1 for the rote group.
4. Under L2 enter the data from Table 13.1 for the imagery group.
5. Under L3 enter the data from Table 13.1 for the story group.
6. Press the STAT key once again and highlight TESTS.
7. Scroll down to ANOVA. Press the ENTER key.
8. Next to "ANOVA" enter (L1,L2,L3) using the 2nd function key with the appropriate number keys. Make sure that you use commas. The finished line should read "ANOVA(L1,L2,L3)."
9. Press ENTER.

The F score of 11.065 should be displayed followed by the significance level of .0005.

CHAPTER 8

Repeated Measures and Two-Factor ANOVAs

In the previous chapter, we discussed designs with more than two levels of an independent variable and the statistics appropriate for analyzing such designs. In this chapter, we will look at the more advanced parametric statistics used to analyze correlated-groups designs with more than two levels of an independent variable and between-subjects designs with more than one independent variable. Thus, in Module 15 we will learn how to calculate a repeated measures ANOVA appropriate for correlated-groups designs.

factorial design A design with more than one independent variable.

In Modules 16 and 17 we will discuss parametric statistics appropriate for more complex designs—those with more than one independent variable— namely, the two-way randomized ANOVA. These more complex designs are usually referred to as factorial designs. The term **factorial design** indicates that more than one factor, or variable, is manipulated in the study. We will discuss the advantages of such designs over more simplistic designs. In addition, we will discuss how to interpret the findings (called main effects and interaction effects) from such designs. Lastly, we will consider the statistical analysis of such designs.

One-Way Repeated Measures ANOVA

Learning Objectives
- Identify what a one-way repeated measures ANOVA is and what it does.
- Use the formulas provided to calculate a one-way repeated measures ANOVA.
- Interpret the results from a one-way repeated measures ANOVA.
- Calculate η^2 for a one-way repeated measures ANOVA.
- Calculate Tukey's post hoc test for a one-way repeated measures ANOVA.

Correlated-Groups Designs

Like between-subjects designs, correlated-groups designs may also use more than two levels of an independent variable. You should remember from Chapter 6 that there are two types of correlated-groups designs—a within-subjects design and a matched-subjects design. The same statistical analyses are used for both designs. We will use a within-subjects design to illustrate the statistical analysis appropriate for a correlated-groups design with more than two levels of an independent variable.

Imagine now that we want to conduct the same study described in Module 14 on the effects of rehearsal type on memory, but using a within-subjects rather than a between-subjects design. Why might we want to do this? As noted in Chapter 6, within-subjects designs—in fact, all correlated-groups designs—are more powerful than between-subjects designs. Therefore, one reason for this choice would be to increase statistical power. In addition, the within-subjects design uses fewer participants and provides almost perfect control across conditions. Because the same people participate in each condition, we know that the individuals in each condition are completely equivalent to each other and that the only difference between conditions will be the type of rehearsal used.

In this study, the same three conditions will be used: rote rehearsal, rehearsal with imagery, and rehearsal with a story. The only difference is that the same 8 subjects serve in every condition. Obviously, we cannot use the

TABLE 15.1 Number of words recalled in a within-subjects study of the effects of rehearsal type on memory

ROTE REHEARSAL	IMAGERY	STORY	
2	4	5	
3	2	3	
3	5	6	
3	7	6	
2	5	8	
5	4	7	
6	8	10	
4	5	9	
$\bar{X} = 3.5$	$\bar{X} = 5$	$\bar{X} = 6.75$	Grand Mean = 5.083

same list of words across conditions because there could be a large practice effect. We therefore have to use three lists of words that are equivalent in difficulty and that are counterbalanced across conditions. In other words, not all participants in each condition will receive the same list of words. Let's assume that we have taken the design problems into account and that the data in Table 15.1 represent the performance of the subjects in this study. The number of words recalled in each condition is out of 10 words.

You can see that the data are similar to those in the between-subjects design described in Module 14. Because of the similarity in the data, we will be able to see how the statistics used with a within-subjects design are more powerful than those used with a between-subjects design. Because we have interval-ratio data, we will once again use an ANOVA to analyze these data. The only difference will be that the ANOVA used in this case is a **one-way repeated measures ANOVA.** The phrase *repeated measures* refers to the fact that measures were taken repeatedly on the same individuals; that is, the same participants served in all conditions. The difference between this ANOVA and the one-way randomized ANOVA is that the conditions are correlated (related); therefore, the ANOVA procedure must be modified to take this relationship into account.

one-way repeated measures ANOVA
An inferential statistical test for comparing the means of three or more groups using a correlated-groups design.

One-Way Repeated Measures ANOVA: What It Is and What It Does ●●

With a one-way repeated measures ANOVA, participants in different conditions are equated prior to the experimental manipulation because the same participants are used in each condition. This means that the single largest factor contributing to error variance (individual differences across subjects) has been removed. This also means that the error variance will be smaller. What part of the F-ratio is the error variance? Remember that the denominator in the F-ratio is made up of error variance. Thus, if error variance (the denominator) is smaller, the resulting F-ratio will be larger. The end result is that a repeated measures ANOVA is more sensitive to small differences between groups.

The null and alternative hypotheses for the repeated measures ANOVA are the same as those for the randomized ANOVA. That is, the null hypothesis is that the means from the conditions tested will be similar or the same, and the alternative hypothesis is that the mean from at least one condition will differ from that of the other conditions:

$H_0: \mu_1 = \mu_2 = \mu_3$

H_a: At least one $\mu \neq$ another μ

A repeated measures ANOVA is calculated in a manner similar to that for a randomized ANOVA. We first determine the sums of squares (SS), then the degrees of freedom (df) and mean squares (MS), and finally the F-ratio. The main difference lies in the calculation of the sums of squares. As with the randomized ANOVA, I will describe what the different sums of squares are, provide the definitional formulas, and show how to use these formulas with the data from Table 15.1. The computational formulas for the sums of squares for a repeated measures ANOVA are presented in Appendix D. If your instructor prefers that you use them (rather than the definitional formulas) with the experimental data from Table 15.1, please refer to this appendix.

Calculations for the One-Way Repeated Measures ANOVA

The total sum of squares is calculated for a repeated measures ANOVA in the same manner as it is for a randomized ANOVA. The total sum of squares (SS_{total}) is the total amount of variability in the entire data set (across all the conditions). It is calculated by summing the squared deviations of each score from the grand mean, or $\Sigma(X - \overline{X}_G)^2$, where X refers to each individual score and $\overline{X}_G$ refers to the grand mean. The total sum of squares for the present example is 115.82. The calculations for this are shown in Table 15.2.

Because there is only one group of subjects, what was referred to as the between-groups sum of squares in a randomized ANOVA is now called a between-treatments, or simply a between, sum of squares. The between sum of squares is the sum of the difference between each condition or treatment mean and the grand mean, squared and multiplied by the number of scores in each treatment. It is calculated in the same manner as in the randomized ANOVA: $\Sigma[(\overline{X}_t - \overline{X}_G)^2 n]$, where $\overline{X}_t$ represents the mean for each treatment, $\overline{X}_G$ represents the grand mean, and n represents the number of scores in each treatment. The between sum of squares in the present example is 42.34 and is calculated in Table 15.3.

Finally, what was the within-groups sum of squares in the randomized ANOVA is split into two sources of variance in the repeated measures

TABLE 15.2   Calculation of SS_{Total} using the definitional formula

ROTE REHEARSAL		IMAGERY		STORY	
X	$(X - \bar{X}_G)^2$	X	$(X - \bar{X}_G)^2$	X	$(X - \bar{X}_G)^2$
2	9.50	4	1.17	5	.01
3	4.34	2	9.50	3	4.34
3	4.34	5	.01	6	.84
3	4.34	7	3.67	6	.84
2	9.50	5	.01	8	8.51
5	.01	4	1.17	7	3.67
6	.84	8	8.51	10	24.18
4	1.17	5	.01	9	15.34
	$\Sigma = 34.04$		$\Sigma = 24.05$		$\Sigma = 57.73$

$SS_{Total} = (34.04 + 24.05 + 57.73) = 115.82$

NOTE: All numbers have been rounded to two decimal places.

TABLE 15.3   Calculation of $SS_{Between}$ using the definitional formula

Rote Rehearsal

$(\bar{X}_t - \bar{X}_G)^2 n = (3.5 - 5.083)^2 8 = (-1.583)^2 8 = (2.51)8 = 20.05$

Imagery

$(\bar{X}_t - \bar{X}_G)^2 n = (5 - 5.083)^2 8 = (-.083)^2 8 = (.007)8 = .06$

Story

$(\bar{X}_t - \bar{X}_G)^2 n = (6.75 - 5.083)^2 8 = (1.667)^2 8 = (2.779)8 = 22.23$

$SS_{Between} = 20.05 + .06 + 22.23 = 42.34$

ANOVA: subject (participant) variance and error (residual) variance. To calculate these sums of squares, we begin by calculating the within-groups sum of squares just as we did in the randomized ANOVA. In other words, we calculate the sum of squared difference scores for each score and its treatment mean, or $\Sigma(X - \bar{X}_t)^2$, where X represents each score and $\bar{X}_t$ represents each treatment mean. The within-groups sum of squares is 73.48. The calculation for this is shown in Table 15.4.

Once we have calculated the within-groups sum of squares, we can determine the subject sum of squares, which is a reflection of the amount of within-groups variance due to individual differences. It is the sum of squared difference scores for the mean of each participant across conditions and the grand mean, multiplied by the number of conditions. In a definitional formula, we would represent this as $\Sigma[(\bar{X}_S - \bar{X}_G)^2 k]$, where

TABLE 15.4   Calculation of SS_{Within} using the definitional formula

ROTE REHEARSAL		IMAGERY		STORY	
X	$(X - \bar{X}_t)^2$	X	$(X - \bar{X}_t)^2$	X	$(X - \bar{X}_t)^2$
2	2.25	4	1	5	3.06
3	.25	2	9	3	14.06
3	.25	5	0	6	.56
3	.25	7	4	6	.56
2	2.25	5	0	8	1.56
5	2.25	4	1	7	.06
6	6.25	8	9	10	10.56
4	.25	5	0	9	5.06
$\Sigma = 14$		$\Sigma = 24$		$\Sigma = 35.48$	

$SS_{Within} = (14 + 24 + 35.48) = 73.48$

NOTE: All numbers have been rounded to two decimal places.

$\bar{X}_S$ represents the mean across treatments for each subject, $\bar{X}_G$ represents the grand mean, and k represents the number of treatments. The subject sum of squares is 52.40. The calculation for this is shown in Table 15.5.

After the variability due to individual differences ($SS_{Subject}$) has been removed from the within-groups sum of squares, what is left is the error sum of squares. In definitional form, this is $SS_{Within} - SS_{Subject}$, or in our example, $73.48 - 52.40 = 21.08$. We will soon see that the final F-ratio is computed by taking the $MS_{Between}$ divided by the MS_{Error}. The main difference, then, between the repeated measures ANOVA and the randomized ANOVA is that the within-groups variance is divided into two sources

TABLE 15.5   Calculation of $SS_{Subject}$ using the definitional formula

ROTE REHEARSAL X	IMAGERY X	STORY X	$\bar{X}_S$	$(\bar{X}_S - \bar{X}_G)^2 3$
2	4	5	3.67	5.99
3	2	3	2.67	17.47
3	5	6	4.67	.51
3	7	6	5.33	.18
2	5	8	5.00	.02
5	4	7	5.33	.18
6	8	10	8.00	25.53
4	5	9	6.00	2.52
			$SS_{Subject} = 52.40$	

NOTE: All numbers have been rounded to two decimal places.

TABLE 15.6   Repeated measures ANOVA summary table: definitional formulas

SOURCE	df	SS	MS	F
Subject	$n - 1$	$\Sigma[(\bar{X}_S - \bar{X}_G)^2 k]$	$\dfrac{SS_S}{df_S}$	
Between	$k - 1$	$\Sigma[(\bar{X}_t - \bar{X}_G)^2 n]$	$\dfrac{SS_B}{df_B}$	$\dfrac{MS_B}{MS_E}$
Error	$(k - 1)(n - 1)$	$\Sigma[(X - \bar{X}_t)^2] - SS_S$	$\dfrac{SS_E}{df_E}$	
Total	$N - 1$	$\Sigma(X - \bar{X}_G)^2$		

of variance (that attributable to individual differences and that attributable to error variance), and only the variance attributable to error is used in the calculation of the MS_{Error} and in the calculation of the final F-ratio.

The next step is to calculate the MS, or mean square, for each term. You may remember that the MS for each term is calculated by dividing the SS by the df. Therefore, in order to calculate the MS for each term, we need to know the degrees of freedom for each term. Table 15.6 provides the definitional formulas for the sums of squares, the formulas for the degrees of freedom and mean squares, and the formula for the F-ratio. The df_{Total} is calculated the same way that it was for the randomized ANOVA, $N - 1$. In this case, large N refers to the total number of scores in the study, not the total number of participants. Thus, the df_{Total} would be $24 - 1 = 23$. The $df_{Subjects}$ is calculated by subtracting 1 from the number of participants $(n - 1)$ and would be $8 - 1 = 7$. The $df_{Between}$ is once again calculated by subtracting 1 from the number of conditions $(k - 1)$, or $3 - 1 = 2$. Lastly, the df_{Error} is calculated by multiplying the $df_{Between}$ by the $df_{Subjects}$: $(k - 1)(n - 1) = 2 \times 7 = 14$.

Once the MS for each term is determined (see Tables 15.6 and 15.7), we can calculate the F-ratio. In the repeated measures ANOVA, as in the randomized ANOVA, we divide the $MS_{Between}$ by the MS_{Error}. The degrees of freedom, sums of squares, mean squares, and F_{obt} calculated for these data are shown in Table 15.7.

TABLE 15.7   Repeated measures ANOVA summary table for the memory study

SOURCE	df	SS	MS	F
Subject	7	52.40	7.49	
Between	2	42.34	21.17	14.02
Error	14	21.08	1.51	
Total	23	115.82		

Interpreting the One-Way Repeated Measures ANOVA

The repeated measures ANOVA is interpreted in the same way as the randomized ANOVA. We use Table A.3 in Appendix A to determine the critical value for the F-ratio. Using the $df_{Between}$ of 2 and the df_{Error} of 14 as the coordinates for Table A.3, we find that the F_{cv} for the .05 level is 3.74. Because our F_{obt} is much larger than this, we know that it is significant at the .05 level. Let's also look at the F_{cv} for the .01 level, which is 6.51. Once again, our F_{obt} is larger than this. In APA publication format, this would be reported as $F(2, 14) = 14.02$, $p < .01$. The use of Excel and SPSS to complete a one-way repeated measures ANOVA is illustrated in the Statistical Software Resources section at the end of this chapter.

If you look back to Table 14.5—the ANOVA summary table for the one-way randomized ANOVA, with very similar data to the repeated measures ANOVA—you can see how much more powerful the repeated measures ANOVA is than the randomized ANOVA. Notice that although the total sums of squares are very similar, the resulting F-ratio for the repeated measures ANOVA is much larger (14.02 versus 11.07). If the F_{obt} is larger, there is a greater probability that it will be statistically significant. Notice also that although the data used to calculate the two ANOVAs are similar, the group means in the repeated measures ANOVA are more similar (closer together) than those from the randomized ANOVA, yet the F_{obt} from the repeated measures ANOVA is larger. Thus, with somewhat similar data, the resulting F-ratio for the repeated measures ANOVA is larger and thus affords more statistical power.

Graphing the Means and Effect Size

As with the one-way randomized ANOVA discussed in Module 14, we should also graph the results of this ANOVA because of the significant difference between the means. The resulting graph appears in Figure 15.1. In addition, we should also compute the effect size using eta-squared. Eta-squared is calculated by dividing $SS_{Between}$ by SS_{Total}. This would be $42.34/115.82 = .366$.

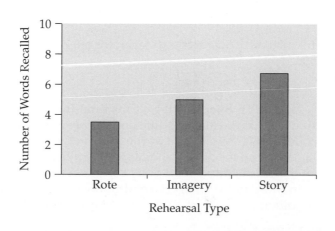

FIGURE 15.1
Number of words recalled as a function of rehearsal type

This tells us that 36.6% of the variability among the scores can be attributed to the various rehearsal conditions. Notice that even though a moderate amount of the variability in the dependent variable is accounted for by knowing the condition to which a participant was assigned, the effect size is not as large as that from the randomized ANOVA we calculated in Module 14. This shows the importance of determining effect size. Although the repeated measures ANOVA may lead to a larger final F-ratio and greater statistical significance, it does not necessarily mean that the independent variable explains more of the variability in the dependent variable.

Assumptions of the One-Way Repeated Measures ANOVA

As with the randomized ANOVA, certain assumptions must be met to ensure that the statistic is being used properly. The first three assumptions for the one-way repeated measures ANOVA are the same as those for the one-way randomized ANOVA:

- The data are on an interval-ratio scale.
- The underlying distribution is normally distributed.
- The variances among the populations being compared are homogeneous.
- The groups are correlated (within-subjects or matched-subjects).

Tukey's Post Hoc Test

As with the randomized ANOVA, we can also perform post hoc tests when the resulting F-ratio is significant. Once again, we will use Tukey's HSD post hoc test:

$$\text{HSD} = Q(k, df_{\text{Error}})\sqrt{\frac{MS_{\text{Error}}}{n}}$$

Remember that we determine Q by using Table A.4 in Appendix A. For our example, the honestly significant difference for the .05 level would be

$$\text{HSD}_{.05} = 3.70\sqrt{\frac{1.51}{8}} = 3.70\sqrt{0.1887} = 3.70(0.434) = 1.61$$

To calculate HSD for the .01 level, we refer to Table A.4 once again and find that

$$\text{HSD}_{.01} = 4.89(0.434) = 2.12$$

Table 15.8 compares the means from the three conditions in the present study. We can see that the difference in means between the Rote and the Story conditions is significant at the .01 level and the difference between the Imagery and the Story conditions is significant at the .05 level. Thus, based on these data, those in the Story condition recalled significantly more words than those in the Imagery condition ($p < .05$) and than those in the Rote condition ($p < .01$).

TABLE 15.8   Differences between each pair of means in the within-subjects study

	ROTE REHEARSAL	IMAGERY	STORY
Rote Rehearsal	—	1.5	3.25
Imagery		—	1.75
Story			—

IN REVIEW

ONE-WAY REPEATED MEASURES ANOVA

Concept	Description
Null Hypothesis (H_0)	The independent variable had no effect—the samples all represent the same population
Alternative Hypothesis (H_a)	The independent variable had an effect—at least one of the samples represents a different population than the others
F-ratio	The ratio formed when the between variance is divided by the error variance
Between Variance	An estimate of the variance of the treatment means about the grand mean; includes both systematic variance and error variance
Subject Variance	The variance due to individual differences; removed from the error variance
Error Variance	An estimate of the variance within each condition in the experiment after variance due to individual differences has been removed
Eta-squared (η^2)	A measure of effect size—the variability in the dependent variable attributable to the independent variable
Tukey's Post Hoc Test	A test conducted to determine which conditions in a study with more than two groups differ significantly from each other

CRITICAL THINKING CHECK 15.1

1. Explain why a repeated measures ANOVA is statistically more powerful than a randomized one-way ANOVA.
2. Identify other advantage(s) associated with using a within-subjects design.

REVIEW OF KEY TERMS

factorial design (p. 252)

one-way repeated measures ANOVA (p. 254)

MODULE EXERCISES

(Answers to odd-numbered questions appear in Appendix B.)

1. What is the difference between a randomized ANOVA and a repeated measures ANOVA?
2. What does the term *one-way* mean with respect to an ANOVA?
3. Why is a repeated measures ANOVA statistically more powerful than a randomized ANOVA?
4. A researcher is interested in the effects of practice on accuracy in a signal detection task. Participants are tested with no practice, after 1 hour of practice, and after 2 hours of practice. Each person participates in all three conditions. The following data indicate how many signals were accurately detected by each participant at each level of practice.

Amount of Practice

Participant	No Practice	1 Hour	2 Hours
1	3	4	6
2	4	5	5
3	2	3	4
4	1	3	5
5	3	6	7
6	3	4	6
7	2	3	4

Source	df	SS	MS	F
Subject		16.27		
Between		25.81		
Error		4.87		
Total		46.95		

a. Complete the ANOVA summary table. (If your instructor wants you to calculate the sums of squares, use the preceding data to do so.)
b. Is F_{obt} significant at $\alpha = .05$? At $\alpha = .01$?
c. Perform post hoc comparisons if necessary.
d. What conclusions can be drawn from the F-ratio and the post hoc comparisons?
e. What is the effect size, and what does this mean?
f. Graph the means.
5. A researcher has been hired by a pizzeria to determine which type of crust is most preferred by customers. The restaurant offers three types of crust: hand-tossed, thick, and thin. Following are the means for each condition, from 10 subjects who tasted each type of crust and rated them on

a 1–10 scale, with 10 as the highest rating. The ANOVA summary table also follows.

Crust Type	Mean	n
Hand-tossed	2.73	10
Thick	4.20	10
Thin	8.50	10

Source	df	SS	MS	F
Subject		2.75		
Between		180.05		
Error		21.65		
Total		204.45		

a. Complete the ANOVA summary table.
b. Is F_{obt} significant at $\alpha = .05$? At $\alpha = .01$?
c. Perform post hoc comparisons if necessary.
d. What conclusions can be drawn from the F-ratio and the post hoc comparisons?
e. What is the effect size, and what does this mean?
f. Graph the means.
6. A researcher is interested in whether massed or spaced studying has a greater impact on grades in a course. The researcher has her class study for 6 hours, all in one day, for one exam (massed-study condition). She has them study for 2 hours each day for 3 days for another exam (3-day spaced condition). Lastly, she has them study 1 hour a day for 6 days for a third exam (6-day spaced condition). The mean exam scores (out of a possible 100 points) for each condition appear next, along with the ANOVA summary table.

Study Condition	Mean	n
Massed	69.13	15
3-day spaced	79.33	15
6-day spaced	90.27	15

Source	df	SS	MS	F
Subject		136.96		
Between		3,350.96		
Error		499.03		
Total		3,986.95		

a. Complete the ANOVA summary table.
b. Is F_{obt} significant at $\alpha = .05$? At $\alpha = .01$?
c. Perform post hoc comparisons if necessary.
d. What conclusions can be drawn from the F-ratio and the post hoc comparisons?
e. What is the effect size, and what does this mean?
f. Graph the means.

CRITICAL THINKING CHECK ANSWERS

Critical Thinking Check 15.1

1. A repeated measures ANOVA is statistically more powerful because the within-groups variance is divided into two sources of variance—that due to individual differences (subject) and that left over (error). Only the error variance is used to calculate the F-ratio. We therefore divide by a smaller number, thus resulting in a larger F-ratio and a greater chance that it will be significant.

2. The within-subjects design also has the advantages of requiring fewer subjects and assuring equivalency of groups.

WEB RESOURCES

The book-specific website at CengageBrain.com offers students a variety of study tools and useful resources such as glossaries, flashcards, quizzes, and Statistics and Research Methods Workshops.

MODULE 16
Using Designs with More than One Independent Variable

Learning Objectives
- Explain factorial notation and the advantages of factorial designs.
- Identify main effects and interaction effects based on looking at graphs.
- Draw graphs for factorial designs based on matrices of means.
- Explain what a two-way randomized ANOVA is and what it does.

Remember the study discussed in Module 14 on the effects of rehearsal on memory. We had subjects use one of three types of rehearsal (rote, imagery, or story) in order to determine their effects on the number of words recalled. Imagine that, upon further analysis of the data, we discovered that concrete words (for example, *desk*, *bike*, *tree*) were recalled better than abstract words (for example, *love*, *truth*, *honesty*) in one rehearsal condition but not in another. Such a result is called an interaction between variables; this concept is discussed in more detail later in the module. One advantage of using factorial designs is that they allow us to assess how variables interact. In the real world, it would be unusual to find that a certain behavior is produced by only one variable; behavior is usually contingent on many variables operating together in an interactive way. Designing experiments with more than one independent variable allows researchers to assess how multiple variables may affect behavior.

Factorial Notation and Factorial Designs

A factorial design, then, is one with more than one factor or independent variable. A *complete factorial design* is one in which all levels of each independent variable are paired with all levels of every other independent variable. An *incomplete factorial design* also has more than one independent variable, but all levels of each variable are not paired with all levels of every other variable. The design illustrated in this module is a complete factorial design.

Remember that an independent variable must have at least two levels—if it does not vary, it is not a variable. Thus, the simplest complete factorial design would be one with two independent variables, each with two levels. Let's consider an example. Suppose we manipulate two independent variables: word type (concrete versus abstract) and rehearsal type (rote versus imagery). The independent variable Word Type has two levels, abstract and concrete; the independent variable Rehearsal Type also has two levels, rote and imagery. This is known as a 2 × 2 factorial design.

The factorial notation (2 × 2) for a factorial design is determined as follows:

[Number of levels of independent variable 1]
  × [Number of levels of independent variable 2]
  × [Number of levels of independent variable 3]...

Thus, the **factorial notation** indicates how many independent variables were used in the study and how many levels were used for each independent variable. This is often a point of confusion for students, who frequently think that in the factorial notation 2 × 2, the first number (2) indicates that there are two independent variables and the second number (2) indicates that they each have two levels. This is not how to interpret factorial notation. Rather, each number in the notation specifies the number of levels of a single independent variable. Thus, a 3 × 6 factorial design is one with two independent variables; the two numbers in the factorial notation each represent a single independent variable. In a 3 × 6 factorial design, one independent variable has three levels, and the other has six levels. Alternatively, in a 2 × 3 × 5 design, there are three independent variables. One variable has two levels, one has three levels, and the remaining independent variable has five levels.

Referring back to our 2 × 2 factorial design, we see that there are two independent variables, each with two levels. This factorial design has four conditions (2 × 2 = 4): abstract words with rote rehearsal, abstract words with imagery rehearsal, concrete words with rote rehearsal, and concrete words with imagery rehearsal. How many conditions would there be in a 3 × 6 factorial design? If you said 18, you are correct. Would it be possible to have a 1 × 3 factorial design? If you answered no, you are correct. It is not possible to have a factor (variable) with one level because it does not vary.

factorial notation The notation that indicates how many independent variables were used in a study and how many levels were used for each variable.

Main Effects and Interaction Effects

Two kinds of information can be gleaned from a factorial design. The first piece of information gained from a factorial design is whether there are any main effects. A **main effect** is an effect of a single independent variable. In our design with two independent variables, two main effects are possible: an effect of word type and an effect of rehearsal type. In other words, there can be as many main effects as there are independent variables. The second piece of information is whether or not there is an interaction effect. As the name implies, this is information regarding how the variables or factors

main effect An effect of a single independent variable.

interaction effect The effect of each independent variable across the levels of the other independent variable.

interact. Specifically, an **interaction effect** indicates the effect of each independent variable across the levels of the other independent variable. When there is an interaction between two independent variables, the effect of one independent variable depends on the level of the other independent variable. If this makes no sense at this point, don't worry; it will become clear as we work through our example.

Let's look at the data from our study on the effects of word type and rehearsal type on memory. Table 16.1 presents the mean performance for participants in each condition. This was a completely between-subjects design—different subjects served in each of the four conditions. There were 8 subjects in each condition, for a total of 32 subjects in the study. Each participant in each condition was given a list of 10 words (either abstract or concrete) to learn using the specified rehearsal technique (rote or imagery).

Typically, researchers begin by assessing whether or not there is an interaction effect because having an interaction effect indicates that the effect of one independent variable depends on the level of the other independent variable. However, when first beginning to interpret two-way designs, students usually find it easier to begin with the main effects and then move on to the interaction effect. What we need to keep in mind is that if we later find an interaction effect, any main effects will have to be qualified. Remember, because we have two independent variables, there is the possibility for two main effects—one for word type (independent variable A in the table) and one for rehearsal type (independent variable B in the table). The main effect of each independent variable tells us about the relationship between that single independent variable and the dependent variable. In other words, did different levels of one independent variable bring about changes in the dependent variable?

We can find the answer to this question by looking at the row and column means in Table 16.1. The column means tell us about the overall effect of independent variable A (word type). The column means indicate that there is a difference in number of words recalled between the concrete and abstract word conditions. More concrete words were recalled (7.5) than abstract words (5). The column means represent the average performance

TABLE 16.1 Results of the 2 × 2 factorial design: effects of word type and rehearsal type on memory

REHEARSAL TYPE (INDEPENDENT VARIABLE B)	WORD TYPE (INDEPENDENT VARIABLE A)		ROW MEANS (MAIN EFFECT OF B)
	CONCRETE	ABSTRACT	
Rote Rehearsal	5	5	5
Imagery Rehearsal	10	5	7.5
Column Means (Main Effect of A)	7.5	5	

for the concrete and abstract word conditions summarized across the rehearsal conditions. In other words, we obtained the column mean of 7.5 for the concrete word conditions by averaging the number of words recalled in the concrete/word rote rehearsal condition and the concrete/word imagery rehearsal condition $[(5 + 10)/2 = 7.5]$. Similarly, the column mean for the abstract word conditions (5) was obtained by averaging the data from the two abstract word conditions $[(5 + 5)/2 = 5]$. (Please note that determining the row and column means in this manner is only possible when the number of participants in each condition is equal. If the number of participants in each condition is unequal, then all individual scores within the single row or column must be used in the calculation of the row or column mean.)

The main effect for independent variable B (rehearsal type) can be assessed by looking at the row means. The row means indicate that there is a difference in the number of words recalled between the rote rehearsal and the imagery rehearsal conditions. More words were recalled when subjects used the imagery rehearsal technique (7.5) than when they used the rote rehearsal technique (5). As with the column means, the row means represent the average performance in the rote and imagery rehearsal conditions, summarized across the word type conditions.

At face value, the main effects tell us that, overall, subjects recall more words when they are concrete and when imagery rehearsal is used. However, we now need to assess whether there is an interaction between the variables. If so, the main effects noted previously will have to be qualified, because an interaction indicates that the effect of one independent variable depends on the level of the other independent variable. In other words, an interaction effect indicates that the effect of one independent variable is different at different levels of the other independent variable.

Look again at the data in Table 16.1. We can see an interaction in these results because when rote rehearsal is used, word type makes no difference (the means are the same—5 words recalled). However, when imagery rehearsal is used, word type makes a large difference. Specifically, when imagery is used with concrete words, participants do very well (recall an average of 10 words); yet when imagery is used with abstract words, participants perform the same as they did in both of the rote rehearsal conditions (recall an average of only 5 words). Think about what this means. When there is an interaction between the two variables, the effect of one independent variable differs at different levels of the other independent variable—there is a contrast or a difference in the way subjects perform across the levels of the independent variables.

Another way to assess whether there is an interaction effect in a study is to graph the means. Figure 16.1 represents a line graph of the data presented in Table 16.1. The interaction may be easier for you to see here. First, when there is an interaction between variables, the lines are not parallel—they have markedly different slopes. You can see in the figure that one line is flat (representing the data from the rote rehearsal conditions), whereas the other line has a positive slope to it (representing the data from the imagery rehearsal conditions). Look at the figure, and think about the interaction. The

FIGURE 16.1
Line graph
representing
interaction between
rehearsal type and
word type

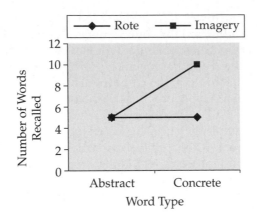

flat line indicates that when rote rehearsal was used, word type had no effect (the line is flat because the means are the same). The line with the positive slope indicates that when imagery rehearsal was used, word type had a large effect—subjects remembered more concrete words than abstract words.

You are probably familiar with the concept of interaction in your own life. When we say "It depends," we are indicating that what we do in one situation depends on some other variable—there is an interaction. In other words, whether or not you go to a party depends on whether you have to work and who is going to be at the party. If you have to work, you will not go to the party under any circumstance. However, if you do not have to work, you might go if a "certain person" is going to be there. If that person is not going to be there, you will not go. See if you can graph this interaction. The dependent variable, which always goes on the y-axis, is the likelihood of going to the party. One independent variable would be placed on the x-axis (whether or not you have to work), and the levels of the other independent variable would be captioned in the graph (whether the certain person is or is not present at the party).

To determine whether main effects or an interaction effect are significant, we need to conduct a statistical analysis. We will discuss the appropriate analysis in Module 17.

Possible Outcomes of a 2 × 2 Factorial Design ●●

A 2 × 2 factorial design has several possible outcomes. Because there are two independent variables, there may or may not be a significant effect of each. In addition, there may or may not be a significant interaction effect. Thus, there are eight possible outcomes in all (possible combinations of significant and nonsignificant effects). Figure 16.2 illustrates these eight possible outcomes for a 2 × 2 factorial design, using the same study we

FIGURE 16.2
Possible outcomes of a 2 × 2 factorial design with rehearsal type and word type as independent variables

a. No Main Effects; No Interaction Effect

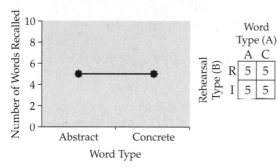

b. Main Effect of A; No Main Effect of B; No Interaction Effect

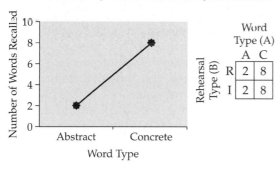

c. No Main Effect of A; Main Effect of B; No Interaction Effect

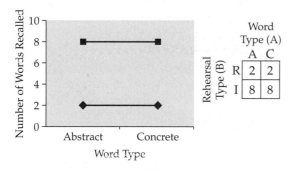

d. Main Effect of A; Main Effect of B; No Interaction Effect

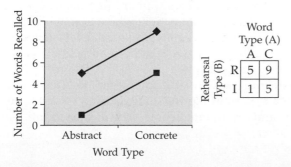

e. Main Effect of A; Main Effect of B; Interaction Effect

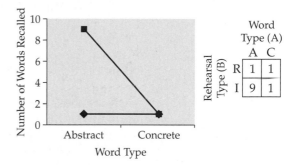

f. Main Effect of A; No Main Effect of B; Interaction Effect

g. No Main Effect of A; Main Effect of B; Interaction Effect

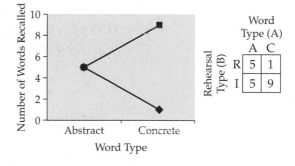

h. No Main Effects; Interaction Effect

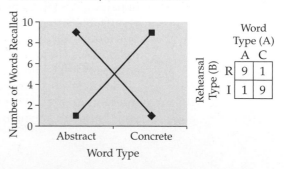

have been discussing as an example. Obviously, only one of these outcomes would be possible in a single study. All eight are graphed here to give you a concrete illustration of each possibility. For each graph, the dependent variable (number of words recalled) is placed on the y-axis, and independent variable A (word type) is placed on the x-axis. The two means for one level of independent variable B (rehearsal type) are plotted, and a line is drawn to represent this level of independent variable B. In the same fashion, the means for the second level of independent variable B are plotted, and a second line is drawn to represent this level of independent variable B. Next to each graph is a matrix showing the means from the four conditions in the study. The graphs were derived by plotting the four means from each matrix. In addition, whether or not there are main effects and an interaction effect is indicated next to each graph.

Can you tell from looking at the graphs which ones represent interaction effects? If you identified graphs a, b, c, and d as not having interaction effects and graphs e, f, g, and h as having interaction effects, you were correct. You should have a greater appreciation for interaction after looking at these graphs. Notice that in graphs a–d, there is no interaction because each level of independent variable A (word type) affects the levels of independent variable B (rehearsal type) in the same way. For example, look at graphs c and d. In graph c, the lines are parallel with no slope. This indicates that for both rote and imagery rehearsal, word type made no difference. In graph d, the lines are parallel and sloped. This indicates that for both rote and imagery rehearsal, word type had the same effect—performance was poorer for abstract words and then increased by the same amount for concrete words.

Now turn to graphs e–h, which represent interaction effects. Sometimes there is an interaction because there is no relationship between the independent variable and the dependent variable at one level of the second independent variable but a strong relationship at the other level of the second independent variable. Look at graphs e and f to see this. In graph e, when rote rehearsal is used, word type makes no difference, whereas when imagery rehearsal is used, word type makes a large difference. In graph f, the interaction is due to a similar result. Sometimes, however, an interaction may indicate that an independent variable has an opposite effect on the dependent variable at different levels of the second independent variable. Graphs g and h illustrate this. In graph g, when imagery rehearsal is used, performance improves for concrete words versus abstract words (a positive relationship). However, when rote rehearsal is used, performance decreases for concrete words versus abstract words (a negative relationship). Finally, graph h shows similar but more dramatic results. Here there is a complete crossover interaction, where exactly the opposite result is occurring for independent variable B at the levels of independent variable A. Notice also in this graph that although there is a large crossover interaction, there are no main effects.

To make sure you completely understand interpreting main effects and interaction effects, cover the answers in Figure 16.2 and quiz yourself on whether there are main effects and/or an interaction effect in each graph.

COMPLEX DESIGNS			IN REVIEW
	Description	Advantage or Example	
Factorial Design	Any design with more than one independent variable.	In the example in this module, word type and rehearsal type were both manipulated in order to determine whether there were main effects and an interaction effect. The advantage of this is that it more closely resembles the real world because the results are due to more than one factor (variable).	
Factorial Notation	The numerical notation corresponding to a factorial design. It indicates, in brief form, the number of independent variables and the number of levels of each variable.	A 3 × 4 design has two independent variables, one with three levels and one with four levels.	
Main Effect	An effect of a single independent variable. A main effect describes the effect of a single variable as if there were no other variables in the study.	In a study with two independent variables, two main effects are possible—one for each variable.	
Interaction Effect	The effect of each independent variable at the levels of the other independent variable.	Interaction effects allow us to assess whether the effect of one variable depends on the level of the other variable. In this way, they allow us to more closely simulate the real world, where multiple variables often interact.	

1. What would be the factorial notation for the following design? A pizza parlor owner is interested in what type of pizza is most preferred by his customers. He manipulates the type of crust for the pizzas by using thin, thick, and hand-tossed crusts. In addition, he manipulates the topping for the pizzas by offering cheese, pepperoni, sausage, veggie, and everything. He then has his customers sample the various pizzas and rate them. After you have determined the factorial notation, indicate how many conditions there are in this study.

2. How many main effect(s) and interaction effect(s) are possible in a 4 × 6 factorial design?

CRITICAL THINKING CHECK 16.1

3. Draw a graph representing the following data from a study using the same independent variables as in the module example. Determine whether there are any main effects or an interaction effect.

Rote rehearsal/Concrete words: $\overline{X} = 10$
Rote rehearsal/Abstract words: $\overline{X} = 1$
Imagery rehearsal/Concrete words: $\overline{X} = 9$
Imagery rehearsal/Abstract words: $\overline{X} = 9$

REVIEW OF KEY TERMS

factorial notation (p. 265)   interaction effect (p. 266)   main effect (p. 265)

MODULE EXERCISES

(Answers to odd-numbered questions appear in Appendix B.)

1. What is the advantage of manipulating more than one independent variable in an experiment?
2. How many independent variables are there in a 3 × 6 factorial design? How many conditions (cells) are there in this design?
3. In a study, a researcher manipulated the number of hours that subjects studied (either 4, 6, or 8), the type of study technique used (shallow processing versus deep processing), and whether subjects studied individually or in groups. What is the factorial notation for this design?
4. What is the difference between a cell (condition) mean and the means used to interpret a main effect?

5. How many main effects and interaction effects are possible in a 2 × 6 factorial design?
6. What is the difference between a complete factorial design and an incomplete factorial design?
7. The cell means for two experiments appear below. Determine whether there are any effects of Factor A, Factor B, and Factor A × B (interaction) for each experiment. In addition, draw a graph representing the data from each experiment.

Experiment 1

	A_1	A_2
B_1	3	5
B_2	5	7

Experiment 2

	A_1	A_2
B_1	12	4
B_2	4	12

CRITICAL THINKING CHECK ANSWERS

Critical Thinking Check 16.1

1. This would be a 3 × 5 design. There are three types of crust and five types of toppings. There would be 15 conditions in this study.
2. A 4 × 6 factorial design has two independent variables. Thus, there is the possibility of two main effects (one for each independent variable) and one interaction effect (the interaction between the two independent variables).
3. There appears to be a main effect of word type, with concrete words recalled better than abstract words. There also appears to be a main effect of rehearsal type, with those who used imagery rehearsal remembering more words than those who used rote rehearsal. In addition, there appears to be an interaction effect: When imagery rehearsal is used, word type makes no difference—recall is very high for both types of words.

When rote rehearsal is used, word type makes a large difference—concrete words are recalled very well and abstract words very poorly.

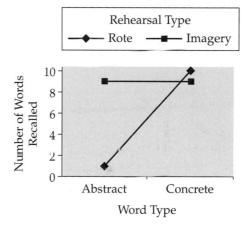

WEB RESOURCES

The book-specific website at CengageBrain.com offers students a variety of study tools and useful resources such as glossaries, flashcards, quizzes, and Statistics and Research Methods Workshops.

Two-Way Randomized ANOVA

Learning Objectives
- Explain what a two-way randomized ANOVA is and what it does.
- Calculate a two-way randomized ANOVA.
- Interpret a two-way randomized ANOVA.
- Explain what a two-way repeated measures ANOVA is.

As discussed in Module 14, the type of statistical analysis most commonly used when interval-ratio data have been collected is an ANOVA. For the factorial designs discussed in the previous module, a two-way ANOVA would be used. The term *two-way* indicates that there are two independent variables in the study. If a design had three independent variables, then we would use a three-way ANOVA; if there were four independent variables, a four-way ANOVA; and so on. With a between-subjects design, a two-way randomized ANOVA is used. With a correlated-groups factorial design, a two-way repeated measures ANOVA is used. If the data in a study are not interval-ratio and the design is complex (more than one independent variable), there are nonparametric statistics that would be appropriate for use. These will not be discussed in this module, but can be found in more advanced statistics texts.

Two-Way Randomized ANOVA: What It Is and What It Does

A two-way ANOVA is similar to a one-way ANOVA in that it analyzes the variance between groups and within groups. The logic is the same: If either of the variables has an effect, the variance between the groups should be greater than the variance within the groups. As with the one-way ANOVA, an *F*-ratio is formed by dividing the between-groups variance by the within-groups variance. The difference is that in the two-way ANOVA, between-groups variance may be attributable to Factor A (one of the independent variables in the study), to Factor B (the second independent variable in the study), and to the interaction of Factors A and B. With two independent variables, there is a possibility of a main effect for each variable, and an F-ratio is calculated to represent each of these effects. In addition, there is the possibility of one interaction effect, and an F-ratio is also needed to represent this effect. Thus, with a two-way ANOVA, there are three F-ratios to calculate and ultimately to interpret.

In a 2×2 factorial design, such as the one we looked at in Module 16, there are three null and alternative hypotheses. The null hypothesis for Factor A states that there is no main effect for Factor A, and the alternative hypothesis states that there is an effect of Factor A (the differences observed between the groups are greater than what would be expected based on chance). In other words, the null hypothesis states that the population means represented by the sample means are from the same population, and the alternative hypothesis states that the population means represented by the sample means are not from the same population. A second null hypothesis states that there is no main effect of Factor B, and the alternative hypothesis states that there is an effect of Factor B. The third null hypothesis states that there is no interaction of Factors A and B, and the alternative hypothesis states that there is an interaction effect.

Let's use the memory study introduced in the previous module to illustrate the calculation of a two-way randomized ANOVA. In this study, Factor A was word type (concrete versus abstract), Factor B was rehearsal type (rote versus imagery), and the dependent variable was the number of words recalled. Table 17.1 presents the number of words recalled by the 32 subjects in the memory study, with 8 subjects in each condition. As in the previous modules, the definitional formulas for the various sums of squares (SS) will be provided and used to calculate each SS. The computational formulas are provided in Appendix D if your instructor prefers that you use them.

Calculations for the Two-Way Randomized ANOVA •●

In a two-way ANOVA, there are several sources of variance; therefore, several sums of squares must be calculated. Let's begin with the sum of squares total (SS_{Total}), which represents the sum of the squared deviation scores for all participants in the study. This is calculated in the same manner as it was in Modules 14 and 15. The definitional formula is $SS_{Total} = \Sigma(X - \overline{X}_G)^2$, where X refers to each individual's score and $\overline{X}_G$ refers to the grand mean for the study. The use of this formula is illustrated in Table 17.2, where we see that $SS_{Total} = 202$. As in the one-way ANOVA, we can use the SS_{Total} as a check on the accuracy of our calculations. In other words, when we finish calculating all of the various other sums of squares, they should sum to the total sum of squares. The df_{Total} is determined in the same manner as in the previous ANOVA examples in Modules 14 and 15, $N - 1$. In this case, $df_{Total} = 31$.

In addition to total variance, there is also variance due to Factor A (word type). This will tell us whether the main effect of Factor A is significant.

TABLE 17.1 Number of words recalled as a function of word type and rehearsal type

| REHEARSAL TYPE (INDEPENDENT VARIABLE B) | WORD TYPE (INDEPENDENT VARIABLE A) | | ROW MEANS (MAIN EFFECT OF B) |
	CONCRETE	ABSTRACT	
Rote rehearsal	4	5	
	5	4	
	3	5	
	6	6	4.5
	2	4	
	2	5	
	6	6	
	4	5	
	Cell mean = 4	Cell mean = 5	
Imagery rehearsal	10	6	
	12	5	
	11	6	
	9	7	8
	8	6	
	10	6	
	10	7	
	10	5	
	Cell mean = 10	Cell mean = 6	
Column means (Main effect of A)	7	5.5	Grand mean = 6.25

TABLE 17.2 Calculation of SS_{Total} using the definitional formula

ROTE/CONCRETE		ROTE/ABSTRACT		IMAGERY/CONCRETE		IMAGERY/ABSTRACT	
X	$(X - \bar{X}_G)^2$	X	$(X - \bar{X}_G)^2$	X	$(X - \bar{X}_G)^2$	X	$(X - \bar{X}_G)^2$
4	5.0625	5	1.5625	10	14.0625	6	0.0625
5	1.5625	4	5.0625	12	33.0625	5	1.5625
3	10.5625	5	1.5625	11	22.5625	6	0.0625
6	0.0625	6	0.0625	9	7.5625	7	0.5625
2	18.0625	4	5.0625	8	3.0625	6	0.0625
2	18.0625	5	1.5625	10	14.0625	6	0.0625
6	0.0625	6	0.0625	10	14.0625	7	0.5625
4	5.0625	5	1.5625	10	14.0625	5	1.5625
Σ =	58.50		16.50		122.50		4.50

$SS_{Total} = 58.50 + 16.50 + 122.50 + 4.50 = 202$

TABLE 17.3 Calculation of SS_A using the definitional formula

$$SS_A = \Sigma[(\bar{X}_A - \bar{X}_G)^2 n_A]$$
$$= [(7 - 6.25)^2 16] + [(5.5 - 6.25)^2 16]$$
$$= [(0.75)^2 16] + [(-0.75)^2 16]$$
$$= [(0.5625)16] + [(0.5625)16]$$
$$= 9 + 9$$
$$= 18$$

Similarly, there is variance due to Factor B (rehearsal type), which will tell us whether the main effect of Factor B is significant. Both of these sources of variance are determined by first calculating the appropriate sums of squares for each term and then dividing by the corresponding degrees of freedom for each term in order to obtain the mean square for each factor. The **sum of squares Factor A** (SS_A) represents the sum of the squared deviation scores of each group mean for Factor A minus the grand mean, times the number of scores in each Factor A condition (column). The definitional formula is $SS_A = \Sigma[(\bar{X}_A - \bar{X}_G)^2 n_A]$, where $\bar{X}_A$ represents the mean for each condition of Factor A, $\bar{X}_G$ represents the grand mean, and n_A represents the number of people in each of the Factor A conditions. The use of this formula is illustrated in Table 17.3. Notice that $n_A = 16$. We use 16 because the column means for Factor A are derived based on the 16 scores that make up the concrete word conditions (8 subjects in the concrete/rote condition and 8 subjects in the concrete/imagery condition) and the 16 scores that make up the abstract word conditions (8 subjects in the abstract/rote condition and 8 subjects in the abstract/imagery condition). As can be seen in Table 17.3, the $SS_A = 18$. The df_A are equal to the number of levels of Factor A minus 1 (A − 1). Because Factor A has two levels, there is 1 degree of freedom. The mean square for Factor A can now be calculated by dividing the SS_A by the df_A. Thus, the mean square for Factor A (MS_A) is equal to 18/1 = 18.

The **sum of squares Factor B** (SS_B) is calculated in a similar manner. In other words, SS_B is the sum of the squared deviation scores of each group mean for Factor B minus the grand mean, times the number of scores in each Factor B condition. The definitional formula is $SS_B = \Sigma[(\bar{X}_B - \bar{X}_G)^2 n_B]$, where $\bar{X}_B$ represents the mean for each condition of Factor B, $\bar{X}_G$ represents the grand mean, and n_B represents the number of people in each of the Factor B conditions. The SS_B calculated in Table 17.4 is 98. Notice that, as with Factor A, n_B is also equal to 16—the total number of scores that contribute to the row means. In addition, as with Factor A, the mean square for Factor B is calculated by dividing the SS_B by the df_B. The df_B is derived by taking the number of levels of Factor B minus 1 (B − 1). This would be 2 − 1 = 1, and the MS_B would therefore be 98/1 = 98.

We also have to consider the variance due to the interaction of Factors A and B, which will tell us whether or not there is a significant interaction

sum of squares Factor A The sum of the squared deviation scores of each group mean for Factor A minus the grand mean, times the number of scores in each Factor A condition.

sum of squares Factor B The sum of the squared deviation scores of each group mean for Factor B minus the grand mean, times the number of scores in each Factor B condition.

TABLE 17.4 Calculation of SS_B using the definitional formula

$SS_B = \sum[(\overline{X}_B - \overline{X}_G)^2 n_B]$
$= [(4.5 - 6.25)^2 16] + [(8 - 6.25)^2 16]$
$= [(-1.75)^2 16] + [(1.75)^2 16]$
$= [(3.0625)16] + [(3.0625)16]$
$= 49 + 49$
$= 98$

sum of squares interaction
The sum of the squared difference of each condition mean minus the grand mean, times the number of scores in each condition. The SS_A and SS_B are then subtracted from this.

effect. The **sum of squares interaction** ($SS_{A \times B}$) is the sum of the squared difference of each condition mean minus the grand mean, times the number of scores in each condition or cell. Because this gives us an estimate of the amount of variance of the scores about their respective condition means, it includes the amount of variance due to Factor A, Factor B, and the interaction. Thus, once this sum is calculated, we must subtract out the variance due solely to Factor A and that due solely to Factor B. The definitional formula is thus $SS_{A \times B} = [(\overline{X}_C - \overline{X}_G)^2 n_C] - SS_A - SS_B$, where $\overline{X}_C$ is the mean for each condition, $\overline{X}_G$ is the grand mean, and n_C is the number of scores in each condition. The calculation of the $SS_{A \times B}$ is illustrated in Table 17.5. As can be seen in this table, the sum of squares for the interaction term is 50. We must divide this number by its corresponding degrees of freedom. The degrees of freedom for the interaction are based on the number of conditions in the study. In the present study, there are four conditions. To determine the degrees of freedom across the conditions, we multiply the degrees of freedom for the factors involved in the interaction. Thus, $df_{A \times B} = (A - 1)(B - 1) = 1$. Using this to determine the $MS_{A \times B}$, we find that $50/1 = 50$.

Lastly, we have to determine the amount of variance due to error—the within-groups variance. As in a one-way ANOVA, the within-groups variance is an indication of the amount of variance in the scores within a cell or condition about that condition mean. The **sum of squares error**

sum of squares error The sum of the squared deviations of each score from its condition (cell) mean.

(SS_{Error}) is the sum of the squared deviations of each score from its condition or cell mean. The definitional formula is $SS_{\text{Error}} = \sum(X - \overline{X}_C)^2$. The calculation of the SS_{Error} is illustrated in Table 17.6. In the present study, the SS_{Error} is 36. We can now check all of our calculations by summing SS_A, SS_B, $SS_{A \times B}$,

TABLE 17.5 Calculation of $SS_{A \times B}$ using the definitional formula

$SS_{A \times B} = \sum[(\overline{X}_C - \overline{X}_G)^2 n_C] - SS_A - SS_B$
$= [(4 - 6.25)^2 8] + [(5 - 6.25)^2 8] + [(10 - 6.25)^2 8] + [(6 - 6.25)^2 8] - 18 - 98$
$= [(-2.25)^2 8] + [(-1.25)^2 8] + [(3.75)^2 8] + [(-0.25)^2 8] - 18 - 98$
$= [(5.0625)8] + [(1.5625)8] + [(14.0625)8] + [(0.0625)8] - 18 - 98$
$= 40.50 + 12.50 + 112.50 + 0.50 - 18 - 98$
$= 50$

TABLE 17.6 Calculation of SS_{Error} using the definitional formula

ROTE/CONCRETE		ROTE/ABSTRACT		IMAGERY/CONCRETE		IMAGERY/ABSTRACT	
X	$(X - \bar{X}_c)^2$	X	$(X - \bar{X}_c)^2$	X	$(X - \bar{X}_c)^2$	X	$(X - \bar{X}_c)^2$
4	0	5	0	10	0	6	0
5	1	4	1	12	4	5	1
3	1	5	0	11	1	6	0
6	4	6	1	9	1	7	1
2	4	4	1	8	4	6	0
2	4	5	0	10	0	6	0
6	4	6	1	10	0	7	1
4	0	5	0	10	0	5	1
$\Sigma =$	18		4		10		4

$SS_{Error} = 18 + 4 + 10 + 4 = 36$

and SS_{Error}: $18 + 98 + 50 + 36 = 202$. We previously found that $SS_{Total} = 202$, so we know that our calculations are correct.

The df_{Error} is determined by assessing the degrees of freedom within each of the design's conditions. In other words, the number of conditions in the study is multiplied by the number of participants in each condition minus the one score not free to vary. In the present example this would be $4(8 - 1)$, or 28. As a check, when we sum the degrees of freedom for A, B, A × B, and error, they should equal the df_{Total}. In this case, $df_A = 1$, $df_B = 1$, $df_{A \times B} = 1$, and $df_{Error} = 28$. They sum to 31, which is the df_{Total} we calculated previously. To determine the MS_{Error}, we divide the SS_{Error} by its degrees of freedom: $36/28 = 1.29$.

"EVERY ONCE IN A WHILE I JUST LIKE TO UNWIND WITH A LITTLE ADDITION AND SUBTRACTION."

TABLE 17.7 ANOVA summary table including formulas

SOURCE	df	SS	MS	F
Factor A (word type)	$A - 1$	$\sum[(\bar{X}_A - \bar{X}_G)^2 n_A]$	$\dfrac{SS_A}{df_A}$	$\dfrac{MS_A}{MS_{Error}}$
Factor B (rehearsal type)	$B - 1$	$\sum[(\bar{X}_B - \bar{X}_G)^2 n_B]$	$\dfrac{SS_B}{df_B}$	$\dfrac{MS_B}{MS_{Error}}$
$A \times B$	$(A - 1)(B - 1)$	$\sum[(\bar{X}_C - \bar{X}_G)^2 n_C] - SS_A - SS_B$	$\dfrac{SS_{A \times B}}{df_{A \times B}}$	$\dfrac{MS_{A \times B}}{MS_{Error}}$
Error	$AB(n - 1)$	$\sum(X - \bar{X}_C)^2$	$\dfrac{SS_{Error}}{df_{Error}}$	
Total	$N - 1$	$\sum(X - \bar{X}_G)^2$		

Now that we have calculated the sum of squares, degrees of freedom, and mean squares for each term, we can determine the corresponding F-ratios. In a two-way ANOVA, there are three F-ratios: one for Factor A, one for Factor B, and one for the interaction of A and B. Each of the F-ratios is determined by dividing the MS for the appropriate term by the MS_{Error}. Thus, for Factor A (word type), the F-ratio equals $18/1.29 = 13.95$. For Factor B (rehearsal type), the F-ratio is determined in the same manner: $98/1.29 = 75.97$. Lastly, for the interaction, the F-ratio is $50/1.29 = 38.76$. The definitional formulas for the sums of squares and the formulas for the degrees of freedom, mean squares, and F-ratios are summarized in Table 17.7. Table 17.8 shows the ANOVA summary table for the data from the present study.

Interpreting the Two-Way Randomized ANOVA

Our obtained F-ratios are all larger than 1.00. To determine whether they are large enough to let us reject the null hypotheses, however, we need to compare our obtained F-ratios with the F_{cv}. As we learned in Module 13, the underlying F distribution is actually a family of distributions, each based on the degrees of freedom between and within each group. Remember that the alternative hypotheses are that the population means represented by the

TABLE 17.8 Two-way ANOVA summary table

SOURCE	df	SS	MS	F
Factor A (word type)	1	18	18	13.95
Factor B (rehearsal type)	1	98	98	75.97
$A \times B$	1	50	50	38.76
Error	28	36	1.29	
Total	31	202		

sample means are not from the same population. Table A.3 in Appendix A provides the critical values for the family of F distributions when $\alpha = .05$ and when $\alpha = .01$. We use this table exactly as we did in the previous modules. That is, we use the df_{Error} (remember df_{Error} represents the degrees of freedom within groups, or the degrees of freedom for error variance) running down the left side of the table and the $df_{Between}$ running across the top of the table. F_{cv} is found where the row and column corresponding to these two numbers intersect. You might be wondering what $df_{Between}$ is in the present example. It always represents the degrees of freedom between groups. However, in a two-way ANOVA, we have three $df_{Betweens}$: one for Factor A, one for Factor B, and one for the interaction term. Therefore, we need to determine three F_{cv}s, one for each of the three terms in the study.

To determine the F_{cv} for Factor A (word type), we look at the degrees of freedom for Factor A ($df_A = 1$). This represents the degrees of freedom between groups for variable A, or the number running across the top of Table A.3. We move down the left side to the df_{Error} (df_{Within}), which is 28. Where 1 and 28 intersect, we find that the F_{cv} for the .05 level is 4.20 and the F_{cv} for the .01 level is 7.64. This means that in order for our F_{obt} to be significant at either of these levels, it has to meet or exceed the F_{cv} for that alpha level. Because our F_{obt} for Factor A exceeds both of these F_{cv}s, it is significant at the .01 level. In APA publication format, this would be written as $F(1, 28) = 13.95, p < .01$. This means that there was a significant main effect of Factor A (word type). If we look at the column means from Table 17.1 for word type, we see that participants did better (remembered more words) when concrete words were used than when abstract words were used. I have initially interpreted the main effect for Factor A at face value, but we will see when we interpret the interaction that concrete words were not remembered better in both of the rehearsal type conditions.

We also need to determine the F_{cv} for variable B and for the interaction term. Because the degrees of freedom are the same for all of the terms in this study (1, 28), we use the same F_{cv}s. In addition, because the F_{obt}s also exceed the F_{cv} of 7.64 for the .01 level, we know that the F_{obt} for Factor B and for the interaction term are also significant at the .01 level. Thus, for Factor B (rehearsal type), $F(1, 28) = 75.97, p < .01$, indicating a significant main effect of rehearsal type. Referring back to the row means from Table 17.1, we see that subjects remembered substantially more words when imagery rehearsal was used than when rote rehearsal was used. Once again, I have interpreted the main effect of Factor B at face value, but we will see that the interaction will qualify this interpretation. In other words, imagery rehearsal led to better performance overall, but not when we break it down by word type. Lastly, for the interaction term, $F(1, 28) = 38.76, p < .01$, indicating that there was a significant interaction effect. When rote rehearsal was used, word type made little difference; however, when imagery rehearsal was used, the performance for the two word types varied. With imagery rehearsal, subjects remembered significantly more concrete words than abstract words. As discussed in the previous module, it is sometimes easier to interpret the interaction effect when looking at a figure. Thus, the condition means from Table 17.1 are graphed in Figure 17.1. You can

FIGURE 17.1
Number of words
recalled as a function
of word type and
rehearsal type

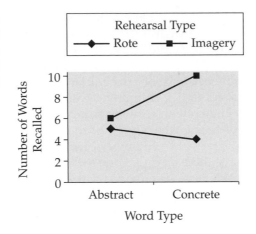

see how to use either Excel or SPSS to complete these calculations in the Statistical Software Resources section at the end of this chapter.

Assumptions of the Two-Way Randomized ANOVA

The two-way randomized ANOVA is used when you have a factorial design. The remaining assumptions are as follows:

- All conditions (cells) contain independent samples of subjects (in other words, there are different subjects in each condition).
- Interval or ratio data were collected.
- The populations represented by the data are roughly normally distributed.
- The populations represented by the data all have homogeneous variances.

Post Hoc Tests and Effect Size

As with a one-way ANOVA, post hoc tests such as Tukey's HSD (honestly significant difference) test are recommended. For the present example, a 2 × 2 design, post hoc tests are not necessary because any significant main effect indicates a significant difference between the two groups comprising that variable. In other words, because each independent variable in the present study has only two conditions, a significant main effect of that variable indicates significant differences between the two groups. If one or both of the independent variables in a factorial design have three or more levels and the main effect(s) is (are) significant, then Tukey's HSD test should be conducted to determine exactly which groups differ significantly from each other. In addition, it is also possible to use a variation of the Tukey HSD test to compare the means from a significant interaction effect. These calculations are beyond the scope of this book but can be found in a more advanced statistics text.

As noted in previous modules, when a significant relationship is observed, you should also calculate the effect size—the proportion of variance in the dependent variable that is accounted for by the manipulation of the independent variables(s). In the previous modules we used eta-squared (η^2)

as a measure of effect size with ANOVAs. You may remember that $\eta^2 = SS_{Between}/SS_{Total}$. When using a two-way ANOVA, we have three $SS_{Between}$s: one for variable A, one for variable B, and one for the interaction term. Referring back to Table 17.8, we can obtain the SS scores needed for these calculations. For Factor A (word type), η^2 would be calculated as follows:

$$\eta^2 = \frac{18}{202} = .089$$

This means that Factor A (word type) can account for 8.9% of the total variance in number of words recalled. We can also calculate the effect sizes for Factor B (rehearsal type) and the interaction term using the same formula. For Factor B, η^2 would be $98/202 = .485$. In other words, Factor B (rehearsal type) can account for 48.5% of the total variance in the number of words recalled. Clearly, rehearsal type is very important in determining the number of words recalled; according to Cohen (1988), this effect size is meaningful. Lastly, for the interaction effect, $\eta^2 = 50/202 = .25$. Thus, the interaction of the Factors A and B can account for 25% of the variance in the number of words recalled. This means that knowing the individual cell or condition (in other words, the Factor A by Factor B condition) that the subjects were in can account for 25% of the variance in the dependent variable. This is also a meaningful effect size.

IN REVIEW

TWO-WAY RANDOMIZED ANOVA	
Concept	Description
Null hypothesis (H_0)	The independent variable had no effect—the samples all represent the same population. In a two-way ANOVA, there are three null hypotheses: one for Factor A, one for Factor B, and one for the interaction of A and B.
Alternative hypothesis (H_a)	The independent variable had an effect—at least one of the samples represents a different population than the others. In a two-way ANOVA, there are three alternative hypotheses: one for Factor A, one for Factor B, and one for the interaction of A and B.
F-ratio	The ratio formed when the between-groups variance is divided by the within-groups variance. In a two-way ANOVA, there are three F-ratios: one for Factor A, one for Factor B, and one for the interaction of A and B.
Between-groups variance	An estimate of the variance of the group means about the grand mean. In a two-way ANOVA, there are three types of between-groups variance: that attributable to Factor A, that attributable to Factor B, and that attributable to the interaction of A and B.
Within-groups variance	An estimate of the variance within each condition in the experiment—also known as error variance, or variance due to chance.
Eta-squared	A measure of effect size—the variability in the dependent variable attributable to the independent variable. In a two-way ANOVA, eta-squared is calculated for Factor A, for Factor B, and for the interaction of A and B.
Tukey's post hoc test	A test conducted to determine which conditions from a variable with more than two conditions differ significantly from each other.

CRITICAL THINKING CHECK 17.1

1. Assuming that there were two significant main effects in a hypothetical 2 × 4 design, would Tukey's HSD need to be calculated for these main effects? Why or why not?

2. A researcher is attempting to determine the effects of practice and gender on a timed task. Participants in the experiment were given a computerized search task. They searched a computer screen of various characters and attempted to find a particular character on each trial. When they found the designated character, they pressed a button, stopping a timer. Their reaction time (in milliseconds) on each trial was recorded. Subjects practiced for either 1, 2, or 3 hours and were either female or male. The ANOVA summary table appears below, along with the means for each condition and the number of subjects in each condition.

Two-Way ANOVA Summary Table

Source	df	SS	MS	F
Factor A (Gender)		684,264		
Factor B (Practice)		989,504		
A × B		489,104		
Error		2,967,768		
Total		5,130,640		

Condition	Mean	n
Female/1 hour	1,778.125	8
Female/2 hours	1,512.375	8
Female/3 hours	1,182.75	8
Male/1 hour	1,763.375	8
Male/2 hours	1,764.25	8
Male/3 hours	1,662	8

a. Identify the factorial notation for the design.
b. Complete the ANOVA summary table.
c. Determine significance levels for any main or interaction effect(s).
d. Explain any significant main or interaction effect(s).
e. Calculate eta-squared for any significant effects.
f. Draw a graph representing the data.

Two-Way Repeated Measures ANOVA

When a complex within-subjects (the same subjects are used in all conditions) or matched-subjects (subjects are matched across conditions) design is used, and the data collected are interval-ratio in scale, then the appropriate statistic would be a two-way repeated measures ANOVA. This

ANOVA is similar to the two-way randomized ANOVA in that it indicates whether there is a significant main effect of either independent variable in the study and whether the interaction effect is significant. However, a correlated-groups design requires slight modifications in the formulas applied. If you find yourself in a situation where it is necessary to use a two-way repeated measures ANOVA, you can find the calculations in a more advanced statistics text.

Beyond the Two-Way ANOVA

In this and the previous section, we have discussed one- and two-way ANOVAs. It is possible to add more factors (independent variables) to a study and to analyze the data with an ANOVA. For example, if a study used three independent variables, then a three-way ANOVA would be used. In this situation, there would be three main effects, three two-way interactions, and one three-way interaction to interpret. This means that there would be seven F-ratios to calculate. Obviously, this complicates the interpretation of the data considerably. Because three-way interactions are so difficult to interpret, most researchers try to design studies that are not quite so complex.

All of the studies discussed so far have had only one dependent variable. Besides adding independent variables, it is also possible to add dependent variables to a study. With one dependent variable, we use *univariate* statistics to analyze the data. Thus, all of the statistics discussed thus far in this text have been univariate statistics. When we have more than one dependent variable, we must use *multivariate* statistics to analyze the data. Many types of multivariate statistics are available, including the multivariate *t* test and the multivariate ANOVA, referred to as a *MANOVA*. These advanced statistics are beyond the scope of this book. However, should you encounter them in the literature, you can interpret them in a similar fashion to those statistics that we have covered. In other words, the larger the *t* score or *F*-ratio, the more likely it is the samples represent different populations and that the test statistic is significant.

Finally, a *meta-analysis* is a statistical procedure (also beyond the scope of this book) that combines, tests, and describes the results from many different studies. Before this technique was developed, researchers had to rely on more subjective reviews of the literature to summarize the general findings from many studies. By allowing researchers to assess the results from a large number of studies through one statistical procedure, a meta-analysis enables us to draw more objective conclusions about the generalizability of research findings.

REVIEW OF KEY TERMS

sum of squares error (p. 278)
sum of squares Factor A (p. 277)

sum of squares Factor B (p. 277)
sum of squares interaction (p. 278)

MODULE EXERCISES

(Answers to odd-numbered questions appear in Appendix B.)

1. How many possible main effects are there in a 3 × 3 factorial design? How many possible interaction effects are there in a 3 × 3 factorial design?
2. How does a two-way ANOVA differ from a one-way ANOVA?
3. If you find two significant main effects in a 2 × 6 factorial design, should you compute Tukey's post hoc comparisons for both main effects?
4. Complete each of the ANOVA summary tables below. In addition, answer the following questions for each of the ANOVA summary tables.
   a. What is the factorial notation?
   b. How many conditions were in the study?
   c. How many subjects were in the study?
   d. Identify significant main effects and interaction effects.

Source	df	SS	MS	F
A	1	60		
B	2	40		
A × B	2	90		
Error	30			
Total	35	390		

Source	df	SS	MS	F
A	2	40		
B	3	60		
A × B	6	150		
Error	72			
Total	83	400		

Source	df	SS	MS	F
A	1	10		
B	1	60		
A × B	1	20		
Error	36			
Total	39	150		

5. In a study, a researcher measures the preference of males and females for two brands of frozen pizza (one low-fat and one regular). The table below shows the preference scores on a 10-point scale for each of the 24 subjects in the study.

	Females	Males
Brand 1	3	9
(Low fat)	4	7
	2	6
	2	8
	5	9
	3	7

	Females	Males
Brand 2	8	4
(Regular)	9	2
	7	5
	10	6
	9	2
	10	5

Source	df	SS	MS	F
Gender		0.167		
Pizza Brand		6.00		
Gender × Pizza		130.67		
Error		35.00		
Total		171.83		

a. Complete the ANOVA summary table. (If your instructor wants you to calculate the sums of squares, use the above data to do so.)
b. Are the F_{obt}s significant at $\alpha = .05$? At $\alpha = .01$?
c. What conclusions can be drawn from the F-ratios?
d. What is the effect size, and what does this mean?
e. Graph the means.

6. A researcher is attempting to determine the effects of practice and gender on a timed task. Participants in an experiment were given a computerized search task. They searched a computer screen of various characters and attempted to find a particular character on each trial. When they found the designated character, they pressed a button, stopping a timer. Their reaction time (in seconds) on each trial was recorded. Participants practiced for either 2, 4, or 6 hours and were either female or male. The reaction time data for the 30 subjects appear below.

	Females	Males
2 Hours	12	11
	13	12
	12	13
	11	12
	11	11
4 Hours	10	8
	10	8
	10	10
	8	10
	7	9
6 Hours	7	5
	5	6
	7	8
	6	6
	7	8

Source	df	SS	MS	F
Gender		0.027		
Practice		140.60		
Gender × Practice		0.073		
Error		28.00		
Total		168.70		

a. Complete the ANOVA summary table. (If your instructor wants you to calculate the sums of squares, use the above data to do so.)

b. Are the F_{obt}s significant at $\alpha = .05$? At $\alpha = .01$?
c. What conclusions can be drawn from the F-ratios?
d. What is the effect size, and what does this mean?
e. Graph the means.

CRITICAL THINKING CHECK ANSWERS

Critical Thinking Check 17.1

1. Tukey's HSD would not need to be calculated for the main effect of the variable with two levels because if there is a significant main effect for a variable with two levels, we know that the difference between those two levels is significant. We would need to calculate Tukey's HSD for the variable with four levels in order to determine exactly which groups among the four differed significantly from each other.

2. a. This is a 2 × 3 design.

	Gender		Row Means
Practice	Female	Male	(Practice)
1 hour	1,778.125	1,763.375	1,770.75
2 hours	1,512.375	1,764.25	1,638.31
3 hours	1,182.75	1,662	1,422.38
Column Means (Gender)	1,491.08	1,729.88	

b. Two-Way ANOVA Summary Table

Source	df	SS	MS	F
Factor A (Gender)	1	684,264	684,264	9.68
Factor B (Practice)	2	989,504	494,752	7.00
A × B	2	489,104	244,552	3.46
Error	42	2,967,768	70,661.143	
Total	47	5,130,640		

c. Gender: $F(1, 42) = 9.68, p < .01$
   Practice: $F(2, 42) = 7.00, p < .01$
   Interaction: $F(2, 42) = 3.46, p < .05$

d. The significant main effect of gender indicates that females performed more quickly than males. The significant main effect of practice indicates that as the amount of time spent practicing increased, reaction time decreased. The significant interaction effect indicates that practice only affected females—the more females practiced, the more quickly they responded. However, practice did not affect males—reaction times for males were consistent across the various practice conditions.

e. Eta-squared was .13 for gender, .19 for practice, and .095 for the interaction. Thus, overall, the proportion of variance in the dependent variable accounted for by the independent variables is .415, or 41.5%.

f.

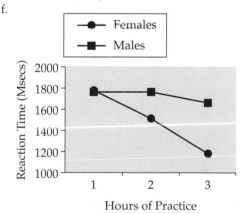

WEB RESOURCES

The book-specific website at CengageBrain.com offers students a variety of study tools and useful resources such as glossaries, flashcards, quizzes, and Statistics and Research Methods Workshops.

CHAPTER EIGHT SUMMARY AND REVIEW
Repeated Measures and Two-Factor ANOVAs

CHAPTER SUMMARY

The first module in this section discussed correlated-groups designs using more than two levels of an independent variable. Advantages to such designs include being able to compare more than two kinds of treatment, using fewer subjects and comparing all treatments to a control group. In addition, the section discussed statistical analyses most appropriate for use with these designs—most commonly, with interval-ratio data, an ANOVA. A repeated measures one-way ANOVA would be used for correlated-groups designs. Also discussed were appropriate post hoc tests (Tukey's HSD) and measures of effect size (eta-squared).

Modules 16 and 17 described designs using more than one independent variable. These modules discussed several advantages of using such designs and introduced the concepts of factorial notation, main effects, and interaction effects. After reading the description of main and interaction effects, you should be able to graph data from a factorial design and interpret what the graph means. Additional topic coverage included the statistical analysis of such designs using a two-way ANOVA. The various calculations necessary to compute a two-way randomized ANOVA were presented, along with the assumptions of the test and a description of how to interpret the results.

CHAPTER 8 REVIEW EXERCISES

(Answers to exercises appear in Appendix B.)

Fill-in Self-Test

Answer the following questions. If you have trouble answering any of the questions, restudy the relevant material before going on to the multiple-choice self-test.

1. The ANOVA for use with one independent variable and a correlated-groups design is the _____ _____.
2. The notation that indicates how many independent variables were used in a study and how many levels there were for each variable is called

   _____.
3. An effect of a single independent variable is a _____.
4. In a 4 × 6 factorial design, there are _____ independent variables, one with _____ levels and one with _____ levels.
5. In a two-way randomized ANOVA, there is the possibility for _____ main effect(s) and _____ interaction effect(s).
6. In a two-way ANOVA, the sum of the squared deviations of each score minus its condition mean is the _____.
7. In an ANOVA, we use _____ to measure effect size.

Multiple-Choice Self-Test

Select the single best answer for each of the following questions. If you have trouble answering any of the questions, restudy the relevant material.

1. One advantage of a correlated-groups design is that the effects of _____ have been removed.
   a. individual differences
   b. experimenter effects
   c. subject bias effects
   d. measurement error

2. When we manipulate more than one independent variable in a study, we
   a. will have significant main effects.
   b. will have at least one significant interaction effect.
   c. are using a factorial design.
   d. all of the above.

3. In a study examining the effects of time of day (morning, afternoon, or evening) and teaching style (lecture only versus lecture with small group discussion) on student attentiveness, how many main effects are possible?
   a. 3
   b. 6
   c. 5
   d. 2

4. In a study examining the effects of time of day (morning, afternoon, or evening) and teaching style (lecture only versus lecture with small group discussion) on student attentiveness, how many interaction effects are possible?
   a. 1
   b. 2
   c. 6
   d. 5

5. In a study examining the effects of time of day (morning, afternoon, or evening) and teaching style (lecture only versus lecture with small group discussion) on student attentiveness, the factorial notation would be
   a. 2 × 2.
   b. 2 × 3.
   c. 2 × 5.
   d. 3 × 3.

6. A 2 × 4 × 5 × 6 factorial design has _____ potential main effects.
   a. 2
   b. 3
   c. 4
   d. 24

7. An experiment with two independent variables each with three levels is a _____ design.
   a. 2 × 3
   b. 3 × 3
   c. 2 × 2 × 2
   d. 3 × 3 × 3

8. If the lines in a graph are not parallel, then there is most likely a(n)
   a. main effect of variable A.
   b. main effect of variable B.
   c. interaction effect.
   d. all of the above.

9. A two-way randomized ANOVA is to _____ as a two-way repeated measures ANOVA is to _____.
   a. two independent variables manipulated between-subjects; two dependent variables manipulated within-subjects
   b. two dependent variables manipulated between-subjects; two independent variables manipulated within-subjects
   c. two independent variables manipulated between-subjects; two independent variables manipulated within-subjects
   d. two dependent variables manipulated between-subjects; two dependent variables manipulated within-subjects

10. When the effect of one independent variable depends on the level of the other independent variable, we have observed a(n)
    a. main effect of one variable.
    b. main effect of a level of an independent variable.
    c. interaction effect.
    d. all of the above.

11. How many conditions would there be in a factorial design with three levels of Factor A and three levels of Factor B?
    a. 6
    b. 3
    c. 9
    d. Unable to determine

12. In a study with two levels of Factor A, four levels of Factor B, and five participants in each condition, the df_{Error} would be
    a. 39.
    b. 32.
    c. 8.
    d. 40.

13. In a study with two levels of Factor A, four levels of Factor B, and five participants in each condition, the dfs for Factors A and B, respectively, would be _____ and _____.
    a. 2; 4
    b. 4; 4
    c. 1; 4
    d. 1; 3

Self-Test Problems

1. The following ANOVA table corresponds to an experiment on pain reliever effectiveness. Three types of pain reliever are used (aspirin, acetaminophen, and ibuprofen), and effectiveness is rated on a 0–10 scale. The rating scores for the six subjects in each treatment follow:

   Aspirin: 4, 6, 4, 4, 3, 5   Acetaminophen: 6, 4, 6, 7, 3, 5
   Ibuprofen: 7, 6, 5, 8, 6, 5

   The sums of squares are provided in the table below. However, for practice, see if you can correctly calculate them by hand.

   ANOVA Summary Table

Source	df	SS	MS	F
Subjects		9.12		
Between		10.19		
Error		13.90		
Total				

a. Complete the ANOVA Summary Table presented above.
b. Is the F_{obt} significant at $\alpha = .05$? At $\alpha = .01$?
c. What conclusions can be drawn from the F-ratio?
d. What is the effect size, and what does this mean?
e. Graph the means.

2. The following ANOVA table corresponds to an experiment with two factors: time of day (morning, afternoon, or evening) and teaching method (lecture only or lecture with small group activities). The attention level (on a 0–10 scale) of college students during the morning, afternoon, or evening is measured in each of the teaching method conditions. This is a completely between-subjects design. The scores for the five participants in each group follow:

Lecture only/Morning: 8, 9, 9, 9, 10
Lecture only/Afternoon: 5, 6, 7, 8, 9
Lecture only/Evening: 5, 5, 6, 7, 7
Lecture and small group/Morning: 3, 4, 5, 6, 7
Lecture and small group/Afternoon: 5, 6, 6, 6, 7
Lecture and small group/Evening: 7, 7, 8, 9, 9

The sums of squares are provided in the table below. However, for practice, see if you can correctly calculate them by hand.

ANOVA Summary Table

Source	df	SS	MS	F
A (Time)		1.67		
B (Teaching Method)		7.50		
A × B		45.02		
Within		32.00		
Total				

a. Construct the matrix showing the means in each condition, and provide the factorial notation.
b. Complete the ANOVA Summary Table presented above.
c. Are the F_{obt}s significant at $\alpha = .05$? At $\alpha = .01$?
d. What conclusions can be drawn from the F-ratio?
e. What is the effect size, and what does this mean?
f. Graph the means.

CHAPTER EIGHT
Statistical Software Resources

If you need help getting started with Excel or SPSS, please see Appendix C: Getting Started with Excel and SPSS.

MODULE 15 One-Way Repeated Measures ANOVA

The problem we'll be using to illustrate how to calculate the one-way randomized ANOVA appears in Module 15.

Let's use the example from Module 15 in which a researcher wants to study the effects on memory performance of rehearsal type. Three types of rehearsal are used (rote, imagery, and story) by three different groups of subjects. The dependent variable is the subjects' scores on a 10-item test of the material. These scores are listed in Table 15.1 in Module 15.

Using Excel

We'll use the data from Table 15.1 (in Module 15) to illustrate the use of Excel to compute a one-way repeated measures ANOVA. In this study, we had subjects use one of three different types of rehearsal (rote, imagery, or story) and then had them perform a recall task. Thus we manipulated rehearsal and measured memory for the 10 words subjects studied. Because there were different subjects in each condition, we use a repeated measures ANOVA. We begin by entering the data into Excel, with the data from each condition appearing in a different column. This can be seen next.

Next, with the **Data** ribbon highlighted, click on the **Data Analysis** tab in the top right corner. You will receive the following dialog box:

Select **Anova: Two-Factor Without Replication,** as in the preceding box, and click **OK.** The following dialog box will appear:

With the cursor in the **Input Range** box, highlight the three columns of data so that they are entered into the Input Range box as they are in the preceding window. Make sure you highlight only the data in columns B, C, and D. Then click **OK.** The output from the ANOVA will appear on a new Worksheet as seen next.

| File | Home | Insert | Page Layout | Formulas | Data | Review | View |

Get External Data | Connections | Sort & Filter

| M15 | | f_x | |

◢	A	B	C	D	E	F	G	H
1	Anova: Two-Factor Without Replication							
2								
3	SUMMARY	Count	Sum	Average	Variance			
4	Row 1	3	11	3.666667	2.333333			
5	Row 2	3	8	2.666667	0.333333			
6	Row 3	3	14	4.666667	2.333333			
7	Row 4	3	16	5.333333	4.333333			
8	Row 5	3	15	5	9			
9	Row 6	3	16	5.333333	2.333333			
10	Row 7	3	24	8	4			
11	Row 8	3	18	6	7			
12								
13	Column 1	8	28	3.5	2			
14	Column 2	8	40	5	3.428571			
15	Column 3	8	54	6.75	5.071429			
16								
17								
18	ANOVA							
19	Source of Variation	SS	df	MS	F	P-value	F crit	
20	Rows	52.5	7	7.5	5	0.00514	2.764199	
21	Columns	42.33333	2	21.16667	14.11111	0.000441	3.738892	
22	Error	21	14	1.5				
23								
24	Total	115.8333	23					
25								

You can see from the ANOVA Summary Table provided by Excel that $F (2, 14) = 14.11$, $p = .000441$. In addition to the full ANOVA Summary Table, Excel also provides the mean and variance for each row (subject) and each condition. Moreover, there is also an F-score reported for the Rows term (the subjects). We report only the F-score for the Columns (this represents between-groups variance/within-groups variance)—the F-score for the Rows term can be ignored.

Using SPSS

(Please Note: In order to conduct this analysis, you need the advanced package in addition to the general SPSS package.)

We'll use the data from Table 15.1 (in Module 15) to illustrate the use of SPSS to compute a one-way repeated measures ANOVA. As in the Excel example earlier in this module, we used the same subjects in each rehearsal condition, and we therefore use a repeated measures ANOVA. We begin by entering the data into SPSS, with the data from each condition appearing in a different column. Remember that the data for each subject have to appear in a single row. To emphasize this, I've used the first column to indicate each subject in the study, followed by their data in the corresponding row.

| File | Edit | View | Data | Transform | Analyze | Direct Marketing | Graphs | Utilitie |

	Subject	Rote	Imagery	Story	var
1	1.00	2.00	4.00	5.00	
2	2.00	3.00	2.00	3.00	
3	3.00	3.00	5.00	6.00	
4	4.00	3.00	7.00	6.00	
5	5.00	2.00	5.00	8.00	
6	6.00	5.00	4.00	7.00	
7	7.00	6.00	8.00	10.00	
8	8.00	4.00	5.00	9.00	
9					

Next, click on **Analyze,** followed by **General Linear Model,** and then **Repeated Measures.** The following dialog box will be produced:

To utilize this dialog box, click in the box beneath **Within-Subject Factor Name.** This represents the independent variable in the study, so enter the name of the independent variable—in this case, Rehearsaltype. Then in the box below this, let SPSS know how many levels there are to the independent variable—in this case, three. Next click on the **Add** button, which should be active once you've accomplished the two previous steps. We now have to indicate to SPSS what the three levels of Rehearsaltype are. We do this by clicking on **Define,** which should produce the dialog box illustrated next.

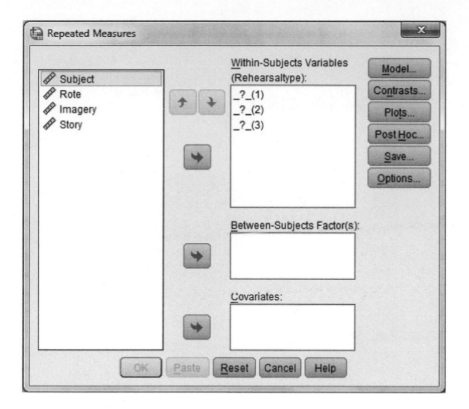

We now must enter the three levels of Rehearsaltype into slots in the **Within-Subjects Variables** box. Do this by highlighting the type of rehearsal and then utilizing the right pointing arrow to enter it into the box. Once all three levels of Rehearsaltype have been entered, click **Options.** This will produce the following dialog box:

Select **Descriptive statistics** and then tell SPSS what variable to calculate descriptive statistics on—Rehearsaltype—by moving this variable into the **Display Means for** box. Click **Continue** and then **OK.** The output will appear in the Output sheet. I included only the output necessary to interpret the ANOVA.

General Linear Model

Within-Subjects Factors

Measure:MEASURE_1

Rehearsaltype	Dependent Variable
1	Rote
2	Imagery
3	Story

Descriptive Statistics

	Mean	Std. Deviation	N
Rote	3.5000	1.41421	8
Imagery	5.0000	1.85164	8
Story	6.7500	2.25198	8

Tests of Within-Subjects Effects

Measure:MEASURE_1

Source		Type III Sum of Squares	df	Mean Square	F	Sig.
Rehearsaltype	Sphericity Assumed	42.333	2	21.167	14.111	.000
	Greenhouse-Geisser	42.333	1.943	21.791	14.111	.001
	Huynh-Feldt	42.333	2.000	21.167	14.111	.000
	Lower-bound	42.333	1.000	42.333	14.111	.007
Error(Rehearsaltype)	Sphericity Assumed	21.000	14	1.500		
	Greenhouse-Geisser	21.000	13.599	1.544		
	Huynh-Feldt	21.000	14.000	1.500		
	Lower-bound	21.000	7.000	3.000		

A legend for the three conditions appears first, followed by descriptive statistics for the three conditions. An ANOVA Summary Table follows. We are concerned only with the data reported for the rows where Sphericity is Assumed—these rows represent the standard repeated measures ANOVA. Thus, for these rows, $F(2, 14) = 14.111$, $p < .0001$.

If you look back to the previous modules that cover the one-way randomized ANOVA (Modules 13 and 14), you can see how much more powerful the repeated measures ANOVA is than the randomized ANOVA. Notice that although the total sums of squares are very similar, the resulting F-ratio for the repeated measures ANOVA is much larger (14.11 versus 11.065). If the F_{obt} is larger, there is a greater probability that it will be statistically significant. Notice also that although the data used to calculate the two ANOVAs are similar, the group means in the repeated measures ANOVA are more similar (closer together) than those from the randomized ANOVA, yet the F_{obt} from the repeated measures ANOVA is larger. Thus, with somewhat similar data, the resulting F-ratio for the repeated measures ANOVA is larger and thus affords more statistical power.

MODULES 16 AND 17 Two-way Randomized ANOVA

The problem we'll be using to illustrate how to calculate the one-way randomized ANOVA appears in Modules 16 and 17.

Using Excel

We'll use the data from Table 17.1 to illustrate the use of Excel to compute a two-way randomized ANOVA. This study is similar to the previous two studies for the one-way ANOVAs, except that we are introducing a second independent variable (word type). Thus, there are two types of rehearsal (rote versus imagery) and two word types that subjects might study (abstract versus concrete). Because we used different subjects in each condition, we use a randomized ANOVA, and because there are two independent variables, the ANOVA is two-way. We begin by entering the data into Excel, with the column headings for Word Type and the row headings for Rehearsal Type included. See the example that follows.

Next, with the **Data** ribbon highlighted, click on the **Data Analysis** tab in the top right corner. You will receive the following dialog box:

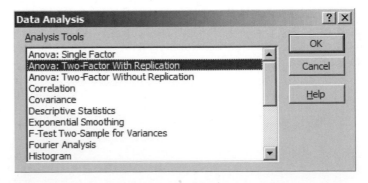

Select **Anova: Two-Factor With Replication,** as in the preceding window, and click **OK.** The following dialog box will appear:

With the cursor in the **Input Range** box, highlight the three columns of labels and data so that they are entered into the Input Range box as they are in the preceding window. Next enter the number of **Rows per sample,** which in this case is 8.Then click **OK.** The output from the ANOVA will appear on a new Worksheet as seen next.

File | Home | Insert | Page Layout | Formulas | Data | Review | View

H35

▲	A	B	C	D	E	F	G	H
1	Anova: Two-Factor With Replication							
2								
3	SUMMARY	Abstract Words	Concrete Words	Total				
4	*Rote Rehearsal*							
5	Count	8	8	16				
6	Sum	40	32	72				
7	Average	5	4	4.5				
8	Variance	0.571428571	2.571428571	1.733333				
9								
10	*Imagery Rehearsal*							
11	Count	8	8	16				
12	Sum	48	80	128				
13	Average	6	10	8				
14	Variance	0.571428571	1.428571429	5.2				
15								
16	*Total*							
17	Count	16	16					
18	Sum	88	112					
19	Average	5.5	7					
20	Variance	0.8	11.46666667					
21								
22								
23	ANOVA							
24	*Source of Variation*	*SS*	*df*	*MS*	*F*	*P-value*	*F crit*	
25	Sample	98	1	98	76.22222	1.76E-09	4.195972	
26	Columns	18	1	18	14	0.000836	4.195972	
27	Interaction	50	1	50	38.88889	9.72E-07	4.195972	
28	Within	36	28	1.285714				
29								
30	Total	202	31					
31								

In the preceding ANOVA Summary Table what is called "Sample" is the independent variable of Rehearsal Type, what is called "Columns" is the independent variable of Word Type, and the interaction is labeled as such. We see that the three F-scores are all significant. In addition, the means and variances for each condition, and summarized across conditions, are reported. Thus, there is an effect of Rehearsal Type, $F (1, 28) = 76.22$, $p = .000000002$, with subjects recalling more words in the Imagery Rehearsal condition. There is also an effect of Word Type, $F (1, 28) = 14$, $p = .0008$, with subjects recalling significantly more concrete words than abstract words. Lastly, there is an interaction effect, $F (1, 28) = 38.89$, $p = .00000097$, showing that subjects recalled abstract words somewhat similarly across the two rehearsal type conditions but that they recalled concrete words much better in the imagery rehearsal condition in comparison to the rote rehearsal condition.

Using SPSS

We'll use the data from Table 17.1 (in Module 17) to illustrate the use of SPSS to compute a two-way randomized ANOVA. We begin by entering the data into SPSS as indicated in the Data Sheet below. The first two columns indicate the condition in which the subjects served, with 1,1, indicating the Abstract Word, Rote Rehearsal condition; 1,2 the Abstract Word, Imagery Rehearsal condition; 2,1 the Concrete Word, Rote Rehearsal condition; and 2,2 the Concrete Word, Imagery Rehearsal condition. The recall data for each of the subjects in these four conditions are entered into the third column.

File Edit View Data Transform Analyze Graphs Utilities Add-ons Window Help

	Wordtype	Rehearsaltype	Wordsrecalled	var	var	var	var	var	var	var
1	1.00	1.00	5.00							
2	1.00	1.00	4.00							
3	1.00	1.00	5.00							
4	1.00	1.00	6.00							
5	1.00	1.00	4.00							
6	1.00	1.00	5.00							
7	1.00	1.00	6.00							
8	1.00	1.00	5.00							
9	1.00	2.00	6.00							
10	1.00	2.00	5.00							
11	1.00	2.00	6.00							
12	1.00	2.00	7.00							
13	1.00	2.00	6.00							
14	1.00	2.00	6.00							
15	1.00	2.00	7.00							
16	1.00	2.00	5.00							
17	2.00	1.00	4.00							
18	2.00	1.00	5.00							
19	2.00	1.00	3.00							
20	2.00	1.00	6.00							
21	2.00	1.00	2.00							
22	2.00	1.00	2.00							
23	2.00	1.00	6.00							
24	2.00	1.00	4.00							
25	2.00	2.00	10.00							
26	2.00	2.00	12.00							
27	2.00	2.00	11.00							
28	2.00	2.00	9.00							
29	2.00	2.00	8.00							
30	2.00	2.00	10.00							
31	2.00	2.00	10.00							
32	2.00	2.00	10.00							
33										
34										
35										

Data View | Variable View

Next, click on **Analyze,** followed by **General Linear Model,** and **Univariate** as indicated below.

File	Edit	View	Data	Transform	Analyze	Graphs	Utilities	Add-ons	Window	Help

	Wordtype	Rehears	Reports ▶			var
1	1.00		Descriptive Statistics ▶			
2	1.00		Compare Means ▶			
3	1.00		General Linear Model ▶	Univariate...		
4	1.00		Correlate ▶			
5	1.00		Regression ▶			
6	1.00		Classify ▶			
7	1.00		Dimension Reduction ▶			
8	1.00		Scale ▶			
9	1.00		Nonparametric Tests ▶			
10	1.00		Forecasting ▶			
			Multiple Response ▶			
			Quality Control ▶			
			ROC Curve...			
11	1.00	2.00	6.00			
12	1.00	2.00	7.00			
13	1.00	2.00	6.00			
14	1.00	2.00	6.00			
15	1.00	2.00	7.00			
16	1.00	2.00	5.00			

The following dialog box will be produced:

Enter the dependent variable (Wordsrecalled) into the **Dependent Variable** box and the two independent variables (Wordtype and Rehearsaltype) into the **Fixed Factors** box by highlighting each variable and utilizing the appropriate arrow keys. Next select **Options,** which will produce the following dialog box:

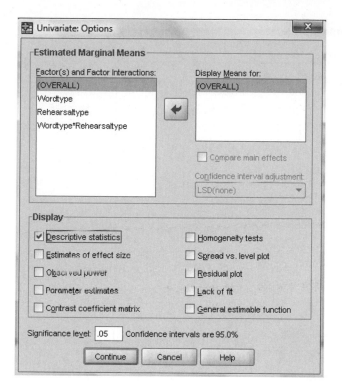

Select **Descriptive statistics,** and then tell SPSS that you want descriptive statistics on all factors by moving OVERALL into the **Display Means for** box. Click Continue and then **OK.** The output will be displayed in an Output window as seen next.

Univariate Analysis of Variance

Between-Subjects Factors

		N
Wordtype	1.00	16
	2.00	16
Rehearsaltype	1.00	16
	2.00	16

Descriptive Statistics

Dependent Variable:Wordsrecalled

Wordtype	Rehearsaltype	Mean	Std. Deviation	N
1.00	1.00	4.0000	1.60357	8
	2.00	10.0000	1.19523	8
	Total	7.0000	3.38625	16
2.00	1.00	5.0000	.75593	8
	2.00	6.0000	.75593	8
	Total	5.5000	.89443	16
Total	1.00	4.5000	1.31656	16
	2.00	8.0000	2.28035	16
	Total	6.2500	2.55267	32

Tests of Between-Subjects Effects

Dependent Variable:Wordsrecalled

Source	Type III Sum of Squares	df	Mean Square	F	Sig.
Corrected Model	166.000[a]	3	55.333	43.037	.000
Intercept	1250.000	1	1250.000	972.222	.000
Wordtype	18.000	1	18.000	14.000	.001
Rehearsaltype	98.000	1	98.000	76.222	.000
Wordtype * Rehearsaltype	50.000	1	50.000	38.889	.000
Error	36.000	28	1.286		
Total	1452.000	32			
Corrected Total	202.000	31			

[a] R Squared = .822 (Adjusted R Squared = .803)

The output begins with a legend for the variables and then is followed by descriptive statistics. The ANOVA Summary Table follows. The rows that correspond to the standard two-way ANOVA are those labeled Word-type through Total. We can see that the three F-ratios reported in these rows correspond to those from the Excel example earlier in the module, and they can be interpreted in the same manner as they were earlier (that is, there is an effect of Rehearsal Type, $F(1, 28) = 76.22$, p $= .000000002$, with subjects recalling more words in the Imagery Rehearsal condition. There is also an effect of Word Type, $F(1, 28) = 14$, $p = .0008$, with subjects recalling significantly more concrete words than abstract words. Lastly, there is an interaction effect, $F(1, 28) = 38.89$, $p = .00000097$, showing that subjects recalled abstract words somewhat similarly across the two rehearsal type conditions but that they recalled concrete words much better in the imagery rehearsal condition in comparison to the rote rehearsal condition.)

Correlational Procedures

In this chapter, we discuss correlational research methods and correlational statistics. As a research method, correlational designs allow us to describe the relationship between two measured variables. A correlation coefficient aids us by assigning a numerical value to the observed relationship. We begin with a discussion of how to conduct correlational research, the magnitude and the direction of correlations, and graphical representations of correlations. We then turn to special considerations when interpreting correlations, how to use correlations for predictive purposes, and how to calculate correlation coefficients. Lastly, we will discuss an advanced correlational technique, regression analysis.

Correlational Research

Learning Objectives
- Describe the difference between strong, moderate, and weak correlation coefficients.
- Draw and interpret scatterplots.
- Explain negative, positive, curvilinear, and no relationship between variables.
- Explain how assuming causality and directionality, the third-variable problem, restrictive ranges, and curvilinear relationships can be problematic when interpreting correlation coefficients.
- Explain how correlations allow us to make predictions.

When conducting correlational studies, researchers determine whether two naturally occurring variables (for example, height and weight, or smoking and cancer) are related to each other. Such studies assess whether the variables are "co-related" in some way—do people who are taller tend to weigh more, or do those who smoke tend to have a higher incidence of cancer? As we saw in Chapter 1, the correlational method is a type of nonexperimental method that describes the relationship between two measured variables. In addition to describing a relationship, correlations also allow us to make predictions from one variable to another. If two variables are correlated, we can predict from one variable to the other with a certain degree of accuracy. For example, knowing that height and weight are correlated would allow us to estimate, within a certain range, an individual's weight based on knowing that person's height.

Correlational studies are conducted for a variety of reasons. Sometimes it is impractical or ethically impossible to do an experimental study. For example, it would be unethical to manipulate smoking and assess whether it caused cancer in humans. How would you, as a subject in an experiment, like to be randomly assigned to the smoking condition and be told that you had to smoke a pack of cigarettes a day? Obviously, this is not a viable experiment, so one means of assessing the relationship between smoking and cancer is through correlational studies. In this type of study, we can examine people who have already chosen to smoke and assess the degree of relationship between smoking and cancer.

Magnitude, Scatterplots, and Types of Relationships

●●

Correlations vary in their **magnitude**—the strength of the relationship. Sometimes there is no relationship between variables, or the relationship may be weak; other relationships are moderate or strong. Correlations can also be represented graphically, in a scatterplot or scattergram. In addition, relationships are of different types—positive, negative, none, or curvilinear.

magnitude An indication of the strength of the relationship between two variables.

Magnitude

The magnitude or strength of a relationship is determined by the correlation coefficient describing the relationship. A **correlation coefficient** is a measure of the degree of relationship between two variables and can vary between −1.00 and +1.00. The stronger the relationship between the variables, the closer the coefficient will be to either −1.00 or +1.00. The weaker the relationship between the variables, the closer the coefficient will be to .00. We typically discuss correlation coefficients as assessing a strong, moderate, or weak relationship, or no relationship. Table 18.1 provides general guidelines for assessing the magnitude of a relationship, but these do not necessarily hold for all variables and all relationships.

A correlation of either −1.00 or +1.00 indicates a perfect correlation—the strongest relationship you can have. For example, if height and weight were perfectly correlated (+1.00) in a group of 20 people, this would mean that the person with the highest weight would also be the tallest person, the person with the second-highest weight would be the second-tallest person, and so on down the line. In addition, in a perfect relationship, each individual's score on one variable goes perfectly with his or her score on the other variable, meaning, for example, that for every increase (decrease) in height of 1 inch, there is a corresponding increase (decrease) in weight of 10 pounds. If height and weight had a perfect negative correlation (−1.00), this would mean that the person with the highest weight would be the shortest, the person with the second-highest weight would be the second shortest, and so on, and that height and weight increased (decreased) by a set amount for each individual. It is very unlikely that you will ever observe a perfect correlation between two variables, but you may observe some very strong relationships between variables (+.70−.99). Whereas a correlation coefficient of ±1.00 represents a perfect relationship, a correlation of .00 indicates no relationship between the variables.

correlation coefficient A measure of the degree of relationship between two sets of scores. It can vary between −1.00 and +1.00.

TABLE 18.1 Estimates for weak, moderate, and strong correlation coefficients

CORRELATION COEFFICIENT	STRENGTH OF RELATIONSHIP
±.70–1.00	Strong
±.30–.69	Moderate
±.00–.29	None (.00) to Weak

Scatterplots

scatterplot A figure that graphically represents the relationship between two variables.

A **scatterplot** or scattergram, a figure showing the relationship between two variables, graphically represents a correlation coefficient. Figure 18.1 presents a scatterplot of the height and weight relationship for 20 adults.

In a scatterplot, two measurements are represented for each participant by the placement of a marker. In Figure 18.1, the horizontal *x*-axis shows the participant's weight and the vertical *y*-axis shows height. The two variables could be reversed on the axes, and it would make no difference in the scatterplot. This scatterplot shows an upward trend, and the points cluster in a linear fashion. The stronger the correlation, the more tightly the data points cluster around an imaginary line through their center. When there is a perfect correlation (± 1.00), the data points all fall on a straight line. In general, a scatterplot may show four basic patterns: a positive relationship, a negative relationship, no relationship, or a curvilinear relationship.

Positive Relationships

positive correlation
A relationship between two variables in which the variables move together—an increase in one is related to an increase in the other, and a decrease in one is related to a decrease in the other.

The relationship represented in Figure 18.2a shows a **positive correlation,** one in which the two variables move in the same direction: An increase in one variable is related to an increase in the other, and a decrease in one is related to a decrease in the other. Notice that this scatterplot is similar to the one in Figure 18.1. The majority of the data points fall along an upward angle (from the lower left corner to the upper right corner). In this example, a person who scored low on one variable also scored low on the other; an individual with a mediocre score on one variable had a mediocre score on the other; and those who scored high on one variable also scored high on the other. In other words, an increase (decrease) in one variable is accompanied by an increase (decrease) in the other variable—as variable *x* increases

**FIGURE 18.1
Scatterplot for
height and weight**

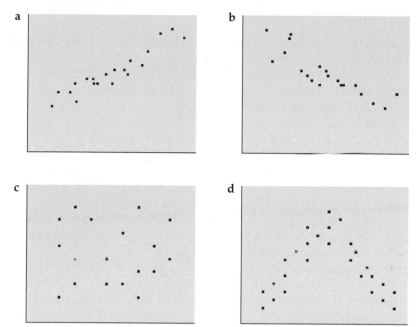

FIGURE 18.2
Possible types of correlational relationships:
(a) positive;
(b) negative;
(c) none;
(d) curvilinear

(or decreases), variable y does the same. If the data in Figure 18.2a represented height and weight measurements, we could say that those who are taller also tend to weigh more, whereas those who are shorter tend to weigh less.

Notice also that the relationship is linear: We could draw a straight line representing the relationship between the variables, and the data points would all fall fairly close to that line.

Negative Relationships

Figure 18.2b represents a negative relationship between two variables. Notice that in this scatterplot the data points extend from the upper left to the lower right. This **negative correlation** indicates that an increase in one variable is accompanied by a *decrease* in the other variable. This represents an inverse relationship: The more of variable x that we have, the less we have of variable y. Assume that this scatterplot represents the relationship between age and eyesight. As age increases, the ability to see clearly tends to decrease—a negative relationship.

No Relationship

As shown in Figure 18.2c, it is also possible to observe no relationship between two variables. In this scatterplot, the data points are scattered in a random fashion. As you would expect, the correlation coefficient for these data is very close to zero ($-.09$).

negative correlation
An inverse relationship between two variables in which an increase in one variable is related to a decrease in the other, and vice versa.

Curvilinear Relationships

A correlation of zero indicates no relationship between two variables. However, it is also possible for a correlation of zero to indicate a curvilinear relationship, illustrated in Figure 18.2d. Imagine that this graph represents the relationship between psychological arousal (the *x*-axis) and performance (the *y*-axis). Individuals perform better when they are moderately aroused than when arousal is either very low or very high. The correlation for these data is also very close to zero (−.05). Think about why this would be so. The strong positive relationship depicted in the left half of the graph essentially cancels out the strong negative relationship in the right half of the graph. Although the correlation coefficient is very low, we would not conclude that there is no relationship between the two variables. As the figure shows, the variables are very strongly related to each other in a curvilinear manner—the points are tightly clustered in an inverted U shape.

Correlation coefficients only tell us about linear relationships. Thus, even though there is a strong relationship between the two variables in Figure 18.2d, the correlation coefficient does not indicate this because the relationship is curvilinear. For this reason, it is important to examine a scatterplot of the data in addition to calculating a correlation coefficient. Alternative statistics (beyond the scope of this text) can be used to assess the degree of curvilinear relationship between two variables.

IN REVIEW

TYPES OF RELATIONSHIPS

	RELATIONSHIP TYPE			
	Positive	**Negative**	**None**	**Curvilinear**
Description of Relationship	Variables increase and decrease together	As one variable increases, the other decreases—an inverse relationship	Variables are unrelated and do not move together in any way	Variables increase together up to a point and then as one continues to increase, the other decreases
Description of Scatterplot	Data points are clustered in a linear pattern extending from lower left to upper right	Data points are clustered in a linear pattern extending from upper left to lower right	There is no pattern to the data points—they are scattered all over the graph	Data points are clustered in a curved linear pattern forming a U shape or an inverted U shape
Example of Variables Related in This Manner	Smoking and cancer	Mountain elevation and temperature	Intelligence level and weight	Memory and age

CRITICAL
THINKING
CHECK
18.1

1. Which of the following correlation coefficients represents the weakest relationship between two variables?
   −.59
   +.10
   −1.00
   +.76
2. Explain why a correlation coefficient of .00 or close to .00 may not mean that there is no relationship between the variables.
3. Draw a scatterplot representing a strong negative correlation between depression and self-esteem. Make sure you label the axes correctly.

Misinterpreting Correlations

Correlational data are frequently misinterpreted, especially when presented by newspaper reporters, talk-show hosts, or television newscasters. Here we discuss some of the most common problems in interpreting correlations. Remember, a correlation simply indicates that there is a weak, moderate, or strong relationship (either positive or negative), or no relationship, between two variables.

The Assumptions of Causality and Directionality

The most common error made when interpreting correlations is assuming that the relationship observed is causal in nature—that a change in variable A causes a change in variable B. Correlations simply identify relationships—they do not indicate causality. For example, I recently saw a commercial on television sponsored by an organization promoting literacy. The statement was made at the beginning of the commercial that a strong positive correlation has been observed between illiteracy and drug use in high school students (those high on the illiteracy variable also tended to be high on the drug-use variable). The commercial concluded with a statement like "Let's stop drug use in high school students by making sure they can all read." Can you see the flaw in this conclusion? The commercial did not air for very long, and I suspect someone pointed out the error in the conclusion.

This commercial made the error of assuming causality and also the error of assuming directionality. **Causality** refers to the assumption that the correlation indicates a causal relationship between two variables, whereas **directionality** refers to the inference made with respect to the direction of a causal relationship between two variables. For example, the commercial assumed that illiteracy was causing drug use; it claimed that if illiteracy were lowered, then drug use would be lowered also. As previously discussed, a correlation between two variables indicates only that they are related—they move together. Although it is possible that one variable causes changes in the other, you cannot draw this conclusion from correlational data.

causality The assumption that a correlation indicates a causal relationship between the two variables.

directionality The inference made with respect to the direction of a relationship between two variables.

Research on smoking and cancer illustrates this limitation of correlational data. For research with humans, we have only correlational data indicating a strong positive correlation between smoking and cancer. Because these data are correlational, we cannot conclude that there is a causal relationship. In this situation, it is probable that the relationship is causal. However, based solely on correlational data, we cannot conclude that it is causal, nor can we assume the direction of the relationship. For example, the tobacco industry could argue that, yes, there is a correlation between smoking and cancer, but maybe cancer causes smoking—maybe those individuals predisposed to cancer are more attracted to smoking cigarettes. Experimental data based on research with laboratory animals do indicate that smoking causes cancer. The tobacco industry, however, frequently denied that this research was applicable to humans and for years continued to insist that no research had produced evidence of a causal link between smoking and cancer in humans.

A classic example of the assumption of causality and directionality with correlational data occurred when researchers observed a strong negative correlation between eye movement patterns and reading ability in children. Poor readers tended to make more erratic eye movements, more movements from right to left, and more stops per line of text. Based on this correlation, some researchers assumed causality and directionality: They assumed that poor oculomotor skills caused poor reading and proposed programs for "eye movement training." Many elementary school students who were poor readers spent time in such training, supposedly developing oculomotor skills in the hope that this would improve their reading ability. Experimental research later provided evidence that the relationship between eye movement patterns and reading ability is indeed causal but that the direction of the relationship is the reverse—poor reading causes more erratic eye movements! Children who are having trouble reading need to go back over the information more and stop and think about it more. When children improve their reading skills (improve recognition and comprehension), their eye movements become smoother (Olson & Forsberg, 1993). Because of the errors of assuming causality and directionality, many children never received the appropriate training to improve their reading ability.

The Third-Variable Problem

third-variable problem
The problem of a correlation between two variables being dependent on another (third) variable.

When interpreting a correlation, it is also important to remember that although the correlation between the variables may be very strong, it may also be that the relationship is the result of some third variable that influences both of the measured variables. The **third-variable problem** results when a correlation between two variables is dependent on another (third) variable.

A good example of the third-variable problem is a well-cited study conducted by social scientists and physicians in Taiwan (Li, 1975). The researchers attempted to identify the variables that best predicted the use of birth control—a question of interest to the researchers because of overpopulation problems in Taiwan. They collected data on various behavioral and environmental variables and found that the variable most strongly correlated with contraceptive use was the number of electrical appliances (yes, electrical appliances—stereos, DVD players, televisions, and so on) in the home. If we take this correlation at face value, it means that individuals with more electrical appliances tend to use contraceptives more, whereas those with fewer electrical appliances tend to use contraceptives less.

It should be obvious to you that this is not a causal relationship (buying electrical appliances does not cause individuals to use birth control, nor does using birth control cause individuals to buy electrical appliances). Thus, we probably do not have to worry about people assuming either causality or directionality when interpreting this correlation. The problem here is that of a third variable. In other words, the relationship between electrical appliances and contraceptive use is not really a meaningful relationship—other variables are tying these two together. Can you think of other dimensions on which individuals who use contraceptives and have a large number of appliances might be similar? If you thought of education, you are beginning to understand what is meant by third variables. Individuals with a higher education level tend to be better informed about contraceptives and also tend to have a higher socioeconomic status (they get better-paying jobs). The higher socioeconomic status would allow them to buy more "things," including electrical appliances.

It is possible statistically to determine the effects of a third variable by using a correlational procedure known as **partial correlation.** This technique involves measuring all three variables and then statistically removing the effect of the third variable from the correlation of the remaining two variables. If the third variable (in this case, education) is responsible for the relationship between electrical appliances and contraceptive use, then the correlation should disappear when the effect of education is removed, or partialed out.

partial correlation
A correlational technique that involves measuring three variables and then statistically removing the effect of the third variable from the correlation of the remaining two variables.

Restrictive Range

The idea behind measuring a correlation is that we assess the degree of relationship between two variables. Variables, by definition, must vary. When a variable is truncated, we say that it has a **restrictive range**—the variable does not vary enough. Look at Figure 18.3a, which represents a scatterplot of SAT scores and college GPAs for a group of students. SAT scores and GPAs are positively correlated. Neither of these variables is restricted in range (SAT scores vary from 400 to 1,600 and GPAs vary from 1.5 to 4.0), so we have the opportunity to observe a relationship between the variables. Now look at Figure 18.3b, which represents the correlation between the same two variables, except that here we have restricted the range on the SAT variable to those who scored between 1,000 and 1,150. The variable has been restricted or truncated and does not "vary" very much. As a result, the opportunity to observe a correlation has been diminished. Even if there were a strong relationship between these variables, we could not observe it because of the restricted range of one of the variables. Thus, when interpreting and using correlations, beware of variables with restricted ranges.

restrictive range
A variable that is truncated and does not vary enough.

Curvilinear Relationships

Curvilinear relationships and the problems in interpreting them were discussed earlier in the module. Remember, correlations are a measure of linear

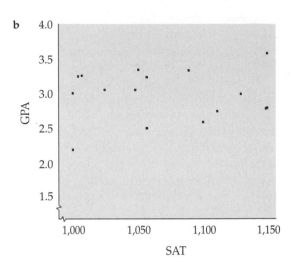

FIGURE 18.3
Restricted range and correlation

relationships. When a curvilinear relationship is present, a correlation coefficient does not adequately indicate the degree of relationship between the variables. If necessary, look back over the previous section on curvilinear relationships to refresh your memory concerning them.

IN REVIEW

MISINTERPRETING CORRELATIONS

TYPES OF MISINTERPRETATIONS

	Causality and Directionality	Third Variable	Restrictive Range	Curvilinear Relationship
Description of Misinterpretation	Assuming the correlation is causal and that one variable causes changes in the other	Other variables are responsible for the observed correlation	One or more of the variables is truncated or restricted and the opportunity to observe a relationship is minimized	The curved nature of the relationship decreases the observed correlation coefficient
Examples	Assuming that smoking causes cancer or that illiteracy causes drug abuse because a correlation has been observed	Finding a strong positive relationship between birth control and number of electrical appliances	If SAT scores are restricted (limited in range), the correlation between SAT and GPA appears to decrease	As arousal increases, performance increases up to a point; as arousal continues to increase, performance decreases

CRITICAL
THINKING
CHECK
18.2

1. I have recently observed a strong negative correlation between depression and self-esteem. Explain what this means. Make sure you avoid the misinterpretations described here.
2. General State University recently investigated the relationship between SAT scores and GPAs (at graduation) for its senior class. It was surprised to find a weak correlation between these two variables. The university knows it has a grade inflation problem (the whole senior class graduated with GPAs of 3.0 or higher), but it is unsure how this might help account for the low correlation observed. Can you explain?

Prediction and Correlation

Correlation coefficients not only describe the relationship between variables; they also allow us to make predictions from one variable to another. Correlations between variables indicate that when one variable is present at a certain level, the other also tends to be present at a certain level. Notice the wording used. The statement is qualified by the use of the phrase "tends to." We are not saying that a prediction is guaranteed, nor that the relationship is causal—but simply that the variables seem to occur together at specific levels. Think about some of the examples used previously in this module. Height and weight are positively correlated. One is not causing the other, nor can we predict exactly what an individual's weight will be based on height (or vice versa). But because the two variables are correlated, we can predict with a certain degree of accuracy what an individual's approximate weight might be if we know the person's height.

Let's take another example. We have noted a correlation between SAT scores and college freshman GPAs. Think about what the purpose of the SAT is. College admissions committees use the test as part of the admissions procedure. Why? They use it because there is a positive correlation between SAT scores and college GPAs. Individuals who score high on the SAT tend to have higher college freshman GPAs; those who score lower on the SAT tend to have lower college freshman GPAs. This means that knowing students' SAT scores can help predict, with a certain degree of accuracy, their freshman GPA and thus their potential for success in college. At this point, some of you are probably saying, "But that isn't true for me—I scored poorly (or very well) on the SAT and my GPA is great (or not so good)." Statistics only tell us what the trend is for most people in the population or sample. There will always be outliers—the few individuals who do not fit the trend. Most people, however, are going to fit the pattern.

Think about another example. We know there is a strong positive correlation between smoking and cancer, but you may know someone who has smoked for 30 or 40 years and does not have cancer or any other health problems. Does this one individual negate the fact that there is a strong relationship between smoking and cancer? No. To claim that it does would be a classic **person-who argument**—arguing that a well-established statistical trend is invalid because we know a "person who" went against the trend (Stanovich, 2007). A counterexample does not change the fact of a strong statistical relationship between the variables and that you are increasing your chance of getting cancer if you smoke. Because of the correlation between the variables, we can predict (with a fairly high degree of accuracy) who might get cancer based on knowing a person's smoking history.

person-who argument
Arguing that a well-established statistical trend is invalid because we know a "person who" went against the trend.

REVIEW OF KEY TERMS

causality (p. 317)
correlation coefficient (p. 313)
directionality (p. 317)
magnitude (p. 313)

negative correlation (p. 315)
partial correlation (p. 319)
person-who argument (p. 322)
positive correlation (p. 314)

restrictive range (p. 319)
scatterplot (p. 314)
third-variable problem (p. 318)

MODULE EXERCISES

(Answers to odd-numbered questions appear in Appendix B.)

1. A health club recently conducted a study of its members and found a positive relationship between exercise and health. It claimed that the correlation coefficient between the variables of exercise and health was +1.25. What is wrong with this statement? In addition, the club stated that this proved that an increase in exercise increases health. What is wrong with this statement?

2. Draw a scatterplot indicating a strong negative relationship between the variables of income and mental illness. Be sure to label the axes correctly.

3. Explain why the correlation coefficient for a curvilinear relationship would be close to .00.

4. Explain why the misinterpretations of causality and directionality always occur together.

5. We have mentioned several times that there is a fairly strong positive correlation between SAT scores and freshman GPAs. The admissions process for graduate school is based on a similar test, the GRE, which also has a potential 400 to 1,600 total point range. If graduate schools do not accept anyone who scores below 1,000 and if a GPA below 3.00 represents failing work in graduate school, what would we expect the correlation between GRE scores and graduate school GPAs to be like in comparison to that between SAT scores and college GPAs? Why would we expect this?

6. Why is the correlational method a predictive method? In other words, how does establishing that two variables are correlated allow us to make predictions?

CRITICAL THINKING CHECK ANSWERS

Critical Thinking Check 18.1

1. +.10
2. A correlation coefficient of .00 or close to .00 may indicate no relationship or a weak relationship. However, if the relationship is curvilinear, the correlation coefficient could also be .00 or close to it. In this case, there would be a relationship between the two variables, but because of the curvilinear nature of the relationship the correlation coefficient would not truly represent the strength of the relationship.

3.

Critical Thinking Check 18.2

1. A strong negative correlation between depression and self-esteem means that individuals who are more depressed also tend to have lower self-esteem, whereas individuals who are less depressed tend to have higher self-esteem. It does not mean that one variable causes changes in the other, but simply that the variables tend to move together in a certain manner.
2. General State University observed such a low correlation between GPAs and SAT scores because of a restrictive range on the GPA variable. Because of grade inflation, the whole senior class graduated with a GPA of 3.0 or higher. This restriction on one of the variables lessens the opportunity to observe a correlation.

WEB RESOURCES

The book-specific website at CengageBrain.com offers students a variety of study tools and useful resources such as glossaries, flashcards, quizzes, and Statistics and Research Methods Workshops.

Correlation Coefficients

Learning Objectives

- Describe when it would be appropriate to use the Pearson product-moment correlation coefficient, the Spearman rank-order correlation coefficient, the point-biserial correlation coefficient, and the phi coefficient.
- Calculate of the Pearson product-moment correlation coefficient for two variables.
- Determine and explain r^2 for a correlation coefficient.

Now that you understand how to interpret a correlation coefficient, let's turn to the actual calculation of correlation coefficients. The type of correlation coefficient used depends on the type of data (nominal, ordinal, interval, or ratio) that were collected.

The Pearson Product-Moment Correlation Coefficient: What It Is and What It Does

Pearson product-moment correlation coefficient (Pearson's *r*) The most commonly used correlation coefficient. It is used when both variables are measured on an interval or ratio scale.

The most commonly used correlation coefficient is the **Pearson product-moment correlation coefficient,** usually referred to as **Pearson's *r*** (*r* is the statistical notation we use to report correlation coefficients). Pearson's *r* is used for data measured on an interval or ratio scale of measurement. Refer back to Figure 18.1 in the previous module, which presents a scatterplot of height and weight data for 20 individuals. Because height and weight are both measured on a ratio scale, Pearson's *r* would be applicable to these data.

The development of this correlation coefficient is typically credited to Karl Pearson (hence the name), who published his formula for calculating *r* in 1895. Actually, Francis Edgeworth published a similar formula for calculating *r* in 1892. Not realizing the significance of his work, however, Edgeworth embedded the formula in a statistical paper that was very difficult to follow, and it was not noted until years later. Thus, although Edgeworth had published the formula three years earlier, Pearson received the recognition (Cowles, 1989).

Calculating the Pearson
Product-Moment Correlation

Table 19.1 presents the raw scores from which the scatterplot in Figure 18.1 (in the previous module) was derived, along with the mean and standard deviation for each distribution. Height is presented in inches and weight in pounds. Let's use these data to demonstrate the calculation of Pearson's r.

To calculate Pearson's r, we need to somehow convert the raw scores on the two different variables into the same unit of measurement. This should sound familiar to you from an earlier module. You may remember from Module 6 that we used z scores to convert data measured on different scales to standard scores measured on the same scale (a z score simply represents the number of standard deviation units a raw score is above or below the mean). Thus, high raw scores will always be above the mean and have positive z scores, and low raw scores will be below the mean and thus have negative z scores.

Think about what will happen if we convert our raw scores on height and weight over to z scores. If the correlation is strong and positive, we should find that positive z scores on one variable go with positive z scores on the other variable and negative z scores on one variable go with negative z scores on the other variable.

After calculating z scores, the next step in calculating Pearson's r is to calculate what is called a *cross-product*—the z score on one variable multiplied by the z score on the other variable. This is also sometimes referred to as a *cross-product of z scores*. Once again, think about what will happen if both z scores used to calculate the cross-product are positive—the cross-product will be positive. What if both z scores are negative? Once again, the cross-product will be positive (a negative number multiplied by a negative number results in a positive number). If we summed all of these positive cross-products and divided by the total number of cases (to obtain the average of the cross-products), we would end up with a large positive correlation coefficient.

What if we found that, when we converted our raw scores to z scores, positive z scores on one variable went with negative z scores on the other variable? These cross-products would be negative and when averaged (that is, summed and divided by the total number of cases) would result in a large negative correlation coefficient.

Lastly, imagine what would happen when there is no linear relationship between the variables being measured. In other words, some individuals who score high on one variable also score high on the other, and some individuals who score low on one variable score low on the other. Each of the previous situations results in positive cross-products. However, you also find that some individuals with high scores on one variable have low scores on the other variable, and vice versa. This would result in negative cross-products. When all of the cross-products are summed and divided by the total number of cases, the positive and negative cross-products would essentially cancel each other out, and the result would be a correlation coefficient close to zero.

TABLE 19.1 Height and weight data for 20 individuals

WEIGHT (IN POUNDS)	HEIGHT (IN INCHES)
100	60
120	61
105	63
115	63
119	65
134	65
129	66
143	67
151	65
163	67
160	68
176	69
165	70
181	72
192	76
208	75
200	77
152	68
134	66
138	65
$\mu = 149.25$	$\mu = 67.4$
$\sigma = 30.42$	$\sigma = 4.57$

TABLE 19.2 Calculating the Pearson correlation coefficient

X (WEIGHT IN POUNDS)	Y (HEIGHT IN INCHES)	Z_X	Z_Y	$Z_X Z_Y$
100	60	−1.62	−1.62	2.62
120	61	−0.96	−1.40	1.34
105	63	−1.45	−0.96	1.39
115	63	−1.13	−0.96	1.08
119	65	−0.99	−0.53	0.52
134	65	−0.50	−0.53	0.27
129	66	−0.67	−0.31	0.21
143	67	−0.21	−0.09	0.02
151	65	0.06	−0.53	−0.03
163	67	0.45	−0.09	−0.04
160	68	0.35	0.13	0.05
176	69	0.88	0.35	0.31
165	70	0.52	0.57	0.30
181	72	1.04	1.01	1.05
192	76	1.41	1.88	2.65
208	75	1.93	1.66	3.20
200	77	1.67	2.10	3.51
152	68	0.09	0.13	0.01
134	66	−0.50	−0.31	0.16
138	65	−0.37	−0.53	0.20
				$\Sigma = +18.82$

Now that you have a basic understanding of the logic behind calculating Pearson's r, let's look at the formula for Pearson's r:

$$r = \frac{\Sigma Z_X Z_Y}{N}$$

where

Σ = the summation of
Z_X = the z score for variable X for each individual
Z_Y = the z score for variable Y for each individual
N = the number of individuals in the sample

Thus, we begin by calculating the z scores for X (weight) and Y (height). This is shown in Table 19.2. Remember, the formula for a z score is

$$z = \frac{X - \mu}{\sigma}$$

where

> X = each individual score
> μ = the population mean
> σ = the population standard deviation

The first two columns in Table 19.2 list the height and weight raw scores for the 20 individuals. As a general rule of thumb, when calculating a correlation coefficient, you should have at least 10 subjects per variable; with two variables, we need a minimum of 20 individuals, which we have. Following the raw scores for variable X (weight) and variable Y (height) are columns representing Z_X, Z_Y, and $Z_X Z_Y$ (the cross-product of z scores). The cross-products column has been summed (Σ) at the bottom of the table.

Now, let's use the information from the table to calculate r:

$$r = \frac{\Sigma Z_X Z_Y}{N} = \frac{18.82}{20} = +.94$$

Interpreting the Pearson Product-Moment Correlation ●●

The obtained correlation between height and weight for the 20 individuals represented in the table is +.94. Can you interpret this correlation coefficient? The positive sign tells us that the variables increase and decrease together. The large magnitude (close to 1.00) tells us that there is a strong positive relationship between height and weight. However, we can also determine whether this correlation coefficient is statistically significant, as we have done with other statistics. The null hypothesis (H_0) when we are testing a correlation coefficient is that the true population correlation coefficient is .00—the variables are not related. The alternative hypothesis (H_a) is that the observed correlation is not equal to .00—the variables are related. In order to test the null hypothesis that the population correlation coefficient is .00, we must consult a table of critical values for r (the Pearson product-moment correlation coefficient). Table A.5 in Appendix A shows critical values for both one- and two-tailed tests of r. A one-tailed test of a correlation coefficient means that you have predicted the expected direction of the correlation coefficient, whereas a two-tailed test means that you have not predicted the direction of the correlation coefficient.

To use this table, we first need to determine the degrees of freedom, which for the Pearson product-moment correlation are equal to $N - 2$, where N represents the total number of pairs of observations. Our correlation coefficient of +.94 is based on 20 pairs of observations; thus, the degrees of freedom are $20 - 2 = 18$. Once the degrees of freedom have been determined, we can consult the critical values table. For 18 degrees of freedom and a one-tailed test (the test is one-tailed because we expect a positive relationship between height and weight) at $\alpha = .05$, the r_{cv} is ±.3783. This means that our r_{obt} must be that large or larger in order to be statistically significant at the .05 level. Because our r_{obt} is that large, we would reject H_0. In other words, the observed correlation coefficient is statistically significant, and we can conclude that those who are taller tend to weigh significantly more, whereas those who are shorter tend to weigh significantly less.

Because r_{obt} was significant at the .05 level, we should check for significance at the .025 and .005 levels provided in Table A.5. Our r_{obt} of $+.94$ is larger than the critical values at all of the levels of significance provided in Table A.5. In APA publication format, this would be reported as $r(18) = +.94, p < .005$, one-tailed. You can see how to use either Excel, SPSS, or the TI-84 calculator to calculate Pearson's r in the Statistical Software Resources section at the end of this chapter.

In addition to interpreting the correlation coefficient, it is important to calculate the **coefficient of determination (r^2)**. Calculated by squaring the correlation coefficient, the coefficient of determination is a measure of the proportion of the variance in one variable that is accounted for by another variable. In our group of 20 individuals, there is variation in both the height and weight variables, and some of the variation in one variable can be accounted for by the other variable. We could say that the variation in the weights of these 20 individuals can be explained by the variation in their heights. Some of the variation in their weights, however, cannot be explained by the variation in height. It might be explained by other factors such as genetic predisposition, age, fitness level, or eating habits. The coefficient of determination tells us how much of the variation in weight is accounted for by the variation in height. Squaring the obtained correlation coefficient of $+.94$, we have $r^2 = .8836$. We typically report r^2 as a percentage. Hence, 88.36% of the variance in weight can be accounted for by the variance in height—a very high coefficient of determination. Depending on the research area, the coefficient of determination could be much lower and still be important. It is up to the researcher to interpret the coefficient of determination accordingly.

coefficient of determination (r^2)
A measure of the proportion of the variance in one variable that is accounted for by another variable; calculated by squaring the correlation coefficient.

Alternative Correlation Coefficients

As noted previously, the type of correlation coefficient used depends on the type of data collected in the research study. Pearson's correlation coefficient is used when both variables are measured on an interval or ratio scale. Alternative correlation coefficients can be used with ordinal and nominal scales of measurement. We will mention three such correlation coefficients but will not present the formulas because our coverage of statistics is necessarily selective. All of the formulas are based on Pearson's formula and can be found in a more advanced statistics text. Each of these coefficients is reported on a scale of -1.00 to $+1.00$. Thus, each is interpreted in a fashion similar to Pearson's r. Lastly, as with Pearson's r, the coefficient of determination (r^2) can be calculated for each of these correlation coefficients to determine the proportion of variance in one variable accounted for by the other variable.

When one or more of the variables is measured on an ordinal (ranking) scale, the appropriate correlation coefficient is **Spearman's rank-order correlation coefficient.** If one of the variables is interval or ratio in nature, it must be ranked (converted to an ordinal scale) before you do the calculations. If one of the variables is measured on a dichotomous (having only two possible values, such as gender) nominal scale and the other is measured on

Spearman's rank-order correlation coefficient
The correlation coefficient used when one or more of the variables is measured on an ordinal (ranking) scale

an interval or ratio scale, the appropriate correlation coefficient is the **point-biserial correlation coefficient.** Lastly, if both variables are dichotomous and nominal, the **phi coefficient** is used.

Although both the point-biserial and phi coefficients are used to calculate correlations with dichotomous nominal variables, you should refer back to one of the cautions mentioned in the previous module concerning potential problems when interpreting correlation coefficients—specifically, the caution regarding restricted ranges. Clearly, a variable with only two levels has a restricted range. Can you think about what the scatterplot for such a correlation would look like? The points would have to be clustered into columns or groups, depending on whether one or both of the variables were dichotomous.

point-biserial correlation coefficient The correlation coefficient used when one of the variables is measured on a dichotomous nominal scale and the other is measured on an interval or ratio scale.

phi coefficient The correlation coefficient used when both measured variables are dichotomous and nominal.

CORRELATION COEFFICIENTS

IN REVIEW

TYPES OF COEFFICIENTS

	Pearson	**Spearman**	**Point-Biserial**	**Phi**
Type of Data	Both variables must be interval or ratio	Both variables are ordinal (ranked)	One variable is interval or ratio, and one variable is nominal and dichotomous	Both variables are nominal and dichotomous
Correlation Reported as	±.00–1.0	±.00–1.0	±.00–1.0	±.00–1.0
r^2 Applicable?	Yes	Yes	Yes	Yes

CRITICAL THINKING CHECK 19.1

1. Professor Hitch found that the Pearson product-moment correlation between the height and weight of the 32 students in her class was +.35. Using Table A.5 in Appendix A, for a one-tailed test, determine whether this is a significant correlation coefficient. Determine the coefficient of determination for the correlation coefficient, and explain what it means.
2. In a recent study, researchers were interested in determining the relationship between gender and amount of time spent studying for a group of college students. Which correlation coefficient should be used to assess this relationship?

REVIEW OF KEY TERMS

coefficient of determination (r^2) (p. 328)

Pearson product-moment correlation coefficient (Pearson's r) (p. 324)

phi coefficient (p. 329)

point-biserial correlation coefficient (p. 329)

Spearman's rank-order correlation coefficient (p. 328)

MODULE EXERCISES

(Answers to odd-numbered questions appear in Appendix B.)

1. Explain when the Pearson product-moment correlation coefficient should be used.
2. In a study of caffeine and stress, college students indicate how many cups of coffee they drink per day and their stress level on a scale of 1 to 10. The data follow:

Number of Cups of Coffee	Stress Level
3	5
2	3
4	3
6	9
5	4
1	2
7	10
3	5

Calculate a Pearson's r to determine the type and strength of the relationship between caffeine and stress level.
3. How much of the variability in stress scores in exercise 2 is accounted for by the number of cups of coffee consumed per day?
4. Given the following data, determine the correlation between IQ scores and psychology exam scores, between IQ scores and statistics exam scores, and between psychology exam scores and statistics exam scores.

Student	IQ Score	Psychology Exam Score	Statistics Exam Score
1	140	48	47
2	98	35	32
3	105	36	38
4	120	43	40
5	119	30	40
6	114	45	43
7	102	37	33
8	112	44	47
9	111	38	46
10	116	46	44

5. Calculate the coefficient of determination for each of the correlation coefficients in exercise 4, and explain what these mean.
6. Explain when it would be appropriate to use the phi coefficient versus the point-biserial coefficient.
7. If one variable is ordinal and the other is interval-ratio, which correlation coefficient should be used?

CRITICAL THINKING CHECK ANSWERS

Critical Thinking Check 19.1

1. Yes. For a one-tailed test, $r(30) = .35, p < .025$. The coefficient of determination (r^2) = .1225. This means that height can explain 12.25% of the variance observed in the weight of these individuals.

2. In this study, gender is nominal in scale, and the amount of time spent studying is ratio in scale. Thus, a point-biserial correlation coefficient would be appropriate.

WEB RESOURCES

The book-specific website at CengageBrain.com offers students a variety of study tools and useful resources such as glossaries, flashcards, quizzes, and Statistics and Research Methods Workshops.

Advanced Correlational Techniques: Regression Analysis

Learning Objectives

- Explain what regression analysis is.
- Determine the regression line for two variables.

As we have seen, the correlational procedure allows us to predict from one variable to another, and the degree of accuracy with which you can predict depends on the strength of the correlation. A tool that enables us to predict an individual's score on one variable based on knowing one or more other variables is known as **regression analysis**. For example, imagine that you are an admissions counselor at a university and you want to predict how well a prospective student might do at your school based on both SAT scores and high school GPA. Or imagine that you work in a human resources office and you want to predict how well future employees might perform based on test scores and performance measures. Regression analysis allows you to make such predictions by developing a regression equation.

To illustrate regression analysis, let's use the height and weight data presented in Table 20.1. When we used these data to calculate Pearson's r (in Module 19), we determined that the correlation coefficient was +.94. Also, we can see in Figure 18.1 (in Module 18) that there is a linear relationship between the variables, meaning that a straight line can be drawn through the data to represent the relationship between the variables. This **regression line** is shown in Figure 20.1; it represents the relationship between height and weight for this group of individuals.

regression analysis
A procedure that allows us to predict an individual's score on one variable based on knowing one or more other variables.

regression line The best-fitting straight line drawn through the center of a scatterplot that indicates the relationship between the variables.

Regression Lines

Regression analysis involves determining the equation for the best-fitting line for a data set. This equation is based on the equation for representing a line you may remember from algebra class: $y = mx + b$, where m is the slope of the line and b is the y-intercept (the place where the line crosses the

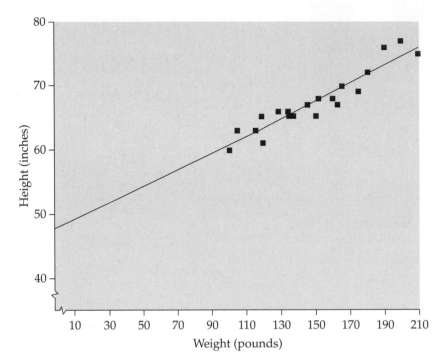

FIGURE 20.1
The relationship between height and weight, with the regression line indicated

TABLE 20.1 Height and weight data for 20 individuals

WEIGHT(IN POUNDS)	HEIGHT (IN INCHES)
100	60
120	61
105	63
115	63
119	65
134	65
129	66
143	67
151	65
163	67
160	68
176	69
165	70
181	72
192	76
208	75
200	77
152	68
134	66
138	65
$\mu = 149.25$	$\mu = 67.4$
$\sigma = 30.42$	$\sigma = 4.57$

y-axis). For a linear regression analysis, the formula is essentially the same, although the symbols differ:

$$Y' = bX + a$$

where Y' is the predicted value on the Y variable, b is the slope of the line, X represents an individual's score on the X variable, and a is the y-intercept.

Using this formula, then, we can predict an individual's approximate score on variable Y based on that person's score on variable X. With the height and weight data, for example, we could predict an individual's approximate height based on knowing the person's weight. You can picture what we are talking about by looking at Figure 20.1 Given the regression line in Figure 20.1, if we know an individual's weight (read from the x-axis), we can then predict the person's height (by finding the corresponding value on the y-axis).

Calculating the Slope and y-intercept

To use the regression line formula, we need to determine both b and a. Let's begin with the slope (b). The formula for computing b is

$$b = r\left[\frac{\sigma_Y}{\sigma_X}\right]$$

This should look fairly simple to you. We have already calculated r in the previous module (+.94) and the standard deviations (σ) for both height and weight (see Table 20.1). Using these calculations, we can compute b as follows:

$$b = .94\left[\frac{4.57}{30.42}\right] = .94(0.150) = 0.141$$

Now that we have computed b, we can compute a. The formula for a is

$$a = \overline{Y} - b(\overline{X})$$

Once again, this should look fairly simple, because we have just calculated b, and $\overline{Y}$ and $\overline{X}$ (the means for the Y and X variables—height and weight, respectively) are presented in Table 20.1. Using these values in the formula for a, we have

$$a = 67.40 - 0.141(149.25)$$
$$= 67.40 - 21.04$$
$$= 46.36$$

Thus, the regression equation for the line for the data in Figure 20.1 is

$$Y' \text{ (height)} = 0.141X \text{ (weight)} + 46.36$$

where 0.141 is the slope and 46.36 is the y-intercept.

Prediction and Regression

Now that we have calculated the equation for the regression line, we can use this line to predict from one variable to another. For example, if we know that an individual weighs 110 pounds, we can predict the person's height using this equation:

$$Y' = 0.141(110) + 46.36$$
$$= 15.51 + 46.36$$
$$= 61.87 \text{ inches}$$

Let's make another prediction using this regression line. If someone weighs 160 pounds, what would we predict their height to be? Using the regression equation, this would be

$$Y' = 0.141(160) + 46.36$$
$$= 22.561 + 46.36$$
$$= 68.92 \text{ inches}$$

As we can see, determining the regression equation for a set of data allows us to predict from one variable to the other. The stronger the relationship between the variables (that is, the stronger the correlation coefficient), the more accurate the prediction will be. The calculations for regression analysis using Excel, SPSS and the TI-84 calculator are presented in the Statistical Software Resources section at the end of this chapter.

Multiple Regression Analysis ●●

A more advanced use of regression analysis is known as *multiple regression analysis.* Multiple regression analysis involves combining several predictor variables into a single regression equation. This is analogous to the factorial ANOVAs we discussed in Modules 16 and 17, in that we can assess the effects of multiple predictor variables (rather than a single predictor variable) on the dependent measure. In our height and weight example, we attempted to predict an individual's height based on knowing the person's weight. There might be other variables we could add to the equation that would increase our predictive ability. For example, if, in addition to the individual's weight, we knew the height of the biological parents, this might increase our ability to accurately predict the person's height.

When using multiple regression, the predicted value of Y' represents the linear combination of all the predictor variables used in the equation. The rationale behind using this more advanced form of regression analysis is that in the real world it is unlikely that one variable is affected by only one other variable. In other words, real life involves the interaction of many variables on other variables. Thus, in order to more accurately predict variable A, it makes sense to consider all possible variables that might influence variable A. In terms of our example, it is doubtful that height is influenced only by weight. There are many other variables that might help us to predict height, such as the variable just mentioned—the height of each biological parent. The calculation of multiple regression is beyond the scope of this book. For further information on it, consult a more advanced statistics text.

IN REVIEW

REGRESSION ANALYSIS	
Concept	**What It Does**
Regression Analysis	A tool that enables one to predict an individual's score on one variable based on knowing one or more other variables
Regression Line	The equation for the best-fitting line for a data set. The equation is based on determining the slope and y-intercept for the best-fitting line and is as follows: $Y' = bX + a$, where Y' is the predicted value on the Y variable, b is the slope of the line, X represents an individual's score on the X variable, and a is the y-intercept
Multiple Regression	A type of regression analysis that involves combining several predictor variables into a singe regression equation

1. How does determining a best-fitting line help us to predict from one variable to another?
2. For the example in the text, if an individual's weight was 125 pounds, what would the predicted height be?

CRITICAL THINKING CHECK 20.1

REVIEW OF KEY TERMS

regression analysis (p. 331)   regression line (p. 331)

MODULE EXERCISES

(Answers to odd-numbered questions appear in Appendix B.)

1. What is a regression analysis and how does it allow us to make predictions from one variable to another?
2. In a study of caffeine and stress, college students indicate how many cups of coffee they drink per day and their stress level on a scale of 1 to 10. The data follow:

Number of Cups of Coffee	Stress Level
3	5
2	3
4	3
6	9
5	4
1	2
7	10
3	5

Determine the regression equation for this correlation coefficient.
3. Given the following data, determine the regression equation for IQ scores and psychology exam scores, IQ scores and statistics exam scores, and psychology exam scores and statistics exam scores.

Student	IQ Score	Psychology Exam Score	Statistics Exam Score
1	140	48	47
2	98	35	32
3	105	36	38
4	120	43	40
5	119	30	40
6	114	45	43
7	102	37	33
8	112	44	47
9	111	38	46
10	116	46	44

4. Assuming that the regression equation for the relationship between IQ score and psychology exam score is $Y' = .274X + 9$, what would you expect the psychology exam score to be for the following individuals, given their IQ exam score?

Individual	IQ Score (X)	Psychology Exam Score (Y')
Tim	118	
Tom	98	
Tina	107	
Tory	103	

CRITICAL THINKING CHECK ANSWERS

Critical Thinking Check 20.1

1. The best-fitting line is the line that comes closest to all of the data points in a scatterplot. Given this line, we can predict from one variable to another by determining where on the line an individual's score on one variable lies and then determining what the score would be on the other variable based on this.

2. If an individual weighed 125 pounds and we used the regression line determined in this module to predict height, then

$$Y' = 0.141(125) + 46.36$$
$$= 17.625 + 46.36$$
$$= 63.985 \text{ inches}$$

WEB RESOURCES

The book-specific website at CengageBrain.com offers students a variety of study tools and useful resources such as glossaries, flashcards, quizzes, and Statistics and Research Methods Workshops.

CHAPTER NINE SUMMARY AND REVIEW
Correlational Procedures

CHAPTER SUMMARY

After reading this chapter, you should have an understanding of correlational research, which allows researchers to observe relationships between variables; correlation coefficients, the statistics that assess that relationship; and regression analysis, a procedure that allows us to predict from one variable to another. Correlations vary in type (positive or negative) and magnitude (weak, moderate, or strong). The pictorial representation of a correlation is a scatterplot. Scatterplots allow us to see the relationship, facilitating its interpretation

When interpreting correlations, several errors are commonly made. These include assuming causality and directionality, the third-variable problem, having a restrictive range on one or both variables, and the problem of assessing a curvilinear relationship. Knowing that two variables are correlated allows researchers to make predictions from one variable to another.

Four different correlation coefficients (Pearson's, Spearman's, point-biserial, and phi) and when each should be used were discussed. The coefficient of determination was also discussed with respect to more fully understanding correlation coefficients. Lastly, regression analysis, which allows us to predict from one variable to another, was described.

CHAPTER 9 REVIEW EXERCISES

(Answers to exercises appear in Appendix B.)

Fill-in Self-Test

Answer the following questions. If you have trouble answering any of the questions, restudy the relevant material before going on to the multiple-choice self-test.

1. A _____ is a figure that graphically represents the relationship between two variables.
2. When an increase in one variable is related to a decrease in the other variable, and vice versa, we have observed an inverse or _____ relationship.
3. When we assume that because we have observed a correlation between two variables, one variable must be causing changes in the other variable, we have made the errors of _____ and _____.
4. A variable that is truncated and does not vary enough is said to have a

_____.
5. The _____ correlation coefficient is used when both variables are measured on an interval-ratio scale.
6. The _____ correlation coefficient is used when one variable is measured on an interval-ratio scale and the other on a nominal scale.

7. To measure the proportion of variance in one of the variables accounted for by the other variable, we use the _____.

8. _____ is a procedure that allows us to predict an individual's score on one variable based on knowing the person's score on a second variable.

Multiple-Choice Self-Test

Select the single best answer for each of the following questions. If you have trouble answering any of the questions, restudy the relevant material.

1. The magnitude of a correlation coefficient is to _____ as the type of correlation is to _____.
   a. absolute value; slope
   b. sign; absolute value
   c. absolute value; sign
   d. none of the above

2. Strong correlation coefficient is to weak correlation coefficient as _____ is to _____.
   a. −1.00; +1.00
   b. −1.00; +.10
   c. +1.00; −1.00
   d. +.10; −1.00

3. Which of the following correlation coefficients represents the variables with the weakest degree of relationship?
   a. +.89
   b. −1.00
   c. +.10
   d. −.47

4. A correlation coefficient of +1.00 is to _____ as a correlation coefficient of −1.00 is to _____.
   a. no relationship; weak relationship
   b. weak relationship; perfect relationship
   c. perfect relationship; perfect relationship
   d. perfect relationship; no relationship

5. If the points on a scatterplot are clustered in a pattern that extends from the upper left to the lower right, this would suggest that the two variables depicted are
   a. normally distributed.
   b. positively correlated.
   c. regressing toward the average.
   d. negatively correlated.

6. We would expect the correlation between height and weight to be _____, whereas we would expect the correlation between age in adults and hearing ability to be _____.
   a. curvilinear; negative
   b. positive; negative
   c. negative; positive
   d. positive; curvilinear

7. When we argue against a statistical trend based on one case, we are using a
   a. third variable.
   b. regression analysis.
   c. partial correlation.
   d. person-who argument.

8. If a relationship is curvilinear, we would expect the correlation coefficient to be
   a. close to .00.
   b. close to +1.00.

c. close to -1.00.

d. an accurate representation of the strength of the relationship.

9. The _____ is the correlation coefficient that should be used when both variables are measured on an ordinal scale.

a. Spearman rank-order correlation coefficient

b. coefficient of determination

c. point-biserial correlation coefficient

d. Pearson product-moment correlation coefficient

10. Suppose that the correlation between age and hearing ability for adults is $-.65$. What proportion (or percentage) of the variability in hearing ability is accounted for by the relationship with age?

a. 65%

b. 35%

c. 42%

d. unable to determine

11. Drew is interested in assessing the degree of relationship between belonging to a Greek organization and number of alcoholic drinks consumed per week. Drew should use the _____ correlation coefficient to assess this.

a. partial

b. point-biserial

c. phi

d. Pearson product-moment

12. Regression analysis allows us to

a. predict an individual's score on one variable based on knowing the person's score on another variable.

b. determine the degree of relationship between two interval-ratio variables.

c. determine the degree of relationship between two nominal variables.

d. predict an individual's score on one variable based on knowing that the variable is interval-ratio in scale.

Self-Test Problem

1. Professor Mumblemore wants to determine the degree of relationship between students' scores on their first and second exams in his chemistry class. The scores received by students on the first and second exams follow:

Student	Score on Exam 1	Score on Exam 2
Sarah	81	87
Ned	74	82
Tim	65	62
Lisa	92	86
Laura	69	75
George	55	70
Tara	89	75
Melissa	84	87
Justin	65	63
Chang	76	70

Calculate a Pearson's r to determine the type and strength of the relationship between exam scores. How much of the variability in Exam 2 is accounted for by knowing an individual's score on Exam 1? Determine the regression equation for this correlation coefficient.

CHAPTER NINE
Statistical Software Resources

If you need help getting started with Excel or SPSS, please see Appendix C: Getting Started with Excel and SPSS.

MODULE 19 Correlation Coefficients

The data we'll be using to illustrate how to calculate correlation coefficients are the weight and height data presented in Table 19.1 in Module 19.

Using Excel

To illustrate how Excel can be used to calculate a correlation coefficient, let's use the data from Table 19.1, on which we will calculate Pearson's product-moment correlation coefficient. In order to do this, we begin by entering the data from Table 19.1 into Excel. The following figure illustrates this—the weight data were entered into column A and the height data into column B.

	A	B	C
1	100	60	
2	120	61	
3	105	63	
4	115	63	
5	119	65	
6	134	65	
7	129	66	
8	143	67	
9	151	65	
10	163	67	
11	160	68	
12	176	69	
13	165	70	
14	181	72	
15	192	76	
16	208	75	
17	200	77	
18	152	68	
19	134	66	
20	138	65	
21			

Next, with the **Data** ribbon active, as in the preceding window, click on **Data Analysis** in the upper right corner. The following dialog box will appear:

Highlight **Correlation,** and then click **OK.** The subsequent dialog box will appear.

With the cursor in the **Input Range** box, highlight the data in columns A and B and click **OK.** The output worksheet generated from this is very small and simply reports the correlation coefficient of +.94, as seen next.

Using SPSS

To illustrate how SPSS can be used to calculate a correlation coefficient, let's use the data from Table 19.1, on which we will calculate Pearson's product-moment correlation coefficient, just as we did earlier. In order to do this, we begin by entering the data from Table 19.1 into SPSS. The following figure illustrates this—the weight data were entered into column A and the height data into column B.

File	Edit	View	Data	Transform	Analyze	Graphs	Utilities	Ad

	Weight	Height	var	var
1	100.00	60.00		
2	120.00	61.00		
3	105.00	63.00		
4	115.00	63.00		
5	119.00	65.00		
6	134.00	65.00		
7	129.00	66.00		
8	143.00	67.00		
9	151.00	65.00		
10	163.00	67.00		
11	160.00	68.00		
12	176.00	69.00		
13	165.00	70.00		
14	181.00	72.00		
15	192.00	76.00		
16	208.00	75.00		
17	200.00	77.00		
18	152.00	68.00		
19	134.00	66.00		
20	138.00	65.00		
21				

Next, click on **Analyze,** followed by **Correlate,** and then **Bivariate.** The dialog box that follows will be produced.

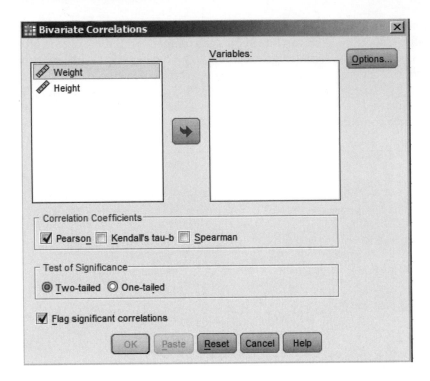

Move the two variables you want correlated (Weight and Height) into the **Variables** box. In addition, click **One-tailed** because this was a one-tailed test, and lastly, click on **Options** and select **Means and standard deviations,** thus letting SPSS know that you want descriptive statistics on the two variables. The dialog box should now appear as follows:

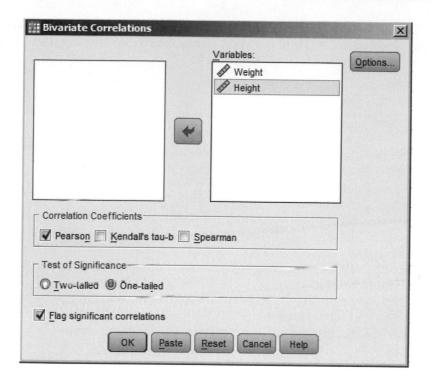

Click **OK** to receive the following output:

Correlations

Descriptive Statistics

	Mean	Std. Deviation	N
Weight	149.2500	31.21213	20
Height	67.4000	4.68368	20

Correlations

		Weight	Height
Weight	Pearson Correlation	1	.941**
	Sig. (2-tailed)		.000
	N	20	20
Height	Pearson Correlation	.941**	1
	Sig. (2-tailed)	.000	
	N	20	20

** Correlation is significant at the 0.01 level (2-tailed).

The correlation coefficient of +.941 is provided along with the one-tailed significance level and the mean and standard deviation for each of the variables.

Using the TI-84

Let's use the data from Table 19.1 to conduct the analysis using the TI-84 calculator.

1. With the calculator on, press the STAT key.
2. EDIT will be highlighted. Press the ENTER key.
3. Under L1 enter the weight data from Table 19.1.
4. Under L2 enter the height data from Table 19.1.
5. Press the 2nd key and 0 [catalog] and scroll down to DiagnosticOn and press ENTER. Press ENTER once again. (The message DONE should appear on the screen.)
6. Press the STAT key and highlight CALC. Scroll down to 8:LinReg(a+bx) and press ENTER.
7. Type L1 (by pressing the 2nd key followed by the 1 key) followed by a comma and L2 (by pressing the 2nd key followed by the 2 key) next to LinReg(a+bx). It should appear as follows on the screen: LinReg(a+bx) L1,L2.
8. Press ENTER.

The values of a (46.31), b (.141), r^2 (.89), and r (.94) should appear on the screen. You can see that r (the correlation coefficient) is the same as that calculated by Excel and SPSS.

MODULE 20 Regression Analysis

The data we'll be using to illustrate how to calculate a regression analysis are the weight and height data presented in Table 20.1, Module 20.

Using Excel

To illustrate how Excel can be used to calculate a regression analysis, let's use the data from Table 20.1, on which we will calculate a regression line. In order to do this, we begin by entering the data from Table 20.1 into Excel. The following figure illustrates this—the weight data were entered into column A and the height data into column B:

Next, with the **Data** ribbon active, as in the preceding window, click on **Data Analysis** in the upper right corner. The following drop-down box will appear:

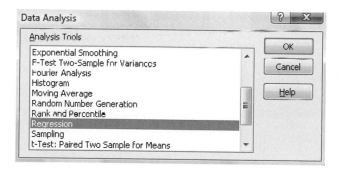

Highlight **Regression,** and then click **OK.** The dialog box that follows will appear.

With the cursor in the **Input Y Range** box, highlight the height data in column B so that it appears in the Input Y Range box. Do the same with the **Input X Range** box and the data from column A (we place the height data in the Y box because this is what we are predicting—height—based on knowing one's weight). Then click **OK**. The following output will be produced:

	A	B	C	D	E	F	G	H	I	J
1	SUMMARY OUTPUT									
2										
3	*Regression Statistics*									
4	Multiple R	0.941472332								
5	R Square	0.886370152								
6	Adjusted R Squ	0.880057383								
7	Standard Error	1.622085773								
8	Observations	20								
9										
10	ANOVA									
11		*df*	*SS*	*MS*	*F*	*Significance F*				
12	Regression	1	369.4390794	369.4391	140.4091	6.1824E-10				
13	Residual	18	47.3609206	2.631162						
14	Total	19	416.8							
15										
16		*Coefficients*	*Standard Error*	*t Stat*	*P-value*	*Lower 95%*	*Upper 95%*	*Lower 95.0%*	*Upper 95.0%*	
17	Intercept	46.31442348	1.816048149	25.50286	1.4E-15	42.4990479	50.1297991	42.4990479	50.12979906	
18	X Variable 1	0.141276895	0.01192267	11.84943	6.18E-10	0.11622829	0.1663255	0.11622829	0.166325496	
19										

We are primarily interested in the data necessary to create the regression line—the Y-intercept and the slope. This can be found on lines 17 and 18 of the output worksheet in the first column labeled Coefficients. We see that the Y-intercept is 46.31 and the slope is .141. Thus, the regression equation would be $Y' = .141(X) + 46.31$.

Using SPSS

To illustrate how SPSS can be used to calculate a regression analysis, let's again use the data from Table 20.1, on which we will calculate a regression line, just as we did with Excel. In order to do this, we begin by entering the data from Table 20.1 into SPSS. The following figure illustrates this—the data were entered just as they were when we used SPSS to calculate a correlation coefficient in Module 20.

| File | Edit | View | Data | Transform | Analyze | Graphs | Utilities | Ad |

	Weight	Height	var	var
1	100.00	60.00		
2	120.00	61.00		
3	105.00	63.00		
4	115.00	63.00		
5	119.00	65.00		
6	134.00	65.00		
7	129.00	66.00		
8	143.00	67.00		
9	151.00	65.00		
10	163.00	67.00		
11	160.00	68.00		
12	176.00	69.00		
13	165.00	70.00		
14	181.00	72.00		
15	192.00	76.00		
16	208.00	75.00		
17	200.00	77.00		
18	152.00	68.00		
19	134.00	66.00		
20	138.00	65.00		
21				

Next, click on **Analyze**, followed by **Regression**, and then **Linear**, as in the following window:

File	Edit	View	Data	Transform	Analyze	Graphs	Utilities	Add-ons	Window	Help

Reports ▶
Descriptive Statistics ▶
Compare Means ▶
General Linear Model ▶
Correlate ▶
Regression ▶   Linear...
Classify ▶   Curve Estimation...
Dimension Reduction ▶   Partial Least Squares...
Scale ▶   Ordinal...
Nonparametric Tests ▶
Forecasting ▶
Multiple Response ▶
Quality Control ▶
ROC Curve...

	Participant	Weig		var	var	var
1	1.00	10				
2	2.00	12				
3	3.00	10				
4	4.00	11				
5	5.00	11				
6	6.00	13				
7	7.00	12				
8	8.00	14				
9	9.00	15				
10	10.00	16				
11	11.00	160.00	68.00			
12	12.00	176.00	69.00			
13	13.00	165.00	70.00			
14	14.00	181.00	72.00			
15	15.00	192.00	76.00			
16	16.00	208.00	75.00			
17	17.00	200.00	77.00			
18	18.00	152.00	68.00			
19	19.00	134.00	66.00			
20	20.00	138.00	65.00			

The dialog box that follows will be produced.

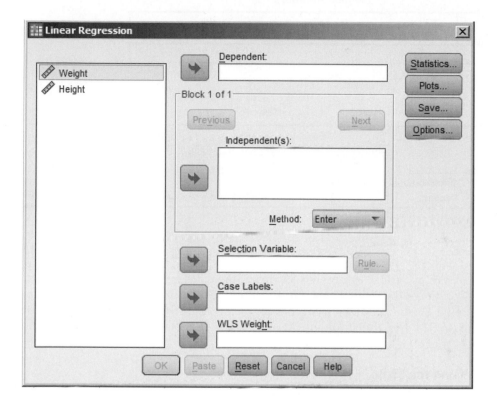

For this regression analysis, we are attempting to predict height based on knowing an individual's weight. Thus, we are using height as the dependent measure in our model and weight as the independent measure. Enter Height into the **Dependent** box and Weight into the **Independent** box by using the appropriate arrows. Then click **OK.** The output will be generated in the output window.

Regression

Variables Entered/Removed[b]

Model	Variables Entered	Variables Removed	Method
1	Weight[a]	.	Enter

[a] All requested variables entered.

[b] Dependent Variable: Height.

Model Summary

Model	R	R Square	Adjusted R Square	Std. Error of the Estimate
1	.941[a]	.886	.880	1.62209

[a] Predictors: (Constant), Weight.

Coefficients[a]

Model		Unstandardized Coefficients		Standardized Coefficients	t	Sig.
		B	Std. Error	Beta		
1	(Constant)	46.314	1.816		25.503	.000
	Weight	.141	.012	.941	11.849	.000

[a] Dependent Variable: Height.

We are most interested in the data necessary to create the regression line—the Y-intercept and the slope. This can be found in the box labeled Unstandardized Coefficients. We see that the Y-intercept (Constant) is 46.314 and the slope is .141. Thus, the regression equation would be $Y' = .141(X) + 46.31$.

Using the TI-84

Let's use the data from Table 20.1 to conduct the regression analysis using the TI-84 calculator.

1. With the calculator on, press the STAT key.
2. EDIT will be highlighted. Press the ENTER key.
3. Under L1 enter the weight data from Table 20.1.
4. Under L2 enter the height data from Table 20.1.
5. Press the 2nd key and 0 [catalog] and scroll down to DiagnosticOn and press ENTER. Press ENTER once again. (The message DONE should appear on the screen.)
6. Press the STAT key and highlight CALC. Scroll down to 8:LinReg(a+bx) and press ENTER.
7. Type L1 (by pressing the 2nd key followed by the 1 key) followed by a comma and L2 (by pressing the 2nd key followed by the 2 key) next to LinReg(a+bx). It should appear as follows on the screen: LinReg(a+bx) L1,L2
8. Press ENTER.

The values of a (46.31), b (.141), r^2 (.89), and r (.94) should appear on the screen.

Statistics used to analyze nominal and ordinal data are referred to as nonparametric tests. You may remember from Module 8 that a nonparametric test is a test that does not involve the use of any population parameters. In other words, μ and σ are not needed, and the underlying distribution does not have to be normal. In addition, most nonparametric tests are based on fewer assumptions than parametric tests. Nonparametric tests are usually easier to compute than parametric tests. They are, however, less powerful than parametric tests, meaning that it is more difficult to reject the null hypothesis when it is false. In this chapter, we will look at two nonparametric tests for nominal data: the χ^2 goodness-of-fit test and the χ^2 test of independence. We will also discuss four tests for ordinal data: the Wilcoxon rank-sum test, used with between-subjects designs with two groups; the Wilcoxon matched-pairs signed-ranks T test, used with correlated-groups two-condition designs; the Kruskal-Wallis test used with between-subjects designs with more than two groups; and the Friedman test used with correlated-groups designs with more than two groups.

MODULE 21
Chi-Square Tests

Learning Objectives
- Explain what the χ^2 goodness-of-fit test is and what it does.
- Calculate a χ^2 goodness-of-fit test.
- List the assumptions of the χ^2 goodness-of-fit test.
- Calculate the χ^2 test of independence.
- Interpret the χ^2 test of independence.
- Explain the assumptions of the χ^2 test of independence.

The Chi-Square (χ^2) Goodness-of-Fit Test: What It Is and What It Does ● ●

The **chi-square (χ^2) goodness-of-fit test** is used for comparing categorical information against what we would expect based on previous knowledge. As such, it tests what are called **observed frequencies** (the frequency with which participants fall into a category) against **expected frequencies** (the frequency expected in a category if the sample data represent the population). It is a nondirectional test, meaning that the alternative hypothesis is neither one-tailed nor two-tailed. The alternative hypothesis for a χ^2 goodness-of-fit test is that the observed data do not fit the expected frequencies for the population, and the null hypothesis is that they do fit the expected frequencies for the population. There is no conventional way to write these hypotheses in symbols, as we have done with the previous statistical tests. To illustrate the χ^2 goodness-of-fit test, let's look at a situation in which its use would be appropriate.

chi-square (χ^2) goodness-of-fit test
A nonparametric inferential procedure that determines how well an observed frequency distribution fits an expected distribution.

observed frequencies
The frequency with which participants fall into a category.

expected frequencies
The frequency expected in a category if the sample data represent the population.

Calculations for the χ^2 Goodness-of-Fit Test

Suppose that a researcher is interested in determining whether the teenage pregnancy rate at a particular high school is different from the rate statewide. Assume that the rate statewide is 17%. A random sample of 80 female students is selected from the target high school. Seven of the students are

TABLE 21.1 Observed and expected frequencies for χ^2 goodness-of-fit example

FREQUENCIES	PREGNANT	NOT PREGNANT
Observed	7	73
Expected	14	66

either pregnant now or have been pregnant previously. The χ^2 goodness-of-fit test measures the observed frequencies against the expected frequencies. The observed and expected frequencies are presented in Table 21.1.

As can be seen in the table, the observed frequencies represent the number of high school females in the sample of 80 who were pregnant versus not pregnant. The expected frequencies represent what we would expect based on chance, given what is known about the population. In this case, we would expect 17% of the females to be pregnant because this is the rate statewide. If we take 17% of 80 (.17 × 80 = 14), we would expect 14 of the students to be pregnant. By the same token, we would expect 83% of the students (.83 × 80 = 66) to be not pregnant. If the calculated expected frequencies are correct, when summed they should equal the sample size (14 + 66 = 80).

Once the observed and expected frequencies have been determined, we can calculate χ^2 using the following formula:

$$\chi^2 = \Sigma \frac{(O - E)^2}{E}$$

where O is the observed frequency, E is the expected frequency, and Σ indicates that we must sum the indicated fraction for each category in the study (in this case, for the pregnant and not-pregnant groups). Using this formula with the present example, we have

$$\chi^2 = \frac{(7 - 14)^2}{14} + \frac{(73 - 66)^2}{66}$$

$$= \frac{(-7)^2}{14} + \frac{(7)^2}{66}$$

$$= \frac{49}{14} + \frac{49}{66}$$

$$= 3.5 + 0.74$$

$$= 4.24$$

Interpreting the χ^2 Goodness-of-Fit Test

The null hypothesis is rejected if the χ^2_{obt} is greater than the χ^2_{cv}. The χ^2_{cv} is found in the χ^2 table in Appendix A at the back of the book (Table A.6). In order to use the table, you need to know the degrees of freedom for the χ^2 test. This is the number of categories minus 1. In our example, we have two categories (pregnant and not pregnant); thus, we have 1 degree of freedom. At $\alpha = .05$, then, $\chi^2_{cv} = 3.84$, according to Table A.6. Our χ^2_{obt} of 4.24 is larger than the critical value, so we can reject the null hypothesis and conclude that the observed frequency of pregnancy is significantly lower than expected by chance. In other words, the female teens at the target high school have a significantly lower pregnancy rate than would be expected based on the statewide rate. In APA style, this would be reported as $\chi^2(1, N = 80) = 4.24, p < .05$. You can see how to use SPSS or the TI-84 calculator to conduct this statistical test in the Statistical Software Resources section at the end of this chapter.

Assumptions and Appropriate Use of the χ^2 Goodness-of-Fit Test

Although the χ^2 goodness-of-fit test is a nonparametric test and therefore less restrictive than a parametric test, it does have its own assumptions. First, the test is appropriate for nominal (categorical) data. If data are measured on a higher scale of measurement, they can be transformed to a nominal scale. Second, the frequencies in each cell should not be too small. If the frequency in any cell is too small (<5), then the χ^2 test should not be conducted. Lastly, to be generalizable to the population, the sample should be randomly selected and the observations must be independent. In other words, each observation must be based on the score of a different subject.

Chi-Square (χ^2) Test of Independence: What It Is and What It Does ●●

The logic of the **chi-square (χ^2) test of independence** is the same as for any χ^2 statistic—we are comparing how well an observed breakdown of people over various categories fits some expected breakdown (such as an equal breakdown). In other words, a χ^2 test compares an observed frequency distribution to an expected frequency distribution. If we observe a difference, we determine whether the difference is greater than what would be expected based on chance. The difference between the χ^2 test of independence and the χ^2 goodness-of-fit test is that the goodness-of-fit test compares how well an observed frequency distribution of *one* nominal variable fits some expected pattern of frequencies, whereas the test of independence compares how well an observed frequency distribution of *two* nominal variables fits some expected pattern of frequencies. The formula we use is the same as for the χ^2 goodness-of-fit test described previously:

$$\chi^2 = \Sigma \frac{(O - E)^2}{E}$$

The null hypothesis and the alternative hypothesis are similar to those used with the *t* tests. The null hypothesis is that there are no observed differences in frequency between the groups we are comparing; the alternative

chi-square (χ^2) test of independence A nonparametric inferential test used when frequency data have been collected to determine how well an observed breakdown of people over various categories fits some expected breakdown.

hypothesis is that there are differences in frequency between the groups and that the differences are greater than we would expect based on chance.

Calculations for the χ^2 Test of Independence

As a means of illustrating the χ^2 test of independence, imagine that teenagers in a randomly chosen sample are categorized as having been employed as babysitters or never having been employed in this capacity. The teenagers are then asked whether they have ever taken a first aid course. In this case, we would like to determine whether babysitters are more likely to have taken first aid than those who have never worked as babysitters. Because we are examining the observed frequency distribution of two nominal variables (babysitting and taking a first aid class), the χ^2 test of independence is appropriate. We find that 65 of the 100 babysitters have had a first aid course and 35 of the babysitters have not. In the non-babysitter group, 43 out of 90 have had a first aid course, and the remaining 47 have not. Table 21.2 is a contingency table showing the observed and expected frequencies.

To determine the expected frequency for each cell, we use this formula:

$$E = \frac{(RT)(CT)}{N}$$

where RT is the row total, CT is the column total, and N is the total number of observations. Thus, the expected frequency for the upper left cell in Table 21.2 would be

$$E = \frac{(100)(108)}{190} = \frac{10,800}{190} = 56.8$$

The expected frequencies appear in parentheses in Table 21.2. Notice that the expected frequencies when summed equal 190, the N in the study. Once we have the observed and expected frequencies, we can calculate χ^2:

$$\chi^2 = \Sigma \frac{(O - E)^2}{E}$$

$$= \frac{(65 - 57)^2}{57} + \frac{(35 - 43)^2}{43} + \frac{(43 - 51)^2}{51} + \frac{(47 - 39)^2}{39}$$

$$= 1.123 + 1.488 + 1.255 + 1.641 = 5.507$$

TABLE 21.2 Observed and expected frequencies for babysitters and non-babysitters having taken a first aid course

	TAKEN FIRST AID COURSE		
	Yes	No	Row Totals
Babysitters	65 (57)	35 (43)	100
Non-babysitters	43 (51)	47 (39)	90
Column Totals	108	82	190

Interpreting the χ^2 Test of Independence

The degrees of freedom for this χ^2 test are equal to $(r - 1)(c - 1)$, where r stands for the number of rows and c stands for the number of columns. In our example, this would be $(2 - 1)(2 - 1) = 1$. We now refer to Table A.6 in Appendix A to identify χ^2_{cv} for $df = 1$. At the .05 level, $\chi^2_{cv} = 3.841$. Our χ^2_{obt} of 5.507 exceeds the critical value, and we reject the null hypothesis. In other words, there is a significant difference between babysitters and non-babysitters in terms of their having taken a first aid class—significantly more babysitters have taken a first aid class. If you were to report this result in APA style, it would appear as $\chi^2(1, N = 190) = 5.507$, $p < .05$. You can see how to use SPSS or the TI-84 calculator to conduct this statistical test in the Statistical Software Resources section at the end of this chapter.

Effect Size: Phi Coefficient

As with many of the statistics discussed in previous chapters, we can also compute the effect size for a χ^2 test of independence. For a 2×2 contingency table, we use the **phi coefficient** (ϕ), where

phi coefficient An inferential test used to determine effect size for a chi-square test.

$$\phi = \sqrt{\frac{\chi^2}{N}}$$

In our example, this would be

$$\phi = \sqrt{\frac{5.507}{190}} = \sqrt{0.02898} = 0.17$$

Cohen's (1988) specifications for the phi coefficient indicate that a phi coefficient of .10 is a small effect, .30 is a medium effect, and .50 is a large effect. Our effect size is small. Hence, even though the χ^2 was significant, there was not a large effect size. In other words, the difference observed in whether a teenager had taken a first aid class was not strongly accounted for by being a babysitter. Why do you think the χ^2 was significant even though the effect size was small? If you attributed this to the large sample size, you were correct.

Assumptions of the χ^2 Test of Independence

The assumptions underlying the χ^2 test of independence are the same as those noted previously for the χ^2 goodness-of-fit test:

- The sample must be random.
- The observations must be independent.
- The data are nominal.

IN REVIEW

	χ^2 **TESTS**	
	χ^2 **Goodness-of-Fit Test**	χ^2 **Test of Independence**
What It Is	A nonparametric test comparing observed frequencies on one nominal variable to expected frequencies based on population data	A nonparametric test comparing observed to expected frequencies for a two-group between-subjects design
What It Does	Will identify how well an observed frequency distribution of one nominal variable fits some expected pattern of frequencies	Will identify differences in frequency on two variables between groups
Assumptions	• Random sample • Independent observations • Nominal data	• Random sample • Independent observations • Nominal data

CRITICAL THINKING CHECK 21.1

1. How do the χ^2 tests differ in use from a t test?
2. Why are the χ^2 tests nonparametric tests, and what does this mean?

REVIEW OF KEY TERMS

chi-square (χ^2) goodness-of-fit test (p. 355)
chi-square (χ^2) test of independence (p. 357)

expected frequencies (p. 355)
observed frequencies (p. 355)

phi coefficient (p. 359)

MODULE EXERCISES

(Answers to odd-numbered questions appear in Appendix B.)

1. When is it appropriate to use a χ^2 test?
2. What is the difference between the χ^2 goodness-of-fit test and the χ^2 test of independence?
3. A researcher believes that the percentage of people who exercise in California is greater than the national exercise rate. The national rate is 20%. The researcher gathers a random sample of 120 individuals who live in California and finds

that the number who exercise regularly is 31 out of 120.
   a. What is χ^2_{obt}?
   b. What is (are) the df for this test?
   c. What is χ^2_{cv}?
   d. What conclusion should be drawn from these results?
4. A teacher believes that the percentage of students at her high school who go on to college is greater than the rate in the general population of high

school students. The rate in the general population is 30%. In the most recent graduating class at her high school, the teacher found that 90 students graduated and that 40 of those went on to college.

a. What is χ^2_{obt}?
b. What is (are) the df for this test?
c. What is χ^2_{cv}?
d. What conclusion should be drawn from these results?

5. You notice in your introductory psychology class that more women tend to sit up front and more men in the back. In order to determine whether this difference is significant, you collect data on the seating preferences for the students in your class. The data follow:

	Males	Females
Front of the Room	15	27
Back of the Room	32	19

a. What is χ^2_{obt}?
b. What is (are) the df for this test?
c. What is χ^2_{cv}?
d. What conclusion should be drawn from these results?

6. What is the phi coefficient? Calculate phi for the previous χ^2 test.

CRITICAL THINKING CHECK ANSWERS

Critical Thinking Check 21.1

1. The χ^2 test is a nonparametric test used with nominal (categorical) data. It examines how well an observed frequency distribution of one or two nominal variables fits some expected pattern of frequencies. The t test is a parametric test for use with interval and ratio data.

2. A nonparametric test is one that does not involve the use of any population parameters, such as the mean and standard deviation. In addition, a nonparametric test does not assume a bell-shaped distribution. The χ^2 tests are nonparametric because they fit this definition.

WEB RESOURCES

The book-specific website at CengageBrain.com offers students a variety of study tools and useful resources such as glossaries, flashcards, quizzes, and Statistics and Research Methods Workshops.

MODULE 22
Tests for Ordinal Data

Learning Objectives
- Calculate Wilcoxon's rank-sum test.
- Interpret Wilcoxon's rank-sum test.
- Explain the assumptions of the Wilcoxon's rank-sum test.
- Calculate Wilcoxon's matched-pairs signed-ranks T test.
- Interpret Wilcoxon's matched-pairs signed-ranks T test.
- Explain the assumptions of the Wilcoxon's matched-pairs signed-ranks T test.
- Calculate the Kruskal-Wallis test.
- Interpret the Kruskal-Wallis test.
- Explain the assumptions of the Kruskal-Wallis test.
- Calculate the Friedman test.
- Interpret the Friedman test.
- Explain the assumptions of the Friedman test.

Wilcoxon rank-sum test
A nonparametric inferential test for comparing sample medians of two independent groups of scores.

Wilcoxon matched-pairs signed-ranks T test
A nonparametric inferential test for comparing sample medians of two dependent or related groups of scores.

Kruskal-Wallis Test An inferential nonparametric test used to determine differences between three or more groups on a ranked variable for a between-subjects design.

Friedman Test An inferential nonparametric test used to determine differences between three or more conditions on a ranked variable for a correlated-groups design.

In this module, we discuss two Wilcoxon tests. The **Wilcoxon rank-sum test** is similar to the independent-groups t test, and the **Wilcoxon matched-pairs signed-ranks T test** is similar to the correlated-groups t test. The Wilcoxon tests, however, are nonparametric tests. As such, they use ordinal data rather than interval-ratio data and allow us to compare the medians of two populations instead of the means. In addition, we will discuss extensions of each of the above tests for use with more than two groups—the **Kruskal-Wallis test** for between-subjects designs and the **Friedman test** for correlated-groups designs.

Wilcoxon Rank-Sum Test: What It Is and What It Does ● ●

Imagine that a teacher of fifth-grade students wants to compare the number of books read per term by female versus male students in her class. Rather than reporting the data as the actual number of books read (interval-ratio data), she ranks the female and male students, giving the student who read the fewest books a rank of 1 and the student who read the most books the

**TABLE 22.1   Number of books read
and corresponding rank for female
and male students**

GIRLS		BOYS	
X	Rank	X	Rank
20	4	10	1
24	8	17	2
29	9	23	7
33	10	19	3
57	12	22	6
35	11	21	5
			$\Sigma = 24$

highest rank. She does this because the distribution representing number of books read is skewed (not normal). She predicts that the girls will read more books than boys. Thus, H_0 is that the median number of books read does not differ between girls and boys ($Md_{girls} = Md_{boys}$, or $Md_{girls} \leq Md_{boys}$), and H_a is that the median number of books read is greater for girls than for boys ($Md_{girls} > Md_{boys}$). The number of books read by each group and the corresponding rankings are presented in Table 22.1.

Calculations for the Wilcoxon Rank-Sum Test

As a check to confirm that the ranking has been done correctly, the highest rank should be equal to $n_1 + n_2$; in our example, $n_1 + n_2 = 12$ and the highest rank is also 12. In addition, the sum of the ranks should equal $N(N + 1)/2$, where N represents the total number of people in the study. In our example, this is $12(12 + 1)/2$. This calculates to 78. If we sum the ranks ($1 + 2 + 3 + 4 + 5 + 6 + 7 + 8 + 9 + 10 + 11 + 12$), they also equal 78. Thus, the ranking was done correctly.

The Wilcoxon test is completed by first summing the ranks for the group expected to have the smaller total. As the teacher expects the males to read less, she sums their ranks. This sum, as seen in the Table 22.1, is 24.

Interpreting the Wilcoxon Rank-Sum Test

Using Table A.7 in Appendix A, we see that for a one-tailed test at the .05 level, if $n_1 = 6$ and $n_2 = 6$, the maximum sum of the ranks in the group expected to be lower is 28. If the sum of the ranks of the group expected to be lower (the males in this situation) exceeds 28, then the result is not significant. Please note that this is the only statistic that we have discussed so far where the obtained value needs to be *equal to or less than* the critical value in order to be statistically significant. When using this table, n_1 is always the smaller of the two groups; if the n's are equal, it does not matter which is n_1 and which is n_2. Moreover, Table A.7 presents the critical values for one-tailed tests only. If a two-tailed test is used, the table can be adapted by dividing the alpha level in half. In other words, we would use the critical values for the .025 level from the table in order to determine the critical value at the .05 level for a two-tailed test. We find that the sum of ranks of the group predicted to have lower scores (24) is less than the cutoff for significance. Our conclusion is to reject the null hypothesis. In other words, we observed that the ranks in the two groups differed, there were not an equal number of high and low ranks in each group, or one group (the girls in this case) read significantly more books than the other. If we were to report this in APA style, it would appear as follows: $W_s(n_1 = 6, n_2 = 6) = 24, p < .05$. You can see how to use SPSS to conduct this statistical test in the Statistical Software Resources section at the end of this chapter.

Assumptions of the Wilcoxon Rank-Sum Test

The Wilcoxon rank-sum test is a nonparametric procedure that is analogous to the independent-groups t test. The assumptions of the test are as follows:

- The data are ratio, interval, or ordinal in scale, all of which must be converted to ranked (ordinal) data before the test is conducted.
- The underlying distribution is not normal.
- The observations are independent.

If the observations are not independent (a correlated-groups design), then the Wilcoxon matched-pairs signed-ranks T test should be used.

Wilcoxon Matched-Pairs Signed-Ranks T Test: What It Is and What It Does ● ●

Imagine that the same teacher in the previous problem wants to compare the number of books read by all students (female and male) over two terms. During the first term, the teacher keeps track of how many books each student reads. During the second term, the teacher institutes a reading reinforcement program through which students can earn prizes based on the number of books read. The number of books read by students is once again measured. As before, the distribution representing number of books read is skewed (not normal). Thus, a nonparametric statistic is necessary. However, in this case, the design is within-subjects—two measures are taken on each student, one before the reading reinforcement program is instituted and one after the program is instituted.

Table 22.2 shows the number of books read by the students across the two terms. Notice that the number of books read during the first term represents the data used in the previous Wilcoxon rank-sum test. The teacher uses a one-tailed test and predicts that students will read more books after the reinforcement program is instituted. Thus, H_0 is that the median number of books read does not differ between the two terms ($Md_{before} = Md_{after}$ or

TABLE 22.2 Number of books read in each term

TERM 1 (NO REINFORCEMENT)	TERM 2 (REINFORCEMENT IMPLEMENTED)	DIFFERENCE SCORE (D) (TERM 1 − TERM 2)	RANK	SIGNED RANK
X	X			
10	15	−5	4.5	−4.5
17	23	−6	6	−6
19	20	−1	1.5	−1.5
20	20	0	—	—
21	28	−7	8	−8
22	26	−4	3	−3
23	24	−1	1.5	−1.5
24	29	−5	4.5	−4.5
29	37	−8	10	−10
33	40	−7	8	−8
57	50	7	8	8
35	55	−20	11	−11
			$+\Sigma = 8$	
			$-\Sigma = 58$	

$Md_{before} \geq Md_{after}$), and H_a is that the median number of books read is greater after the reinforcement program is instituted ($Md_{before} < Md_{after}$).

Calculations for the Wilcoxon Matched-Pairs Signed-Ranks T Test

The first step in completing the Wilcoxon signed-ranks test is to compute a difference score for each individual. In this case, we have subtracted the number of books read in Term 2 from the number of books read in Term 1. Keep in mind the logic of a matched-pairs test. If the reinforcement program had no effect, we would expect all of the difference scores to be 0 or very close to 0. Columns 1–3 in Table 22.2 represent the number of books read in each term and the difference scores. Next, we rank the absolute value of each difference score. This is shown in column 4 of Table 22.2. Notice that the difference score of zero is not ranked. Also note what happens when ranks are tied—for example, there are two difference scores of 1. These difference scores take positions 1 and 2 in the ranking; they are each given a rank of 1.5 (halfway between the ranks of 1 and 2), and the next rank assigned is 3. As a check, the highest rank should equal the number of ranked scores. In our problem, we ranked 11 difference scores; thus, the highest rank should be 11, and it is.

Once the ranks have been determined, we attach to each rank the sign of the previously calculated difference score. This is represented in the last column of Table 22.2. The final step necessary to complete the Wilcoxon signed-ranks test is to sum the positive ranks and then sum the negative ranks. Once again, if there is no difference in number of books read across the two terms, we would expect the sum of the positive ranks to equal or be very close to the sum of the negative ranks. The sums of the positive and negative ranks are shown at the bottom of the last column in Table 22.2.

For a two-tailed test, the T_{obt} is equal to the smaller of the summed ranks. Thus, if we were computing a two-tailed test, our T_{obt} would equal 8. However, our test is one-tailed; the teacher predicted that the number of books read would increase during the reinforcement program. For a one-tailed test, we predict whether we expect more positive or negative difference scores. Because we subtracted Term 2 (the term in which they were reinforced for reading) from Term 1, we would expect more negative differences. The T_{obt} for a one-tailed test is the sum of the signed ranks predicted to be smaller. In this case, we would predict the summed ranks for the positive differences to be smaller than that for negative differences. Thus, T_{obt} for a one-tailed test is also 8.

Interpreting the Wilcoxon Matched-Pairs Signed-Ranks T Test

Using Table A.8 in Appendix A, we see that for a one-tailed test at the .05 level with $N = 11$ (we use $N = 11$ and not 12 because we ranked only 11 of the 12 difference scores), the maximum sum of the ranks in the group expected to be lower is 13. If the sum of the ranks for the group expected to be lower exceeds 13, then the result is not significant. Please note that, as with the previous Wilcoxon rank-sum test, the obtained value needs to be *equal to or less than* the critical value in order to be statistically significant. Our conclusion is to reject the null hypothesis. In other words, we observed that the sum of the positive versus the negative ranks differed, or the number of books read in the two conditions differed; significantly more books were read in the reinforcement condition than in the no-reinforcement condition. If we were to report this in APA style, it would appear as follows: $T(N = 11) = 8, p < .05$. You can see how to use SPSS to conduct this statistical test in the Statistical Software Resources section at the end of this chapter.

Assumptions of the Wilcoxon Matched-Pairs Signed-Ranks T Test

The Wilcoxon matched-pairs signed-ranks T test is a nonparametric procedure that is analogous to the correlated-groups t test. The assumptions of the test are as follows:

- The data are ratio, interval, or ordinal in scale, all of which must be converted to ranked (ordinal) data before the test is conducted.
- The underlying distribution is not normal.
- The observations are dependent or related (a correlated-groups design).

WILCOXON TESTS		IN REVIEW
TYPE OF TEST		

	Wilcoxon Rank-Sum Test	**Wilcoxon Matched-Pairs Signed-Ranks *T* Test**
What It Is	A nonparametric test for a two-group between-subjects design	A nonparametric test for a two-group correlated-groups (within- or matched-subjects) design
What It Does	Will identify differences in ranks on a variable between groups	Will identify differences in signed-ranks on a variable for correlated groups
Assumptions	• Ordinal data • Distribution is not normal • Independent observations	• Ordinal data • Distribution is not normal • Dependent or related observations

CRITICAL THINKING CHECK 22.1

1. I have recently conducted a study in which I ranked my subjects (college students) on height and weight. I am interested in whether there are any differences in height and weight depending upon whether the subject is an athlete (defined by being a member of a sports team) or not an athlete. Which statistic would you recommend using to analyze these data? If the actual height (in inches) and weight (in pounds) data were available, what statistic would be appropriate?

2. Determine the difference scores and ranks for the following set of matched-pairs data. Finally, calculate T for these data, and determine whether the T score is significant for a two-tailed test.

Subject	Score 1	Score 2
1	12	15
2	10	9
3	15	14
4	17	23
5	17	16
6	22	19
7	20	30
8	22	25

Beyond the Wilcoxon Tests ● ●

Just as the ANOVA is an extension of a *t* test, the Wilcoxon tests have an analogous extension. For a between-subjects design with more than two groups, the Kruskal-Wallis test is appropriate. As with the Wilcoxon tests, the Kruskal-Wallis test is appropriate when the data are ordinal or if the involved populations are not normally distributed or homogeneity of variance is in question. The analogous test (more than two groups, ordinal data, and/or skewed distributions) for use with a correlated-groups design is the Friedman test.

The Kruskal-Wallis Test: What It Is and What It Does

As with a one-way randomized ANOVA, the Kruskal-Wallis test is used in situations where there is one independent variable with three or more levels and the design is between-subjects. However, unlike the ANOVA, the Kruskal-Wallis test is used either when the data are ordinal or when the assumptions of population normality or homogeneity of variance are questionable. The data used to calculate the Kruskal-Wallis test are always ordinal (ranked).

Let's use a study similar to that from Module 14 in which a researcher is studying the difference in recall performance between three different types of rehearsal (rote, imagery, and story). Subjects are given a list of 15 words to learn utilizing one of three rehearsal types. Because the data are interval-ratio in scale, when we studied this problem in Module 14 we used the one-way randomized ANOVA to analyze the data. In this situation, however, the researcher is worried that the data are somewhat skewed, thus affecting the normality and homogeneity of variances assumptions associated with the ANOVA test. The researcher therefore correctly decides to use the Kruskal-Wallis test. The number of words recalled by the subjects in each condition appears in Table 22.3.

Calculations for the Kruskal-Wallis Test   In order to use the Kruskal-Wallis test, the number of words recalled must be converted to an ordinal ranking scale. Thus, each of the subjects' recall scores is converted to a rank, with

TABLE 22.3   Number of words recalled correctly in rote, imagery, and story rehearsal conditions

ROTE	IMAGERY	STORY
2	6	10
4	8	9
3	9	12
2	7	8
8	6	4
4	11	13

TABLE 22.4 Number of words recalled correctly and corresponding ranks in rote, imagery, and story rehearsal conditions

ROTE	RANK	IMAGERY	RANK	STORY	RANK
2	1.5	6	7.5	10	15
4	5	8	11	9	13.5
3	3	9	13.5	12	17
2	1.5	7	9	8	11
8	11	6	7.5	4	5
4	5	11	16	13	18
	$T = 27$		$T = 64.5$		$T = 79.5$

the lowest score receiving a rank of 1, the second-lowest a rank of 2, etc. When two subjects recall the same number of words—for example, the two subjects who both recalled 2 words in the Rote condition—they take positions 1 and 2 in the ranking and are each given a rank of 1.5. This is illustrated in Table 22.4.

As a check to confirm that the ranking has been completed correctly, the highest rank should be equal to $n_1 + n_2 + n_3$; in our example $n_1 + n_2 + n_3 = 18$, and the highest rank is also 18. In addition, the sum of the ranks should equal $N(N + 1)/2$, where N is the total number of people in the study. In our example, $18(18 + 1)/2 = 171$, and if we add the ranks ($1.5 + 1.5 + 3 + 5 + 5 + 5 + 7.5 + 7.5 + 9 + 11 + 11 + 11 + 13.5 + 13.5 + 15 + 16 + 17 + 18$), they sum to 171 also. Thus the ranking was completed correctly. The null hypothesis for the Kruskal-Wallis test states that there are no systematic differences in the ranks between conditions, whereas the alternative hypothesis states that we expect systematic differences in the ranks between conditions.

Once the ranks have been determined, the ranks within each condition are summed or totaled, as can be seen in Table 22.4 in which the symbol T has been used to indicate the sum of the ranks in each condition. The T values will be used in the calculation of the Kruskal-Wallis test. The formula used for the Kruskal-Wallis test produces a chi-square statistic and is calculated as follows:

$$\chi^2 = \frac{12}{N(N + 1)}\left(\sum \frac{T^2}{n}\right) - 3(N + 1)$$

We can now use the data from Table 22.4 to calculate the chi-square value.

$$\chi^2 = \frac{12}{18(18 + 1)}\left(\frac{27^2}{6} + \frac{64.5^2}{6} + \frac{79.5^2}{6}\right) - 3(18 + 1)$$

$$= \frac{12}{(18)(19)}\left(\frac{729}{6} + \frac{4{,}160.25}{6} + \frac{6{,}320.25}{6}\right) - 3(19)$$

$$= \frac{12}{342}(121.5 + 693.38 + 1{,}053.38) - 57$$

$$= .035(1{,}868.26) - 57$$

$$= 65.39 - 57$$

$$= 8.39$$

Interpreting the Kruskal-Wallis Test   The degrees of freedom for the Kruskal-Wallis test are calculated in a similar manner to the degrees of freedom for a chi-square test; in other words, the number of conditions minus 1. In this example we have $df = 3 - 1 = 2$. In addition, the Kruskal-Wallis test is based on approximately the same distribution as the chi-square test, so we can use the chi-square probability table to determine whether the obtained statistic is significant. Thus, referring to Table A.6 in Appendix A, we find that the χ^2_{cv} when $df = 2$ is 5.992. Because our $\chi^2_{obt} = 8.39$ and exceeds the critical value, we can reject H_0. Thus, there are significant differences in number of words recalled between the three rehearsal type conditions. In addition, because our χ^2_{obt} is so large we should check the critical values at the .01 and .005 levels provided in Table A.6. When we check these we find that $\chi^2 = 8.39(2, N = 18), p < .005$.

Assumptions of the Kruskal-Wallis Test   The assumptions of the Kruskal-Wallis test are that the data are ranked (ordinal), the distribution is not normal, there are at least five scores in each condition, and that the observations are independent (there are different subjects in each condition).

The Friedman Test: What It Is and What It Does

If the Kruskal-Wallis is the nonparametric version of the one-way randomized ANOVA, the Friedman test is the nonparametric version of the one-way repeated measures ANOVA and is used in situations where there is one independent variable with three or more levels and the design is correlated-groups. As with the Kruskal-Wallis, the Friedman test is used either when the data are ordinal or when the assumptions of population normality or homogeneity of variance have been violated. The data used to calculate the Friedman test are always ordinal (ranked).

Let's use the same study and data as we did earlier with the Kruskal-Wallis test, except in this situation imagine that we used the same subjects in each of the conditions—a within-subjects correlated-groups design. Thus, each subject serves in each of the three rehearsal conditions (rote, imagery, and story) and studies a list of equally difficult words in each condition. The null hypothesis for the Friedman test states that there are no systematic differences in the ranks between conditions, whereas the alternative hypothesis states that we expect systematic differences in the ranks between conditions. The number of words recalled by the subjects in each condition appears in Table 22.5.

Calculations for the Friedman Test   In order to use the Friedman test, the number of words recalled across the three conditions for each subject must be converted to an ordinal ranking scale. Thus, each subject's recall scores across the three conditions is converted to a rank, with the lowest score receiving a

TABLE 22.5 Number of words recalled correctly in rote, imagery, and story rehearsal conditions

ROTE	IMAGERY	STORY
2	6	10
4	8	9
3	9	12
2	7	8
6	4	8
4	11	13

TABLE 22.6 Number of words recalled correctly and corresponding ranks in rote, imagery, and story rehearsal conditions for each subject

SUBJECT	ROTE	RANK	IMAGERY	RANK	STORY	RANK
1	2	1	6	2	10	3
2	4	1	8	2	9	3
3	3	1	9	2	12	3
4	2	1	7	2	8	3
5	6	2	4	1	8	3
6	4	1	11	2	13	3
		$R = 7$		$R = 11$		$R = 18$

rank of 1, the second-lowest a rank of 2, and the highest score a rank of 3 for each subject. Therefore, in a study with three conditions, such as this one, the highest rank a single subject's score can receive is 3. If scores within a single subject's data are the same, they split the ranks. For example, if one subject recalled 2 words in both the Rote and Imagery conditions, that subject would receive a rank of 1.5 in each of those conditions. This situation has not occurred in our data. The ranks for each participant appear in Table 22.6.

Once the ranks have been determined, the ranks within each condition are summed or totaled, as can be seen in Table 22.6 in which the symbol R (for Rank) has been used to indicate the sum of the ranks in each condition. The R values will be used in the calculation of the Friedman test. The formula used for the Friedman test produces a chi-square statistic and is calculated as follows:

$$\chi^2 = \frac{12}{nk(k+1)}(\Sigma R^2) - 3n(k+1),$$

where n refers to the number of subjects and k refers to the number of conditions. We can now use the data from Table 22.6 to calculate the chi-square value.

$$\chi^2 = \frac{12}{6 \times 3(3 + 1)}(\Sigma R^2) - 3 \times 6(3 + 1)$$

$$= \frac{12}{18(4)}(7^2 + 11^2 + 18^2) - 18(4)$$

$$= \frac{12}{72}(49 + 121 + 324) - 72$$

$$= .167(494) - 72$$

$$= 82.5 - 72$$

$$= 10.5$$

Interpreting the Friedman Test   The degrees of freedom for the Friedman test are calculated in a similar manner to the degrees of freedom for any chi-square test; in other words, the number of conditions minus 1. In this example, we have $df = 3 - 1 = 2$. In addition, the Friedman test is based on approximately the same distribution as the chi-square test, so we can use the chi-square probability table to determine whether the obtained statistic is significant. Thus, referring to Table A.6 in Appendix A, we find that the χ^2_{cv} when $df = 2$ is 5.992. Because our $\chi^2_{obt} = 10.5$ and exceeds the critical value, we can reject H_0. Thus, there are significant differences in number of words recalled between the three rehearsal type conditions. In addition, because our χ^2_{obt} is so large we should check the critical values at the .01 and .005 levels in Table A.6. When we check these we find that $\chi^2 = 10.50(2, N = 6)$, $p < .005$.

Assumptions of the Friedman Test   The assumptions of the Friedman test are that the data are ranked (ordinal), the distribution is not normal, there are at least five scores in each condition, and that the observations are not independent (a correlated-groups design was used).

IN REVIEW

NONPARAMETRIC TESTS FOR MORE THAN TWO GROUPS

	TYPE OF TEST	
	Kruskal-Wallis Test	**Friedman Test**
What It Is	A nonparametric test for a between-subjects design with more than two groups	A nonparametric test for a correlated-groups (within- or matched-subjects) design with more than two groups
What It Does	Will identify differences in ranks on a variable between groups	Will identify differences in ranks on a variable for correlated groups
Assumptions	• Ordinal data • Distribution is not normal • Independent observations • More than five observations per condition	• Ordinal data • Distribution is not normal • Dependent or related observations • More than five observations per condition

1. Explain when you would use the Kruskal-Wallis test versus the Friedman test.
2. Determine the ranks for the data below, which represent subject preference for ketchups of differing colors. The preference scores are on a 1–5 scale with a score of 5 indicating the highest preference. In addition, there are five people in each condition for a total of 15 subjects in the experiment.

Ketchup Color

Red	Green	Blue
4	2	5
3	1	3
5	1	4
4	3	5
3	2	4

REVIEW OF KEY TERMS

Friedman test (p. 362)
Kruskall-Wallis test (p. 362)

Wilcoxon matched-pairs signed-
ranks *T* test (p. 362)

Wilcoxon rank-sum test (p. 362)

MODULE EXERCISES

(Answers to odd-numbered questions appear in Appendix B.)

1. Explain how the nonparametric tests in this module differ from the chi-square tests discussed in the previous module.
2. Explain when it would be appropriate to use the Wilcoxon rank-sum test versus the Wilcoxon matched-pairs signed-ranks *T* test.
3. What is the difference in interpretation when comparing the obtained Wilcoxon values to the Wilcoxon critical values compared to all of the other statistics covered in this text?
4. A researcher is interested in comparing the maturity level of students who volunteer for community service versus those who do not. The researcher assumes that those who complete community service will have higher maturity scores. Maturity scores tend to be skewed (not normally distributed). The maturity scores follow. Higher scores indicate higher maturity levels.

No Community Service	Community Service
33	41
41	48
54	61
13	72
22	83
26	55

a. What statistical test should be used to analyze these data?
b. Identify H_0 and H_a for this study.
c. Conduct the appropriate analysis.
d. Should H_0 be rejected? What should the researcher conclude?

5. Researchers at a food company are interested in how a new spaghetti sauce made from green tomatoes (and green in color) will compare to its traditional red spaghetti sauce. The company is worried that the green color will adversely affect the tastiness scores. It randomly assigns subjects to either the green or red sauce condition.

Subjects indicate the tastiness of the sauce on a 10-point scale. Tastiness scores tend to be skewed. The scores follow:

Red Sauce	Green Sauce
7	4
6	5
9	6
10	8
6	7
7	6
8	9

a. What statistical test should be used to analyze these data?
b. Identify H_0 and H_a for this study.
c. Conduct the appropriate analysis.
d. Should H_0 be rejected? What should the researcher conclude?

6. Imagine that the researchers in exercise 5 want to conduct the same study as a within-subjects design. Subjects rate both the green and red sauces by indicating the tastiness of the sauce on a 10-point scale. As in the previous problem, researchers are concerned that the color of the green sauce will adversely affect tastiness scores. Tastiness scores tend to be skewed. The scores follow:

Subject	Red Sauce	Green Sauce
1	7	4
2	6	3
3	9	6
4	10	8
5	6	7
6	7	5
7	8	9

a. What statistical test should be used to analyze these data?
b. Identify H_0 and H_a for this study.
c. Conduct the appropriate analysis.
d. Should H_0 be rejected? What should the researcher conclude?
7. Explain when you would use the Kruskal-Wallis test versus the Wilcoxon rank-sum test.
8. Explain when you would use the Friedman test versus the Wilcoxon matched-pairs signed-ranks T test.
9. Imagine that marketing researchers working for a food company want to determine whether children would prefer ketchup of a different color. They develop red, green, and blue ketchups that all taste the same and have children ($N = 7$) taste each of the ketchups (a correlated-groups design) and rank them on a 5-point scale with 5 indicating the highest preference. The data from the 7 subjects appear below.

Ketchup Color

Subject	Red	Green	Blue
1	4	2	5
2	3	1	3
3	5	1	4
4	4	3	5
5	3	2	4
6	5	1	3
7	3	1	5

a. What statistical test should be used to analyze these data?
b. Identify H_0 and H_a for this study.
c. Conduct the appropriate analysis.
d. Should H_0 be rejected? What should the researcher conclude?

CRITICAL THINKING CHECK ANSWERS

Critical Thinking Check 22.1

1. Because the subjects have been ranked (ordinal data) on height and weight, Wilcoxon's rank-sum test would be appropriate. If the actual height (in inches) and weight (in pounds) were reported, the data would be interval-ratio. In this case, the independent-groups t test would be appropriate.

2.

Subject	Score 1	Score 2	Difference Score	Rank	Signed Rank
1	12	15	−3	5	−5
2	10	9	1	2	2
3	15	14	1	2	2
4	17	23	−6	7	−7
5	17	16	1	2	2
6	22	19	3	5	5
7	20	30	−10	8	−8
8	22	25	−3	5	−5
				$+\Sigma = 11$	
				$-\Sigma = 25$	

$T (N = 8) = 11$, not significant

Critical Thinking Check 22.2

1. Both tests are nonparametric tests that are used with ordinal data when the distribution is skewed. In addition, both tests are also used when there is one independent variable with more than two levels. The difference is that the Kruskal-Wallis test is used for between-subjects designs and the Friedman test is used for correlated-groups designs.

2.

		Ketchup Color			
Red	Rank	Green	Rank	Blue	Rank
4	10.5	2	3.5	5	14
3	6.5	1	1.5	3	6.5
5	14	1	1.5	4	10.5
4	10.5	3	6.5	5	14
3	6.5	2	3.5	4	10.5

WEB RESOURCES

The book-specific website at CengageBrain.com offers students a variety of study tools and useful resources such as glossaries, flashcards, quizzes, and Statistics and Research Methods Workshops.

CHAPTER TEN SUMMARY AND REVIEW
Nonparametric Procedures

CHAPTER SUMMARY

In this chapter, we discussed nonparametric statistics. Nonparametric tests are those for which population parameters (μ and σ) are not known. In addition, the underlying distribution of scores is assumed to be not normal, and the data are most commonly nominal or ordinal.

We discussed six different nonparametric statistics. The χ^2 goodness-of-fit test examines how well an observed frequency distribution of one nominal variable fits some expected pattern of frequencies. The χ^2 test of independence once again compares observed frequencies to expected frequencies. The difference here is that it compares how well an observed frequency distribution of two nominal variables fits some expected pattern of frequencies.

The final four nonparametric statistics covered are used with ordinal data. The Wilcoxon rank-sum test compares ranked data for two groups of different subjects—a between-subjects design—in order to determine whether there are significant differences in the rankings in one group versus the other group. The Wilcoxon matched-pairs signed-ranks T test compares ranked data for a single group of subjects (or two groups of matched subjects) on two measures. In other words, the Wilcoxon matched-pairs signed-ranks T test is used with correlated-groups designs to determine whether there are differences in subjects' scores across the two conditions in which they served. The Kruskal-Wallis test is used with between-subjects designs when there are more than two groups being compared, whereas the Friedman test is used with correlated-groups designs when there are more than two conditions being compared.

CHAPTER 10 REVIEW EXERCISES

(Answers to exercises appear in Appendix B.)

Fill-in Self-Test

Answer the following questions. If you have trouble answering any of the questions, restudy the relevant material before going on to the multiple-choice self-test.

1. _____ and _____ frequencies are used in the calculation of the χ^2 statistic.
2. The nonparametric inferential statistic for comparing two groups of different people when ordinal data are collected is the _____.
3. When frequency data are collected, we use the _____ to determine how well an observed frequency distribution of two nominal variables fits some expected breakdown.

4. Effect size for a chi-square test is determined by using the _____.
5. The Wilcoxon _____ test is used with within-subjects designs.
6. The Wilcoxon rank-sum test is used with _____ designs.
7. Chi-square tests use _____ data, whereas Wilcoxon tests use _____ data.
8. The extension of the Wilcoxon rank-sum test for use with more than two groups is the _____.

Multiple-Choice Self-Test

Select the single best answer for each of the following questions. If you have trouble answering any of the questions, restudy the relevant material.

1. Parametric is to nonparametric as _____ is to _____.
   a. z test; t test
   b. t test; z test
   c. χ^2 test; z test
   d. t test; χ^2 test
2. Which of the following is an assumption of χ^2 tests?
   a. It is a parametric test.
   b. It is appropriate only for ordinal data.
   c. The frequency in each cell should be less than 5.
   d. The sample should be randomly selected.
3. The calculation of the *df* for the _____ is $(r-1)(c-1)$.
   a. independent-groups t test
   b. correlated-groups t test
   c. χ^2 test of independence
   d. Wilcoxon rank-sum test
4. The _____ is a measure of effect size for the _____.
   a. phi coefficient; χ^2 goodness-of-fit test
   b. eta-squared; χ^2 goodness-of-fit test
   c. phi coefficient; χ^2 test of independence
   d. eta-squared; Wilcoxon rank-sum test
5. The Wilcoxon rank-sum test is used with _____ data.
   a. interval
   b. ordinal
   c. nominal
   d. ratio
6. Wilcoxon rank-sum test is to _____ design as Wilcoxon matched-pairs signed-ranks T test is to _____ design.
   a. between-subjects; within-subjects
   b. correlated-groups; within-subjects
   c. correlated-groups; between-subjects
   d. within-subjects; matched-subjects
7. When using a between-subjects design, and comparing three or more groups on an ordinal variable we would use the:
   a. Kruskal-Wallis test
   b. Friedman test
   c. Wilcoxon rank-sum test
   d. Wilcoxon matched-pairs signed-ranks T test.

Self-Test Problems

1. A researcher believes that the percentage of people who smoke in the South is greater than in the nation as a whole. The national rate is 15%. The researcher gathers a random sample of 110 individuals who live in the South and finds that the number who smoke is 21 out of 110.
   a. What statistical test should be used to analyze these data?
   b. Identify H_0 and H_a for this study.
   c. Conduct the appropriate analysis.
   d. Should H_0 be rejected? What should the researcher conclude?

2. You notice at the gym that it appears more women tend to work out together, whereas more men tend to work out alone. In order to determine whether this difference is significant, you collect data on the workout preferences for a sample of men and women at your gym. The data follow:

	Males	Females
Together	12	24
Alone	22	10

   a. What statistical test should be used to analyze these data?
   b. Identify H_0 and H_a for this study.
   c. Conduct the appropriate analysis.
   d. Should H_0 be rejected? What should the researcher conclude?

3. Researchers at a food company are interested in how a new ketchup made from green tomatoes (and green in color) will compare to their traditional red ketchup. They are worried that the green color will adversely affect the tastiness scores. They randomly assign subjects to either the green or red ketchup condition. Subjects indicate the tastiness of the sauce on a 20-point scale. Tastiness scores tend to be skewed. The scores follow:

Green Ketchup	Red Ketchup
14	16
15	16
16	19
18	20
16	17
16	17
19	18

   a. What statistical test should be used to analyze these data?
   b. Identify H_0 and H_a for this study.
   c. Conduct the appropriate analysis.
   d. Should H_0 be rejected? What should the researcher conclude?

CHAPTER TEN
Statistical Software Resources

If you need help getting started with Excel or SPSS, please see Appendix C: Getting Started with Excel and SPSS.

MODULE 21 Chi-Square Tests

CHI-SQUARE GOODNESS-OF-FIT TEST

Using SPSS

To begin using SPSS to calculate this chi-square test, we must enter the data into the Data Editor. We'll use the problem from Module 21 to illustrate this test. The data appear in Table 21.1 in Module 21. We have 80 individuals in the sample, thus there will be 80 scores entered. A score of 1 indicates that the individual was pregnant (there are 7 scores of 1 entered), and a score of 2 indicates that the individual was not pregnant (there are 73 scores of 2 entered). A portion of the Data Editor with the data entered appears next. I've named the variable Observedpregnancy to indicate that we are interested in the pregnancy rate observed in the sample.

File	Edit	View	Data	Transform	Analyze	Graphs	Utilities	Add-ons	Window	Help

	Observedpregnancy	var	var	var	var
1	1				
2	1				
3	1				
4	1				
5	1				
6	1				
7	1				
8	2				
9	2				
10	2				
11	2				
12	2				
13	2				
14	2				
15	2				
16	2				
17	2				
18	2				
19	2				
20	2				
21	2				
22	2				
23	2				
24	2				
25	2				
26	2				
27	2				
28	2				
29	2				
30	2				
31	2				
32	2				
33	2				
34	2				
35	2				

Data View | Variable View

Next, we click on **Analyze,** then **Nonparametric Tests, Legacy Dialogs,** and finally **Chi-square.** This is illustrated in the following screen capture:

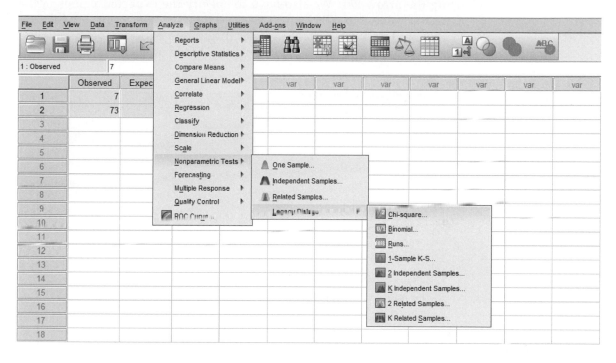

This will produce the following dialog box:

Our **Test Variable List** is the data in the Observedpregnancy variable. Thus, move the Observedpregnancy variable over to the **Test Variable List** using the arrow key. We also have to specify the expected values in the Expected Values box. Click on **Values** and then type the first value (14) into the box and click on **Add.** Next enter the second expected value (66) and enter it by clicking on **Add.** The dialog box should now appear as follows:

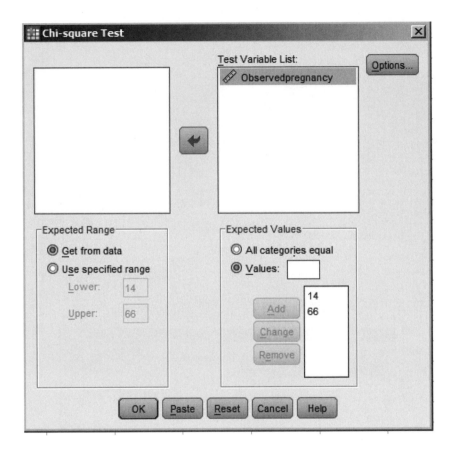

Click **OK** and you should receive the output that appears next.

NPar Tests

Chi-Square Test

Frequencies

Observedpregnancy

	Observed N	Expected N	Residual
1	7	14.0	-7.0
2	73	66.0	7.0
Total	80		

Test Statistics

	Observedpreg nancy
Chi-square	4.242[a]
df	1
Asymp. Sig.	.039

a. 0 cells (.0%) have
expected frequencies
less than 5. The
minimum expected cell
frequency is 14.0.

We can reject the null hypothesis and conclude that the observed frequency of pregnancy is significantly lower than expected by chance. In other words, the female teens at the target high school have a significantly lower pregnancy rate than would be expected based on the statewide rate. In APA style, this would be reported as $\chi^2(1, N = 80) = 4.24, p = .039$.

Using the TI-84

Let's use the data from Table 21.1 to conduct the calculation using the TI-84 calculator.

1. With the calculator on, press the STAT key.
2. Highlight EDIT and press ENTER.
3. Enter the Observed Scores in L1 and the Expected Scores in L2.
4. Press the STAT key and highlight TESTS.
5. Scroll down to D: χ^2 GOF Test and press ENTER.
6. The calculator should show Observed: L1, Expected: L2, and df = 1.
7. Scroll down and highlight Calculate and press ENTER.

The χ^2 value of 4.24 should appear on the screen, along with the $df = 1$ and $p = .039$.

CHI-SQUARE TEST OF INDEPENDENCE

Using SPSS

We'll use the problem from Module 21 to illustrate this test. The data can be found in Table 21.2 in Module 21. We begin by entering the data into SPSS. We enter the data by indicating whether the individual is a babysitter (1) or not a babysitter (2) and whether they have taken a first aid class (1) or not (2). Thus, a 1, 1 is a babysitter who has taken a first aid class whereas a 2, 1 is a non-babysitter who has taken a first aid class. This coding system is illustrated in the following screen capture of the Data Editor:

| File Edit View Data Transform Analyze Graphs Utilities Add-ons Win |

	BabysitterNonbabysitter	FirstAidNoFirst...	var	var
1	1	1		
2	1	1		
3	1	1		
4	1	1		
5	1	1		
6	1	1		
7	1	1		
8	1	1		
9	1	1		
10	1	1		
11	1	1		
12	1	1		
13	1	2		
14	1	2		
15	1	2		
16	1	2		
17	1	2		
18	1	2		
19	2	1		
20	2	1		
21	2	1		
22	2	1		
23	2	1		
24	2	2		
25	2	2		
26	2	2		
27	2	2		
28	2	2		
29	2	2		
30	2	2		
31	2	2		
32	2	2		
33	2	2		
34	2	2		

Please note that not all of the data are visible in the preceding screen capture, so enter the data from Table 14.2 in which there is data for 36 individuals.

Next, click on **Analyze, Descriptive Statistics,** and then **Crosstabs** as indicated in the following screen capture:

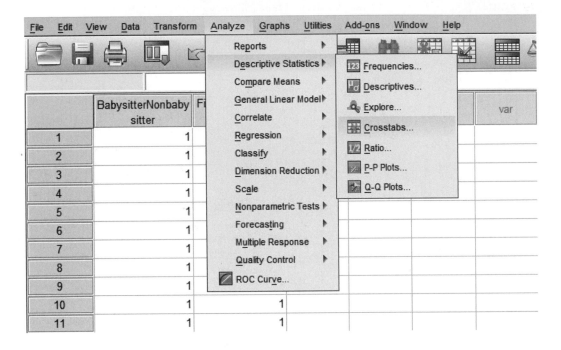

This will produce the dialog box seen next.

Next move one of the variables to the **Rows** box using the arrow keys and move the second variable to the **Columns** box (it does not matter which variable is entered into rows versus columns). The dialog box should now look as follows:

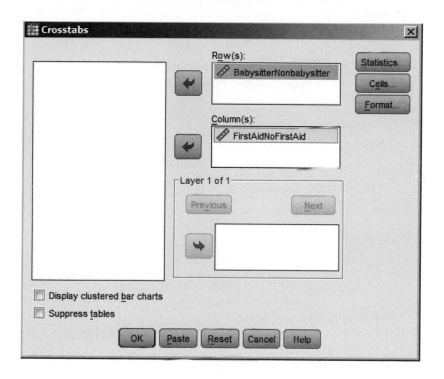

Click on **Statistics** and check the **Chi-square** box and click **Continue.**

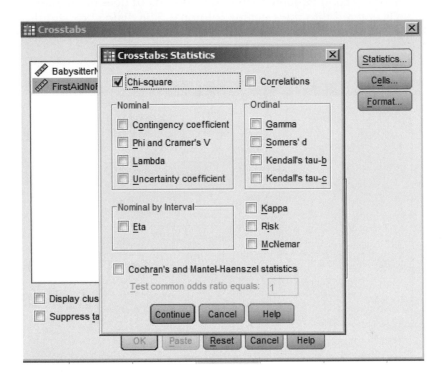

Next click on **Cells** and check the **Observed** and **Expected** boxes as seen next.

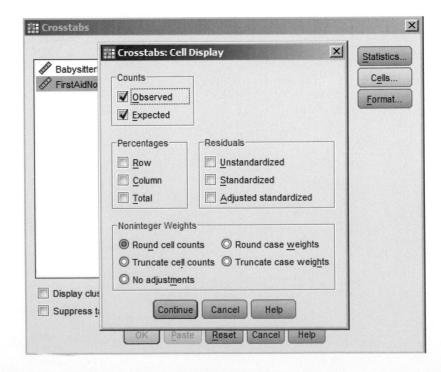

Click **Continue** and then **OK.** The output should appear as follows:

Crosstabs

Case Processing Summary

	Cases					
	Valid		Missing		Total	
	N	Percent	N	Percent	N	Percent
BabysitterNonbabysitter * FirstAidNoFirstAid	36	33.0%	73	67.0%	109	100.0%

BabysitterNonbabysitter * FirstAidNoFirstAid Crosstabulation

			FirstAidNoFirstAid		Total
			1	2	
BabysitterNonbabysitter	1	Count	12	6	18
		Expected Count	8.5	9.5	18.0
	2	Count	5	13	18
		Expected Count	8.5	9.5	18.0
Total		Count	17	19	36
		Expected Count	17.0	19.0	36.0

Chi-Square Tests

	Value	df	Asymp. Sig. (2-sided)	Exact Sig. (2-sided)	Exact Sig. (1-sided)
Pearson Chi-Square	5.461[a]	1	.019		
Continuity Correction[b]	4.012	1	.045		
Likelihood Ratio	5.611	1	.018		
Fisher's Exact Test				.044	.022
Linear-by-Linear Association	5.310	1	.021		
N of Valid Cases	36				

a. 0 cells (.0%) have expected count less than 5. The minimum expected count is 8.50.

b. Computed only for a 2x2 table

We are most interested in the data reported in the Chi-Square Tests box above. The chi-square test of independence is reported as Pearson Chi-Square by SPSS. Thus, based on this, we reject the null hypothesis. In other words, there is a significant difference between babysitters and non-babysitters in terms of their having taken a first aid class—significantly more babysitters have taken a first aid class. If you were to report this result in APA style, it would appear as $\chi^2(1, N = 190) = 5.461, p = .019$.

Using the TI-84

Let's use the data from Table 21.2 to conduct the calculation using the TI-84 calculator.

1. With the calculator on, press the 2nd key followed by the MATRIX [X^{-1}] key.
2. Highlight EDIT and 1:[A] and press ENTER.
3. Enter the dimensions for the matrix. Our matrix is 2 × 2. Press ENTER.
4. Enter each observed frequency from Table 21.2 followed by ENTER.
5. Press the STAT key and highlight TESTS.
6. Scroll down to C: χ^2-Test and press ENTER.
7. The calculator should show Observed: [A] and Expected: [B].
8. Scroll down and highlight Calculate and press ENTER.

The χ^2 value of 5.73 (the TI-84 does not round the expected frequencies to whole numbers, thus the chi-square it calculates is slightly larger than that calculated in Module 21 and by SPSS) should appear on the screen, along with the $df = 1$ and $p = .017$.

MODULE 22 Tests for Ordinal Data

WILCOXON RANK-SUM TEST

Let's use the example from Module 22 in which a teacher of fifth-grade students wants to compare the number of books read per term by female versus male students in her class. The distribution representing number of books read is skewed (not normal), thus a nonparametric test is used (Table 22.1).

Using SPSS

To begin using SPSS to calculate this Wilcoxon rank-sum test, we must enter the data into the Data Editor. This is illustrated in the following screen capture of the Data Editor in which you can see that the first column is labeled Gender, with females as 1's and males as 2's. The number of books read by each student is indicated in the second column. These data can be found in Table 22.1 in Module 22.

	File	Edit	View	Data	Transform	Analyze	Graphs	Utilities	Add-ons	Windo

1 : Gender		1.00

	Gender	BooksRead	var	var	var
1	1.00	20.00			
2	1.00	24.00			
3	1.00	29.00			
4	1.00	33.00			
5	1.00	57.00			
6	1.00	35.00			
7	2.00	10.00			
8	2.00	17.00			
9	2.00	23.00			
10	2.00	19.00			
11	2.00	22.00			
12	2.00	21.00			
13					

To conduct the statistical test, begin by clicking on **Analyze,** then **Non-parametric Tests, Legacy Dialogs,** and finally **2 Independent Samples** as is indicated in the following screen capture:

This will produce the following dialog box:

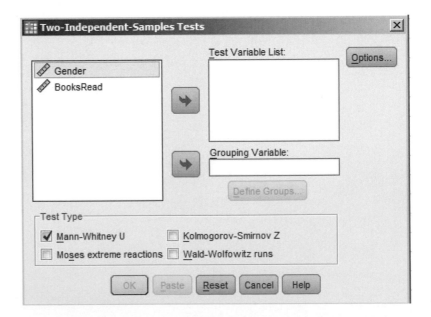

Gender is the **Grouping Variable,** so use the arrow key to enter it into the appropriate box. The **Test Variable** is BooksRead, so enter it into that box. With the **Grouping Variable** box highlighted, click on the **Define Groups...** box to receive the dialog box presented next.

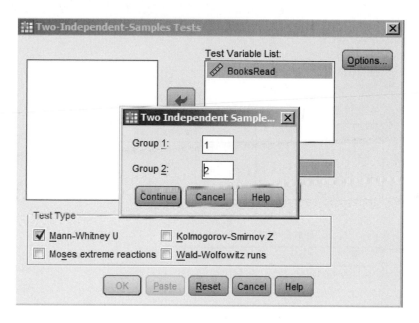

Let SPSS know how the groups are defined, in other words that you have 1's and 2's defining your groups, and then click **Continue.** Your completed dialog box should appear as follows:

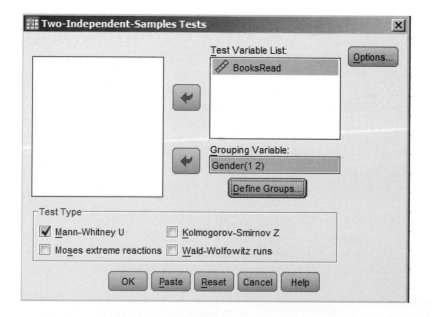

Please note that the **Test Type** selected should be **Mann-Whitney;** however, the output you receive will have both the Mann-Whitney test and the Wilcoxon test statistics. Now click on **OK** to receive the following analysis output:

NPar Tests

Mann-Whitney Test

Ranks

	Gender	N	Mean Rank	Sum of Ranks
BooksRead	1.00	6	9.00	54.00
	2.00	6	4.00	24.00
	Total	12		

Test Statistics[b]

	BooksRead
Mann-Whitney U	3.000
Wilcoxon W	24.000
Z	-2.402
Asymp. Sig. (2-tailed)	.016
Exact Sig. [2*(1-tailed Sig.)]	.015[a]

a. Not corrected for ties.

b. Grouping Variable: Gender

Notice that in the Test Statistics box, both the Mann-Whitney U test and the Wilcoxon W test statistics are provided. We can see that the mean rank for girls is 9, whereas the mean rank for boys is 4. The easiest way to interpret both the Mann-Whitney and Wilcoxon tests is based on the z score provided. Based on this score we can conclude that girls read significantly more books than boys, $z = -2.402$, $p = .0075$ (the two-tailed significance level is provided, but because this was a one-tailed test, we divide that in half).

WILCOXON MATCHED-PAIRS SIGNED-RANKS T TEST

Let's use the example from Module 22 in which the same teacher in the previous problem wants to compare the number of books read by all students (female and male) over two terms to illustrate this test.

Using SPSS

To begin using SPSS to calculate this test statistic, we must enter the data from Table 22.2 in Module 22 into the Data Editor, as illustrated in the following screen capture:

File	Edit	View	Data	Transform	Analyze	Graphs	Utilities	Add-

1 : TermI   20.00

	TermI	TermII	var	var
1	20.00	20.00		
2	24.00	29.00		
3	29.00	37.00		
4	33.00	40.00		
5	57.00	50.00		
6	35.00	55.00		
7	10.00	15.00		
8	17.00	23.00		
9	23.00	24.00		
10	19.00	20.00		
11	22.00	26.00		
12	21.00	28.00		
13				
14				

Notice that the variables are simply labeled TermI and TermII. Next, click on **Analyze, Nonparametric, Legacy Dialogs,** and finally **2 Related Samples…** as is indicated in the following screen capture:

This will produce the following dialog box:

Highlight TermI and use the arrow key to move it to the **Variable1** box. Do the same for the TermII variable. In addition, make sure that **Wilcoxon** is selected in the **Test Type** box. The dialog box should appear as follows:

Next, click on the **Options...** box to receive the dialog box illustrated next.

Click **Descriptive** and then **Continue.** Finally, click **OK** to receive the following analysis output:

NPar Tests

Descriptive Statistics

	N	Mean	Std. Deviation	Minimum	Maximum
TermI	12	25.8333	11.96839	10.00	57.00
TermII	12	30.5833	12.43498	15.00	55.00

Wilcoxon Signed Ranks Test

Ranks

		N	Mean Rank	Sum of Ranks
TermII - TermI	Negative Ranks	1[a]	8.00	8.00
	Positive Ranks	10[b]	5.80	58.00
	Ties	1[c]		
	Total	12		

a. TermII < TermI

b. TermII > TermI

c. TermII = TermI

Test Statistics[b]

	TermII - TermI
Z	-2.229[a]
Asymp. Sig. (2-tailed)	.026

a. Based on negative ranks.

b. Wilcoxon Signed Ranks Test

We can see that the mean number of books read in Term I is 25.83, whereas the mean number of books read in Term II is 30.58. In order to conduct the Wilcoxon test, the number of books read in Term I is subtracted from the number of books read in Term II for each student. These difference scores are then ranked (an ordinal variable). We can see that there was 1 negative rank, 10 positive ranks, and 1 tie. Based on these results, we can conclude that students read significantly more books in Term II in comparison to Term I, $z = -2.229$, $p - .013$ (the two-tailed significance level is provided, but because this was a one-tailed test, we divide that in half).

KRUSKAL-WALLIS TEST

Let's use the example from Module 22 in which we measured number of words recalled by subjects who used one of three different types of rehearsal.

Using SPSS

To begin using SPSS to calculate this test statistic, we must enter the data from Table 22.3 in Module 22 into the Data Editor as illustrated in the following screen capture. In the screen capture, the first variable, RehearsalType, indicates which type of rehearsal subjects used (1 for rote, 2 for imagery, and 3 for story). The variable WordsRecalled shows how many words each subject recalled.

	File	Edit	View	Data	Transform	Analyze	Direct Mark

13 :			
	RehearsalType	WordsRecalled	var
1	1.00	2.00	
2	1.00	4.00	
3	1.00	3.00	
4	1.00	2.00	
5	1.00	8.00	
6	1.00	4.00	
7	2.00	6.00	
8	2.00	8.00	
9	2.00	9.00	
10	2.00	7.00	
11	2.00	6.00	
12	2.00	11.00	
13	3.00	10.00	
14	3.00	9.00	
15	3.00	12.00	
16	3.00	8.00	
17	3.00	4.00	
18	3.00	13.00	
19			

After the data have been entered, click on **Analyze, Nonparametric Tests, Legacy Dialogs, K Independent Samples,** as in the following screen capture:

This will produce the following dialog box:

Move the **WordsRecalled** variable to the **Test Variable List** box by using the arrow button and then move the **RehearsalType** variable to the **Grouping Variable** box by using the arrow button. **Kruskal-Wallis H** should be checked in the **Test Type** box. The dialog box should appear as follows:

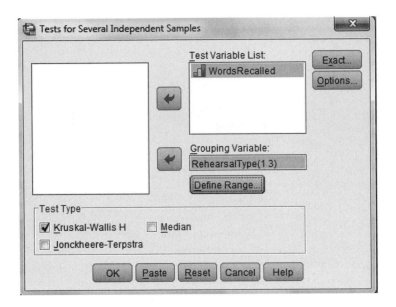

Now click on the **Define Range** box to define the range of the grouping variable. You should receive the following pop-up window:

Enter 1 into the **Minimum** box and 3 in the **Maximum** box as appears below.

Click **Continue** and then **OK** to produce the following output in which we can see the reported chi-square test statistic—$\chi^2 = 8.65(2, N = 18)\, p = .013$, indicating that there were significant differences in numbers of words recalled across the three conditions.

Kruskal-Wallis Test

Ranks

	RehearsalType	N	Mean Rank
WordsRecalled	1.00	6	4.50
	2.00	6	10.75
	3.00	6	13.25
	Total	18	

Test Statistics[a,b]

	WordsRecalled
Chi-Square	8.651
df	2
Asymp. Sig.	.013

a. Kruskal Wallis Test
b. Grouping Variable: RehearsalType

FRIEDMAN TEST

Let's use the example from Module 22 in which we measured number of words recalled by subjects who used one of three different types of rehearsal.

Using SPSS

To begin using SPSS to calculate this test statistic we must enter the data from Table 22.5 in Module 22 into the Data Editor, as illustrated in the following screen capture:

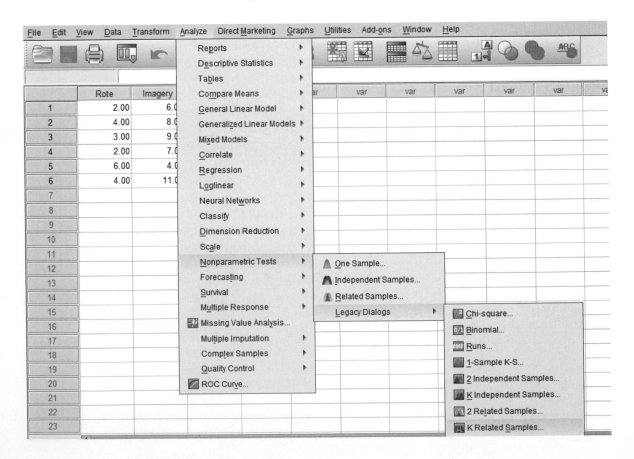

	Rote	Imagery	Story	var
1	2.00	6.00	10.00	
2	4.00	8.00	9.00	
3	3.00	9.00	12.00	
4	2.00	7.00	8.00	
5	6.00	4.00	8.00	
6	4.00	11.00	13.00	
7				

In the preceding screen capture the data from each condition appear in a separate column in the Data Editor. After the data have been entered, click on **Analyze, Nonparametric Tests, Legacy Dialogs, K Related Samples,** as in the following screen capture:

The following dialog box will be produced:

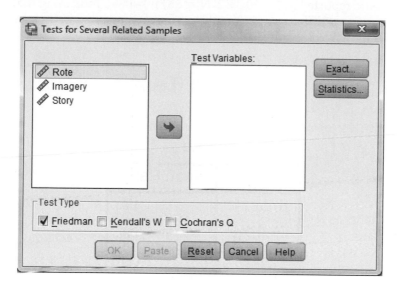

Using the arrow button in the center of the dialog box, move the three levels of the independent variable over to the **Test Variables** box. In addition, ensure that the **Friedman** box is checked under **Test Type.** The dialog box should appear as below.

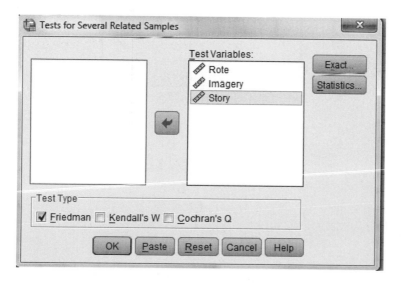

Click **OK** to receive the following output in which we see the chi-square test statistic reported [$\chi^2 = 10.33(2, N = 18)\ p = 006$], indicating that there were significant differences in numbers of words recalled across the three conditions.

Friedman Test

Ranks

	Mean Rank
Rote	1.17
Imagery	1.83
Story	3.00

Test Statistics[a]

N	6
Chi-Square	10.333
df	2
Asymp. Sig.	.006

a. Friedman Test

APPENDIX A
Statistical Tables

TABLE A.1 Areas Under the Normal Curve (z Table)

z	AREA BETWEEN MEAN AND z	AREA BEYOND z	z	AREA BETWEEN MEAN AND z	AREA BEYOND z
0.00	0.00000	0.50000	0.34	0.13307	0.36693
0.01	0.00400	0.49600	0.35	0.13684	0.36316
0.02	0.00798	0.49202	0.36	0.14058	0.35942
0.03	0.01198	0.48802	0.37	0.14432	0.35568
0.04	0.01595	0.48405	0.38	0.14803	0.35197
0.05	0.01995	0.48005	0.39	0.15174	0.34826
0.06	0.02392	0.47608	0.40	0.15542	0.34458
0.07	0.02791	0.47209	0.41	0.15911	0.34089
0.08	0.03188	0.46812	0.42	0.16276	0.33724
0.09	0.03587	0.46413	0.43	0.16641	0.33359
0.10	0.03983	0.46017	0.44	0.17003	0.32997
0.11	0.04381	0.45619	0.45	0.17366	0.32634
0.12	0.04776	0.45224	0.46	0.17724	0.32276
0.13	0.05173	0.44827	0.47	0.18083	0.31917
0.14	0.05567	0.44433	0.48	0.18439	0.31561
0.15	0.05963	0.44037	0.49	0.18794	0.31206
0.16	0.06356	0.43644	0.50	0.19146	0.30854
0.17	0.06751	0.43249	0.51	0.19498	0.30502
0.18	0.07142	0.42858	0.52	0.19847	0.30153
0.19	0.07536	0.42464	0.53	0.20195	0.29805
0.20	0.07926	0.42074	0.54	0.20540	0.29460
0.21	0.08318	0.41682	0.55	0.20885	0.29115
0.22	0.08706	0.41294	0.56	0.21226	0.28774
0.23	0.09096	0.40904	0.57	0.21567	0.28433
0.24	0.09483	0.40517	0.58	0.21904	0.28096
0.25	0.09872	0.40128	0.59	0.22242	0.27758
0.26	0.10257	0.39743	0.60	0.22575	0.27425
0.27	0.10643	0.39357	0.61	0.22908	0.27092
0.28	0.11026	0.38974	0.62	0.23237	0.26763
0.29	0.11410	0.38590	0.63	0.23566	0.26434
0.30	0.11791	0.38209	0.64	0.23891	0.26109
0.31	0.12173	0.37827	0.65	0.24216	0.25784
0.32	0.12552	0.37448	0.66	0.24537	0.25463
0.33	0.12931	0.37069	0.67	0.24858	0.25142

(continued)

TABLE A.1 Areas Under the Normal Curve (z Table) (continued)

z	AREA BETWEEN MEAN AND Z	AREA BEYOND Z	z	AREA BETWEEN MEAN AND Z	AREA BEYOND Z
0.68	0.25175	0.24825	1.01	0.34376	0.15624
0.69	0.25491	0.24509	1.02	0.34614	0.15386
0.70	0.25804	0.24196	1.03	0.34851	0.15149
0.71	0.26116	0.23884	1.04	0.35083	0.14917
0.72	0.26424	0.23576	1.05	0.35315	0.14685
0.73	0.26732	0.23268	1.06	0.35543	0.14457
0.74	0.27035	0.22965	1.07	0.35770	0.14230
0.75	0.27338	0.22662	1.08	0.35993	0.14007
0.76	0.27637	0.22363	1.09	0.36215	0.13785
0.77	0.27936	0.22064	1.10	0.36433	0.13567
0.78	0.28230	0.21770	1.11	0.36651	0.13349
0.79	0.28525	0.21475	1.12	0.36864	0.13136
0.80	0.28814	0.21186	1.13	0.37077	0.12923
0.81	0.29104	0.20896	1.14	0.37286	0.12714
0.82	0.29389	0.20611	1.15	0.37494	0.12506
0.83	0.29674	0.20326	1.16	0.37698	0.12302
0.84	0.29955	0.20045	1.17	0.37901	0.12099
0.85	0.30235	0.19765	1.18	0.38100	0.11900
0.86	0.30511	0.19489	1.19	0.38299	0.11701
0.87	0.30786	0.19214	1.20	0.38493	0.11507
0.88	0.31057	0.18943	1.21	0.38687	0.11313
0.89	0.31328	0.18672	1.22	0.38877	0.11123
0.90	0.31594	0.18406	1.23	0.39066	0.10934
0.91	0.31860	0.18140	1.24	0.39251	0.10749
0.92	0.32121	0.17879	1.25	0.39436	0.10564
0.93	0.32383	0.17617	1.26	0.39617	0.10383
0.94	0.32639	0.17361	1.27	0.39797	0.10203
0.95	0.32895	0.17105	1.28	0.39973	0.10027
0.96	0.33147	0.16853	1.29	0.40149	0.09851
0.97	0.33399	0.16601	1.30	0.40320	0.09680
0.98	0.33646	0.16354	1.31	0.40491	0.09509
0.99	0.33892	0.16108	1.32	0.40658	0.09342
1.00	0.34134	0.15866	1.33	0.40825	0.09175

(continued)

TABLE A.1   Areas Under the Normal Curve (z Table) (*continued*)

z	AREA BETWEEN MEAN AND z	AREA BEYOND z	z	AREA BETWEEN MEAN AND z	AREA BEYOND z
1.34	0.40988	0.09012	1.67	0.45255	0.04745
1.35	0.41150	0.08850	1.68	0.45352	0.04648
1.36	0.41309	0.08691	1.69	0.45450	0.04550
1.37	0.41467	0.08533	1.70	0.45543	0.04457
1.38	0.41621	0.08379	1.71	0.45638	0.04362
1.39	0.41775	0.08225	1.72	0.45728	0.04272
1.40	0.41924	0.08076	1.73	0.45820	0.04180
1.41	0.42074	0.07926	1.74	0.45907	0.04093
1.42	0.42220	0.07780	1.75	0.45995	0.04005
1.43	0.42365	0.07635	1.76	0.46080	0.03920
1.44	0.42507	0.07493	1.77	0.46165	0.03835
1.45	0.42648	0.07352	1.78	0.46246	0.03754
1.46	0.42785	0.07215	1.79	0.46328	0.03672
1.47	0.42923	0.07077	1.80	0.46407	0.03593
1.48	0.43056	0.06944	1.81	0.46486	0.03514
1.49	0.43190	0.06810	1.82	0.46562	0.03438
1.50	0.43319	0.06681	1.83	0.46639	0.03361
1.51	0.43449	0.06551	1.84	0.46712	0.03288
1.52	0.43574	0.06426	1.85	0.46785	0.03215
1.53	0.43700	0.06300	1.86	0.46856	0.03144
1.54	0.43822	0.06178	1.87	0.46927	0.03073
1.55	0.43944	0.06056	1.88	0.46995	0.03005
1.56	0.44062	0.05938	1.89	0.47063	0.02937
1.57	0.44180	0.05820	1.90	0.47128	0.02872
1.58	0.44295	0.05705	1.91	0.47194	0.02806
1.59	0.44409	0.05591	1.92	0.47257	0.02743
1.60	0.44520	0.05480	1.93	0.47321	0.02679
1.61	0.44631	0.05369	1.94	0.47381	0.02619
1.62	0.44738	0.05262	1.95	0.47442	0.02558
1.63	0.44846	0.05154	1.96	0.47500	0.02500
1.64	0.44950	0.05050	1.97	0.47559	0.02441
1.65	0.45054	0.04946	1.98	0.47615	0.02385
1.66	0.45154	0.04846	1.99	0.47672	0.02328

TABLE A.1 Areas Under the Normal Curve (z Table) (*continued*)

z	AREA BETWEEN MEAN AND z	AREA BEYOND z	z	AREA BETWEEN MEAN AND z	AREA BEYOND z
2.00	0.47725	0.02275	2.33	0.49011	0.00989
2.01	0.47780	0.02220	2.34	0.49036	0.00964
2.02	0.47831	0.02169	2.35	0.49062	0.00938
2.03	0.47883	0.02117	2.36	0.49086	0.00914
2.04	0.47932	0.02068	2.37	0.49112	0.00888
2.05	0.47983	0.02017	2.38	0.49134	0.00866
2.06	0.48030	0.01970	2.39	0.49159	0.00841
2.07	0.48078	0.01922	2.40	0.49180	0.00820
2.08	0.48124	0.01876	2.41	0.49203	0.00797
2.09	0.48170	0.01830	2.42	0.49224	0.00776
2.10	0.48214	0.01786	2.43	0.49246	0.00754
2.11	0.48258	0.01742	2.44	0.49266	0.00734
2.12	0.48300	0.01700	2.45	0.49287	0.00713
2.13	0.48342	0.01658	2.46	0.49305	0.00695
2.14	0.48382	0.01618	2.47	0.49325	0.00675
2.15	0.48423	0.01577	2.48	0.49343	0.00657
2.16	0.48461	0.01539	2.49	0.49362	0.00638
2.17	0.48501	0.01499	2.50	0.49379	0.00621
2.18	0.48537	0.01463	2.51	0.49397	0.00603
2.19	0.48575	0.01425	2.52	0.49413	0.00587
2.20	0.48610	0.01390	2.53	0.49431	0.00569
2.21	0.48646	0.01354	2.54	0.49446	0.00554
2.22	0.48679	0.01321	2.55	0.49462	0.00538
2.23	0.48714	0.01286	2.56	0.49477	0.00523
2.24	0.48745	0.01255	2.57	0.49493	0.00507
2.25	0.48779	0.01221	2.58	0.49506	0.00494
2.26	0.48809	0.01191	2.59	0.49521	0.00479
2.27	0.48841	0.01159	2.60	0.49534	0.00466
2.28	0.48870	0.01130	2.61	0.49548	0.00452
2.29	0.48900	0.01100	2.62	0.49560	0.00440
2.30	0.48928	0.01072	2.63	0.49574	0.00426
2.31	0.48957	0.01043	2.64	0.49585	0.00415
2.32	0.48983	0.01017	2.65	0.49599	0.00401

(*continued*)

TABLE A.1 Areas Under the Normal Curve (z Table)

z	AREA BETWEEN MEAN AND z	AREA BEYOND z	z	AREA BETWEEN MEAN AND z	AREA BEYOND z
2.66	0.49609	0.00391	2.94	0.49836	0.00164
2.67	0.49622	0.00378	2.95	0.49842	0.00158
2.68	0.49632	0.00368	2.96	0.49846	0.00154
2.69	0.49644	0.00356	2.97	0.49852	0.00148
2.70	0.49653	0.00347	2.98	0.49856	0.00144
2.71	0.49665	0.00335	2.99	0.49862	0.00138
2.72	0.49674	0.00326	3.00	0.49865	0.00135
2.73	0.49684	0.00316	3.02	0.49874	0.00126
2.74	0.49693	0.00307	3.04	0.49882	0.00118
2.75	0.49703	0.00297	3.06	0.49889	0.00111
2.76	0.49711	0.00289	3.08	0.49896	0.00104
2.77	0.49721	0.00279	3.10	0.49903	0.00097
2.78	0.49728	0.00272	3.12	0.49910	0.00090
2.79	0.49738	0.00262	3.14	0.49916	0.00084
2.80	0.49744	0.00256	3.16	0.49921	0.00079
2.81	0.49753	0.00247	3.18	0.49926	0.00074
2.82	0.49760	0.00240	3.20	0.49931	0.00069
2.83	0.49768	0.00232	3.25	0.49943	0.00057
2.84	0.49774	0.00226	3.30	0.49952	0.00048
2.85	0.49782	0.00218	3.35	0.49961	0.00039
2.86	0.49788	0.00212	3.40	0.49966	0.00034
2.87	0.49796	0.00204	3.45	0.49973	0.00027
2.88	0.49801	0.00199	3.50	0.49977	0.00023
2.89	0.49808	0.00192	3.60	0.49984	0.00016
2.90	0.49813	0.00187	3.70	0.49989	0.00011
2.91	0.49820	0.00180	3.80	0.49993	0.00007
2.92	0.49825	0.00175	3.90	0.49995	0.00005
2.93	0.49832	0.00168	4.00	0.49997	0.00003

Source: Lehman, R. S. (1995). *Statistics in the Behavioral Sciences: A Conceptual Introduction*. Pacific Grove, CA: Brooks/Cole Publishing.

TABLE A.2   Critical Values for the Student's *t* Distribution

	LEVEL OF SIGNIFICANCE FOR ONE-TAILED TEST					
	.10	.05	.025	.01	.005	.0005
	LEVEL OF SIGNIFICANCE FOR TWO-TAILED TEST					
df	.20	.10	.05	.02	.01	.001
1	3.078	6.314	12.706	31.821	63.657	636.619
2	1.886	2.920	4.303	6.965	9.925	31.598
3	1.638	2.353	3.182	4.541	5.841	12.941
4	1.533	2.132	2.776	3.747	4.604	8.610
5	1.476	2.015	2.571	3.365	4.032	6.859
6	1.440	1.943	2.447	3.143	3.707	5.959
7	1.415	1.895	2.365	2.998	3.499	5.405
8	1.397	1.860	2.306	2.896	3.355	5.041
9	1.383	1.833	2.262	2.821	3.250	4.781
10	1.372	1.812	2.228	2.764	3.169	4.587
11	1.363	1.796	2.201	2.718	3.106	4.437
12	1.356	1.782	2.179	2.681	3.055	4.318
13	1.350	1.771	2.160	2.650	3.012	4.221
14	1.345	1.761	2.145	2.624	2.977	4.140
15	1.341	1.753	2.131	2.602	2.947	4.073
16	1.337	1.746	2.120	2.583	2.921	4.015
17	1.333	1.740	2.110	2.567	2.898	3.965

(continued)

TABLE A.2   Critical Values for the Student's *t* Distribution

	LEVEL OF SIGNIFICANCE FOR ONE-TAILED TEST					
	.10	.05	.025	.01	.005	.0005
	LEVEL OF SIGNIFICANCE FOR TWO-TAILED TEST					
df	.20	.10	.05	.02	.01	.001
18	1.330	1.734	2.101	2.552	2.878	3.922
19	1.328	1.729	2.093	2.539	2.861	3.883
20	1.325	1.725	2.086	2.528	2.845	3.850
21	1.323	1.721	2.080	2.518	2.831	3.819
22	1.321	1.717	2.074	2.508	2.819	3.792
23	1.319	1.714	2.069	2.500	2.807	3.767
24	1.318	1.711	2.064	2.492	2.797	3.745
25	1.316	1.708	2.060	2.485	2.787	3.725
26	1.315	1.706	2.056	2.479	2.779	3.707
27	1.314	1.703	2.052	2.473	2.771	3.690
28	1.313	1.701	2.048	2.467	2.763	3.674
29	1.311	1.699	2.045	2.462	2.756	3.659
30	1.310	1.697	2.042	2.457	2.750	3.646
40	1.303	1.684	2.021	2.423	2.704	3.551
60	1.296	1.671	2.000	2.390	2.660	3.460
120	1.289	1.658	1.980	2.358	2.617	3.373
∞	1.282	1.645	1.960	2.326	2.576	3.291

SOURCE: Lehman, R. S. (1995). *Statistics in the Behavioral Sciences: A Conceptual Introduction*. Pacific Grove, CA: Brooks/Cole Publishing.

TABLE A.3 Critical Values for the F Distribution

df FOR DENOMINATOR (df WITHIN OR ERROR)	α	df FOR NUMERATOR (df BETWEEN) 1	2	3	4	5	6	7	8	9	10	11	12
1	.05	161	200	216	225	230	234	237	239	241	242	243	244
2	.05	18.5	19.0	19.2	19.2	19.3	19.3	19.4	19.4	19.4	19.4	19.4	19.4
	.01	98.5	99.0	99.2	99.2	99.3	99.3	99.4	99.4	99.4	99.4	99.4	99.4
3	.05	10.1	9.55	9.28	9.12	9.01	8.94	8.89	8.85	8.81	8.79	8.76	8.74
	.01	34.1	30.8	29.5	28.7	28.2	27.9	27.7	27.5	27.3	27.2	27.1	27.1
4	.05	7.71	6.94	6.59	6.39	6.26	6.16	6.09	6.04	6.00	5.96	5.94	5.91
	.01	21.2	18.0	16.7	16.0	15.5	15.2	15.0	14.8	14.7	14.5	14.4	14.4
5	.05	6.61	5.79	5.41	5.19	5.05	4.95	4.88	4.82	4.77	4.74	4.71	4.68
	.01	16.3	13.3	12.1	11.4	11.0	10.7	10.5	10.3	10.2	10.1	9.96	9.89
6	.05	5.99	5.14	4.76	4.53	4.39	4.28	4.21	4.15	4.10	4.06	4.03	4.00
	.01	13.7	10.9	9.78	9.15	8.75	8.47	8.26	8.10	7.98	7.87	7.79	7.72
7	.05	5.59	4.74	4.35	4.12	3.97	3.87	3.79	3.73	3.68	3.64	3.60	3.57
	.01	12.2	9.55	8.45	7.85	7.46	7.19	6.99	6.84	6.72	6.62	6.54	6.47
8	.05	5.32	4.46	4.07	3.84	3.69	3.58	3.50	3.44	3.39	3.35	3.31	3.28
	.01	11.3	8.65	7.59	7.01	6.63	6.37	6.18	6.03	5.91	5.81	5.73	5.67
9	.05	5.12	4.26	3.86	3.63	3.48	3.37	3.29	3.23	3.18	3.14	3.10	3.07
	.01	10.6	8.02	6.99	6.42	6.06	5.80	5.61	5.47	5.35	5.26	5.18	5.11
10	.05	4.96	4.10	3.71	3.48	3.33	3.22	3.14	3.07	3.02	2.98	2.94	2.91
	.01	10.0	7.56	6.55	5.99	5.64	5.39	5.20	5.06	4.94	4.85	4.77	4.71
11	.05	4.84	3.98	3.59	3.36	3.20	3.09	3.01	2.95	2.90	2.85	2.82	2.79
	.01	9.65	7.21	6.22	5.67	5.32	5.07	4.89	4.74	4.63	4.54	4.46	4.40
12	.05	4.75	3.89	3.49	3.26	3.11	3.00	2.91	2.85	2.80	2.75	2.72	2.69
	.01	9.33	6.93	5.95	5.41	5.06	4.82	4.64	4.50	439	4.30	4.22	4.16
13	.05	4.67	3.81	3.41	3.18	3.03	2.92	2.83	2.77	2.71	2.67	2.63	2.60
	.01	9.07	6.70	5.74	5.21	4.86	4.62	4.44	4.30	4.19	4.10	4.02	3.96
14	.05	4.60	3.74	3.34	3.11	2.96	2.85	2.76	2.70	2.65	2.60	2.57	2.53
	.01	8.86	6.51	5.56	5.04	4.69	4.46	4.28	4.14	4.03	3.94	3.86	3.80
15	.05	4.54	3.68	3.29	3.06	2.90	2.79	2.71	2.64	2.59	2.54	2.51	2.48
	.01	8.68	6.36	5.42	4.89	4.56	4.32	4.14	4.00	3.89	3.80	3.73	3.67
16	.05	4.49	3.63	3.24	3.01	2.85	2.74	2.66	2.59	2.54	2.49	2.46	2.42
	.01	8.53	6.23	5.29	4.77	4.44	4.20	4.03	3.89	3.78	3.69	3.62	3.55
17	.05	4.45	3.59	3.20	2.96	2.81	2.70	2.61	2.55	2.49	2.45	2.41	2.38
	.01	8.40	6.11	5.18	4.67	4.34	4.10	3.93	3.79	3.68	3.59	3.52	3.46
18	.05	4.41	3.55	3.16	2.93	2.77	2.66	2.58	2.51	2.46	2.41	2.37	2.34
	.01	8.29	6.01	5.09	4.58	4.25	4.01	3.84	3.71	3.60	3.51	3.43	3.37
19	.05	4.38	3.52	3.13	2.90	2.74	2.63	2.54	2.48	2.42	2.38	2.34	2.31
	.01	8.18	5.93	5.01	4.50	4.17	3.94	3.77	3.63	3.52	3.43	3.36	3.30

(continued)

TABLE A.3 Critical Values for the F Distribution (*continued*)

df FOR NUMERATOR (df BETWEEN)															df FOR DENOMINATOR
15	20	24	30	40	50	60	100	120	200	500	∞	α	(df WITHIN OR ERROR)
246	248	249	250	251	252	252	253	253	254	254	254	.05	1
19.4	19.4	19.5	19.5	19.5	19.5	19.5	19.5	19.5	19.5	19.5	19.5	.05	2
99.4	99.4	99.5	99.5	99.5	99.5	99.5	99.5	99.5	99.5	99.5	99.5	.01	
8.70	8.66	8.64	8.62	8.59	8.58	8.57	8.55	8.55	8.54	8.53	8.53	.05	3
26.9	26.7	26.6	26.5	26.4	26.4	26.3	26.2	26.2	26.2	26.1	26.1	.01	
5.86	5.80	5.77	5.75	5.72	5.70	5.69	5.66	5.66	5.65	5.64	5.63	.05	4
14.2	14.0	13.9	13.8	13.7	13.7	13.7	13.6	13.6	13.5	13.5	13.5	.01	
4.62	4.56	4.53	4.50	4.46	4.44	4.43	4.41	4.40	4.39	4.37	4.36	.05	5
9.72	9.55	9.47	9.38	9.29	9.24	9.20	9.13	9.11	9.08	9.04	9.02	.01	
3.94	3.87	3.84	3.81	3.77	3.75	3.74	3.71	3.70	3.69	3.68	3.67	.05	6
7.56	7.40	7.31	7.23	7.14	7.09	7.06	6.99	6.97	6.93	6.90	6.88	.01	
3.51	3.44	3.41	3.38	3.34	3.32	3.30	3.27	3.27	3.25	3.24	3.23	.05	7
6.31	6.16	6.07	5.99	5.91	5.86	5.82	5.75	5.74	5.70	5.67	5.65	.01	
3.22	3.15	3.12	3.08	3.04	3.02	3.01	2.97	2.97	2.95	2.94	2.93	.05	8
5.52	5.36	5.28	5.20	5.12	5.07	5.03	4.96	4.95	4.91	4.88	4.86	.01	
3.01	2.94	2.90	2.86	2.83	2.80	2.79	2.76	2.75	2.73	2.72	2.71	.05	9
4.96	4.81	4.73	4.65	4.57	4.52	4.48	4.42	4.40	4.36	4.33	4.31	.01	
2.85	2.77	2.74	2.70	2.66	2.64	2.62	2.59	2.58	2.56	2.55	2.54	.05	10
4.56	4.41	4.33	4.25	4.17	4.12	4.08	4.01	4.00	3.96	3.93	3.91	.01	
2.72	2.65	2.61	2.57	2.53	2.51	2.49	2.46	2.45	2.43	2.42	2.40	.05	11
4.25	4.10	4.02	3.94	3.86	3.81	3.78	3.71	3.69	3.66	3.62	3.60	.01	
2.62	2.54	2.51	2.47	2.43	2.40	2.38	2.35	2.34	2.32	2.31	2.30	.05	12
4.01	3.86	3.78	3.70	3.62	3.57	3.54	3.47	3.45	3.41	3.38	3.36	.01	
2.53	2.46	2.42	2.38	2.34	2.31	2.30	2.26	2.25	2.23	2.22	2.21	.05	13
3.82	3.66	3.59	3.51	3.43	3.38	3.34	3.27	3.25	3.22	3.19	3.17	.01	
2.46	2.39	2.35	2.31	2.27	2.24	2.22	2.19	2.18	2.16	2.14	2.13	.05	14
3.66	3.51	3.43	3.35	3.27	3.22	3.18	3.11	3.09	3.06	3.03	3.00	.01	
2.40	2.33	2.29	2.25	2.20	2.18	2.16	2.12	2.11	2.10	2.08	2.07	.05	15
3.52	3.37	3.29	3.21	3.13	3.08	3.05	2.98	2.96	2.92	2.89	2.87	.01	
2.35	2.28	2.24	2.19	2.15	2.12	2.11	2.07	2.06	2.04	2.02	2.01	.05	16
3.41	3.26	3.18	3.10	3.02	2.97	2.93	2.86	2.84	2.81	2.78	2.75	.01	
2.31	2.23	2.19	2.15	2.10	2.08	2.06	2.02	2.01	1.99	1.97	1.96	.05	17
3.31	3.16	3.08	3.00	2.92	2.87	2.83	2.76	2.75	2.71	2.68	2.65	.01	
2.27	2.19	2.15	2.11	2.06	2.04	2.02	1.98	1.97	1.95	1.93	1.92	.05	18
3.23	3.08	3.00	2.92	2.84	2.78	2.75	2.68	2.66	2.62	2.59	2.57	.01	
2.23	2.16	2.11	2.07	2.03	2.00	1.98	1.94	1.93	1.91	1.89	1.88	.05	19
3.15	3.00	2.92	2.84	2.76	2.71	2.67	2.60	2.58	2.55	2.51	2.49	.01	

TABLE A.3 Critical Values for the F Distribution (*continued*)

df FOR DENOMINATOR (df WITHIN OR ERROR)	α	1	2	3	4	5	6	7	8	9	10	11	12
		df FOR NUMERATOR (df BETWEEN)											
20	.05	4.35	3.49	3.10	2.87	2.71	2.60	2.51	2.45	2.39	2.35	2.31	2.28
	.01	8.10	5.85	4.94	4.43	4.10	3.87	3.70	3.56	3.46	3.37	3.29	3.23
22	.05	4.30	3.44	3.05	2.82	2.66	2.55	2.46	2.40	2.34	2.30	2.26	2.23
	.01	7.95	5.72	4.82	4.31	3.99	3.76	3.59	3.45	3.35	3.26	3.18	3.12
24	.05	4.26	3.40	3.01	2.78	2.62	2.51	2.42	2.36	2.30	2.25	2.21	2.18
	.01	7.82	5.61	4.72	4.22	3.90	3.67	3.50	3.36	3.26	3.17	3.09	3.03
26	.05	4.23	3.37	2.98	2.74	2.59	2.47	2.39	2.32	2.27	2.22	2.18	2.15
	.01	7.72	5.53	4.64	4.14	3.82	3.59	3.42	3.29	3.18	3.09	3.02	2.96
28	.05	4.20	3.34	2.95	2.71	2.56	2.45	2.36	2.29	2.24	2.19	2.15	2.12
	.01	7.64	5.45	4.57	4.07	3.76	3.53	3.36	3.23	3.12	3.03	2.96	2.90
30	.05	4.17	3.32	2.92	2.69	2.53	2.42	2.33	2.27	2.21	2.16	2.13	2.09
	.01	7.56	5.39	4.51	4.02	3.70	3.47	3.30	3.17	3.07	2.98	2.91	2.84
40	.05	4.08	3.23	2.84	2.61	2.45	2.34	2.25	2.18	2.12	2.08	2.04	2.00
	.01	7.31	5.18	4.31	3.83	3.51	3.29	3.12	2.99	2.89	2.80	2.73	2.66
60	.05	4.00	3.15	2.76	2.53	2.37	2.25	2.17	2.10	2.04	1.99	1.95	1.92
	.01	7.08	4.98	4.13	3.65	3.34	3.12	2.95	2.82	2.72	2.63	2.56	2.50
120	.05	3.92	3.07	2.68	2.45	2.29	2.17	2.09	2.02	1.96	1.91	1.87	1.83
	.01	6.85	4.79	3.95	3.48	3.17	2.96	2.79	2.66	2.56	2.47	2.40	2.34
200	.05	3.89	3.04	2.65	2.42	2.26	2.14	2.06	1.98	1.93	1.88	1.84	1.80
	.01	6.76	4.71	3.88	3.41	3.11	2.89	2.73	2.60	2.50	2.41	2.34	2.27
∞	.05	3.84	3.00	2.60	2.37	2.21	2.10	2.01	1.94	1.88	1.83	1.79	1.75
	.01	6.63	4.61	3.78	3.32	3.02	2.80	2.64	2.51	2.41	2.32	2.25	2.18

(*continued*)

TABLE A.3 Critical Values for the *F* Distribution

15	20	24	30	40	50	60	100	120	200	500	∞	α	*df* FOR DENOMINATOR (*df* WITHIN OR ERROR)
2.20	2.12	2.08	2.04	1.99	1.97	1.95	1.91	1.90	1.88	1.86	1.84	.05	20
3.09	2.94	2.86	2.78	2.69	2.64	2.61	2.54	2.52	2.48	2.44	2.42	.01	
2.15	2.07	2.03	1.98	1.94	1.91	1.89	1.85	1.84	1.82	1.80	1.78	.05	22
2.98	2.83	2.75	2.67	2.58	2.53	2.50	2.42	2.40	2.36	2.33	2.31	.01	
2.11	2.03	1.98	1.94	1.89	1.86	1.84	1.80	1.79	1.77	1.75	1.73	.05	24
2.89	2.74	2.66	2.58	2.49	2.44	2.40	2.33	2.31	2.27	2.24	2.21	.01	
2.07	1.99	1.95	1.90	1.85	1.82	1.80	1.76	1.75	1.73	1.71	1.69	.05	26
2.81	2.66	2.58	2.50	2.42	2.36	2.33	2.25	2.23	2.19	2.16	2.13	.01	
2.04	1.96	1.91	1.87	1.82	1.79	1.77	1.73	1.71	1.69	1.67	1.65	.05	28
2.75	2.60	2.52	2.44	2.35	2.30	2.26	2.19	2.17	2.13	2.09	2.06	.01	
2.01	1.93	1.89	1.84	1.79	1.76	1.74	1.70	1.68	1.66	1.64	1.62	.05	30
2.70	2.55	2.47	2.39	2.30	2.25	2.21	2.13	2.11	2.07	2.03	2.01	.01	
1.92	1.84	1.79	1.74	1.69	1.66	1.64	1.59	1.58	1.55	1.53	1.51	.05	40
2.52	2.37	2.29	2.20	2.11	2.06	2.02	1.94	1.92	1.87	1.83	1.80	.01	
1.84	1.75	1.70	1.65	1.59	1.56	1.53	1.48	1.47	1.44	1.41	1.39	.05	60
2.35	2.20	2.12	2.03	1.94	1.88	1.84	1.75	1.73	1.68	1.63	1.60	.01	
1.75	1.66	1.61	1.55	1.50	1.46	1.43	1.37	1.35	1.32	1.28	1.25	.05	120
2.19	2.03	1.95	1.86	1.76	1.70	1.66	1.56	1.53	1.48	1.42	1.38	.01	
1.72	1.62	1.57	1.52	1.46	1.41	1.39	1.32	1.29	1.26	1.22	1.19	.05	200
2.13	1.97	1.89	1.79	1.69	1.63	1.58	1.48	1.44	1.39	1.33	1.28	.01	
1.67	1.57	1.52	1.46	1.39	1.35	1.32	1.24	1.22	1.17	1.11	1.00	.05	∞
2.04	1.88	1.79	1.70	1.59	1.52	1.47	1.36	1.32	1.25	1.15	1.00	.01	

df FOR NUMERATOR (*df* BETWEEN)

SOURCE: Lehman, R. S. (1995). *Statistics in the Behavioral Sciences: A Conceptual Introduction*. Pacific Grove, CA: Brooks/Cole Publishing.

TABLE A.4 Studentized Range Statistic (Q)

ERROR df (df WITHIN)	α	K = NUMBER OF MEANS OR NUMBER OF STEPS BETWEEN ORDERED MEANS									
		2	3	4	5	6	7	8	9	10	11
5	.05	3.64	4.60	5.22	5.67	6.03	6.33	6.58	6.80	6.99	7.17
	.01	5.70	6.98	7.80	8.42	8.91	9.32	9.67	9.97	10.24	10.48
6	.05	3.46	4.34	4.90	5.30	5.63	5.90	6.12	6.32	6.49	6.65
	.01	5.24	6.33	7.03	7.56	7.97	8.32	8.61	8.87	9.10	9.30
7	.05	3.34	4.16	4.68	5.06	5.36	5.61	5.82	6.00	6.16	6.30
	.01	4.95	5.92	6.54	7.01	7.37	7.68	7.94	8.17	8.37	8.55
8	.05	3.26	4.04	4.53	4.89	5.17	5.40	5.60	5.77	5.92	6.05
	.01	4.75	5.64	6.20	6.62	6.96	7.24	7.47	7.68	7.86	8.03
9	.05	3.20	3.95	4.41	4.76	5.02	5.24	5.43	5.59	5.74	5.87
	.01	4.60	5.43	5.96	6.35	6.66	6.91	7.13	7.33	7.49	7.65
10	.05	3.15	3.88	4.33	4.65	4.91	5.12	5.30	5.46	5.60	5.72
	.01	4.48	5.27	5.77	6.14	6.43	6.67	6.87	7.05	7.21	7.36
11	.05	3.11	3.82	4.26	4.57	4.82	5.03	5.20	5.35	5.49	5.61
	.01	4.39	5.15	5.62	5.97	6.25	6.48	6.67	6.84	6.99	7.13
12	.05	3.08	3.77	4.20	4.51	4.75	4.95	5.12	5.27	5.39	5.51
	.01	4.32	5.05	5.50	5.84	6.10	6.32	6.51	6.67	6.81	6.94
13	.05	3.06	3.73	4.15	4.45	4.69	4.88	5.05	5.19	5.32	5.43
	.01	4.26	4.96	5.40	5.73	5.98	6.19	6.37	6.53	6.67	6.79
14	.05	3.03	3.70	4.11	4.41	4.64	4.83	4.99	5.13	5.25	5.36
	.01	4.21	4.89	5.32	5.63	5.88	6.08	6.26	6.41	6.54	6.66
15	.05	3.01	3.67	4.08	4.37	4.59	4.78	4.94	5.08	5.20	5.31
	.01	4.17	4.84	5.25	5.56	5.80	5.99	6.16	6.31	6.44	6.55
16	.05	3.00	3.65	4.05	4.33	4.56	4.74	4.90	5.03	5.15	5.26
	.01	4.13	4.79	5.19	5.49	5.72	5.92	6.08	6.22	6.35	6.46
17	.05	2.98	3.63	4.02	4.30	4.52	4.70	4.86	4.99	5.11	5.21
	.01	4.10	4.74	5.14	5.43	5.66	5.85	6.01	6.15	6.27	6.38
18	.05	2.97	3.61	4.00	4.28	4.49	4.67	4.82	4.96	5.07	5.17
	.01	4.07	4.70	5.09	5.38	5.60	5.79	5.94	6.08	6.20	6.31
19	.05	2.96	3.59	3.98	4.25	4.47	4.65	4.79	4.92	5.04	5.14
	.01	4.05	4.67	5.05	5.33	5.55	5.73	5.89	6.02	6.14	6.25
20	.05	2.95	3.58	3.96	4.23	4.45	4.62	4.77	4.90	5.01	5.11
	.01	4.02	4.64	5.02	5.29	5.51	5.69	5.84	5.97	6.09	6.19
24	.05	2.92	3.53	3.90	4.17	4.37	4.54	4.68	4.81	4.92	5.01
	.01	3.96	4.55	4.91	5.17	5.37	5.54	5.69	5.81	5.92	6.02
30	.05	2.89	3.49	3.85	4.10	4.30	4.46	4.60	4.72	4.82	4.92
	.01	3.89	4.45	4.80	5.05	5.24	5.40	5.54	5.65	5.76	5.85
40	.05	2.86	3.44	3.79	4.04	4.23	4.39	4.52	4.63	4.73	4.82
	.01	3.82	4.37	4.70	4.93	5.11	5.26	5.39	5.50	5.60	5.69
60	.05	2.83	3.40	3.74	3.98	4.16	4.31	4.44	4.55	4.65	4.73
	.01	3.76	4.28	4.59	4.82	4.99	5.13	5.25	5.36	5.45	5.53
120	.05	2.80	3.36	3.68	3.92	4.10	4.24	4.36	4.47	4.56	4.64
	.01	3.70	4.20	4.50	4.71	4.87	5.01	5.12	5.21	5.30	5.37
∞	.05	2.77	3.31	3.63	3.86	4.03	4.17	4.29	4.39	4.47	4.55
	.01	3.64	4.12	4.40	4.60	4.76	4.88	4.99	5.08	5.16	5.23

(continued)

TABLE A.4   Studentized Range Statistic (Q)

K = NUMBER OF MEANS OR NUMBER OF STEPS BETWEEN ORDERED MEANS										
12	13	14	15	16	17	18	19	20	α	ERROR *df* (*df* WITHIN)
7.32	7.47	7.60	7.72	7.83	7.93	8.03	8.12	8.21	.05	5
10.70	10.89	11.08	11.24	11.40	11.55	11.68	11.81	11.93	.01	
6.79	6.92	7.03	7.14	7.24	7.34	7.43	7.51	7.59	.05	6
9.48	9.65	9.81	9.95	10.08	10.21	10.32	10.43	10.54	.01	
6.43	6.55	6.66	6.76	6.85	6.94	7.02	7.10	7.17	.05	7
8.71	8.86	9.00	9.12	9.24	9.35	9.46	9.55	9.65	.01	
6.18	6.29	6.39	6.48	6.57	6.65	6.73	6.80	6.87	.05	8
8.18	8.31	8.44	8.55	8.66	8.76	8.85	8.94	9.03	.01	
5.98	6.09	6.19	6.28	6.36	6.44	6.51	6.58	6.64	.05	9
7.78	7.91	8.03	8.13	8.23	8.33	8.41	8.49	8.57	.01	
5.83	5.93	6.03	6.11	6.19	6.27	6.34	6.40	6.47	.05	10
7.49	7.60	7.71	7.81	7.91	7.99	8.08	8.15	8.23	.01	
5.71	5.81	5.90	5.98	6.06	6.13	6.20	6.27	6.33	.05	11
7.25	7.36	7.46	7.56	7.65	7.73	7.81	7.88	7.95	.01	
5.61	5.71	5.80	5.88	5.95	6.02	6.09	6.15	6.21	.05	12
7.06	7.17	7.26	7.36	7.44	7.52	7.59	7.66	7.73	.01	
5.53	5.63	5.71	5.79	5.86	5.93	5.99	6.05	6.11	.05	13
6.90	7.01	7.10	7.19	7.27	7.35	7.42	7.48	7.55	.01	
5.46	5.55	5.64	5.71	5.79	5.85	5.91	5.97	6.03	.05	14
6.77	6.87	6.96	7.05	7.13	7.20	7.27	7.33	7.39	.01	
5.40	5.49	5.57	5.65	5.72	5.78	5.85	5.90	5.96	.05	15
6.66	6.76	6.84	6.93	7.00	7.07	7.14	7.20	7.26	.01	
5.35	5.44	5.52	5.59	5.66	5.73	5.79	5.84	5.90	.05	16
6.56	6.66	6.74	6.82	6.90	6.97	7.03	7.09	7.15	.01	
5.31	5.39	5.47	5.54	5.61	5.67	5.73	5.79	5.84	.05	17
6.48	6.57	6.66	6.73	6.81	6.87	6.94	7.00	7.05	.01	
5.27	5.35	5.43	5.50	5.57	5.63	5.69	5.74	5.79	.05	18
6.41	6.50	6.58	6.65	6.73	6.79	6.85	6.91	6.97	.01	
5.23	5.31	5.39	5.46	5.53	5.59	5.65	5.70	5.75	.05	19
6.34	6.43	6.51	6.58	6.65	6.72	6.78	6.84	6.89	.01	
5.20	5.28	5.36	5.43	5.49	5.55	5.61	5.66	5.71	.05	20
6.28	6.37	6.45	6.52	6.59	6.65	6.71	6.77	6.82	.01	
5.10	5.18	5.25	5.32	5.38	5.44	5.49	5.55	5.59	.05	24
6.11	6.19	6.26	6.33	6.39	6.45	6.51	6.56	6.61	.01	
5.00	5.08	5.15	5.21	5.27	5.33	5.38	5.43	5.47	.05	30
5.93	6.01	6.08	6.14	6.20	6.26	6.31	6.36	6.41	.01	
4.90	4.98	5.04	5.11	5.16	5.22	5.27	5.31	5.36	.05	40
5.76	5.83	5.90	5.96	6.02	6.07	6.12	6.16	6.21	.01	
4.81	4.88	4.94	5.00	5.06	5.11	5.15	5.20	5.24	.05	60
5.60	5.67	5.73	5.78	5.84	5.89	5.93	5.97	6.01	.01	
4.71	4.78	4.84	4.90	4.95	5.00	5.04	5.09	5.13	.05	120
5.44	5.50	5.56	5.61	5.66	5.71	5.75	5.79	5.83	.01	
4.62	4.68	4.74	4.80	4.85	4.89	4.93	4.97	5.01	.05	∞
5.29	5.35	5.40	5.45	5.49	5.54	5.57	5.61	5.65	.01	

TABLE A.5   Critical Values of the Pearson *r*
(Pearson Product-Moment Correlation Coefficient)

	LEVEL OF SIGNIFICANCE FOR ONE-TAILED TEST		
	.05	.025	.005
	LEVEL OF SIGNIFICANCE FOR TWO-TAILED TEST		
df	.10	.05	.01
1	.98769	.99692	.999877
2	.90000	.95000	.990000
3	.8054	.8783	.95873
4	.7293	.8114	.91720
5	.6694	.7545	.8745
6	.6215	.7067	.8343
7	.5822	.6664	.7977
8	.5494	.6319	.7646
9	.5214	.6021	.7348
10	.4973	.5760	.7079
11	.4762	.5529	.6835
12	.4575	.5324	.6614
13	.4409	.5139	.6411
14	.4259	.4973	.6226
15	.4124	.4821	.6055
16	.4000	.4683	.5897
17	.3887	.4555	.5751
18	.3783	.4438	.5614
19	.3687	.4329	.5487
20	.3598	.4227	.5368
25	.3233	.3809	.4869
30	.2960	.3494	.4487
35	.2746	.3246	.4182
40	.2573	.3044	.3932
45	.2428	.2875	.3721
50	.2306	.2732	.3541
60	.2108	.2500	.3248
70	.1954	.2319	.3017
80	.1829	.2172	.2830
90	.1726	.2050	.2673
100	.1638	.1946	.2540

SOURCE: Abridged from Table VII in R. A. Fisher and F. Yates, *Statistical Tables for Biological, Agricultural, and Medical Research*, 6th ed., 1974, p. 63. © 1963 R. A. Fisher and F. Yates, reprinted by permission of Pearson Education Limited.

TABLE A.6 Critical Values for the χ^2 Distribution

df	.10	.05	.025	.01	.005
1	2.706	3.841	5.024	6.635	7.879
2	4.605	5.992	7.378	9.210	10.597
3	6.251	7.815	9.348	11.345	12.838
4	7.779	9.488	11.143	13.277	14.860
5	9.236	11.071	12.833	15.086	16.750
6	10.645	12.592	14.449	16.812	18.548
7	12.017	14.067	16.013	18.475	20.278
8	13.362	15.507	17.535	20.090	21.955
9	14.684	16.919	19.023	21.666	23.589
10	15.987	18.307	20.483	23.209	25.188
11	17.275	19.675	21.920	24.725	26.757
12	18.549	21.026	23.337	26.217	28.300
13	19.812	22.362	24.736	27.688	29.819
14	21.064	23.685	26.119	29.141	31.319
15	22.307	24.996	27.488	30.578	32.801
16	23.542	26.296	28.845	32.000	34.267
17	24.769	27.587	30.191	33.409	35.718
18	25.989	28.869	31.526	34.805	37.156
19	27.204	30.144	32.852	36.191	38.582
20	28.412	31.410	34.170	37.566	39.997
21	29.615	32.671	35.479	38.932	41.401
22	30.813	33.925	36.781	40.290	42.796
23	32.007	35.172	38.076	41.638	44.181
24	33.196	36.415	39.364	42.980	45.559
25	34.382	37.653	40.647	44.314	46.929
26	35.563	38.885	41.923	45.642	48.290
27	36.741	40.113	43.195	46.963	49.645
28	37.916	41.337	44.461	48.278	50.994
29	39.087	42.557	45.722	49.588	52.336
30	40.256	43.773	46.979	50.892	53.672
40	51.805	55.759	59.342	63.691	66.767
50	63.167	67.505	71.420	76.154	79.490
60	74.397	79.082	83.298	88.381	91.955
70	85.527	90.531	95.023	100.424	104.213

SOURCE: Lehman, R. S. (1995). *Statistics in the Behavioral Sciences: A Conceptual Introduction*. Pacific Grove, CA: Brooks/Cole Publishing.

TABLE A.7 Critical Values for W (Wilcoxon Rank-Sum Test)

	$N_1 = 1$							$N_1 = 2$							
N_2	0.001	0.005	0.010	0.025	0.05	0.10	$2\overline{W}$	0.001	0.005	0.010	0.025	0.05	0.10	$2\overline{W}$	N_2
2							4						—	10	2
3							5						3	12	3
4							6					—	3	14	4
5							7					3	4	16	5
6							8					3	4	18	6
7							9				—	3	4	20	7
8						—	10				3	4	5	22	8
9						1	11				3	4	5	24	9
10						1	12				3	4	6	26	10
11						1	13				3	4	6	28	11
12						1	14			—	4	5	7	30	12
13						1	15			3	4	5	7	32	13
14						1	16			3	4	6	8	34	14
15						1	17			3	4	6	8	36	15
16						1	18			3	4	6	8	38	16
17						1	19			3	5	6	9	40	17
18				—		1	20		—	3	5	7	9	42	18
19					1	2	21		3	4	5	7	10	44	19
20					1	2	22		3	4	5	7	10	46	20
21					1	2	23		3	4	6	8	11	48	21
22					1	2	24		3	4	6	8	11	50	22
23					1	2	25		3	4	6	8	12	52	23
24					1	2	26		3	4	6	9	12	54	24
25	—	—	—	—	1	2	27	—	3	4	6	9	12	56	25

	$N_1 = 3$							$N_1 = 4$							
N_2	0.001	0.005	0.010	0.025	0.05	0.10	$2\overline{W}$	0.001	0.005	0.010	0.025	0.05	0.10	$2\overline{W}$	N_2
3					6	7	21								
4				—	6	7	24			—	10	11	13	36	4
5				6	7	8	27		—	10	11	12	14	40	5
6			—	7	8	9	30		10	11	12	13	15	44	6
7			6	7	8	10	33		10	11	13	14	16	48	7
8		—	6	8	9	11	36		11	12	14	15	17	52	8
9		6	7	8	10	11	39	—	11	13	14	16	19	56	9
10		6	7	9	10	12	42	10	12	13	15	17	20	60	10
11		6	7	9	11	13	45	10	12	14	16	18	21	64	11
12		7	8	10	11	14	48	10	13	15	17	19	22	68	12
13		7	8	10	12	15	51	11	13	15	18	20	23	72	13
14		7	8	11	13	16	54	11	14	16	19	21	25	76	14
15		8	9	11	13	16	57	11	15	17	20	22	26	80	15
16	—	8	9	12	14	17	60	12	15	17	21	24	27	84	16
17	6	8	10	12	15	18	63	12	16	18	21	25	28	88	17
18	6	8	10	13	15	19	66	13	16	19	22	26	30	92	18
19	6	9	10	13	15	20	69	13	17	19	23	27	31	96	19
20	6	9	11	14	17	21	72	13	18	20	24	28	32	100	20
21	7	9	11	14	17	21	75	14	18	21	25	29	33	104	21
22	7	10	12	15	18	22	78	14	19	21	26	30	35	108	22
23	7	10	12	15	19	23	81	14	19	22	27	31	36	112	23
24	7	10	12	16	19	24	84	15	20	23	27	32	38	116	24
25	7	11	13	16	20	25	87	15	20	23	28	33	38	120	25

(continued)

TABLE A.7 Critical Values for W (Wilcoxon Rank-Sum Test) (*continued*)

	$N_1 = 5$								$N_1 = 6$							
N_2	0.001	0.005	0.010	0.025	0.05	0.10	$2\overline{W}$	0.001	0.005	0.010	0.025	0.05	0.10	$2\overline{W}$	N_2
5		15	16	17	19	20	55								
6		16	17	18	20	22	60	—	23	24	26	28	30	78	6
7	—	16	18	20	21	23	65	21	24	25	27	29	32	84	7
8	15	17	19	21	23	25	70	22	25	27	29	31	34	90	8
9	16	18	20	22	24	27	75	23	26	23	31	33	36	96	9
10	16	19	21	23	26	28	80	24	27	29	32	35	38	102	10
11	17	20	22	24	27	30	85	25	28	30	34	37	40	108	11
12	17	21	23	26	28	32	90	25	30	32	35	38	42	114	12
13	18	22	24	27	30	33	95	26	31	33	37	40	44	120	13
14	18	22	25	28	31	35	100	27	32	34	38	42	46	126	14
15	19	23	26	29	33	37	105	28	33	36	40	44	48	132	15
16	20	24	27	30	34	38	110	29	34	37	42	46	50	138	16
17	20	25	28	32	35	40	115	30	36	39	43	47	52	144	17
18	21	26	29	33	37	42	120	31	37	40	45	49	55	150	18
19	22	27	30	34	38	43	125	32	38	41	46	51	57	156	19
20	22	28	31	35	40	45	130	33	39	43	48	53	59	162	20
21	23	29	32	37	41	47	135	33	40	44	50	55	61	168	21
22	23	29	33	38	43	48	140	34	42	45	51	57	63	174	22
23	24	30	34	39	44	50	145	35	43	47	53	58	65	180	23
24	25	31	35	40	45	51	150	36	44	48	54	60	67	186	24
25	25	32	36	42	47	53	155	37	45	50	56	62	69	192	25

	$N_1 = 7$								$N_1 = 8$							
N_2	0.001	0.005	0.010	0.025	0.05	0.10	$2\overline{W}$	0.001	0.005	0.010	0.025	0.05	0.10	$2\overline{W}$	N_2
7	29	32	34	36	39	41	105								
8	30	34	35	38	41	44	112	40	43	45	49	51	55	136	8
9	31	35	37	40	43	46	119	41	45	47	51	54	58	144	9
10	33	37	39	42	45	49	126	42	47	49	53	56	60	152	10
11	34	38	40	44	47	51	133	44	49	51	55	59	63	160	11
12	35	40	42	46	49	54	140	45	51	53	58	62	66	168	12
13	36	41	44	48	52	56	147	47	53	56	60	64	69	176	13
14	37	43	45	50	54	59	154	48	54	58	62	67	72	184	14
15	38	44	47	52	56	61	161	50	56	60	65	69	75	192	15
16	39	46	49	54	58	64	168	51	58	62	67	72	78	200	16
17	41	47	51	56	61	66	175	53	60	64	70	75	81	208	17
18	42	49	32	58	63	69	182	54	62	66	72	77	84	216	18
19	43	50	54	60	65	71	189	56	64	68	74	80	87	224	19
20	44	52	56	62	67	74	196	57	66	70	77	83	90	232	20
21	46	53	58	64	69	76	203	59	68	72	79	33	92	240	21
22	47	55	59	66	72	79	210	60	70	74	81	88	95	248	22
23	48	57	61	68	74	81	217	62	71	76	84	90	98	256	23
24	49	58	63	70	76	84	224	64	73	78	86	93	101	264	24
25	50	60	64	72	78	86	231	65	75	81	89	96	104	272	25

	$N_1 = 9$								$N_1 = 10$							
N_2	0.001	0.005	0.010	0.025	0.05	0.10	$2\overline{W}$	0.001	0.005	0.010	0.025	0.05	0.10	$2\overline{W}$	N_2
9	52	56	59	62	66	70	171								
10	53	58	61	65	69	73	180	65	71	74	78	82	87	210	10
11	55	61	63	68	72	76	189	67	73	77	81	86	91	220	11
12	57	63	66	71	75	80	198	69	76	79	84	89	94	230	12

TABLE A.7 Critical Values for W (Wilcoxon Rank-Sum Test) (continued)

	$N_1 = 9$							$N_1 = 10$							
N_2	0.001	0.005	0.010	0.025	0.05	0.10	$2\overline{W}$	0.001	0.005	0.010	0.025	0.05	0.10	$2\overline{W}$	N_2
13	59	65	68	73	78	83	207	72	79	82	88	92	98	240	13
14	60	67	71	76	81	86	216	74	81	85	91	96	102	250	14
15	62	69	73	79	84	90	225	76	84	88	94	99	106	260	15
16	64	72	76	82	87	93	234	78	86	91	97	103	109	270	16
17	66	74	78	84	90	97	243	80	89	93	100	106	113	280	17
18	68	76	81	87	93	100	252	82	92	96	103	110	117	290	18
19	70	78	83	90	96	103	261	84	94	99	107	113	121	300	19
20	71	81	85	93	99	107	270	87	97	102	110	117	125	310	20
21	73	83	88	95	102	110	279	89	99	105	113	120	128	320	21
22	75	85	90	98	105	113	288	91	102	108	116	123	132	330	22
23	77	88	93	101	108	117	297	93	105	110	119	127	136	340	23
24	79	90	95	104	111	120	306	95	107	113	122	130	140	350	24
25	81	92	98	107	114	123	315	98	110	116	126	134	144	360	25

	$N_1 = 11$							$N_1 = 12$							
N_2	0.001	0.005	0.010	0.025	0.05	0.10	$2\overline{W}$	0.001	0.005	0.010	0.025	0.05	0.10	$2\overline{W}$	N_2
11	81	87	91	96	100	106	253								
12	83	90	94	99	104	110	264	98	105	109	115	120	127	300	12
13	86	93	97	103	108	114	275	101	109	113	119	125	131	312	13
14	88	96	100	106	112	118	286	103	112	116	123	129	136	324	14
15	90	99	103	110	116	123	297	106	115	120	127	133	141	336	15
16	93	102	107	113	120	127	308	109	119	124	131	138	145	348	16
17	95	105	110	117	123	131	319	112	122	127	135	142	150	360	17
18	98	108	113	121	127	135	330	115	125	131	139	146	155	372	18
19	100	111	116	124	131	139	341	118	129	134	143	150	159	384	19
20	103	114	119	128	135	144	352	120	132	138	147	155	164	396	20
21	106	117	123	131	139	148	363	123	136	142	151	159	169	408	21
22	108	120	126	135	143	152	374	126	139	145	155	163	173	420	22
23	111	123	129	139	147	156	385	129	142	149	159	168	178	432	23
24	113	126	132	142	151	161	396	132	146	153	163	172	183	444	24
25	116	129	136	146	155	165	407	135	149	156	167	176	187	456	25

	$N_1 = 13$							$N_1 = 14$							
N_2	0.001	0.005	0.010	0.025	0.05	0.10	$2\overline{W}$	0.001	0.005	0.010	0.025	0.05	0.10	$2\overline{W}$	N_2
13	117	125	130	136	142	149	351								
14	120	129	134	141	147	154	364	137	147	152	160	166	174	406	14
15	123	133	138	145	152	159	377	141	151	156	164	171	179	420	15
16	126	136	142	150	156	165	390	144	155	161	169	176	185	434	16
17	129	140	146	154	161	170	403	148	159	165	174	182	190	448	17
18	133	144	150	158	166	175	416	151	163	170	179	187	196	462	18
19	136	148	154	163	171	180	429	155	168	174	183	192	202	476	19
20	139	151	158	167	175	185	442	159	172	178	188	197	207	490	20
21	142	155	162	171	180	190	455	162	176	183	193	202	213	504	21
22	145	159	166	176	185	195	468	166	180	187	198	207	218	518	22
23	149	163	170	180	189	200	481	169	184	192	203	212	224	532	23
24	152	166	174	185	194	205	494	173	188	196	207	218	229	546	24
25	155	170	178	189	199	211	507	177	192	200	212	223	235	560	25

(continued)

TABLE A.7 Critical Values for W (Wilcoxon Rank-Sum Test)

	$N_1 = 15$							$N_1 = 16$							
N_2	0.001	0.005	0.010	0.025	0.05	0.10	$2\overline{W}$	0.001	0.005	0.010	0.025	0.05	0.10	$2\overline{W}$	N_2
15	160	171	176	184	192	200	465								
16	163	175	181	190	197	206	480	184	196	202	211	219	229	528	16
17	167	180	186	195	203	212	495	188	201	207	217	225	235	544	17
18	171	184	190	200	208	218	510	192	206	212	222	231	242	560	18
19	175	189	195	205	214	224	525	196	210	213	228	237	248	576	19
20	179	193	200	210	220	230	540	201	215	223	234	243	255	592	20
21	183	198	205	216	225	236	555	205	220	228	239	249	261	608	21
22	187	202	210	221	231	242	370	209	225	233	245	255	267	624	22
23	191	207	214	226	236	248	585	214	230	238	251	261	274	640	23
24	195	211	219	231	242	254	600	218	235	244	256	267	280	656	24
25	199	216	224	237	248	260	615	222	240	249	262	273	287	672	25

	$N_1 = 17$							$N_1 = 18$							
N_2	0.001	0.005	0.010	0.025	0.05	0.10	$2\overline{W}$	0.001	0.005	0.010	0.025	0.05	0.10	$2\overline{W}$	N_2
17	210	223	230	240	249	259	595								
18	214	228	235	246	255	266	612	237	252	259	270	280	291	666	18
19	219	234	241	252	262	273	629	242	258	265	277	287	299	684	19
20	223	239	246	258	268	280	646	247	263	271	283	294	306	702	20
21	228	244	252	264	274	287	663	252	269	277	290	301	313	720	21
22	233	249	258	270	281	294	680	257	275	283	296	307	321	738	22
23	238	255	263	276	287	300	697	262	280	289	303	314	328	756	23
24	242	260	269	282	294	307	714	267	286	295	309	321	335	774	24
25	247	265	275	288	300	314	731	273	292	301	316	323	343	792	25

	$N_1 = 19$							$N_1 = 20$							
N_2	0.001	0.005	0.010	0.025	0.05	0.10	$2\overline{W}$	0.001	0.005	0.010	0.025	0.05	0.10	$2\overline{W}$	N_2
19	267	283	291	303	313	325	741								
20	272	239	297	309	320	333	760	298	315	324	337	348	361	820	20
21	277	295	303	316	328	341	779	304	322	331	344	356	370	840	21
22	283	301	310	323	335	349	798	309	328	337	351	364	378	860	22
23	288	307	316	330	342	357	817	315	335	344	359	371	386	880	23
24	294	313	323	337	350	364	836	321	341	351	366	379	394	900	24
25	299	319	329	344	357	372	855	327	348	358	373	387	403	920	25

	$N_1 = 21$							$N_1 = 22$							
N_2	0.001	0.005	0.010	0.025	0.05	0.10	$2\overline{W}$	0.001	0.005	0.010	0.025	0.05	0.10	$2\overline{W}$	N_2
21	331	349	359	373	385	399	903								
22	337	356	366	381	393	408	924	365	386	396	411	424	439	990	22
23	343	363	373	388	401	417	945	372	393	403	419	432	448	1012	23
24	349	370	381	396	410	425	966	379	400	411	427	441	457	1034	24
25	356	377	388	404	418	434	987	385	408	419	435	450	467	1056	25

	$N_1 = 23$							$N_1 = 24$							
N_2	0.001	0.005	0.010	0.025	0.05	0.10	$2\overline{W}$	0.001	0.005	0.010	0.025	0.05	0.10	$2\overline{W}$	N_2
23	402	424	434	451	465	481	1081								
24	409	431	443	459	474	491	1104	440	464	475	492	507	525	1176	24
25	416	439	451	468	483	500	1127	448	472	484	501	517	535	1200	25

	$N_1 = 25$						
N_2	0.001	0.005	0.010	0.025	0.05	0.10	$2\overline{W}$
25	480	505	517	536	552	570	1275

Source: Table 1 in L. R. Verdooren. Extended tables of critical values for Wilcoxon's test statistic. *Biometrika*, 1963, Volume 50, pp. 177–186. Reprinted by permission of the Biometrika Trustees.

TABLE A.8   Critical Values for the Wilcoxon Matched-Pairs Signed-Ranks T Test*

	α LEVELS FOR A ONE-TAILED TEST					α LEVELS FOR A ONE-TAILED TEST			
	.05	.025	.01	.005		.05	.025	.01	.005
No. of Pairs	α LEVELS FOR A TWO-TAILED TEST					α LEVELS FOR A TWO-TAILED TEST			
N	.10	.05	.02	.01	N	.10	.05	.02	.01
5	0	—	—	—	28	130	116	101	91
6	2	0	—	—	29	140	126	110	100
7	3	2	0	—	30	151	137	120	109
8	5	3	1	0	31	163	147	130	118
9	8	5	3	1	32	175	159	140	128
10	10	8	5	3	33	187	170	151	138
11	13	10	7	5	34	200	182	162	148
12	17	13	9	7	35	213	195	173	159
13	21	17	12	9	36	227	208	185	171
14	25	21	15	12	37	241	221	198	182
15	30	25	19	15	38	256	235	211	194
16	35	29	23	19	39	271	249	224	207
17	41	34	27	23	40	286	264	238	220
18	47	40	32	27	41	302	279	252	233
19	53	46	37	32	42	319	294	266	247
20	60	52	43	37	43	336	310	281	261
21	67	58	49	42	44	353	327	296	276
22	75	65	55	48	45	371	343	312	291
23	83	73	62	54	46	389	361	328	307
24	91	81	69	61	47	407	378	345	322
25	100	89	76	68	48	426	396	362	339
26	110	98	84	75	49	446	415	379	355
27	119	107	92	83	50	466	434	397	373

*To be significant the T obtained from the data must be equal to or less than the value shown in the table.

Source: From KIRK. *Statistics*, 5E. © 2008 Wadsworth, a part of Cengage Learning, Inc. Reproduced by permission.

Answers to Module and Chapter Summary Exercises

CHAPTER 1
Module 1

1. Because a theory is an organized system of assumptions and principles that attempts to explain certain phenomena and how they are related, it is doubtful that your doctor's explanation of your symptoms is actually a theory. More accurate would have been a statement that he or she had a hypothesis (a prediction describing the potential relationship between at least two variables) regarding your symptoms.

3. Both types of observation have the advantage of flexibility and the disadvantage of affording the researcher little control over the situation.

5 a. The independent variable is the type of study used.
   b. The dependent variable is exam performance.
   c. The control group would be the traditional means of studying (studying alone), whereas the experimental group would be those who studied in interactive groups.
   d. The independent variable is manipulated.

7 a. The independent variable is age.
   b. The dependent variable is reaction time.
   c. The control group might be viewed as those of a more average age (25–45 years), whereas the experimental group might be viewed as those who are elderly (55–75 years).
   d. The independent variable is a nonmanipulated participant variable (age).

Module 2

1. An operational definition is a definition of the variable in terms of the operations or activities the researcher uses to measure or manipulate it. Operational definitions allow us to quantify observations.

3. The four properties are **identity** (objects that are different receive different scores), **magnitude** (the ordering of the numbers reflects the ordering of the variable), **equal unit size** (a difference of 1 is the same amount throughout the entire scale), and **absolute zero** (a score of zero indicates an absence of the variable being measured).

5. An interval scale has the first three properties of measurement (identity, magnitude, and equal unit size), whereas a ratio scale has all four properties of measurement. Examples of an interval scale are the Fahrenheit temperature scale and scores on the SAT. Examples of a ratio scale are percentage correct on an exam or weight.

7. Number of college classes completed would be a discrete variable because you cannot complete a portion of a class. In other words, you are only assigned credit hours based on completing a whole class. The scale of measurement for this variable would be ratio because there is an absolute zero in addition to the other properties of measurement.

Chapter 1 Summary and Review

Fill-in Self-Test Answers

1. hypothesis
2. description, prediction, explanation
3. case study
4. population
5. correlational
6. participant (subject)
7. independent
8. control
9. operational definition
10. Magnitude
11. nominal
12. interval

Multiple-Choice Self-Test Answers

1. b
2. c
3. b
4. b
5. c
6. b
7. d
8. d
9. d
10. b
11. a
12. b
13. a

CHAPTER 2
Module 3

1.

Speed	f	rf
62	1	.05
64	3	.15
65	4	.20
67	3	.15
68	2	.10
70	2	.10
72	1	.05
73	1	.05
76	1	.05
79	1	.05
80	1	.05
	20	1.00

3. Either a histogram or a frequency polygon could be used to graph these data. However, due to the continuous nature of the speed data, a frequency polygon might be most appropriate. Both a

histogram and a frequency polygon of the data are presented.

5. It would be appropriate to use a bar graph when the variable being measured is nominal or qualitative, whereas a histogram is appropriate when the data collected represent a quantitative variable measured on an ordinal, interval, or ratio scale. Moreover, a histogram is most appropriate for discrete data. If the data are continuous, neither of these types of graphs would be appropriate.

Module 4

1. $\overline{X} = 68.55$
   $Md = 67$
   $Mo = 65$
3. $\overline{X} = 7.3$
   $Md = 8.5$
   $Mo = 11$

5. $\overline{X} = 6.12$
   $Md = 6.5$
   $Mo = 3$ and 8 (a bimodal distribution)
7. For distribution A, the mean, median, and mode
   are all 12, thus any of these measures would
   be appropriate because this distribution has no
   extreme scores and thus all three measures of
   central tendency are good measures. For distribution B however, there is one extreme score (100)
   and thus although the median and the mode
   are both 12, the mean is 21.56—a number higher
   than 8 out of 9 of the scores in the distribution.
   Thus, because of this extreme score, the mean is
   not a good measure of central tendency for this
   distribution.

Chapter 2 Summary and Review

Fill-in Self-Test Answers

1. frequency distribution
2. qualitative
3. histogram
4. central tendency
5. median

Multiple-Choice Self-Test Answers

1. c
2. d
3. d
4. c
5. b
6. b
7. c

Answers to Self-Test Problems

1.

X	f	rf
1	2	.17
2	2	.17
4	1	.08
5	1	.08
8	1	.08
9	1	.08
10	1	.08
11	3	.25

2. $\overline{X} = 6.25, Md = 6.5, Mo = 11$

CHAPTER 3
Module 5

1. range $= 8$
   $AD = 2.22$
   $s = 2.74, \sigma = 2.58$

3. range $= 80$
   $AD = 22.22$
   $s = 27.39, \sigma = 25.82$
5. range $= 800$
   $AD = 222.22$
   $s = 273.86, \sigma = 258.20$
7. The data are skewed positively, or
   right-skewed.

Module 6

1. $z = +2.57$
   Proportion of cars that cost an equal amount
   or more $= .0051$
3. $z = +2.0$
   Percentile rank $= 97.72$
5. $z = -3.14, z = +2.0$
   Proportion between $= .4992 + .4772 = .9764$
7. $z = +1.33$
   Proportion studying more $= .0918$
9. $z = -2.0, z = 1.33$
   Proportion between $= .4773 + .4083 = .8856$
11. $z = -.67$
    Percentile rank $= 25.14$
13.

	X	z Score	Percentile Rank
Ken	73.00	$-.22$	41.29
Drew	88.95	$+1.55$	93.94
Cecil	83.28	$+.92$	82.00

Chapter 3 Summary and Review

Fill-in Self-Test Answers

1. variation
2. average deviation
3. unbiased estimator
4. population; sample
5. positively or right
6. z score
7. standard normal distribution

Multiple-Choice Self-Test Answers

1. a
2. a
3. a
4. b
5. b
6. b
7. a
8. c

Answers to Self-Test Problems

1. range $= 6, AD = 2, \sigma = 2.26$

2. a. $z = -1.67$, proportion $= .9525$
   b. $z = +.80$, percentile rank $= 78.81$
   c. $87,400

CHAPTER 4
Module 7

1. a. $20/70 = .29$
   b. $50/70 = .71$
   c. $(20 + 50)/70 = 1.0$
   d. $(20/70) \times (50/70) = .21$
3. $(4/52) + (4/52) = .15$
5. $z = -0.80$, probability $= .21186$
7. $z = 0.40$, $z = -0.80$,
   probability $= .34458 \times .21186 = .073$

Module 8

1. H_0: $\mu_{freshmen} = \mu_{all\ other\ classes}$, or
   H_0: $\mu_{freshmen} \leq \mu_{all\ other\ classes}$
   H_a: $\mu_{freshmen} > \mu_{all\ other\ classes}$
   This is a one-tailed test.
3. H_0: $\mu_{size\ now} = \mu_{family\ size\ in\ previous\ decade}$, or
   H_0: $\mu_{family\ size\ now} \leq \mu_{family\ size\ in\ previous\ decade}$
   H_a: $\mu_{family\ size\ now} > \mu_{family\ size\ in\ previous\ decade}$
   This is a one-tailed test.
5. a. Type I error
   b. Type II error
   c. Type I error
   d. Type II error

Chapter 4 Summary and Review

Fill-in Self-Test Answers

1. Probability
2. multiplication
3. addition
4. null hypothesis
5. directional or one-tailed hypothesis
6. Type I
7. statistical significance
8. Nonparametric

Multiple-Choice Self-Test Answers

1. c
2. a
3. d
4. a
5. d
6. a
7. d
8. b
9. b

10. c
11. c
12. a
13. d
14. b
15. d

CHAPTER 5
Module 9

1. The sampling distribution is a distribution of sample means in which each sample is the same size.
3. The z_{cv} for a one-tailed test needs to be far enough away from the mean that only 5% of the scores are beyond it. This z score is ±1.645 standard deviations from the mean. For a two-tailed test, the z score needs to be far enough away from the mean that only 5% of the scores are beyond it taking both sides (two-tailed) of the distribution into account. Thus, this is 2.5% on one side and 2.5% on the other side. This z score is ±1.96 standard deviations from the mean.
5. a. This is a one-tailed test.
   b. H_0: $\mu_{private\ HS} = \mu_{HS\ in\ general}$, or
      H_0: $\mu_{private\ HS} \leq \mu_{HS\ in\ general}$
      H_a: $\mu_{private\ HS} > \mu_{HS\ in\ general}$
   c. $z_{obt} = 2.37$
   d. $z_{cv} = \pm 1.645$ (one-tailed critical value)
   e. Reject H_0. High school students at private high schools score significantly higher on the SAT.
   d. 95% $CI = 1008.68 - 1091.32$

Module 10

1. A t test differs from a z test mainly in terms of the sample size for which each test is appropriate. We use a t test when the sample size is small (30 or less) and a z test when the sample size is larger than 30. The t test becomes the z test when the sample sizes are large. Both tests allow us to determine how far away from the population mean the sample mean is.
3. t_{cv} changes because the t distributions are a family of symmetric distributions that involve different distributions for each sample size. Therefore, t_{cv} changes for samples of different sizes. We must compute the degrees of freedom in order to determine the t_{cv}.
5. a. This is a one-tailed test.
   b. H_0: $\mu_{headphones} = \mu_{no\ headphones}$, or
      H_0: $\mu_{headphones} \geq \mu_{no\ headphones}$
      H_a: $\mu_{headphones} < \mu_{no\ headphones}$
   c. $t_{obt} = -3.37$

d. $t_{cv} = \pm 1.796$
e. Reject H_0. Those who listen to music via headphones score significantly lower on a hearing test.
f. 95% $CI = 16.43 - 21.23$

Chapter 5 Summary and Review

Fill-in Self-Test Answers

1. sampling distribution
2. standard error of the mean
3. z test
4. t distribution
5. t test
6. t test

Multiple-Choice Self-Test Answers

1. a
2. a
3. b
4. a
5. a
6. d

Answers to Self-Test Problems

1. a. one-tailed
   b. H_0: $\mu_{chess} = \mu_{general\ population}$, or
      H_0: $\mu_{chess} \leq \mu_{general\ population}$
      H_a: $\mu_{chess} > \mu_{general\ population}$
   c. $z_{obt} = +3.03$
   d. $z_{cv} = \pm 1.645$
   e. Reject H_0. Students who play chess score significantly higher on the SAT.
   f. 95% $CI = 1,024.74 - 1,115.26$
2. a. one-tailed
   b. H_0: $\mu_{classical\ music} = \mu_{general\ population}$, or
      H_0: $\mu_{classical\ music} \leq \mu_{general\ population}$
      H_a: $\mu_{classical\ music} > \mu_{general\ population}$
   c. $t_{obt} = +3.05$
   d. $t_{cv} = \pm 1.796$
   e. Reject H_0. Those who listen to classical music score significantly higher on the concentration test.
   f. 95% $CI = 16.43 - 21.23$

CHAPTER 6
Module 11

1. An independent-groups t test would be appropriate when the data collected are interval ratio in scale, there is one independent variable with two levels,

and the design is between-participants (different people randomly assigned to the two conditions).
3. The APA recommends we calculate a measure of effect size because effect size tells us the proportion of variance in the dependent variable that is accounted for by the manipulation of the independent variable. In other words, effect size indicates how big a role the conditions of the independent variable play in determining scores on the dependent variable. Moreover, effect size provides an estimate of the effect of the independent variable, regardless of sample size.
5. a. An independent samples t test should be used.
   b. H_0: $\mu_{Music} = \mu_{No\ music}$, or H_0: $\mu_{Music} \geq \mu_{No\ music}$
      H_a: $\mu_{Music} < \mu_{No\ music}$
   c. $t(16) = 2.58, p < .025$.
   d. Reject H_0. Studying with no music leads to significantly higher test scores.
   e. $d = 1.22$ and $r^2 = .29$—there is a large effect size.
   f.

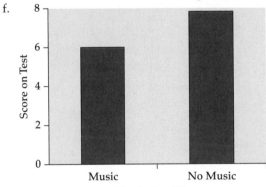

g. The 95% confidence interval is $-2.83 - -29$.

Module 12

1. The difference between the two tests is that the independent-groups t test should be used when there are different participants serving in the two groups being compared (a between-participants design) and a correlated-groups t test should be used when either the same participants are used in both conditions (a within-participants design) or different participants who have been matched on one or more variables are used in the two conditions (a matched-participants design).
3. In order to turn the two scores recorded for each participant into one score for each participant, we calculate a difference score for each individual (their score for one condition minus their score in the other conditions). If the independent variable

had no effect, we would expect the difference scores to be zero, whereas if the independent variable had an effect, we would expect the difference scores to be greater than zero.

5. a. A correlated-groups t test should be used.
   b. $H_0: \mu_{before} = \mu_{after}$, or $H_0: \mu_{before} \geq \mu_{after}$
      $H_a: \mu_{before} < \mu_{after}$
   c. $t(5) = 6.82$ (or 6.71 if calculated by hand and each step is rounded to two decimal places), $p < .005$
   d. Reject H_0. Participating in sports leads to significantly higher self-esteem scores.
   e. $d = 2.73$ and $r^2 = .90$. There is a large effect size.
   f.

Sports Condition

   g. 95% $CI = -2.08 - -.92$

Chapter 6 Summary and Review

Fill-in Self-Test Answers

1. independent-groups t test
2. Cohen's d, or r^2
3. correlated-groups t test
4. difference scores
5. standard error of the difference scores

Multiple-Choice Self-Test Answers

1. b
2. a
3. a
4. b
5. c
6. d
7. b
8. c
9. a
10. c
11. a

Answers to Self-Test Problems

1. a. An independent-groups t test
   b. $H_0: \mu_1 = \mu_2$; $H_a: \mu_1 \neq \mu_2$
   c. $t(10) = -2.99$, $p < .02$ or $t(10) = 2.99$, $p < .02$ (depending on which mean you place first)
   d. Reject H_0. Females spend significantly more time volunteering than males.
   e. $d = 1.73$, or $r^2 = .47$. This is a moderate to large effect size.
   f.

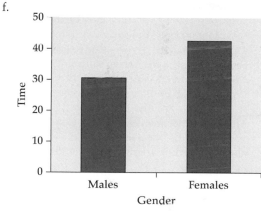

Gender

   g. 95% $CI = -21.51 - -3.15$.
2. a. A correlated-groups t test
   b. $H_0: \mu_1 = \mu_2$; $H_a: \mu_1 \neq \mu_2$
   c. $t(5) = 2.78$, $p < .05$
   d. Reject H_0. When participants studied with music, they scored significantly lower on the quiz.
   e.

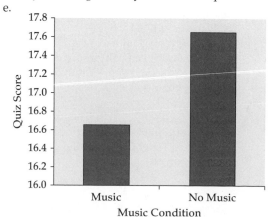

Music Condition

   f. 95% $CI = -1.93 - -.07$

CHAPTER 7
Module 13

1. Conducting a study with three or more levels of the independent variable allows a researcher to compare more than two kinds of treatment in one study, to compare two or more kinds of treatment with a control group, and to compare a placebo group to both the control and experimental groups.
3. Between-groups variance is the variance attributable to both systematic variance and error variance. Systematic variance may be due either to the effects of the independent variable or to confounds. Error variance may be due to chance, sampling error, or individual differences. Within-groups variance is always due to error variance (once again due to chance, sampling error, or individual differences).
5. If H_0 is true, then there is no effect of the independent variable and the F-ratio should be close to 1. This is because there would be no systematic variance. Thus, the F-ratio would be error variance over error variance and should be equal to approximately 1.

Module 14

1. a.

Source	df	SS	MS	F
Between groups	3	187.75	62.58	18.14
Within groups	16	55.20	3.45	
Total	19	242.95		

b. Yes, $F(3, 16) = 18.14, p < .01$
c. $HSD_{.05} = 3.36$ $HSD_{.01} = 4.31$
d. The amount of sleep had a significant effect on creativity. Specifically, those who slept for 6 or 8 hours scored significantly higher on creativity than those who slept for either 2 or 4 hours.
e. The effect size (η^2) is 77%. Thus, knowing the sleep condition to which participants were assigned can explain 77% of the variability in creativity scores.

f.

3. a.

Source	df	SS	MS	F
Between groups	2	4,689.27	2,344.64	.77
Within groups	27	82,604.20	3,059.41	
Total	29	87,293.47		

b. No, $F(2, 27) = .77$, not significant.
c. Not necessary.
d. The level of exercise did not affect stress level. There was, however, a very large amount of error variance.
e. The effect size (η^2) is 5%. Knowing the exercise condition to which a participant was assigned does not account for much of the variability in stress scores.

f.

5. Post hoc comparisons should be performed when three or more groups are being compared and the F-ratio is significant. The post hoc tests allow us to make multiple comparisons between the groups.

Chapter 7 Summary and Review

Fill-in Self-Test Answers

1. Bonferroni adjustment
2. One-Way ANOVA
3. grand mean
4. between-groups
5. total sum of squares
6. mean square
7. Eta-squared
8. post hoc tests or Tukey's HSD

Multiple-Choice Self-Test Answers

1. b
2. d
3. b
4. b
5. a
6. c
7. a
8. d
9. c
10. a

Answers to Self-Test Problems

1. $HSD_{.05} = 3.21$, $HSD_{.01} = 4.18$, $\eta^2 = 60\%$

CHAPTER 8
Module 15

1. A randomized ANOVA is used with a between-participants design. The term *randomized* indicates that participants were randomly assigned to conditions. A repeated measures ANOVA is used with correlated-groups designs. The term *repeated measures* indicates that measures were taken repeatedly on the same participants.
3. A repeated measures ANOVA is statistically more powerful than a randomized ANOVA because the variance due to individual differences is removed from the denominator in the F-ratio (remember that because we use the same participants, or matched-participants in each condition, the individual differences are minimized). Thus, in the final F-ratio, we divide by a smaller number, which results in a larger final F score, and as with most statistics, a larger final test statistic has a greater likelihood of being statistically significant.

5. a.

Source	df	SS	MS	F
Participant	9	2.75	.306	
Between	2	180.05	90.025	75.02
Error	18	21.65	1.20	
Total	29	204.45		

b. Yes, $F(2, 18) = 75.02$, $p < .01$.
c. $HSD_{.05} = 1.26$
   $HSD_{.01} = 1.65$
d. Type of crust significantly affected pizza preference. Specifically, thin crust was preferred significantly more than thick or hand-tossed crusts, and thick crust was preferred significantly more than hand-tossed crust.
e. The effect size (η^2) is 88%. Thus, knowing the type of crust eaten by a participant can account for 88% of the variability in pizza preference scores.

f.

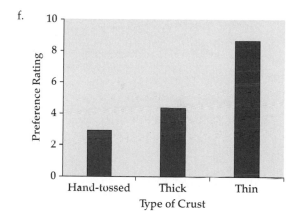

Module 16

1. One advantage is that manipulating more than one independent variable allows us to assess how the variables interact, called an interaction effect. In addition, because in the real world behavior is usually contingent upon more than one variable, designing experiments with more than one variable allows researchers to simulate a real-world setting more effectively.
3. This is a 3 × 2 × 2 design (or a 2 × 2 × 3). The independent variable of number of hours studied has three levels, the independent variable of type of processing has two levels, and the independent variable of group or individual study has two levels.

5. In a 2 × 6 factorial design, there is the possibility for two main effects—one for each of the independent variables. There is the possibility for only one interaction—that between the two independent variables in the study.

7. *Experiment 1*

	A_1	A_2
B_1	3	5
B_2	5	7

A: Yes
B: Yes
A × B: No

Experiment 2

	A_1	A_2
B_1	12	4
B_2	4	12

A: No
B: No
A × B: Yes

Module 17

1. In a 3 × 3 design, there are two possible main effects (one for each independent variable) and one possible interaction between the two independent variables.

3. No, one of the variables has only two levels. Thus, if the F-ratio for that main effect is significant, it means that there were significant differences between those two groups and Tukey's post hoc test is not necessary. However, it is necessary to compute Tukey's post hoc test for the main effect of the variable with six levels because the F-ratio simply tells us that there is a significant difference between two of the groups. Therefore, we need to determine how many of the groups differ significantly from each other.

5. a.

Source	df	SS	MS	F
Gender	1	0.167	0.167	0.095
Pizza Brand	1	6.00	6.00	3.43
Gender×Pizza	1	130.67	130.67	74.67
Error	20	35.00	1.75	
Total	23	171.83		

Note: If calculated by hand, your SS scores may vary slightly due to rounding.

   b. The only significant F-ratio is that for the interaction, $F(1, 20) = 74.67, p < .01$.

   c. There is no significant effect of gender on pizza preference. There is no significant effect of type of pizza on pizza preference. There is a significant interaction effect: The males prefer the low-fat pizza over the regular pizza, whereas the females prefer the opposite (the regular over the low-fat pizza).

   d. The effect size (η^2) is .09% for gender (gender accounts for less than .10% of the variability in preference scores), 3.5% for type of pizza (type of pizza accounts for 3.5% of the variability in preference scores), and 76% for the interaction (the interaction of gender and type of pizza accounts for 76% of the variability in preference scores).

   e. Because the variable of gender is not continuous, a bar graph would be appropriate. Because most students find it easier to interpret interactions with a line graph, this type of graph is also provided and may be used.

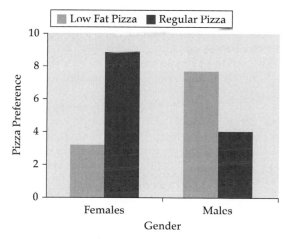

Chapter 8 Summary and Review

Fill-in Self-Test Answers

1. repeated-measures one-way ANOVA
2. factorial notation
3. main effect
4. two; four; six
5. two; one
6. SS_{Error}
7. eta-squared

Multiple-Choice Self-Test Answers

1. a
2. c
3. d
4. a
5. b
6. c
7. b

8. c
9. c
10. c
11. c
12. b
13. d

Answers to Self-Test Problems

1. a.

Source	df	SS	MS	F
Participant	5	9.12	1.82	
Between	2	10.19	5.10	3.67
Error	10	13.90	1.39	
Total	17	33.21		

Note: If calculated by hand, your SS scores may vary slightly due to rounding.

b. No, $F(2, 10) = 3.67$; not significant.
c. Type of pain killer did not significantly affect effectiveness rating.
d. Because the F score was not significant, calculation of the effect size is not necessary. However, if you did calculate it, it would be 31%.
e.

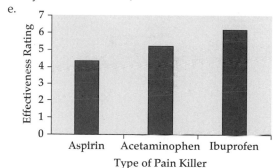

2. a.

	Morning	Afternoon	Evening
Lecture only	9	7	6
Lecture/small-group	5	6	8

This is a 2×3 factorial design.

b.

ANOVA Summary Table

Source	df	SS	MS	F
A (Time)	2	1.67	0.835	0.63
B (Teaching Method)	1	7.50	7.50	5.64
A × B	2	45.02	22.51	16.92
Within	24	32.00	1.33	
Total	29	86.19		

Note: If calculated by hand, your SS scores may vary slightly due to rounding.

c. Factor A: $F(2, 24) = .63$; not significant
   Factor B: $F(1, 24) = 5.64, p < .05$
   Interaction: $F(2, 24) = 16.92, p < .01$
d. There is no significant effect of time of day on attentiveness. There is a significant effect of teaching method on attentiveness: Those in the lecture-only groups were more attentive. There is a significant interaction effect: As time of day increased, attentiveness decreased for the lecture-only conditions, whereas attentiveness increased for the lecture-with-small-group-activities conditions.
e. The effect size (η^2) is 2% for time of day (time of day accounts for less than 2% of the variability in attentiveness scores), 9% for teaching method (teaching method accounts for 9% of the variability in attentiveness scores), and 52% for the interaction (the interaction of time of day and teaching method accounts for 52% of the variability in attentiveness scores).
f.

CHAPTER 9
Module 18

1. The first problem is with the correlation coefficient that was calculated. Correlation coefficients can vary between -1.00 and $+1.00$. They cannot be greater than ± 1.00. Thus, the calculated correlation coefficient is incorrect. Second, correlation does not mean causation. Thus, observing a correlation between exercise and health does not mean that we can conclude that exercise causes better health—they are simply related.
3. The correlation coefficient for a curvilinear relationship would be close to 0.00 because the positive correlation represented by half of the curve would essentially cancel out the negative correlations represented by the other half of the curve.
5. We would expect the correlation between GRE scores and graduate school GPAs to be much lower than that between SAT scores and undergraduate GPAs because both GRE scores and graduate school GPAs are restricted in range.

Module 19

1. The Pearson product-moment correlation coefficient should be used when both variables are measured on an interval-ratio scale of measurement.
3. Based on the strong, positive correlation coefficient, 72.6% of the variability in stress scores is accounted for by the number of cups of coffee consumed per day.
5. IQ with psychology exam—$r^2 = 30.6\%$; thus 30.6% of the variability in intelligence test scores is accounted for by the psychology exam score, and vice versa. IQ exam with statistics exam—$r^2 = 46.5\%$; thus 46.5% of the variability in intelligence test scores is accounted for by the statistics exam score, and vice versa. Psychology exam with statistics exam—$r^2 = 39.2\%$; thus 39.2% of the variability in psychology exam scores is accounted for by the statistics exam score.
7. The Spearman rank-order correlation coefficient should be used. In order to do so, the variable measured on the interval-ratio scale needs to be converted to an ordinal scale.

Module 20

1. A regression analysis is based on determining the regression line—determining the equation for the best-fitting line for a data set. Once the regression line has been determined, we can predict from one variable to another by determining where on the line an individual's score on one variable lies and then determining what value this corresponds to on the second variable (the predicted score).
3. IQ and psychology exam —$Y' = .27(X) + 9.00$
   IQ and statistics exam—$Y' = .32 (X) + 4.98$
   Psychology exam and statistics exam—$Y' = .59(X) + 17.43$

Chapter 9 Summary and Review

Fill-in Self-Test Answers

1. scatterplot
2. negative
3. causality; directionality
4. restrictive range
5. Pearson product-moment
6. point-biserial
7. coefficient of determination
8. Regression analysis

Multiple-Choice Self-Test Answers

1. c
2. b
3. c
4. c
5. d
6. b
7. d
8. a
9. a
10. c
11. b
12. a

Answer to Self-Test Problem

1. $r = .70$
   $r^2 = .49$ (49%)
   Regression equation: $Y' = .569(X) + 33.06$

CHAPTER 10
Module 21

1. It is appropriate to use a chi-square test when the data are nominal and no parameters are known.
3. a. $\chi^2_{obt} = 2.55$
   b. $df = 1$
   c. $\chi^2_{cv} = 3.841$
   d. There is no significant difference between the percent who exercise in California and the national exercise rate.
5. a. χ^2 $(N = 93) = 6.74, p < .01$
   b. $df = 1$
   c. $\chi^2_{cv} = 3.841$
   d. Reject H_0. There is a significant difference in seating preferences for males versus females. More males sit in the back and more females sit in the front.

Module 22

1. The nonparametric tests in this module are used when the data collected are ordinal in scale, whereas the tests in the previous module are used when the data collected are nominal in scale. Both types of tests are nonparametric.
3. For all other statistics covered in this text, the obtained value for the statistic has to be as large as, or larger than, the critical value. For the Wilcoxon tests, however, the obtained value must be equal to or less than the critical value.
5. a. The Wilcoxon's rank-sum test should be used.
   b. H_0: $Md_{Red} = Md_{Green}$, or $Md_{Red} \leq Md_{Green}$
   H_a: $Md_{Red} > Md_{Green}$
   c. $W(n_1 = 7, n_2 = 7) = 43$; not significant
   d. Fail to reject H_0. Tastiness scores for the two different colored sauces did not differ significantly.
7. The Kruskal-Wallis test is used when there is one independent variable with more than two levels and a between-subjects design, whereas the Wilcoxon rank-sum test is used when there is one independent variable with only two levels and a between-subjects design.
9. a. The Friedman test.
   b. H_0: There are no systematic differences in ranks across the three conditions.
   H_a: There are systematic differences in ranks across the three conditions.
   c. $\chi^2 = 10.79$ (2, $N = 7$), $p < .005$.
   d. Reject H_0, children prefer blue ketchup most, then red, and they least prefer green ketchup.

Chapter 10 Summary and Review

Fill-in Self-Test Answers

1. observed; expected
2. Wilcoxon rank-sum test
3. χ^2 test
4. phi coefficient
5. matched-pairs signed-ranks T
6. between-participants
7. nominal; ordinal
8. Kruskal-Wallis test

Multiple-Choice Self-Test Answers

1. d
2. d
3. c
4. c
5. b
6. a
7. a

Answers to Self-Test Problems

1. a. χ^2 goodness-of-fit test
   b. H_0: The observed data fit the expected frequencies for the population.
   H_a: The observed data do not fit the expected frequencies for the population.
   c. $\chi^2_{obt} = 1.45$
   $df = 1$
   $\chi^2_{cv} = 3.841$
   d. Fail to reject H_0. The percentage of people who smoke in the South does not differ significantly from that in the general population.

2. a. χ^2 test of independence
   b. H_0: There is no difference in the frequency of workout preferences for males and females.
   H_a: There is a difference in the frequency of workout preferences for males and females.
   c. $\chi^2 (N = 68) = 8.5, p < .01$
   d. Reject H_0. There is a significant difference in the frequency of workout preferences for males and females. Females prefer to work out together more than males.

3. a. Wilcoxon rank-sum test
   b. H_0: $Md_{Red} = Md_{Green}$, or $Md_{Red} \leq Md_{Green}$
   H_a: $Md_{Red} > Md_{Green}$
   c. $W_s (n_1 = 7, n_2 = 7) = 41$; not significant
   d. Fail to reject H_0. There is no significant difference in tastiness scores.

Getting Started with Excel, SPSS, and the TI-84 Calculator

USING EXCEL 2007 OR 2010

Installing the Analysis ToolPak Before you begin to use Excel to analyze data, you may need to install the Data Analysis ToolPak. For Excel 2007, this can be accomplished by launching Excel and then clicking on the Microsoft Office icon at the top left of the page. At the bottom of the drop-down menu, there is a tab labeled **Excel Options.**

Click on **Excel Options,** and a dialog box of options will appear. On the left-hand side of the dialog box is a list of options; click on **Add-Ins** to open a pop-up window. The very top option in the pop-up window should be **Analysis ToolPak**. Click on this and then **GO.**

A dialog box in which **Analysis ToolPak** is the first option will appear. Check this and then click **OK.**

The ToolPak should now be installed on your computer.

For Excel 2010, the process is similar. Begin by clicking on the **File** tab at the top left of the screen (this tab replaces the Microsoft Office icon from 2007).

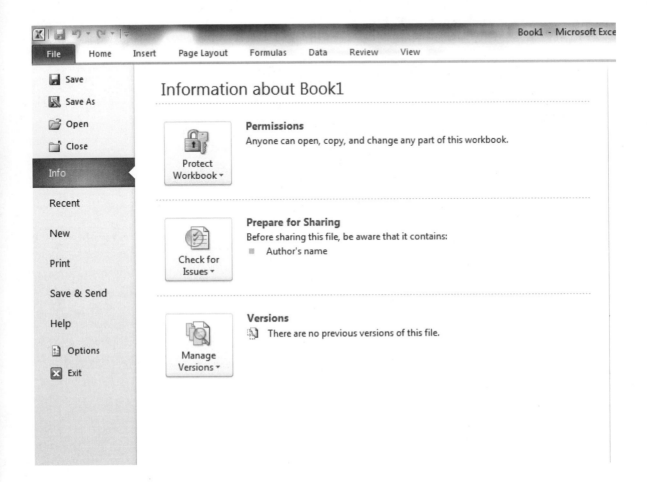

Next, click on **Options** toward the bottom of the drop-down menu. From here the process is similar to that for 2007. A dialog box of options will appear. On the left-hand side of the dialog box is a list of options; click on **Add-Ins** to open a pop-up window. The very top option in the pop-up window should be **Analysis ToolPak.** Click on this and then **GO.** A dialog box in which **Analysis ToolPak** is the first option will appear. Check this and then click **OK.**

Launching Excel When you open Excel, you will be presented with a spreadsheet.

File tab Home tab Data tab

Worksheet tab

You can see in the preceding worksheet where the **File** tab is (in Excel 2007, the Office Button is here), along with the **Home, Data,** and **Worksheet** tabs. The spreadsheet has a series of columns and rows. The columns are labeled with letters, and the rows with numbers. A cell is the point at which a column and row intersect. Thus, cell A1 is highlighted in the preceding screen capture. We typically refer to cells with the column letter first and the row number second (e.g., D5). We will be entering data into the cells for the analyses we'll be conducting using Excel in subsequent modules. In addition, we'll be using the Data Analysis ToolPak for most of our analyses. The ToolPak can be accessed when the **Data** ribbon is active (see the following screen capture).

When the **Data** ribbon is active, as in the preceding image, you can see the **Data Analysis** option at the upper right of the screen. This option indicates that the ToolPak has been installed properly. If the **Data Analysis** option is not visible at the top right of the ribbon, then the ToolPak was not installed properly (see previous instructions on installing the ToolPak).

Entering Data   We can enter data into Excel by simply entering the numbers in the cells. For example, in the following image, I've entered some annual salary data for a small business. You can see that I labeled the data **Salary** in the first cell and then entered the numerical data in a column below the heading.

If I want the data to have a different appearance—for example, to indicate that it is currency—I can format the number type through the **Home** ribbon, **Number** window. To begin, highlight the data in column A (see the preceding image). Then activate the **Home** ribbon by clicking on it (this has been done in the preceding image). You should see the **Number** window in the top right-hand side of the **Home** ribbon in the preceding image.

You can activate the **Number** window by clicking on the arrow in the bottom right of the window; you will receive a dialog box as in the following screen capture that will allow you to format the way you want the numerical data to appear in the cells. Because these data are salaries, let's choose **Currency** and then click **OK.**

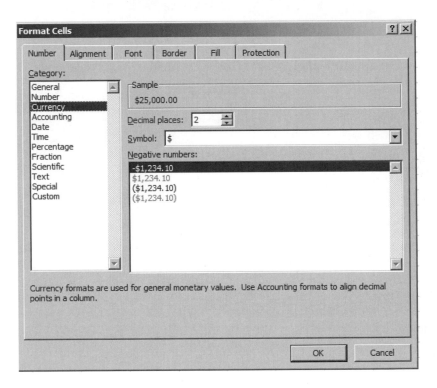

The data in column A now appear as currency, as can be seen in the following image.

USING SPSS 18 OR 19

To begin using SPSS, launch the SPSS program. When you initially start the program, you may receive a startup window such as the one below. Unless otherwise instructed by your professor, click **Cancel.** (Please note: SPSS 18 was marketed as PASW Statistics; it returned to being named SPSS in version 19.)

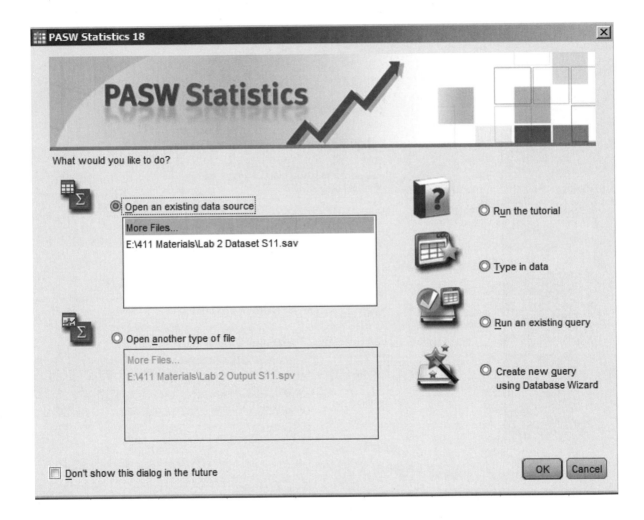

You should now have a view of the data spreadsheet, or the Data Editor, similar to the following image.

The main menu in SPSS runs across the top of the Data Editor and gives you the options from **File** on the far left to **Help** on the far right. We'll mainly be using the **Analyze** option to statistically analyze data. You can see the drop-down menu for the **Analyze** tab in the following image.

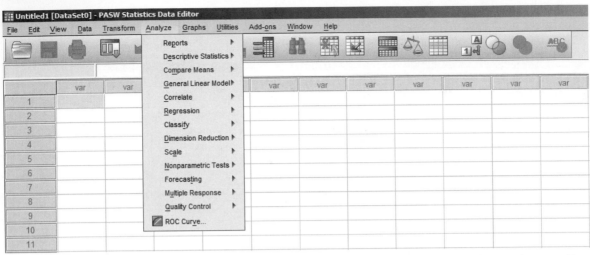

The icons that appear below the main menu provide some shortcut keys to allow you to do such things as Open Files, Save, Insert Cases, Insert Variables, and so on.

Entering Data To enter the data into an SPSS spreadsheet, launch SPSS and enter the data into a column, as in the following spreadsheet in which I have entered the salary data from the previous Excel example. Given that I had already entered the data into Excel, I simply cut and pasted the data column into SPSS, minus the **Salary** heading.

Notice that the variable is simply named VAR0001. To rename the variable to something appropriate for your data set, click on the **Variable View** tab at the bottom left of the screen. You will see the **Variable View** window active in the following image.

File	Edit	View	Data	Transform	Analyze	Graphs	Utilities	Add-ons	Window	Help

	Name	Type	Width	Decimals	Label	Values	Missing	Columns	Align	Measure	Role
1	Salary	Numeric	8	2		None	None	8	Right	Scale	Input
2											
3											
4											
5											
6											
7											
8											
9											
10											
11											
12											
13											
14											
15											
16											
17											
18											
19											
20											
21											
22											
23											
24											
25											
26											
27											
28											
29											
30											
31											
32											
33											
34											
35											
36											

Data View | Variable View

Type the name you wish to give the variable in the first column (labeled **Name**). The variable name cannot have any spaces in it. Because these data represent salary data, we'll type in **Salary.** You can also see that we can format this variable while the **Variable View** window is active by specifying the type of data, the width of the data, the number of decimals, and so on. To get back to the original spreadsheet, highlight the **Data View** tab at the bottom left of the screen. In the **Data View** window, we can now see that the **Salary** heading appears at the top of the column.

	Salary	var	var	var	var	var	var	var	var	var	var
1	25000.00										
2	30000.00										
3	30000.00										
4	32000.00										
5	33000.00										
6	33000.00										
7	35000.00										
8	35000.00										
9	35000.00										
10	35000.00										
11	37000.00										
12	37000.00										
13	40000.00										
14	40000.00										
15	40000.00										
16	45000.00										
17	45000.00										
18	52000.00										
19	55000.00										
20	56000.00										
21	65000.00										
22	90000.00										

If I had not had data to paste into the Data Editor, I could have entered the data by highlighting each cell and typing in the data.

USING THE TI-84 CALCULATOR

Entering data into the TI-84 calculator is considerably easier than entering it into Excel or SPSS. With the calculator on, press the **STAT** key. **EDIT** should be highlighted at the top left of the screen along with **1:Edit** in the first row under the menu. Press the **ENTER** key at the bottom right of the calculator. You should now have a spreadsheet with six columns labeled **L1** through **L6** (you may only be able to see L1 through L3, but if you scroll to the right, columns L4 through L6 become available). To enter data into L1, move the cursor to the first position under L1 and type in the data. Press **ENTER** after you type each number. Your data should now be entered into L1 and be displayed in the column under L1.

To clear the data from a column, highlight the column heading (for example, L1) and press the **CLEAR** key on the calculator. Never press the **DEL** key after highlighting a column heading because this action will delete the entire column. However, if you make this mistake, you can recover the column by pressing the **STAT** key, scrolling down to **5: SetUpEditor,** and pressing **ENTER.** You will receive the command **SetUpEditor** with a flashing cursor. Press **ENTER** on the calculator, and you should receive the message **DONE.** Your variable should now be restored.

Computational Supplement

Independent Groups t test formula for unequal sample sizes

Begin by calculating s^2_{Pooled}:

$$s^2_p = \frac{(n_1 - 1)s_1^2 + (n_2 - 1)s_2^2}{n_1 + n_2 - 2}$$

Next, calculate the standard error of the difference between means:

$$S_{\bar{X}_1 - \bar{X}_2} = \sqrt{\frac{s_p^2}{n_1} + \frac{s_p^2}{n_2}}$$

Lastly, use the standard error of the difference between means to calculate the final t score:

$$t = \frac{\bar{X}_1 - \bar{X}_2}{S_{\bar{X}_1 - \bar{X}_2}}$$

Alternative post hoc test for use with ANOVAs—Fisher's protected t test formula:

$$t = \frac{\bar{X}_1 - \bar{X}_2}{\sqrt{MS_w\left(\frac{1}{n_1} + \frac{1}{n_2}\right)}}$$

Use the t critical values table from Appendix A for a two-tailed test and df_w to determine whether the difference between all pairs of means is significant.

One-Way Randomized ANOVA summary table using computational formulas

SOURCE	df	SS	MS	F
Between-groups	$k - 1$	$\Sigma\left[\dfrac{(\Sigma X_g)^2}{n_g}\right] - \dfrac{(\Sigma X)^2}{N}$	$\dfrac{SS_b}{df_b}$	$\dfrac{MS_b}{MS_w}$
Within-groups	$N - k$	$\Sigma\left[\Sigma X_g^2 - \dfrac{(\Sigma X_g)^2}{n_g}\right]$	$\dfrac{SS_w}{df_w}$	
Total	$N - 1$	$\Sigma X^2 - \dfrac{(\Sigma X)^2}{N}$		

One-Way Repeated Measures ANOVA summary table using computational formulas

SOURCE	df	SS	MS	F
Subject	$n - 1$	$\Sigma\left[\dfrac{(\Sigma X_s)^2}{k}\right] - \dfrac{(\Sigma X)^2}{N}$		
Between	$K - 1$	$\Sigma\left[\dfrac{(\Sigma X_t)^2}{n_t}\right] - \dfrac{(\Sigma X)^2}{N}$	$\dfrac{SS_b}{df_b}$	$\dfrac{MS_b}{MS_e}$
Error	$(k - 1)(n - 1)$	$\Sigma X^2 - \Sigma\left[\dfrac{(\Sigma X_s)^2}{k}\right] - \Sigma\left[\dfrac{(\Sigma X_t)^2}{n_t}\right] + \dfrac{(\Sigma X)^2}{N}$	$\dfrac{SS_e}{df_e}$	
Total	$N - 1$	$\Sigma X^2 - \dfrac{(\Sigma X)^2}{N}$		

Two-Way Randomized ANOVA summary table using computational formulas

SOURCE	df	SS	MS	F
Factor A	$A - 1$	$\sum\left[\dfrac{(\Sigma X_A)^2}{n_A}\right] - \dfrac{(\Sigma X)^2}{N}$	$\dfrac{SS_A}{df_A}$	$\dfrac{MS_A}{MS_{Error}}$
Factor B	$B - 1$	$\sum\left[\dfrac{(\Sigma X_B)^2}{n_B}\right] - \dfrac{(\Sigma X)^2}{N}$	$\dfrac{SS_B}{df_B}$	$\dfrac{MS_B}{MS_{Error}}$
A × B	$(A - 1)(B - 1)$	$\sum\left[\dfrac{(\Sigma X_C)^2}{n_C}\right] - \dfrac{(\Sigma X)^2}{N} - SS_A - SS_B$	$\dfrac{SS_{A \times B}}{df_{A \times B}}$	$\dfrac{MS_{A \times B}}{MS_{Error}}$
Error	$AB(n - 1)$	$\Sigma X^2 - \sum\left[\dfrac{(\Sigma X_C)^2}{n_C}\right]$	$\dfrac{SS_{Error}}{df_{Error}}$	
Total	$N - 1$	$\Sigma X^2 - \dfrac{(\Sigma X)^2}{N}$		

References

American Psychological Association. (2001). *Publication manual of the American Psychological Association* (5th ed.). Washington, DC: Author.

Arkes, H. R., & Hammond, K. R. (Eds.) (1986). *Judgment and decision making: An interdisciplinary reader*. Cambridge, England: Cambridge University Press.

Aron, A., & Aron, E. N. (1999). *Statistics for psychology* (2nd ed.). Upper Saddle River, NJ: Prentice Hall.

Cohen, J. (1988). *Statistical power analysis for the behavioral sciences*. Hillsdale, NJ: Erlbaum.

Cohen, J. (1992). A power primer. *Psychological Bulletin, 112,* 115–159.

Cowles, M. (1989). *Statistics in psychology: An historical perspective*. Hillside, NJ: Erlbaum.

Gould, S. J. (1985, June). The median isn't the message. *Discover, 6*(6), 40–42.

Griggs, R. A., & Cox, J. R. (1982). The elusive thematic-materials effect in Wason's selection task. *British Journal of Psychology, 73,* 407–420.

Halpern, D. F. (1996). *Thought and knowldege: An introduction to critical thinking* (3rd ed.). Mahwah, NJ: Lawrence Erlbaum Associates, Inc.

Hinkel, D. E., Wiersma, W., & Jurs, S. G. (1988). *Applied statistics for the behavioral sciences* (2nd ed.). Boston, MA: Houghton Mifflin.

Huck, S. W., & Cormier, W. H. (1996). *Reading statistics and research,* (2nd ed.). New York: HarperCollins.

Kerlinger, F. N. (1986). *Foundations of behavioral research* (4th ed.). New York: Holt, Rinehart & Winston.

Kranzler, J. H. (2007). *Statistics for the terrified* (4th ed.). Englewood Cliffs, NJ: Pearson Prentice Hall.

Li, C. (1975). *Path analysis: A primer*. Pacific Grove, CA: Boxwood Press.

Mitchell, M., & Jolley, J. (2001). *Research design explained* (4th ed.). Fort Worth, TX: Harcourt.

Olson, R. K., & Forsberg, H. (1993). Disabled and normal readers' eye movements in reading and non-reading tasks. In D. M. Willows, R. Kruk, & E. Corcos (Eds.), *Visual processes in reading and reading disabilities* (pp. 377–391). Hillsdale, NJ: Erlbaum.

Paul, G. L. (1966). *Insight vs. desensitization in psychotherapy*. Stanford, CA: Stanford University Press.

Paul, G. L. (1967). Insight vs. desensitization in psychotherapy two years after termination. *Journal of Consulting Psychology, 31,* 333–348.

Peters, W. S. (1987). *Counting for something: Statistical principles and personalities*. New York: Springer-Verlag.

Schweigert, W. A. (1994). *Research methods & statistics for psychology*. Belmont, CA: Brooks/Cole.

Stanovich, K. E. (2007). *How to think straight about psychology* (8th ed.). Boston: Allyn & Bacon.

Stigler, S. M. (1986). *The history of statistics*. Cambridge, MA: Belknap Press.

Tankard, J., Jr. (1984). *The statistical pioneers*. Cambridge, MA: Schenkman.

Wallis, C. (1987, October 12). Back off, buddy. *Time,* pp. 68–73.

Glossary

absolute zero   A property of measurement in which assigning a score of 0 indicates an absence of the variable being measured.

addition rule   A probability rule stating that the probability of one outcome or another outcome occurring on a particular trial is the sum of their individual probabilities, when the outcomes are mutually exclusive.

alternative hypothesis (research hypothesis)
The hypothesis that the researcher wants to support, predicting that a significant difference exists between the groups being compared.

ANOVA (analysis of variance)   An inferential parametric statistical test for comparing the means of three or more groups.

average deviation   An alternative measure of variation that also indicates the average difference between the scores in a distribution and the mean of the distribution.

bar graph   A graphical representation of a frequency distribution in which vertical bars are centered above each category along the x-axis and are separated from each other by a space indicating that the levels of the variable represent distinct, unrelated categories.

between-groups sum of squares (sum of squares between)   The sum of the squared deviations of each group's mean from the grand mean, multiplied by the number of participants in each group.

between-groups variance   An estimate of the effect of the independent variable *and* error variance.

Bonferroni adjustment   A means of setting a more stringent alpha level in order to minimize Type I errors.

case study method   An in-depth study of one or more individuals.

causality   The assumption that a correlation indicates a causal relationship between the two variables.

central limit theorem   A theorem which states that for any population with mean μ and standard deviation σ, the distribution of sample means for sample size N will have a mean of μ and a standard deviation of $\sigma/\sqrt{N}$ and will approach a normal distribution as N approaches infinity.

chi-square goodness-of-fit test   A nonparametric inferential procedure that determines how well an observed frequency distribution fits an expected distribution.

chi-square test of independence   A nonparametric inferential test used when frequency data have been collected to determine how well an observed breakdown of people over various categories fits some expected breakdown.

class interval frequency distribution   A table in which the scores are grouped into intervals and listed along with the frequency of scores in each interval.

coefficient of determination (r^2)   A measure of the proportion of the variance in one variable that is accounted for by another variable; calculated by squaring the correlation coefficient.

Cohen's *d*   An inferential statistic for measuring effect size.

confidence interval   An interval of a certain width that we feel confident will contain μ.

continuous variables   Variables that usually fall along a continuum and allow for fractional amounts.

correlated-groups *t* test A parametric inferential test used to compare the means of two related (within- or matched-participants) samples.

correlation coefficient A measure of the degree of relationship between two sets of scores. It can vary between -1.00 and $+1.00$.

correlational method A method in which the degree of relationship between at least two variables is assessed.

critical value The value of a test statistic that marks the edge of the region of rejection in a sampling distribution, where values equal to it or beyond it fall in the region of rejection.

degrees of freedom (*df*) The number of scores in a sample that are free to vary.

dependent variable The variable in a study measured by the researcher.

description Carefully observing behavior in order to describe it.

descriptive statistics Numerical measures that describe a distribution by providing information on the central tendency of the distribution, the width of the distribution, and the shape of the distribution.

difference scores Scores representing the difference between participants' performance in one condition and their performance in a second condition.

directionality The inference made with respect to the direction of a relationship between two variables.

discrete variables Variables that usually consist of whole-number units or categories and are made up of chunks or units that are detached and distinct from one another.

effect size The proportion of variance in the dependent variable that is accounted for by the manipulation of the independent variable.

equal unit size A property of measurement in which a difference of 1 means the same amount throughout the entire scale.

error variance The amount of variability among the scores caused by chance or uncontrolled variables.

estimated standard error of the mean An estimate of the standard deviation of the sampling distribution.

eta-squared An inferential statistic for measuring effect size with an ANOVA.

expected frequencies The frequency expected in a category if the sample data represent the population.

experimental method A research method that allows a researcher to establish a cause-and-effect relationship through manipulation of a variable and control of the situation.

explanation Identifying the causes that determine when and why a behavior occurs.

factorial design A design with more than one independent variable.

factorial notation The notation that indicates how many independent variables were used in a study and how many levels were used for each variable.

F-ratio The ratio of between-groups variance to within-groups variance.

frequency distribution A table in which all of the scores are listed along with the frequency with which each occurs.

frequency polygon A line graph of the frequencies of individual scores.

Friedman test An inferential nonparametric test used to determine differences between three or more conditions on a ranked variable for a correlated-groups design.

grand mean The mean performance across all participants in a study.

histogram A graphical representation of a frequency distribution in which vertical bars centered above scores on the *x*-axis touch each other to indicate that the scores on the variable represent related, increasing values.

hypothesis A prediction regarding the outcome of a study. It often involves a prediction regarding the relationship between two variables in a study.

hypothesis testing The process of determining whether a hypothesis is supported by the results of a research study.

identity A property of measurement in which objects that are different receive different scores.

independent variable The variable in a study manipulated by the researcher.

independent-groups *t* test A parametric inferential test for comparing sample means of two independent groups of scores.

inferential statistics Procedures for drawing conclusions about a population based on data collected from a sample.

interaction effect The effect of each independent variable across the levels of the other independent variable.

interval scale A scale in which the units of measurement (intervals) between the numbers on the scale are all equal in size.

Kruskal-Wallis test An inferential nonparametric test used to determine differences between three or more groups on a ranked variable for a between-subjects design.

magnitude (1) A property of measurement in which the ordering of numbers reflects the ordering of the variable. (2) An indication of the strength of the relationship between two variables.

main effect An effect of a single independent variable.

mean A measure of central tendency; the arithmetic average of a distribution.

mean square An estimate of either total variance, variance between groups, or variance within groups.

measure of central tendency A number intended to characterize an entire distribution.

measure of variation A number that indicates how dispersed scores are around the mean of the distribution.

median A measure of central tendency; the middle score in a distribution after the scores have been arranged from highest to lowest or lowest to highest.

mode A measure of central tendency; the score in the distribution that occurs with the greatest frequency.

multiplication rule A probability rule stating that the probability of a series of outcomes occurring on successive trials is the product of their individual probabilities, when the sequence of outcomes is independent.

negative correlation An inverse relationship between two variables in which an increase in one variable is related to a decrease in the other, and vice versa.

negative relationship A relationship between two variables in which an increase in one variable is accompanied by a decrease in the other variable.

negatively skewed distribution A distribution in which the peak is to the right of the center point and the tail extends toward the left, or in the negative direction.

nominal scale A scale in which objects or individuals are broken into categories that have no numerical properties.

nonparametric test A statistical test that does not involve the use of any population parameters—μ and σ are not needed, and the underlying distribution does not have to be normal.

normal curve A symmetrical, bell-shaped frequency polygon representing a normal distribution.

normal distribution A theoretical frequency distribution having certain special characteristics.

null hypothesis The hypothesis predicting that no difference exists between the groups being compared.

observational method Making observations of human or other animal behavior.

observed frequencies The frequency with which participants fall into a category.

one-tailed hypothesis (directional hypothesis) An alternative hypothesis in which the researcher predicts the direction of the expected difference between the groups.

one-way randomized ANOVA An inferential statistical test for comparing the means of three or more groups using a between-participants design.

one-way repeated measures ANOVA An inferential statistical test for comparing the means of three or more groups using a correlated-groups design.

operational definition A definition of a variable in terms of the operations (activities) a researcher uses to measure or manipulate it.

ordinal scale A scale in which objects or individuals are categorized and the categories form a rank order along a continuum.

parametric test A statistical test that involves making assumptions about estimates of population characteristics, or parameters.

partial correlation A correlational technique that involves measuring three variables and then statistically removing the effect of the third variable from the correlation of the remaining two variables.

Pearson product-moment correlation coefficient (Pearson's r) The most commonly used correlation coefficient when both variables are measured on an interval or ratio scale.

percentile rank A score that indicates the percentage of people who scored at or below a given raw score.

person-who argument Arguing that a well-established statistical trend is invalid because we know a "person who" went against the trend.

phi coefficient (1) The correlation coefficient used when both measured variables are dichotomous and nominal. (2) An inferential test used to determine effect size for a chi-square test.

point-biserial correlation coefficient The correlation coefficient used when one of the variables is measured on a dichotomous nominal scale and the other is measured on an interval or ratio scale.

population All of the people about whom a study is meant to generalize.

positive correlation A relationship between two variables in which the variables move together—an increase in one is related to an increase in the other, and a decrease in one is related to a decrease in the other.

positive relationship A relationship between two variables in which an increase in one variable is accompanied by an increase in the other variable.

positively skewed distribution A distribution in which the peak is to the left of the center point and the tail extends toward the right, or in the positive direction.

post hoc test When using an ANOVA, a means of comparing all possible pairs of groups to determine which ones differ significantly from each other.

prediction Identifying the factors that indicate when an event or events will occur.

probability The study of likelihood and uncertainty; the number of ways a particular outcome can occur, divided by the total number of outcomes.

qualitative variable A categorical variable for which each value represents a discrete category.

quantitative variable A variable for which the scores represent a change in quantity.

quasi-experimental method A study in which the variable of interest cannot be manipulated.

range A measure of variation; the difference between the lowest and the highest scores in a distribution.

ratio scale A scale in which, in addition to order and equal units of measurement, there is an absolute zero that indicates an absence of the variable being measured.

regression analysis A procedure that allows us to predict an individual's score on one variable based on knowing one or more other variables.

regression line The best-fitting straight line drawn through the center of a scatterplot that indicates the relationship between the variables.

restrictive range A variable that is truncated and does not vary enough.

sample The group of people who participate in a study.

sampling distribution A distribution of sample means based on random samples of a fixed size from a population.

scatterplot A figure that graphically represents the relationship between two variables.

single-group design A research study in which there is only one group of participants.

Spearman's rank-order correlation coefficient The correlation coefficient used when both of the variables are measured on an ordinal (ranking) scale.

standard deviation A measure of variation; the average difference between the scores in the distribution and the mean or central point of the distribution, or more precisely, the square root of the average squared deviation from the mean.

standard error of the difference between means The standard deviation of the sampling distribution of differences between the means of independent samples in a two-sample experiment.

standard error of the difference scores The standard deviation of the sampling distribution of mean differences between dependent samples in a two-group experiment.

standard error of the mean The standard deviation of the sampling distribution.

standard normal distribution A normal distribution with a mean of 0 and a standard deviation of 1.

statistical power The probability of correctly rejecting a false H_0.

statistical significance An observed difference between two descriptive statistics (such as means) that is unlikely to have occurred by chance.

Student's _t_ distribution A set of distributions that, although symmetrical and bell-shaped, are _not_ normally distributed.

sum of squares error (sum of squares within-groups) The sum of the squared deviations of each score from its group (cell) mean.

sum of squares Factor A The sum of the squared deviation scores of each group mean for Factor A minus the grand mean, times the number of scores in each Factor A condition.

sum of squares Factor B   The sum of the squared deviation scores of each group mean for Factor B minus the grand mean, times the number of scores in each Factor B condition.

sum of squares interaction   The sum of the squared difference of each condition mean minus the grand mean, times the number of scores in each condition. The SS_A and SS_B are then subtracted from this.

survey method   Questioning individuals on a topic or topics and then describing their responses.

t test   A parametric inferential statistical test of the null hypothesis for a single sample where the population variance is not known.

theory   An organized system of assumptions and principles that attempts to explain certain phenomena and how they are related.

third-variable problem   The problem of a correlation between two variables being dependent on another (third) variable.

total sum of squares (sum of squares total)   The sum of the squared deviations of each score from the grand mean.

Tukey's honestly significant difference (HSD)   A post hoc test used with ANOVAs for making all pairwise comparisons when conditions have equal n.

two-tailed hypothesis (nondirectional hypothesis)   An alternative hypothesis in which the researcher predicts that the groups being compared differ, but does not predict the direction of the difference.

Type I error   An error in hypothesis testing in which the null hypothesis is rejected when it is true.

Type II error   An error in hypothesis testing in which there is a failure to reject the null hypothesis when it is false.

variable   An event or behavior that has at least two values.

Wilcoxon matched-pairs signed-ranks *T* test   A nonparametric inferential test for comparing sample medians of two dependent or related groups of scores.

Wilcoxon rank-sum test   A nonparametric inferential test for comparing sample medians of two independent groups of scores.

within-groups sum of squares (sum of squares error)   The sum of the squared deviations of each score from its group (cell) mean.

within-groups variance   The variance within each condition; an estimate of the population error variance.

z score (standard score)   A number that indicates how many standard deviation units a raw score is from the mean of a distribution.

z test   A parametric inferential statistical test of the null hypothesis for a single sample where the population variance is known.

Index